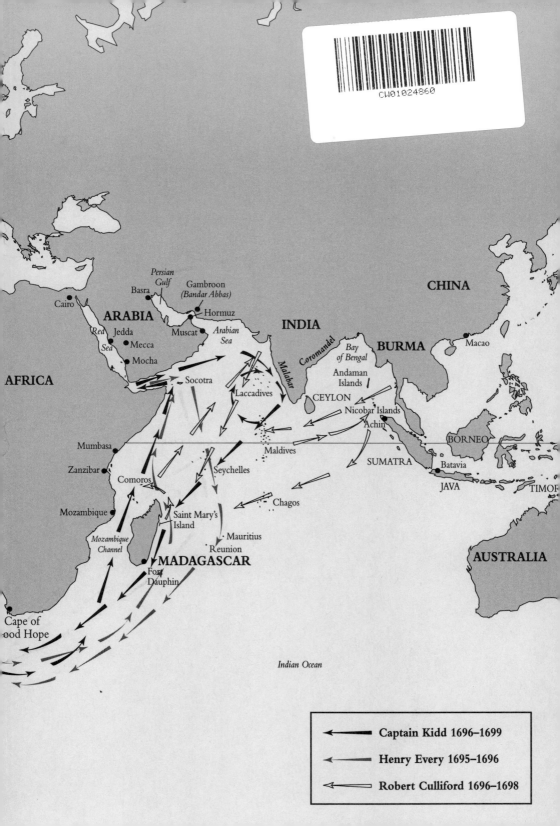

CW01024860

Persian Gulf

Basra

Gambroon
(Bandar Abbas)

Cairo

Hormuz

ARABIA

Muscat

INDIA

CHINA

Red Sea

Jedda

Arabian Sea

Mecca

Socotra

Malabar

Coromandel

BURMA

Macao

Mocha

Laccadives

Bay of Bengal

AFRICA

Andaman Islands

CEYLON

Nicobar Islands

Achin

Mumbasa

Maldives

BORNEO

Zanzibar

Comoros

Seychelles

SUMATRA

Batavia

Mozambique

Chagos

JAVA

TIMOR

Saint Mary's Island

· Mauritius

Reunion

Mozambique Channel

MADAGASCAR

AUSTRALIA

Fort Dauphin

Cape of Good Hope

Indian Ocean

⟵ **Captain Kidd 1696–1699**

⟵ **Henry Every 1695–1696**

⟵ **Robert Culliford 1696–1698**

HONOR AMONG THIEVES

Captain Kidd, Henry Every, and the Pirate Democracy in the Indian Ocean

JAN ROGOZIŃSKI

STACKPOLE BOOKS

Published by
STACKPOLE BOOKS
5067 Ritter Road
Mechanicsburg, PA 17055
www.stackpolebooks.com

Printed in the United States of America

10 9 8 7 6 5 4 3 2 1

FIRST EDITION

Library of Congress Cataloging-in-Publication Data

Rogozinski, Jan.
    Honor among thieves : Captain Kidd, Henry Every, and the Pirate Democracy
in the Indian Ocean / Jan Rogozinski.— 1st ed.
        p. cm.
    Includes bibliographical references (p.).
    ISBN 0-8117-1529-9
        1. Libertalia. 2. Pirates—Madagascar—History. I. Title.

DT469.M37 L537 2000
969.1—dc21

                                        99-089801

For Paul, who makes everything possible.

And in admiration of Daniel Defoe,
the greatest liar that ever lived.

CONTENTS

MAPS AND TABLES

The illustrations are contained in two sections between pages 74 and 75 and between pages 170 and 171.

INTRODUCTION

*He [John Taylor] enrolled among the pirates, who soon elected him
their captain. Certainly, they could not have found a man more
capable of commanding a ship than he was. Leaving aside the nature of
his infamous and hateful profession and his own private vices, Taylor
brought together in one person all that one could hope to find in a
seaman, a soldier, and a leader. . . .*

*At sea, they perform their duties with a great deal of order, better
even than on the ships of the Dutch East India Company; the pirates
take a great deal of pride in doing things right. They practice
continually, firing their guns at targets and fencing with sabers and
rapiers made of wood; while they are exercising, their musicians play a
variety of songs, so that their days pass very agreeably.*

—Jacob de Bucquoy (1744)

Saint Mary's Island, history's only true pirate island, is located east of
Africa, just off the northeast coast of Madagascar. For more than thirty
years from the late 1680s, ships from Saint Mary's scoured the Indian
Ocean, the Red Sea, the Persian Gulf, and waters as far east as Burma. The
most successful criminals in human history, their crews returned to Saint
Mary's with immensely valuable booty. There they enjoyed their treasures
in safety without fear of arrest. There were no rulers to bribe because the
pirates ruled themselves. They *were* the island's government, electing their
own officials and following their own laws.

THE MOST SUCCESSFUL CRIMINALS IN HISTORY

By the 1690s, the waters east of Cape Hope were a pirate's paradise. Merchant vessels routinely carried valuable cargoes, much richer than those
hauled by vessels in the Atlantic and Mediterranean. Each year, for exam-

ple, Indian ships carried Muslim pilgrims and rare luxury goods to Mecca and Jiddah. When the monsoon set in, they gathered at Mocha and returned in a single fleet loaded with gold and silver.

To reach their destinations on time, captains had to take into account both the great distances between ports and the yearly oscillation of the monsoon winds. Merchantmen generally traveled in convoys, following fixed routes and unvarying schedules. Raiders did not have to chase their prey. They could wait at strategic points with complete assurance that the ships would eventually come within easy striking distance.

European shipping also offered tempting targets. Portuguese carracks carried very rich cargoes, as did the vessels owned by the East India Companies of England, France, and the Netherlands. Ships heading east carried cash to finance European traders. Those returning to Europe were loaded with silks, cloth, jewels, spices, and drugs.

Corsairs sailing from Saint Mary's hold the record for the richest hauls taken by any pirates. Henry Every in 1695 captured an Indian warship carrying gold and gems with a value of $200 million in modern currency. Three years later, the crews of the *Soldado* and *Mocha* split $65 million in cash taken from the *Great Mahomet*. At the mouth of the Red Sea in 1700, John Bowen and his men shared out $50 million from another Indian vessel. In 1721, John Taylor and Oliver La Buse took a Portuguese carrack with diamonds, gold, and cargo worth more than $400 million.

Compared to the loot captured by ships from Saint Mary's, the booty won by Caribbean buccaneers pales into insignificance. In all of history, only one or two other pirates even came close.[1] And rich hauls were a routine occurrence. Saint Mary's pirates seized coins and gems on almost every cruise. In the late seventeenth century a man with £500 was set for the rest of his life, and the raiders shared out that much or more nearly ever time they returned to port.

Moreover, most pirates succeeded in retiring with their booty intact. Despite the wealth on board, most ships had to fend for themselves, unprotected by any government or navy. Suffering from starvation wages and tormented by tyrannical captains, merchant seamen had little incentive to fend off attackers. Raiders were killed by exotic fevers or in shipwrecks, and a few were tricked into surrendering by false promises of pardon. But not a single pirate was ever captured at sea.

Booty taken by Saint Mary's Raiders, 1688–1721 (in Descending Order)

Ship's Crew and Captain	Estimated Amount of Booty	Where captured
John Taylor commanding the *Cassandra* and Oliver la Bouche commanding the *Victory* (1721)	More than $400 million, including $250 million in diamonds and treasure. Divided into equal shares, each man receiving loot valued at some $1.8 million	*Nostra Senhora de Cabo* (*Our Lady of the Cape*), a Portuguese vessel taken at Réunion Island in the Indian Ocean
Captain Condent commanding the *Flying Dragon* (1720)	$375 million in coins, drugs, spices, and silk. Shared out at about $1 million per man	A large Muslim ship taken off India's northwestern coast near Bombay
Henry Every in the *Fancy*, accompanied by five other vessels (1695)	At least $200 million. The crew of the *Fancy* kept most of the loot, about $500,000 in cash per man plus a share of the jewels	*Fateh Mohammed* and *Gang-i-Saway* (*Gunsway*) taken in the Red Sea
William May in the *Charming Mary* (1697)	Returns to New York with booty estimated at $150 million by Governor Bellomont	
John Bowen in the *Speedy Return* and Thomas Howard with the *Prosperous* (1703)	$100 million	Two Indian vessels taken in the Red Sea
Dirk Chivers in the *Soldado* and Robert Culliford commanding the *Mocha* (1698)	$50 million in cash. More than $375,000 per share	*Great Mohammed*, Indian ship taken in the Red Sea
Thomas Tew in the *Amity* (1693)	$50 million in all, with each man receiving $600,000	
John Bowen in the *Speaker* (1700 or 1701)	$50 million	Indian vessel taken near the mouth of the Red Sea
George Raynor in the *Batchelor's Delight* (1690–1691)	About $40 million	Two Portuguese galleons and an English East Indiaman, seized in the Indian Ocean
Edward England with the *Fancy* and the *Victory* (1720)	$38 million	*Cassandra*, an East Indian Company vessel taken at Johanna Island in the Comoros
John Halsey with the *Charles* (1707)	$25 million in cash	Two British ships taken off Mocha in the Red Sea
William Kidd in the *Adventure Galley* (1698)	$23 million (claimed as loss by Indian merchants), $11 million (estimate by East India Company officials)	*Quedah Merchant*, an Indian vessel taken off Cochin, India
William Mason and Edward Coats in the *Jacob* (1692)	Between $16 and $20 million, mostly in gold and coins	Four Muslim ships in the Red Sea

THE LONG JOURNEY TO THE EAST

These rich hunting grounds tempted hundreds of adventurers. Many more who wanted to come were frightened off by the long and daunting voyage to the Indian Ocean. Merchantmen could break their journey at Saint Helena and the Cape of Good Hope, but pirates were barred from these ports. To reach the east coast of Africa, American raiders had to sail across some 15,000 miles of open ocean in a voyage that might last for six months. With the Suez Canal still two centuries in the future, they fought through the stormy waters around the Cape of Good Hope. By the time they arrived at Africa's east coast, food and water were in short supply. The pirates' small wooden ships desperately needed repairs. Often, on the way east, so many crewmen died of disease that the ships literally could not man their cannon. No vessel powered by sails and oars could make it all the way from North America to India without some safe haven.

From the early 1690s, Saint Mary's Island became the voyagers' main base. There they created a pirate utopia, supplying every need of both resident and visiting mariner. A narrow island about 35 miles long, Saint Mary's lies twelve miles northeast of Madagascar, a much larger island 200 miles east of Africa. At Saint Mary's southwestern end, a narrow and easily fortified channel protects a circular lagoon. In this natural and easily defensible harbor, pirate craft could safely ride out the region's violent storms.

The pirates got along with and even were adopted by the island's native population. The inhabitants along Madagascar's eastern coast were descended from Polynesian seafarers, who had immigrated from Indonesia a thousand years before. Accustomed to a racially mixed society in which lighter-skinned lords governed darker-skinned slaves, the Malagasy thought of European captains as the counterpart of their own native rulers. They welcomed European mariners—provided that they respected Malagasy traditions. A proud and warlike people, the Malagasy had repelled Portuguese, Dutch, English, and French attempts to establish colonies; the French needed modern cannon and machine guns to conquer Madagascar at the end of the nineteenth century. It is easy to explain the very different receptions given to the pirates and the would-be colonists: The pirates respected the Malagasy, while the settlers sought to conquer and enslave them.

THE PIRATE REPUBLIC OF LIBERTALIA

On this lush tropical island, successive groups of pirates formed a free and independent community, with its own institutions, customs, rules, and flag.

Everyone on Saint Mary's owed his livelihood to piracy. Having retired from active duty, some men acted as resident fences, buying the pirates' booty and selling them ammunition and other European goods. The Malagasy shared in the spoils, as native women happily married successful raiders.

Saint Mary's Island is the only pirate island in human history. At all other havens, sea rovers were only one among several groups sharing power. At other ports, the pirate community may have freely regulated its own affairs and enjoyed considerable influence with the government. But they had no final say in important matters. They answered to the city's rulers, who had to retain the support of other, non-piratical constituencies.

Algiers, for example, was the most important center for Muslim raiders, the so-called Barbary Pirates, beginning in 1515. Sea captains governed their own profession, and corsair squadrons were the main support of Algiers' economy for three centuries. While the city's rulers did respond to corsair requests, they also had to consider the needs of other groups—the soldiers protecting against bedouin attacks, the landowners supplying the city's food, and the officials governing the Ottoman Empire from Istanbul.

The buccaneers at Port Royal, Jamaica, never had things entirely their own way either. Some governors favored the buccaneers, but they also sought to placate sugar planters and slave traders. And colonial officials either obeyed direct orders from London, or faced warships sent from England.

Saint Mary's Island was entirely different. On Saint Mary's, the pirates formed what may well be the most democratic and egalitarian society in human history. Pirate crews elected and fired their officers even while at sea. The ship's articles became a sacred covenant, and each crewman received an equal share of the booty. Physical punishments were rare and imposed only by majority vote. In the perfect freedom of the pirate republic of Libertalia, every marauder could come and go as he pleased. Between voyages, crewmen might spend months or years on Saint Mary's. Once they had made their fortune, some men went back to the Americas or retired in India, while others bought sugar plantations at the nearby French colony of Réunion Island. Many stayed on at Saint Mary's itself: Surrounded by harems of beautiful women, they lived out their lives as White Malagasy.

Some notorious captains—Thomas Tew, Henry Every, William Kidd—did not settle down at Saint Mary's. Nevertheless, their contemporaries were correct in linking them to the island. Had the pirate republic not existed, they never would have made it to the Indian Ocean. On their way east, Tew and Every stopped at Saint Mary's to recruit crewmen. After marauding in the Red Sea, Kidd spent six months at Saint Mary's before returning to New York. More clever than their captain, most of Kidd's crew stayed on at Saint Mary's and thus avoided the hangman's noose.

WHO SAILED FROM SAINT MARY'S?

The story of this pirate utopia was told wherever seamen congregated. Hundreds of young men enlisted under captains bound for India. The historian of Saint Mary's Island is unusually lucky in knowing something about the lives of individual marauders. Most tales about a pirate's youth are pure fantasy. During the seventeenth and eighteenth centuries, ordinary folk lived and died without leaving a mark. In this case, by exception, more than a hundred pirates retired on Réunion Island and thus became subject to the assiduous French bureaucracy.

Piracy was a young man's game. On average, men enlisted in their early twenties and retired a decade later after making their fortunes. Most came from the Caribbean or from cities along the Atlantic coasts of Europe and America. Not all were sailors. Some were skilled craftsmen and could read and write; at least one was a nobleman. Whatever their origins, once aboard ship, they grew into a closely knit community bound together by lasting friendships—although not usually by sexual love.[2]

Pirates were normal men differing from their fellows in their willingness to take risks. As a practical matter, only those living in port cities were likely to join up. Within seafaring communities, the dangers and rigors of a piratical voyage attracted the ambitious, who were frustrated by a lack of opportunities at home.[3] George Noel was literate and apprenticed to a clockmaker. One can easily imagine him—bored with this tedious work—finding his way to the docks and ending up at Madagascar. His adventures were well rewarded. Having sailed under Captain John Bowen, Noel was able to retire on Réunion in 1704 at the young age of twenty-five. He was no fool and invested his wealth wisely. Fifteen years later, he owned a large plantation worked by thirty-one slaves.[4]

THE EXTRAORDINARY TALENTS OF PIRATE CAPTAINS

Anyone undertaking the long voyage to the Indian Ocean wanted his commander to be an expert in navigation and seamanship. Captains were usually experienced mariners, somewhat older than most crewmen. Before he was anything else, a pirate had to be a competent mariner. Although some had the aid of expert pilots, the captain and crew lived with—or died with—his vessel. Through superior seamanship, they ran down and captured their prey, preferably without harming passengers or cargo.

Like other entrepreneurs, pirates sought to hold down expenses and maximize revenues. A captain had to decide where to hunt, evaluate the probable value of his prey, and calculate whether it was worth carrying away. He had to "know the market," both locally and internationally. When he took a prize, the captain had to fence the loot and buy supplies without being outrageously cheated. Captains also had to be effective leaders in battle. Although they tried to avoid it, pirates could not always escape combat, as the occasional merchantmen suddenly turned and fought back.

Above all, a captain had to manage, lead, and inspire his men. Pirates are comparable to land bandits in some regards. But while brigands ashore can succeed by themselves or with a few friends, one or two men can not sail a ship. Every pirate belonged to a sea-going community with up to 200 other men. The officers had to keep their crew contented during the voyage and unified during battles.

Captains could be charming and persuasive when they dealt with government officials. Governor Benjamin Fletcher of New York remarked that he genuinely enjoyed Thomas Tew's company. Tew was, Fletcher said, a brave man and more intelligent than most sea captains. "He was allso what they call as very pleasant man; soe that . . . it was some divertisment as well as information to me, to heare him talke."[5] The French governors of Réunion Island also found that pirate captains made surprisingly affable companions.

Captains had to charm their crews as well, and they also had to dominate the men by the power of their will. Ironically, the very social equality aboard pirate ships actually made captains stand out sharply from their followers. Governments appointed naval commanders; the owners of merchantmen hired their captains. In both cases, second-rate men tried to flog the crew into obedience. A pirate captain, in contrast, stayed in business only if men freely volunteered to join his cruise. At sea, he maintained order by persuading and motivating his men. A captain had to be a strong, assertive, and forceful.

Saint Mary's men elected their officers and insisted they follow the ship's rules. Except during the heat of battle, officers were expected to consult the men on important matters. The men imposed a democratic regime because they wanted a captain they could trust. At the same time, they most certainly did not want a weak leader. Since it often was necessary to make decisions rapidly, there had to be one final authority on board. As did other sailing ships, pirate vessels stayed afloat by maintaining discipline. Expecting the worst, prisoners often were surprised by the good order found among their captors.

Captains of merchantmen and naval warships imposed their will by savage brutality. In contrast, successful pirate captains—Thoms Tew, Henry Every, Robert Culliford, Dirk Chivers, John Bowen, John Taylor—won the obedience and affection of their men through a combination of persuasion, bullying, and encouragement. Seventeenth-century Europeans believed in monarchy, and legends turned Henry Every into a crowned king. In fact, Every was elected by the men, who could remove him at any time. Nevertheless, these romances tell a kind of truth. Through his personality he became a kind of sovereign lord at whose command men suffered and died.

In their energy, toleration of pain, and tight masculine bonding, the young men aboard pirate cruisers resemble a modern-day athletic team. To lead the crew, captains exercised the talents of a winning coach. When he was in one of his blind rages, the men fled from Captain Taylor. Yet they went with him from ship to ship and ocean to ocean because they knew he would bring them victory at sea and a safe retirement with their loot.

THE REAL CAPTAIN KIDD

The history of Saint Mary's Island lifts the curtain of mystery that has veiled Captain William Kidd's famous voyage. Whether they have written as his friend or his foe, Kidd's biographers have discussed him in isolation and without referring to other Saint Mary's captains. Yet Kidd was only one among dozens of captains cruising in the Indian Ocean. Absent the Saint Mary's pirate community, he never would have attempted his voyage. He was personally acquainted with other Saint Mary's captains, and their success inspired his own efforts. On the way home, he spent six months at Saint Mary's before sailing to North America.

William Kidd was temperamentally unfit to be a pirate captain. His personality and methods were exactly the opposite of those of successful captains. Kidd was obsequious to his superiors and expected instant obedience from his subordinates. Instead of consulting the men, he expected them to follow his orders without questioning them. His authoritarian personality brought success in the rigidly stratified societies of England and its colonies, and his ways might have been tolerated on a warship or an East Indiaman. Aboard a pirate vessel, however, Kidd was certain to fail.

By the time the ship reached the safety of the Saint Mary's community, Kidd was hated by both crewmen and officers. Once on shore, the entire crew deserted—just as another of Kidd's crews had done some years before. None of the other ship's companies in port would have him aboard. Even though he knew he would be accused of piracy, Kidd was forced to return to North America. He was cast into exile by the citizens of the democratic community at Saint Mary's.

THE PIRATES CHANGE HISTORY

The pirates permanently changed the several worlds in which they operated. On Saint Mary's Island and the adjacent parts of Madagascar, their half-breed descendants remembered their European heritage with pride. Until the pirates arrived, raiders from the south and west had harassed the tribes along Madagascar's northeastern coast. Their liberty was gained by the half-Malagasy son of an English pirate named Ratsimilao. During the 1720s, Ratsimilao succeeded in uniting the various tribes, who took the new name Betsimisaraka ("the many inseparable"). Under his leadership, they threw out the invaders and then turned to the sea. Taking up their fathers' profession of piracy, they raided the Comoro Islands and East Africa for more than a century.

In America and England, the pirates' very success forced an end to seven centuries of collusion between the English government and sea raiders. Until then, English officials had been able to control the pirates, from whom they took bribes. Suddenly a distant colony of seamen totally escaped supervision and ravished English commerce. It was their success at self-rule that made the Saint Mary's marauders so dangerous to the English government. They made up the entire non-Malagasy population of the island. They took care of themselves and shared with no one. Above all, they sank ships of every country, including their own.

For the first time ever, a large group of English pirates operated without the government's approval. For centuries, England had been a "nation of pirates." Now the pirates had escaped the control of the nation. In desperation, the government reversed a centuries-old policy, outlawed piracy, and sent out fleets to chase down marauders. None of the naval expeditions dared to attack the pirates resident on Madagascar and Saint Mary's, but colonial officials did manage to hinder the flourishing trade between North America and Madagascar. Without more recruits, the pirate utopia gradually came to an end as its residents died natural deaths.

The men of Saint Mary's left a lasting impression on the English literature of piracy. While the pirates frightened government officials, their extraordinary success and exotic life on Saint Mary's fascinated ordinary Englishmen and Anglo-Americans. Responding to public demand, journalists and authors produced pamphlets, books, and plays about Saint Mary's. Some recorded true accounts by former pirates and their victims; most were wholly fictional.

Daniel Defoe, the great English novelist, produced the most compelling and best-remembered stories in his *General History of the Pyrates.* Writing decades later and without any way of getting at the truth, Defoe created his own version of the events. In some cases, it is obvious that he made up his facts—as when, for instance, he quotes the thoughts of a man dying alone.[6] Often, however, fact and fiction are mixed so cleverly that it is difficult to know where one ends and the other begins. One sentence may describe a real event; the very next sentence contains an invented story. Moreover, in the Indian Ocean, even reality sometimes seem fantastic, so the difference between fact and fiction is not apparent on the surface.

There is considerable truth to the judgment that Daniel Defoe was the "greatest liar that ever lived."[7] Even professional historians have been fooled by the *General History of the Pyrates.*[8] His fantasies have found their way into numerous articles in the *Dictionary of American Biography* and the [British] *Dictionary of National Biography.* Works of history quote speeches Defoe invented.[9] Even more mischievously, historians have mined Defoe's biographies of fictional captains for statistics about the age, origins, and family ties of seamen. With true Defovean audacity, they then provide percentages calculated by mixing together statistics of real pirates and Defoe's fictional counterfeits.[10] The entire process has a quality of surreal absurdity.

FROM MADAGASCAR TO TREASURE ISLAND

Defoe's stories about the Madagascar pirates have diverted attention from the historical facts. At the same time, the same stories serve as the source of subsequent pirate literature. Copied and recopied over the years, Defoe's fables have become the basis for a lush pirate mythology that continues to enrich modern fiction and films.

Over the centuries, there have been many curious twists and turns in the evolution of pirate legends. When the word *pirates* is used, for example, most Americans automatically picture a Caribbean buccaneer lurking under the "Jolly Roger"—a black flag carrying the Skull n' Cross Bones. How-

ever, this characteristic pirate flag and clothing originally were created by
Defoe in his biographies of Madagascar pirates. Later authors then transferred these pirate legends from the Indian Ocean to the Caribbean. In particular, Robert Louis Stevenson is indebted to the *General History of the
Pyrates* for characters such as Long John Silver as well as for many of the
details that make *Treasure Island* seem authentic.

Drawing on Defoe, pirate mythology has exaggerated even his most
outrageous fictions. In pirate legends, as they have developed over three
centuries, sea rovers belong to one of three separate types. The Pirate Fiend
was invented by Defoe and earlier by Exquemelin, whose best-selling *Buccaneers of America* inspired Defoe's stories about Madagascar. In this tradition,
pirates are villains of the darkest hue, who enjoy unlimited freedom and
power. Pirate crewmen are big, brutish males who ignore every rule of
middle-class behavior. Dirty and unwashed, they wear tattered clothing, and
disfigure their bodies with earrings and tattoos. Acting out their cruel lusts
without hesitation, they torture for the sheer pleasure of giving pain, and
they brutally rape any woman who crosses their path.

Fictional pirates reject the disciplines society imposes, but they also lack
self-discipline. They do as little work as possible and spend their spare time
in foul drunkenness, sporting with women at low taverns until their money
is gone. They capture more loot only by submitting to a captain who uses
their muscle-ripped bodies.

The fictional pirate captain—Defoe's Captain Lewis, Captain Cornelius,
or Captain John Condent, for example—often shares the physical lusts of his
crewman. He rises above them and commands them only because of his iron
will. Off duty, he may appear as lazy and debauched as his henchmen. Like
them, he enjoys physical pleasures and has large appetites for food, alcohol,
and sex. But he also lusts after power and dominates all those around him.

In other biographies—those, for example, of Captain Mission, Thomas
Howard, Nathaniel North—Daniel Defoe also invented a second and alternative fictional tradition—that of the Noble Hero.[11] All fictional pirate captains are at war with society and create their own alternative world. The
pirate fiend turns against society because he is evil and the laws of civilization would restrain his desires. In an alternative incarnation, the pirate king
is noble, and he fights society because its rules are unjust. Often, he is an
aristocrat, and wicked men have stolen his rightful inheritance.

Forced into exile, the noble hero takes up piracy. But he remains
morally superior both to his victims and to other pirates, including his

brutish followers. In fact, his traits are exactly the opposite of those attached to the pirate fiend. He fights for freedom, not for gold, and does not torture prisoners. He is enormously beautiful rather than coarse and hairy. He is clean and well dressed rather than tattooed. Faithful to one woman, he ignores the most voluptuous wenches.

By the 1870s, melodrama and vaudeville had invented a third type—the Comic Captain. Demented rather than superhuman, the comic captain rages, twists his face into ridiculous shapes, and bellows out nautical-sounding nonsense. But his shenanigans serve no purpose. He may kill and torture, but most of his mannerisms are simply wasted energy. He is so silly and ineffectual that no one gets hurt.[12]

The authors of novels, stories, poems, and movies have created a complex and compelling pirate mythology, embracing a wealth of colorful legends and distinctive symbols. By presenting the real events exactly as they happened, *Honor Among Thieves* does not intend to denigrate pirate mythology. That would be both foolhardy and arrogant: foolhardy because a thousand books could never remove a popular myth already embedded in the culture, arrogant because Defoe's fiends and heroes are remarkable creations of the human mind and spirit.

In removing the thick patina of falsehood from their collective portrait, *Honor Among Thieves* simply seeks to give the men of Saint Mary's their due. They were neither fiends, heroes, nor clowns. They were lavishly rewarded for running risks, and overcoming adversity. Curiously, the real sea raiders accomplished much more than their fictional counterparts. At a time when few men traveled more than a mile or two from their homes, the Madagascar pirates sailed across vast oceans to exotic lands inhabited by alien races. They became partners with the Malagasy, who spurned other foreigners. Fighting pitched battles, they overcame larger and better-armed vessels. Having captured great treasures, they divided their loot fairly and according to their code. Instead of frivolously burying it in the sand, each man kept his fortune safe until he could retire from piracy—some at Madagascar or nearby Réunion Island, others back home in America or Europe. Truly they were criminals. But they were grand and not petty thieves, and their adventures merit our attention.

>·+◂▸·•○•·◂▸+·◂

Men writing in the 1690s gave the value of pirate booty in terms of the monetary standards of their time, such as the British pound sterling. Three hundred years later, we naturally wonder how much their loot is worth in the British pounds and United States dollars of our own time.

Take, for example, the two Indian vessels captured by Henry Every in 1695. The East India Company claimed the pirates took cargoes worth £325,000. In attempting to translate its value into current dollars, historians sometimes ask how much Every's booty would buy today. That is, given inflation, how did prices in 1695 compare to prices three centuries later? What is the purchasing power of a 1695 pound?

A precise answer is not possible. Part of the difficulty lies in identifying comparable commodities and products. In 1695, no one could buy what one can buy today. No one can buy today the products available in 1695. Some items (such as food and housing) were much less expensive in the seventeenth century. Other products cost much more than they do today, including iron and some kinds of clothing. (This is why the Madagascar pirates were so eager to seize Indian cloth; fancy silks and cotton literally were worth their weight in gold.) And some items that Captain Every desperately needed—such as antibiotics, radios, depth-finders, and accurate cannon—could not be obtained at any price in 1695.

While they are aware that their data are imprecise, economic historians nevertheless insist that it is possible to make "broad-brush comparisons" across historical periods. Based on the prices of basic consumable goods (grains, vegetables, meat, fish, butter, cheese, drink, fuel, light, and textiles), recent studies suggest that the ratio was at least 100 to one. That is, a 1695 British pound could purchase at least as many goods as 100 pounds bought in 1995.[13]

The United States and the United States dollar did not exist in 1695. However, when the U.S. gained independence in 1783, one British pound was equivalent to about five U.S. dollars, and this ratio of roughly five to one was maintained for more than a century until World War I. Moreover, price levels in Europe and North America were closely linked throughout the entire eighteenth century.[14] Thus, it seems plausible to assume that the ratio also would have been five to one in 1695, had there been a U.S. dollar then. In other words, when it came to buying everyday consumer goods, one 1695 pound is estimated to have had the buying power of some five hundred dollars.

Anecdotal evidence confirms the rough validity of this approximation. Captains of large merchant vessels were paid £60 to £120 a year in 1700. Using a multiplier of 500 implies that a sea captain earned some $30,000 to

$60,000 annually; in fact, the captain of an American oil tanker, for example, earns considerably more than that. A colonial governor's wife spent the winter in Bermuda. For a household of twenty-one, she enjoyed five months of comparative warmth at a cost of £100.[15] In 1689, when war broke out, Connecticut's government wanted volunteers against Canada, and it increased a private's wages to nine shillings a week. Using a multiplier of 500, this was equivalent to $11,700 a year in today's money. (This seems a little high for a private, but the job was not meant to last a full year.)

Assume that the East India Company was accurate in assessing Every's booty at £375,000. In today's currencies, Every's take thus was worth £37 million or $188 million. To understand why men were eager to make the long voyage to Madagascar, consider that a private returning to North America with £500 in coins or gems had the equivalent in his sea chest of about $250,000.

But comparisons of currency do not measure the political and economic influence enjoyed by persons with money. In terms of power, making a 1695 pound equivalent to five hundred present-day dollars probably understates the greater value of money back then. There was simply less of everything in 1695, so a rich person controlled more of the total economic output. One way of getting at this is to compare a monetary value to the gross domestic product (GDP)—the total amount of goods and services produced each year. In 1695 £500 bought a greater percentage of England's GDP than $250,000 bought of America's GDP in 1999.

The greater social inequality of earlier centuries is also significant. Given the absence of the modern progressive tax system and welfare state, the distribution of income and wealth was far more unequal than in our own day. A man with £500 cash in his pocket possessed more wealth than 99 percent of the population of Europe and North America.[16]

DANIEL DEFOE WROTE THE *GENERAL HISTORY OF THE PYRATES*

Until recently, literary critics agreed that Daniel Defoe (1661?–1731) was indeed the author of works crucial to understanding Madagascar piracy, including *A General History of the Pyrates*, *The King of Pirates*, and *Madagascar; or Robert Drury's Journal*. Some years ago, evidence was found proving both that a Robert Drury actually existed and that some parts of *Robert Drury's Journal* may not be totally fictional. More recently, P. N. Furbank and W. R. Owens argued on literary grounds that Daniel Defoe was not the author of *A General History of the Pyrates*.[17] Credit for writing this book would thus revert to the "Captain Charles Johnson" listed on the title page of the first edition (about whom nothing is known). However, Defoe continues to be listed as the author of both works by the Library of Congress.

The following pages attribute *A General History of the Pyrates* to Defoe. There is no room in this book to discuss why I am not persuaded by the revisionist argument. In a sense, the entire issue of authorship is irrelevant here. The *General History* is an impressive work. Its cunning confusion of fact and fiction has—for better and for worse—determined and distorted the history of piracy for three centuries. If the *General History* was not written by Daniel Defoe, then it was written by someone who was as clever as Defoe in all the ways that Defoe was clever. Any reader who wants to do so is free to put quotation marks around Defoe's name whenever the following pages mention *Robert Drury's Journal* and the *General History of the Pyrates*.

MEASURING TIME AND DISTANCE

During the seventeenth and early eighteenth centuries, Englishmen used the Julian calendar, which was at that time ten days behind the modern or Gregorian calendar. I have edited dates to conform to Gregorian usage only when absolutely necessary. Some historians of piracy and editors of original documents fail to indicate whether they have corrected the dates found in their sources. I mention the possible problems caused by these discrepancies in dates only when a precise chronology is necessary to understand the sequence of events.

Distances at sea as well as on land have been stated in United States statute miles. To convert distances at sea to nautical miles, a reader can multiply these statute miles by 0.87.

›‹◊›‹•‹O›•‹‹◊‹‹

For her courtesy and commitment to excellence, the author is grateful to Leigh Ann Berry, the editor of this book.

Part One

THE BUCCANEERS HEAD EAST, 1689–1695

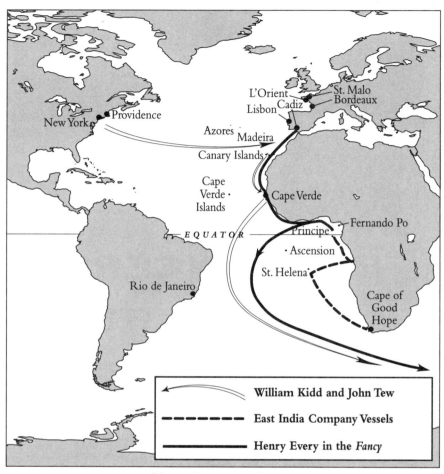

L'Orient
St. Malo
Cadiz
Bordeaux
Lisbon

New York
Providence

Azores
Madeira

Canary Islands

Cape
Verde ·
Islands
Cape Verde

Fernando Po

EQUATOR
Principe
· Ascension

St. Helena·

Rio de Janeiro

Cape of
Good
Hope

William Kidd and John Tew

East India Company Vessels

Henry Every in the *Fancy*

THE ROUTE EAST

CHAPTER ONE

PIRATES ARRIVE AT SAINT MARY'S

Jamaica [was] the seminary, where pirates have commenced Masters of Art, after having practised upon the Spaniard and then launched for the Red and Arabian Seas.

—William Penn, 1700

In the Spring of 1689, the Reverend John Ovington set out for India as chaplain of the *Benjamin,* an East India Company merchant vessel. Sailing in April 1689, the *Benjamin* followed the customary route taken by Company vessels. From England, the ship sailed down Africa's western coast, with stops at the Portuguese colonies of Madeira and São Tiago, the largest of the Cape Verde Islands. Entering the region of the trade winds, the *Benjamin* touched at the tiny island of Malemba near the mouth of the Congo River. From there she rode the trades west to Saint Helena before attempting the perilous journey around the Cape of Good Hope.

Throughout the voyage, Reverend Ovington kept a journal, which he later published, after the Saint Mary's pirates had made the Indian Ocean newsworthy. While the *Benjamin* was anchored at Saint Helena, a slave ship arrived, carrying blacks from Madagascar and bound for New York. The captain of the slaver told Ovington about

> three Pirates which she left Rendezvouzing in St *Augustin's Bay,* a Port belonging to that Island [Madagascar]. Two of the Ships were *English,* and the other *Dutch,* and were all richly Laden with store of Silks, which they had taken in the *Red Sea,* from the *Asian* Merchants that traded from *Mecha* to *Suratt,* and the other coasts of

Indostan. Their Rigging was much worn and Weather-beaten, and for want of a New suit of Sails, they were forced to employ double Silk instead of Canvas, and proffer'd that Exchange to this Commander. They had spent so much time in the Naval surprizes of the *Moors,* and loading themselves with the Rich Booties which were easily taken in the *Red Sea,* that their Ships became almost useless and unfit for Navigation, which brought them thither for Recruits. They were Prodigal in the Expences of their unjust Gain, and quencht their Thirst with *Europe* Liquor at any rate this Commander would put upon it.[1]

In 1689, for Reverend Ovington and other Englishmen, the Madagascar pirates clearly were a new curiosity. In only a few years, almost everyone in England and North America will have heard of their exploits. For these two English pirate vessels were among the first to head for India from North America and England itself. An occasional English pirate ship earlier had made it as far as Madagascar, often with official sponsorship. During the 1630s, for example, King Charles I—always desperate for money—sent two fleets to the Indian Ocean to attack "Moorish" vessels. But these were isolated incidents.

THE CARIBBEAN: SEMINARY FOR BUCCANEERS

During most of the seventeenth century, pirates stayed at home in Caribbean ports. So long as they primarily raided Spanish shipping and cities, they were made welcome by colonial governors, who took a generous cut of their booty. Adventurers of all sorts—including renegade Spaniards, Negro slaves, and American Indians—flocked to Port Royal, near Kingston in the English colony of Jamaica, as well as to several ports on the French island of Saint Domingue (modern Haiti).

From these bases, the Caribbean buccaneers launched ferocious attacks on Spanish shipping and ravished Spain's American ports. Jamaican piracy reached its peak during the 1660s under Sir Thomas Modyford. With Governor Modyford's official authorization, the infamous Sir Henry Morgan commanded hundreds of men in raids on the Spanish treasure ports at Portobelo and Panama City. While the London government publicly scolded Governor Modyford, officials privately condoned the raids to force territorial concessions from Spain.[2]

Morgan's Panama raid, occurring after a peace treaty in 1670, infuriated the Spanish government. When Sir Thomas Lynch became governor, he arrested Modyford and Morgan and sent them to England for trial. Lynch offered pardons to those quitting piracy, but he lacked the naval force to pursue those who continued to cruise. Jamaican piracy died out only when the island's landowners decided that growing sugar was more profitable than fencing pirate booty.[3]

Jamaica's legislature finally outlawed piracy in 1681, and the governor sent out armed vessels to pursue sea rovers. French officials in Haiti continued to tolerate pirates for a few years longer. But these belated buccaneers took relatively little booty. By the 1680s, Spanish merchant shipping already had been driven from the seas. Every major city and large village from Venezuela to Mexico had been raided, often more than once. Earlier attackers had so thoroughly devastated the region that frequently there was literally nothing left for them to loot. In 1702 when raiders captured Tolú, Colombia, they found that the townsmen had "not so much as a Silver Candlestick in their Churches."[4]

After Jamaican authorities acted against them, some English seamen sought haven in the Bahamas or the Carolinas, which still tolerated freebooters. However, while these raiders were willing to attack ships of their own nation, the infant English and French colonies in North America produced few products worth stealing. Pirates always have preferred easily portable and highly valuable booty. Beginning in 1680, the most ambitious abandoned the Caribbean and followed Spanish silver ships back to their ports of origin on South America's west coast.[5]

THE GREAT "SOUTH SEA" RAIDS

As European and Caribbean marauders were fully aware, Spain's wealth had its sources in the Pacific. The route of the Panamanian treasure ships began in Peru. In addition, the fabled Manila Galleon yearly brought immensely valuable cargoes from the Philippines to Acapulco.[6] The "South Sea" had tempted raiders since Sir Francis Drake sailed through Magellan's Strait in 1578 and snatched the enormously rich silver ship *Cacafuego.*

During the 1680s, several thousand men hunted for Peruvian treasure ships in the Pacific Ocean. At least four companies sailed from North America or England, around Cape Horn, and north along the coast toward Panama. Isolated at sea for months at a time, these men navigated thousand of miles of ocean by dead reckoning. Others walked and canoed across the eastern end of the Isthmus, taking a dangerous route through Panama's unchartered swamps and rain forest.

These were extraordinarily daring voyages. Captains feared Pacific waters because there were no havens to welcome their vessel. The passage through Magellan's Strait or around Cape Horn was one of the most difficult in the world. No pirate captain had maps of the South American coast. Once he left the Caribbean, no port would give him refuge if trouble occurred. A voyage to the Pacific took longer than a voyage to the moon does today. The nearest supplier and the nearest fence (assuming booty was taken) were months away.

In the Pacific as in the Caribbean, the buccaneers controlled the open seas. Roaming at will, they had taken two thirds of the Spanish merchant marine in the Pacific by 1686.[7] But they signally failed to capture great treasures—the silver ships were too well guarded, the colonial ports too poor to reward their labors.

The defining moment in the great Pacific raids came in June 1685. Waiting off Panama for the Peruvian treasure ships, almost a thousand men were crammed into a variety of captured coastal craft and two armed cruisers, the *Batchelor's Delight* and the *Cygnet*. Aware that buccaneers were lurking in wait, Peruvian officials sent two galleons and three smaller warships to protect the king's silver, worth over 500,000 pesos ($88 million). By taking a more westerly course than was usual, the warships evaded the raiders and secretly landed the treasure. Then on June 8, 1685, the Peruvian fleet turned and routed the pirates, chasing them away from Panama to Coiba Island.

Squabbling over their defeats, the raiders broke up into smaller and smaller groups. Peruvian defenders killed some, and fever took many more. Some made it back to the Caribbean and retired from buccaneering. The most ambitious among their leaders headed for the Indian Ocean, pinning their hopes on the fabled treasures of the Orient. This time their daring seamanship was more richly rewarded than in Peru.

THE *CYGNET*'S UNENDING, INTERMINABLE CRUISE

Among the men-of-war rendezvousing at Saint Augustine's Bay in 1689 were the *Batchelor's Delight* and the *Cygnet,* the same pirate warships defeated by the Peruvians off Panama four years earlier. The two vessels had followed very different routes to their rendezvous. The *Delight* had taken her buccaneer crew straight back to Jamaica before setting out for Madagascar. In contrast, the *Cygnet* arrived at Saint Augustine's only after an extraordinary three-year voyage, zigzagging across the width and breadth of the Pacific Ocean.

The voyage of the *Cygnet* began with Charles Swann, a Jamaican buccaneer who had sacked Panama in 1671 with Henry Morgan.[8] While visiting London, Swann had run across Basil Ringrose, another Jamaican and one of the first buccaneers to invade the Pacific. Convinced by Ringrose that great riches waited in Peru, Swann rebuilt and outfitted the *Cygnet* ("Baby Swan") as a strong pirate cruiser with sixteen guns. Taking personal command of the vessel, Swan took her from London to South America's Pacific Coast in 1684.

Until it reached India, the *Cygnet* had an extraordinary string of bad luck. After the pirates' defeat off Panama in June 1685, Captain Swann took the ship north toward Acapulco, Mexico, looking for the fabled Manila Galleon. In November, the pirates failed to take a Peruvian treasure ship guarded by Acapulco's guns, and they also sailed past the Galleon in January 1686.

Seeking better luck in Asia, the *Cygnet*'s crew turned due west into the Pacific. Swann made it to Guam and then to the Philippines. He was aided by William Dampier, a pirate scientist, who described the voyage in his best-selling *A New Voyage Round the World*.[9] However, Swann was too arrogant to succeed as a pirate captain. In January 1687, his crew left him behind in Manila, where John Read took over as captain. Still hoping to run into the Manila Galleon, Read cruised the China Sea, visiting Cambodia, southern China, Formosa, and the Celebes Islands. Turning south, the *Cygnet*'s crew became the first Englishmen to reach Australia. Captain Read continued on to the northwest and made for Ceylon. But the *Cygnet* was driven ashore on India's southeastern coast, where more than half the crew deserted.

The *Cygnet* finally took a rich Portuguese prize near Ceylon. Captain Read then headed for the Red Sea, but the fierce northwest monsoon drove the ship back. By accident the *Cygnet* landed at Madagascar, where the crew helped one of the native chiefs war on his enemies. Eventually Read and five or six other crewmen stole away and took passage on a ship visiting from New York. Half wrecked and worm eaten, the *Cygnet* continued cruising but took no more prizes. Not long after, it ran into the slaver that John Ovington had met in Saint Helena, the vessel sank in Saint Augustine's Bay. There the remaining crew members camped out until they were picked up by another pirate vessel.[10]

Once back home Captain Read may well have talked about his Indian Ocean adventures, thus spurring interest in Madagascar. By the time Read arrived in New York, however, some Caribbean buccaneers already knew about the booty waiting in the East. One source of information was the crews of the slave ships that had visited Madagascar from the late 1670s. At least three ships sold their cargo at Port Royal, Jamaica, during the 1680s, and eleven more carried slaves to Barbados.[11]

As early as 1686, a buccaneer vessel had made the long voyage from Caribbean to the Indian Ocean. The pirates called at the tiny French colony on Réunion Island and spent lavishly for food and water.[12] They went on to the Persian Gulf and plundered a Portugese settlement.[13] In January 1687, the pirate warship returned to Réunion, where twenty-two English and Dutch mariners left with their booty.[14] At this point, the vessel disappears from the records and may well have been lost at sea. It was the sticking success of the *Batchelor's Delight,* the *Cygnet's* former consort in Peru, that convinced American pirates to make the seven-thousand-mile voyage to Madagascar.

THE *BATCHELOR'S DELIGHT* IN AFRICA AND SOUTH AMERICA

The *Batchelor's Delight* began her career as a stoutly built Danish slave ship of 180 tons, strongly armed with thirty-six guns. In 1683, she was off West Africa, near Cape Sierra Leone. A buccaneer vessel suddenly appeared, chased her down, and overpowered her much smaller crew. The pirates were among those heading for Peru, but in crossing the Atlantic from Virginia to Africa, their vessel's faults had become all too apparent. They wanted a ship of greater strength and seaworthiness before attempting the difficult passage into the Pacific.

Several of those capturing the *Delight* kept diaries, including William Dampier (who later transferred to the *Cygnet.*) However, Dampier does not mention the incident, and the other diarists also are uncharacteristically reticent. They presumably saw little to boast about in a sneak attack on innocent slavers. What happened to the Danish crew is uncertain.

There is conflicting evidence about the fate of the pirates' own vessel. One account says she was burned "by reason she should tell no tales." But according to another version, the buccaneers traded their previous ship for sixty young black girls, who served as a diversion until they later perished one by one in the icy wastes of the Antarctic. Perhaps the latter tale is true, for the buccaneers renamed their new warship the *Batchelor's Delight.*[15]

Sailing around the tip of South America, the *Delight* reached the Pacific early in 1684, where her captain died. To replace him, the crew elected Edward Davis. Although only about thirty-five years old,[16] Davis had commanded pirate raiders in the Caribbean before joining the first invasion of the Pacific in 1680. Under Davis's command, the *Delight*'s crew spent the next three years cruising up and down South America's Pacific coast, vainly hunting treasure ships. The pirates captured merchant vessels and ransacked coastal towns but took little of great value. As Lionel Wafer, the ship's surgeon, sorrowfully notes,

> We continued thus Rambling about to little purpose, sometimes at Sea, and sometimes ashore; till having spent much time, and visited many Places, were got again to the *Gallapago*'s under the Liene; and were then resolv'd to make the best of our Way out of these Seas.[17]

On their way home, the buccaneers may have been the first Europeans to discover Easter Island.[18] As the *Delight* tried to pass around Cape Horn, a powerful storm drove her far to the south toward Antarctica. But the ship held together and reached the Caribbean early in 1688. There Captain Davis and Lionel Wafer left the *Batchelor's Delight*. Davis took along his personal slave, Peter Cloise, while Wafer was accompanied by Edward Hingson, a close friend.[19]

The four men bought passage to Philadelphia and continued on to Virginia. In June 1688, as they were scudding down the Chesapeake in a tiny shallop, they caught the attention of HMS *Dumbarton,* charged with protecting the tidewater against pirates and privateers. All four were arrested, put in irons, and taken to Jamestown. To Davis's great surprise, Peter Cloise turned against the white men and recounted their raid in the Pacific. They were kept in jail until 1690, and the court sequestered their property, said to be worth £2,316 ($1.2 million).[20] One document lists Edward Davis's wealth after at least a dozen arduous years of piracy—three bags of Spanish money, 142 pounds of broken silver, and some "fowle lynnen."[21]

Peter Cloise died suspiciously soon after his deposition. After their release, the three white men traveled to London. Hingson and Wafer gave up piracy, and Wafer gained some fame for his *New Voyage and Description of the Isthmus of America.* However, Edward Davis—still looking for wealth and adventure—abandoned England and joined the pirates cruising the Indian Ocean and the Red Sea.[22]

THE *BATCHELOR'S DELIGHT* HEADS EAST

After Davis, Wafer, and Hingson had gotten off, the rest of the *Delight's* crew took the ship to Jamaica and accepted royal pardons.[23] Jamaican proclamations of pardon offered each pirate who retired thirty acres of land.[24] But this offer had little appeal to men used to the sea. The *Delight* was soon off again for foreign waters, this time commanded by Captain George Raynor (or Reiner).

Some of the seventy or eighty seamen crowded onto the *Delight* previously had been among those invading Peru under Captain Edward Davis. But the South Sea riches had proved a chimera. This time, the *Delight* instead made for Madagascar, stopping at Saint Augustine's Bay in May 1689. While the *Delight* was being readied to put out to sea again, her former partner in the Pacific, the *Cygnet,* also pulled into port.

By now, after her three-year trans-Pacific odyssey, the *Cygnet* was in extremely poor shape. Deciding not to consort with their old comrades from the South Seas invasion, the *Delight's* crew went up the eastern coast of Africa. Off Sofala, they captured a Portuguese ship bound for Goa. To search their prize more thoroughly than could be done at sea, the men took the Portuguese ship to Mohilla Bay. There they found another Portuguese merchantman, also carrying valuable cargo. After looting both vessels, the pirates allowed them to go on to Goa.[25]

Making toward the northeast, the *Batchelor's Delight* rode the summer monsoon to the Indian Coast. Near Bombay in January 1691, the *Delight* seized the East India Company merchantman *Unity.* The officers were set adrift, while the entire crew of the *Unity* joined the pirates. After choosing Edward Kelley, the *Delight's* quartermaster, as their new captain, the men of the *Unity* went off on their own.

The *Delight's* luck now changed, and she cruised around with little profit. It was time to head home. The pirates made for Madagascar to prepare for the long voyage around the Cape of Good Hope and then across the Atlantic. But instead of returning to Saint Augustine's Bay, they sailed to Madagascar's northeast coast. They had learned that Adam Baldridge had recently built a fort and trading post at Saint Mary's Island. There they could take on European wines and tobacco as well as Madagascar beef and fruit.

ADAM BALDRIDGE, KING OF SAINT MARY'S

In 1689, when he told John Ovington about his encounter with the *Cygnet* and *Batchelor's Delight,* the slave ship's captain remarked that pirates careened

Pirate Warships
at Saint Mary's, 1688–1694

Ship	*Batchelor's Delight*	*Jacob*	*Unity*	*Amity*	*Pearl*
Captain	George Raynor	William Mason, Edward Coats	John Kelley, George Paris	Thomas Tew	William May
1688	Leaves Jamaica, mid-1688?				
1689	Seen at Saint Augustine's Bay, May				
1690	Captures two Portuguese merchantmen	Leaves New York, Dec.			
1691	Captures *Unity*, Jan. At Saint Mary's, Oct.–Nov.	Saint Augustine's Bay, Aug.–Sept.	Seized by *Batchelor's Delight*. When Kelley is arrested, Paris elected captain		
1692	Arrives South Carolina early in 1692	Red Sea, June; Saint Mary's, Oct.	Arrives in New York, share out £1,000 each, June		
1693		Arrives New York, July		Leaves Bermuda, Jan. Takes rich plunder in Red Sea	Leaves Rhode Island, July
1694				Arrives Rhode Island, mid-1694	

their vessels and took on supplies at Saint Augustine's Bay, at Madagascar's southwestern tip. Beginning with the Portuguese in the early 1500s, merchants and slavers often stopped at Saint Augustine's. Although the surrounding country was an arid desert, the bay was the first harbor encountered by exhausted mariners after the harrowing passage around the Cape of Good Hope.

Dealers looking for slaves went on from Saint Augustine's to other Madagascar harbors. While each had good points and bad, they all had one disadvantage: None sheltered a European settlement. Portuguese vessels had entered the Indian Ocean in the early 1500s; and Dutch, French, and British merchants had followed a century later. The French and British East India Companies both had tried to settle Madagascar, but the colonists sent to the island made enemies of the Malagasy, who drove them into the sea. After two centuries, no European had succeeded in establishing a permanent camp anywhere along Madagascar's long coastlines.

Saint Mary's Island became the main resort for pirates when Adam Baldridge built his trading post early in 1691. Some pirate craft already had used the harbor at Saint Mary's. But the presence of Baldridge's fort and the availability of European supplies settled the issue. The island became the headquarters for marauders operating anywhere in eastern waters, in the Red Sea and the Persian Gulf as well as throughout the vast expanse of the Indian Ocean and as far east as China.

Adam Baldridge is an important and enigmatic figure. His history is a bit murky—perhaps he used other names before finally settling on Madagascar. In the summer of 1697, after six successful years trading European goods for pirate booty, Baldridge became greedy. Tricking many natives on board a slave ship that had stopped at Saint Mary's Island, he sold them to French colonists on Réunion Island.[26] In July 1697, the Malagasy took their revenge, killing at least thirty pirates and destroying Baldridge's warehouse. Fortunately for Baldridge, he was away from Saint Mary's on a trading mission. He made for North America, apparently carrying some of his profits with him in the form of gold and other valuables.

After arriving in New York, Adam Baldridge initially charmed Lord Bellomont, the state's new governor. On July I, 1698, Bellomont even wrote to the Board of Trade on Baldridge's behalf.

> There is a proposal made to me, by Captain Adam Balderidge for the settlement of the Island of St Mary's . . .; on your Lordships

examination of it I am sure your Lordships will give it all incouragement and furtherance. Mr Balderidge is now here [but] he hath lived many years in Saint Mary's and Madagascar and appears to be a sober man and reputed wealthy by his long trading in these parts.[27]

Lord Bellomont often was a poor judge of men. In their reply, the Board's members tartly informed the ingenuous earl that Baldridge himself had been the "Chief Manager and transactor" in fencing pirate loot.[28] Amazingly, nothing Adam Baldridge had done at Saint Mary's was illegal at that time. However, Bellomont did examine Baldridge under oath and sent his deposition to London in May 1699.[29] This testimony, undoubtedly self-serving, provides most of our information about the founder of Saint Mary's Island.

Even his pirate guests on Saint Mary's had known little about Baldridge's life before he headed east. The rumors ran that Baldrige had turned pirate around 1685, after killing a man.[30] If true, his piratical career in the Caribbean had been brief and unprofitable.[31] According to the account he prepared for Lord Bellomont, Baldrige joined the crew of a slave ship that landed at Saint Mary's in July 1690.

Something about the island attracted the errant seaman. When the ship left in January 1691, Baldridge stayed behind, helped Malagasy tribesmen raid their enemies, and was rewarded with cattle and captives. He also acquired one or more wives, the daughters of Malagasy chiefs.[32] Baldridge's slaves built his home near a landlocked bay at the island's southwestern end. Initially they erected a simple settlement similar to those found among the Malagasy of that region. A log stockade surrounded huts raised off the ground and roofed with bamboo or the leaves of the banana or traveler's tree.[33]

Baldridge was in the right place at the right time. Malagasy tribesmen fled from the war-torn mainland to his camp on Saint Mary's, hitherto an almost uninhabited island.[34] Just at this time large numbers of pirate ships suddenly headed for the Indian Ocean. At pirate hangouts along the way or farther out along the Indian coast, their captains and crews learned that this white chief of the Malagasy could supply them with fresh food as well as with a safe anchorage in which to careen their vessels.

Baldridge decided to turn his camp into an impregnable fortress. In exchange for cattle and fruit, he demanded payment in cannon and gunpowder. This was a high price, but visiting seamen were willing to pay it. Saint Mary's was a very pleasant place to stay. And Baldridge's demands were backed up by tribesmen carrying round bucklers and sharply pointed javelins known as *assagai*.

The *Batchelor's Delight* was the first of many warships welcomed to Baldridge's settlement, where she arrived in October 1691, about three years after leaving Jamaica. Her crew stayed for three weeks, careening their vessel and feasting on freshly killed beef. Before leaving, they gave Baldridge the colored beads that the Malagasy used for ornaments as well as some powder and shot and "five great Guns for a fortification."[35]

Perhaps Captain Raynor consented to abandon his guns because he was headed for home. Leaving Saint Mary's on November 1691, the *Batchelor's Delight* was wrecked on the coast of South Carolina the following year. The crew arrived safely in Charleston, where they boasted—probably exaggerating—of having plundered the Grand Mogul of India.[36]

Edward Randolph, surveyor of His Majesty's custom in North America, became apoplectic in reporting that Carolinians entertained the men from the *Delight,* "who had liberty to stay or go to any other place."[37] Charleston in 1692 was a pioneer city very short of coins or any kind of money. Its citizens gave a warm welcome when visitors possessed what Randolph describes as "a vast quantity of gold from the Red Sea."[38]

Although South Carolina's governor plundered the now useless *Delight,*[39] the pirates gave its owners £3,000 for the "Ruin of the Ship." In addition, each man received a £1,100 share, worth perhaps half a million dollars in modern money.[40] Captain Raynor used his share to purchase an estate in South Carolina and later was elected to the colonial legislature.[41] Even with their wealth, however, some of the crew could not settle down. With the *Delight* gone, they found other ships to carry them back to Saint Mary's Island.

THE *JACOB* AND THE NEW YORK CONNECTION

Other Caribbean buccaneers soon followed the *Batchelor's Delight* to Madagascar. As had the *Delight's* crew, these men often stuck together for years during several voyages. One such closely-knit group was found on the *Jacob,* which reached Saint Mary's in October 1692, the second pirate ship to visit Baldridge's fort.[42] While at Saint Mary's, the crew split the booty from a two-year cruise, each man receiving a share worth £500 (about $250,000). Despite their wealth, almost half the crew, about thirty men, decided to remain at Saint Mary's when the rest set off for New York. Some may have wanted to win even greater riches before making the tedious voyage to

North America. Others perhaps stayed to remain with friends or because they wanted to spend more time in the East.

The *Jacob's* crew had been buccaneers in the Carribean at the beginning of the Nine Years' War (1688–1697) alongside William Kidd, perhaps the most famous pirate of all time. When war was declared, Kidd and other crewmen stole a twenty-gun French pirate vessel and sailed it to the English colony of Nevis. There the vessel, renamed the *Blessed William,* received a crew of eighty or ninety men. Christopher Codrington, governor of Nevis, appointed Kidd captain and assigned the *William* to a small squadron assembled to harass French shipping and islands. Kidd came under the command of Captain Thomas Hewetson of the navy's warship *Lion.*

Hewetson began the campaign by having his squadron sack the small French island of Marie Galante. Arriving there on December 30, 1689, the English seamen and soldiers chased the French settlers into the hills, destroyed the only town, set fire to every sugar plantation, then took what they pleased back to their ships. Hewetson in the *Lion* and Kidd in the *Blessed William* returned to Nevis before the rest of the squadron. Without waiting for the others, the two ships plus a small sloop immediately set out again to rescue English troops trapped on the French island of Saint Martin.[43]

After landing on the island, the soldiers had been surrounded by superior forces when French ships arrived with reinforcements. Hewetson and Kidd arrived to discover that they were outgunned by five larger French ships. Since he had the wind in his favor, Hewetson nevertheless ordered an attack. Each side formed a line of battle, the two squadrons passing back and forth with cannon and small arms blazing. As was often the case, the cannon fire did little damage, and neither side was in a position to board the other. The next morning, Hewetson's squadron again sailed toward the French ships blockading the shore. But instead of going into battle formation, the French ships sailed toward Anguilla. The English troops were rescued and taken back to Nevis.[44]

Although there were few casualties during this battle, the crew of the *Blessed William* decided that piracy was less dangerous than battle. A few days later, in mid January 1690, Kidd went ashore while the *Blessed William* was anchored in Antigua. In Kidd's absence, William Mason, Robert Culliford, Samuel Burgess, and eighteen or twenty others sailed away with the vessel. The men elected Mason captain, and they all agreed to marauder in the East Indies.[45] As had the *Batchelor's Delight,* the *Blessed William* could have sailed directly to Africa from Antigua. However, before undertaking so long a voyage, the crew needed to refit and supply their ship. Since they had absconded with a vessel under British naval command, they fled the area and headed for New York, where no one knew them. On the way, Mason and his crew captured two Spanish ships and raided the island of Blanquilla, taking slaves, food, and some money.

The *Blessed William* arrived in New York in May 1690 during a civil war. The crew sold its cargo, including the slaves, and used the profits to outfit the ship. That done, they accepted a privateering commission from Jacob Leisler, who had proclaimed himself governor and taken control of the colony the previous year. Leisler commissioned three ships to attack French vessels in the Saint Lawrence River. As "admiral" of the little fleet, William Mason snapped up six prizes carrying fish, salt, and some furs. The Canadian booty was valued at only £229, and the crew aboard one of the vessels accused Mason of stealing their prize money.[46]

Returning to New York, Captain Mason and the men sold the *Blessed William* and transferred to one of their prizes, renamed the *Jacob* in Leisler's honor. The *Jacob* left New York in November with another commission from Leisler.[47] With a stop at Rhode Island, the former Caribbean bucca-neers finally sailed for the East at the end of December 1690. Samuel Burgess was elected quartermaster and assumed responsibility for supplying the ship and guarding any loot until its later division.

William Mason's record of success had made it easy to find recruits. The 170-ton *Jacob* was crowded with about eighty-five men, who suffered through a long voyage. The ship did not sight the Cape Verde Islands until March, and the men ran short of food and water. Just before the *Jacob* reached the Cape Verde chain, the men seized the longboat of a Dutch East Indiaman and took guns, cutlasses, and water casks. They also plundered the island of Saint Nicholas for food, wine, and clothes.[48]

The voyage continued to be plagued by delays, and it took another four months to round the Cape of Good Hope. During August and September 1691, the *Jacob* stopped at Saint Augustine's Bay. On departure, the men left Burgess behind, convinced he had cheated them as quartermaster. Catching the tail end of a southwest monsoon, the *Jacob* went to India's west coast, but cruised with little success. Arguments continued, and William Mason, Robert Culliford, and eighteen other men left the ship at Mangalore.

Edward Coats became captain, took the *Jacob* back to Saint Augustine's Bay in April 1692, and retrieved Samuel Burgess. After careening and tak-ing on supplies, the pirates made for the Red Sea in June. There they seized four ships,[49] looting them of gold and currency said to be worth about £400 to £500 ($200,000 to $250,000) per man.[50]

The *Jacob* retired to Saint Mary's, where Adam Baldridge had established his trading post. Baldridge again traded food for cannon and acquired "six great guns" from the *Jacob*. In December, the crew split up amiably. Half the men stayed on Saint Mary's with Baldridge, while the rest made for New York. The return voyage again took six months, and the *Jacob* dropped anchor at Southold on the east end of Long Island in July 1693.

The *Jacob* had been away for almost three years, during which time Jacob Leisler had been convicted of treason and royal government reimposed. Since the crown had annulled Leisler's acts, the crew feared that his commission to William Mason and the *Jacob* was worthless. Edward Taylor was sent ashore to negotiate with the authorities. According to Taylor's testimony five years later, he received a willing reception from William Nicoll, a local political leader and member of the governor's council. Taylor claimed that he initially paid Governor Benjamin Fletcher £700 to let the ship enter the port at New York City. However, when he returned to the *Jacob*, many of the crew already had made off. So Captain Coats gave the *Jacob* to Governor Fletcher, who promptly sold it for £800. There also was testimony that Coats and some of the others paid Fletcher an additional fee to issue safe-conduct passes.[51]

CHAPTER TWO

TREASURES OF THE ORIENT

*On first coming out they generally go first to the Isle of May for salt,
then to Fernando for water, then round the Cape of Good Hope to
Madagascar to victual and water and so for Batsky [sic], where they
wait for the traders between Surat and Mecca and Tuda, who must
come at a certain time because of the trade-wind.*
   —T. South to the Lords Justices of Ireland, August 1696

By creating a safe haven for pirates at Saint Mary's Island, Adam Baldridge made possible piracy's Golden Age. During the seventeenth and
eighteenth centuries, every sea voyage was an adventure. The journey to
India from North America or Europe was especially long and difficult, and
the risk was great. A navigator heading to Asia from North America had to
cross two separate oceans and deal with a series of weather systems.

Once they arrived in the Indian Ocean, however, raiders found that the
trip had been well worth it. Ships there were much more likely to hold
valuable cargoes, and they were easier to catch than vessels in Atlantic and
Pacific waters. Merchant vessels traveled in large convoys that stayed close
to shore and seldom ventured into the open ocean. Moreover, because of
the predictable twice-yearly alternation of the monsoon winds, ships took
the same routes and sailed at the same times year after year.

The fate of the Manila Galleon shows how difficult it was to intercept
a vessel on the high seas. For more than two centuries, sea raiders diligently
hunted for these extraordinarily rich merchant ships, which traveled across
the Pacific from the Philippines to Acapulco, Mexico, every year from
1565–1811. During this entire span of 247 years, only four Manila Galleons
ever were captured—two by English pirates, two by British naval ships.[1]
Because they hugged the coasts and traveled on a fixed schedule, it was

much easier to catch the fleets traveling between India and the Red Sea or Persian Gulf.

Before they could hunt for treasure ships, however, raiders from North America or Europe first had to reach the Indian Ocean. Even on a jet plane, India is still far away. Bombay is some 7,800 miles from New York and 4,500 miles from London But a ship can not travel on a straight line more or less due east over the continent of Africa. It instead has to go far south to reach the Cape of Good Hope, then turn north and east to cross the Indian Ocean. A steam ship taking the route around the Cape travels more than 12,000 miles from London to Bombay. Modern vessels often use the Suez Canal instead, which cuts the distance by sea almost in half. But this shortcut was not built until the late nineteenth century.

In terms of the time needed to travel between ports, India is even farther away when one takes a sailing ship, which relies on the wind and currents for propulsion. To make optimum use of winds and currents, a sailing master can not simply plot straight lines on his map and take the ship southeast from New York to the Cape and northeast from the Cape to Bombay. A motor vessel going from New York to Saint Augustine's Bay via Cape Town covers some 10,000 miles. During the eighteenth century, both merchant vessels and warships had to follow much more circuitous routes that multiplied the distance by more than half.

In 1696, Captain Kidd's *Adventure Galley* followed the customary route east across the Atlantic to the Madeira Islands and then south to the Cape Verdes. About half way down the African coast, the *Galley* had to tack to the southwest almost as far as Brazil. In the middle of the south Atlantic, Kidd again turned to the southeast and went far below Cape Town to cross over to the Indian Ocean and Madagascar. Taking his roundabout route into consideration, Kidd made good time, arriving at Saint Augustine's Bay 137 days after leaving New York, having traveled perhaps 90 miles a day on average.

PLAY OF THE WINDS

Several bands of prevailing winds encircle the earth. In crossing the Atlantic or the Pacific, mariners were affected by the Trade Winds and the prevailing westerlies. In the Indian Ocean, sailors also had to take into account the twice-yearly alternation of the winds known as the monsoon. These worldwide atmospheric systems are powered by the sun, which transmits its heat unevenly to the surface of the oceans and continents. Warm air at the equator rises and moves out toward the poles. Cooler air flows toward the equa-

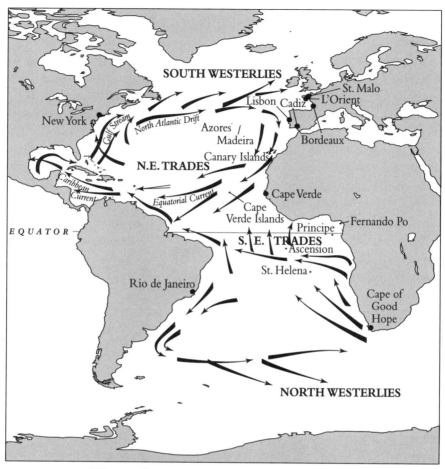

WIND SYSTEMS IN THE ATLANTIC

tor from both the north and south. This cooler air sweeps into the empty space left by the rising warm air, creating a huge convection current. The earth's own rotation around its axis breaks up this planetary big wind system into smaller, circular wind systems.

In the regions immediately north and south of the equator—from about 30° north to 30° south—the oceans are swept by the Trade Winds. Over the oceans, where there are no great land masses to break their course, the Trade Winds are remarkable for their steadiness or constancy, particularly in the Atlantic Ocean. Over the course of an entire year, the northeast trades blow at an average eight knots while the stronger southeast trades average 12 knots an hour. In the northern hemisphere, the trades blow from the northeast; below the equator, they prevail from the southeast. Here again, the Indian Ocean is exceptional. The southeast trades are very powerful below the equator, but there are no northeast trade winds above the equator in the Indian Ocean.[2]

Moving toward the two poles, the earth's rotation creates the zones of the westerlies, located approximately between 35° and 50° both north and south of the equator. Here the winds prevail from the west during all seasons of the year and with considerable power. During the nineteenth century, sailing ships averaged about 150 miles a day traveling from North America to Europe, whereas vessels heading east toward Australia could make more than 200 miles daily.[3]

Sailing masters also took the great ocean currents in account, since these could either aid or thwart their progress. Probably the strongest, and certainly the most studied, of these currents is the Gulf Stream. Beginning in the Gulf of Mexico, the Gulf Stream passes through the straits between Cuba and Florida, continues up the entire coast of North America, then turns toward the northwest off northern Maine. Crossing the Atlantic, it carries warm water to the western and northwestern coasts of the European continent (where it also is known as the North Atlantic Current).

THE MONSOONS OF THE INDIAN OCEAN

Although the Trades and the westerlies move north in the winter and south during the summer, they tend to blow from the same direction year around. Unique to the Indian Ocean is the seasonal reversal of the winds known as the monsoon, which occurs at more or less fixed times each year. From April through September, the winds drive from the southwest, from eastern Africa toward India. From October through March, the winds come from the northeast, from India toward Africa. The changeover from one system roughly coincides with the equinoxes, when the sun crosses the equator.[4] (Above the equator in India, the southwest monsoon thus comes in the summer, the northeast monsoon in the winter. But these seasons are reversed in Madagascar and other regions south of the equator.)

The northeast monsoon generally is dry and accompanied by the light winds and fair weather associated with high pressure. This was the season for traveling from east to west, from Asia toward Africa. During the days of sail, Indian and Asian seaman also preferred to voyage along the coasts during the months of these northeast winds.

The southwest monsoon brings humidity and rain. From April to September, low barometric pressure prevails from the equator all the way north to the Himalayan heights. Driving from the southwest (the "roaring forties"), winds laden with moisture create a great surge and carry strong storms. The time for sailing in an easterly direction, from Africa toward Asia, began just as the southwest monsoon set in. During the three months from June through August, when the winds were at their strongest, the ports on India's western and eastern coasts were closed to shipping.

Most of Asia's populated areas, including India, lie north of the equator. Here the monsoon winds are both regular and predictable. The southwest or summer monsoon always is impatiently awaited in India, for it supplies the subcontinent with much-needed water. In some years, however, it unleashes fearful floods. And the changeover from one monsoon to the other often brings violent cyclones in the Arabian Sea and in the Bay of Bengal.

South of the equator, the southeast trade winds also tend to bring storms and cyclones, especially in the vicinity of Madagascar and mainly during the southern hemisphere's summer. The area of greatest hazard to mariners is the belt that lies between latitudes 10° and 30° south and longitudes 60° and 90° east. Mountainous waves and a swell at times traveling up to four hundred miles an hour signal the approach of a tropical storm. Even the strongest ships face extreme dangers if they sail in the southern Indian Ocean out of season.[5]

Partly because of the hazards of the southeast trades, ancient seamen stuck close to the coasts of India, Asia, and Africa, trusting to the seasonal play of the winds. In any case, there was no reason to sail directly from east to west. The geographical center of the Indian Ocean is filled with insignificant atolls and islands. For navigators, the true center of the Indian Ocean

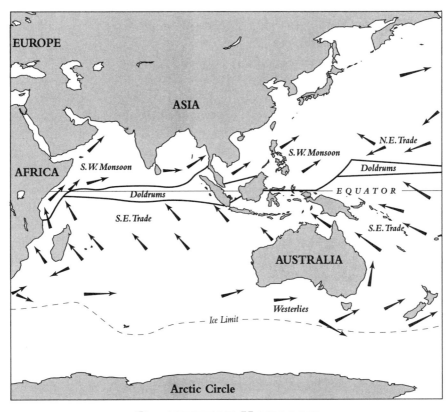

SOUTHWEST MONSOON
(APRIL/MAY THROUGH SEPTEMBER/OCTOBER)

was always the country for which it is named—India, for centuries a fabled fountain of wealth.

Another factor encouraged sailors to stick close to land. The Indian Ocean carries few strong currents, such as the Gulf Stream of the Atlantic. There is one exception. South of the equator, a strong current runs west from the Pacific, leaving the Timor Sea between Australia and Indonesia and ending up at the Mozambique Channel between eastern Africa and Madagascar. However, the distance, sailing directly west from Indonesia to Madagascar, is more than four thousand miles. This current helps to explain why Madagascar is inhabited by peoples of Indonesian extraction but never became part of any regular trade route.

Despite the risk of storm and cyclones, the Indian Ocean is relatively friendly to shipping—provided that one travels during the correct season. Because of its essentially tropical character, the Indian Ocean is free from fog, mist, drift ice, and other hazardous conditions. For centuries, Asian and Indian mariners successfully traveled in fragile vessels that would soon have foundered in the Atlantic or the Pacific.[6]

One threat to wooden ships was more intense than in colder oceans—the deadly teredo worm, which gnaws the hull and quickly transforms it into a sieve, if the wood is not sufficiently resistant.[7] To prevent disaster, mariners had to regularly clean the hulls of their vessels. In this process, known as "careening," they sailed into shallow water until the ship ran aground. The cargo, cannons, and gear were moved to one side, causing the ship to lean heavily in the other direction and exposing the area of the hull below the water. The wood was scraped clean, and hull was treated with a daubing of tallow and sulphur. A safe harbor was essential, since the ship was defenseless while it was careened.

EUROPE'S EAST INDIA COMPANIES INVADE ASIA

Around the year 1700, three systems of mercantile trade coexisted in the Indian Ocean. Thousands of ships, both large and small, took cargoes between Asian ports. Most of these "country traders" were owned and sailed by Indians, although an increasing number belonged to Europeans. The goods they carried and the routes they sailed often had been established for centuries. Superimposed upon this system of coastal traders since the 1500s was the commerce in luxury goods carried from Asia to Europe, normally in large vessels. In addition, from the 1670s, English and Anglo-Americans purchased slaves at Madagascar for sale at Barbados and Jamaica.[8]

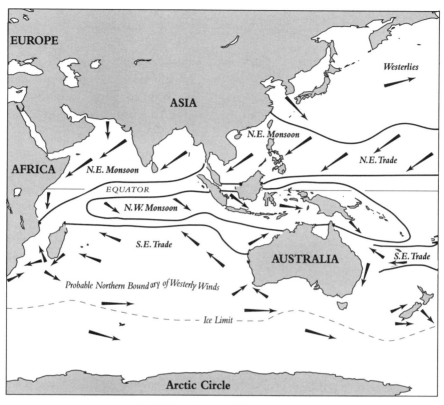

EUROPE

ASIA

AFRICA

Westerlies

N.E. Monsoon

N.E. Trade

N.E. Monsoon

EQUATOR

N.W. Monsoon

S.E. Trade

AUSTRALIA

S.E. Trade

Probable Northern Boundary of Westerly Winds

Ice Limit

Arctic Circle

NORTHEAST MONSOON
(NOVEMBER TO APRIL)

Although not as large as East Indiamen, slave ships were built to carry considerable cargo.

Ships bound for Europe mainly carried rich cargoes—lightweight Oriental products that were sold for very high prices. At first, pepper and other spices made up the bulk of the shipments. Imports of silk and cotton swelled from the 1670s, as Europeans and Latin Americans wanted finer and more comfortable clothes. The demand for coffee, tea, and Chinese porcelains also began to increase.[9]

Importing and reselling these luxury goods was very profitable; moreover, people at the time considered the eastern trade even more lucrative than it really was. Every government wanted to keep these real and imagined profits within its own borders. National trading companies were created and granted monopolies to help them acquire the large sums needed in the precarious business of trading with the Orient. Every voyage—both to the East and back to Europe—had to overcome enormous physical privations, the dangers of the sea, pirates, and European competitors (often more cutthroat than any pirate). In many cases, goods had to be purchased from local merchants who drove a hard bargain. Since Europeans produced relatively few goods that Indians and Asians wanted to purchase, ships heading east were loaded with gold and silver coins.

Portuguese vessels, the first to travel from Europe to India, were financed and managed as a monopoly of the crown or royal government. For about a century, the Portuguese king enjoyed a virtual lock over the sea routes to the Orient. Then the Dutch and English East India Companies entered into competition, determined to snatch away the lucrative Eastern trade. The Dutch company, chartered in 1602, was given jurisdiction over all lands and seas between the Cape of Good Hope and the Strait of Magellan. The English company, founded on December 31, 1600, enjoyed similar privileges. Both East India companies combined entrepreneurial and governmental functions. They acquired most of their capital from private investors, and they were was governed by boards of directors, who were largely independent of English and Dutch rulers. But the companies also functioned as governments in the regions they entered, where they built fortresses, exercised civil and criminal jurisdiction, coined money, waged land and sea wars, and made treaties and alliances.[10]

During the next seventy years, the Dutch East India Company succeeded in taking most Oriental trade away from the Portuguese. Throughout its long life, the Dutch Company sought more than merely a monopoly of Dutch trade with the Orient; wherever this was possible, it tried to control *all* trade, both local and international. Using brutal force, the company succeeded in expelling the Portuguese and English from much of East Asia and India. Portuguese traders and soldiers were driven out of Malacca and Java (later the Dutch East Indies and now Indonesia) as well as Ceylon and Japan. During the 1650s and 1660s, troops of the Dutch East India Company went on to seize Portuguese factories on India's western and eastern coasts. However, the Portugese retained a role in Indian trade by holding onto their forts at Goa, Daman, and Diu in India as well as at Macao in China.[11]

Although it made progress more slowly than its Dutch competitor, the English East India Company began to gain strength at the end of the 1600s. An alliance between the English and Dutch companies against the Portugese ended with the Massacre of Amboina in 1623. The Dutch had agreed that English merchants could trade on Amboina Island in the southern Moluccas. Despite this and alleging an English conspiracy to capture the fort by surprise, the Dutch governor arrested and tortured eighteen English traders, twelve of whom were executed. The English company gave up attempts to gain a foothold in the East Indies where the Dutch fiercely defended their monopoly.

The English East India Company also made slow progress on the Indian subcontinent, party because it lacked good bases of operations. On the east coast, a concession was obtained at Madras in 1639, and Fort Saint George was built to defend the Company's holdings. But Bombay, on the west coast, was acquired only in 1668, and Calcutta, in Bengal, was founded during the 1690s.[12] By then the English company had numerous smaller outposts up and down both coasts as well as the three regional headquarters, called Presidencies, at Bombay, Madras, and Calcutta.[13] The Dutch maintained their supremacy in commerce between Europe and the East into the eighteenth century. Nevertheless there was a relative fall in the volume of Indian commerce controlled by the Dutch, suggesting that the English Company might be gaining the upper hand.[14]

The French East India Company was even slower to get off the ground than the English Company. The first French East India Company, founded in 1642, poured its efforts and money into the colony at Fort Dauphin on Madagascar. A savage massacre by the Malagasy ended these efforts in 1674. Those who escaped took refuge on Réunion Island, but that tiny colony also vegetated until the beginning of the eighteenth century.

Karachi

Diu

Gujarat (Province)
Ahmadabad

Surat

Bombay

Dabhol

Rajapur

Carwar
Goa

Mangalore

Malabar Coast

Tellicherry
Mahe
Calicut
Cochin
Purakadd
Quilon
Anjengo

Cape
Comorin
Tuticorin

CEYLON
Kandy

Coromandel Coast

Madras
Pondicherry
Ft. St. David
Tranquebar
Negapatam

Viravasaram
Masulipatam

Calcutta

Dacca

Mrauk-U

Chittagong

Mandalay
Ava

Rangoon

Negrais

Andaman Is.

Nicobar Is.

INDIA

France's second East India Company was formally established in 1664 and paid more attention to India itself. In 1668, a west coast trading factory was opened at Surat. On the east coast, Pondicherry was founded in 1672 and formally granted to the French company by Emperor Aurangzib sixteen years later. A foundation had been laid for the eighteenth-century battle with England to control India. Up until the 1720s, however, the number of ships and cargoes traveling between France and India remained far below the volume of trade conducted by the Dutch and English companies.

The English and French companies did not hit their stride until the end of the seventeenth century. The Danish East India Company, in contrast, got off to a fine start by obtaining a concession in 1621 at Tranquebar on India's east coast. However, the company could not turn a profit after expenses and went bankrupt in 1634. A second company replaced it, followed by a third in 1686, and a fourth in 1732. By the 1690s, the Danes in India barely hung on to their trading posts. They lived by their wits, trading with pirates and sometimes turning pirates themselves.

EAST INDIAMEN CARRY IMMENSELY RICH BOOTY

Pirates rarely captured East Indiamen. Few were available to be hunted, since only a small number sailed each year. Their routes took them well out to sea, while pirates stayed close to the coasts. Moreover, as the years passed, the East Indiamen became better armed and more likely to fiercely resist attack. During the entire Saint Mary's period, only three were taken—none through assaults at sea.

The first was captured in 1696, when Ralph Stout and William Kelley infiltrated the crew of the *Mocha* and incited a mutiny that took the ship. The other two East Indiamen were seized while anchored at the Comoro Islands. In 1703, John Bowen and Thomas Howard took over the *Pembroke,* which had gotten stuck in the anchorage at Mayotte. In August 1720, John Taylor and Edward England pounced on the *Cassandra* while it was anchored at Johanna Island. In both cases, the Company ships, unlike smaller merchantmen, put up a fierce battle.

Company ships proved to be worth fighting for, as the *Mocha* and the *Cassandra* carried veritable treasures in gold and silver. The cargoes shipped in East Indiamen also are evidence of the great wealth that brought pirates to the Indian Ocean. Because so many bizarre legends have been foisted on the Madagascar raiders, one comes to suspect undocumented claims about their deeds. It is natural to wonder whether they really did capture as much booty as was claimed at the time. Did a hundred or two hundred men really share out treasure and goods worth millions or even hundreds of millions of dollars in modern currency?

Although pirate booty was exaggerated in some cases, there is no question that extremely valuable cargoes routinely passed through the Indian Ocean, the Red Sea, and the Persian Gulf. The merchandise carried by the East Indiamen—spices, cloth, drugs, and precious jewelry—was the same as the merchandise that traveled between Asian ports. If the pirates took only a few East Indiamen, they captured literally hundreds of coastal traders (the ships themselves of considerable value) carrying rich cargoes. Persons that sell stolen goods to fences seldom receive their full value. So rich were the cargoes they seized, however, that the pirates became wealthy men even when they got only a tenth of the value.

Although the types of cargos brought to England changed, the overall amount imported from India remained relatively constant between 1688 and 1713. Each season, East Indiamen made about thirteen round-trip voyages. During the 1680s, the goods from India brought in about £1 million a year (about $500 million today). On average, each ship contained merchandise worth around $40 million in modern money. And the vessels returning to the East also held great riches. To pay for spices and cloth, East India Company ships carried to India more than 500,000 pounds of silver coins and 15,000 pounds of gold coins.[15]

Dutch fleets carried even larger amounts of silk and fine cotton. In 1695, Company vessels brought in textiles worth 2.35 million Dutch guilders (about $120 million). The East India Company partially paid for this cloth by selling Indonesian spices to the Indians. However, during the 1690s, the Company also shipped to India silver coins and bars worth 29 million guilders ($1.5 billion).[16]

The smallest and least successful of the European competitors, the French East India Company could not send out a fleet every year. When merchantmen did make it back to France, they carried equally costly cargo. In 1691, the merchandise from three vessels brought in 1.7 million French livres (about $42 million). In 1702, six ships from India carried goods that sold for 3.7 million livres ($92 million).[17]

THE PIRATES' ASIAN HUNTING GROUNDS
The establishment of European trading companies had not yet diminished India's commerce with the Ottoman Empire and Southeast Asia. Around

1700, the coastal waters of the Arabian and Bengal Seas were home to thousands of vessels, ranging in size from small Arabian dhows to stately 1,300-ton vessels built of teak. (The larger ships, intended for long-distance trade, looked much like those found in Atlantic waters. Following the arrival of the Portuguese, Indian shipbuilders adapted European designs both for vessels and for naval cannon.) Although their crews were Indian, officers might be as ethnically diverse as their craft. Indian shipowners gladly employed Europeans, especially as gunners and navigating officers.[18]

Native merchants continued to dominate commerce within the Indian Ocean. Farther east, the Dutch East India Company had seized most of the ports in the Java Sea and used force to keep non-Dutch traders out of its Indonesian empire. (Only Achin in Sumatra was still open to other European and Asian merchants.) Goods from all Dutch factories were taken to Batavia (now known as Jakarta or Djakarta) on Company-owned vessels and redistributed to other parts of Asia as well as to Europe.[19] But the Dutch failed to duplicate this monopoly in India, and the English and French Companies lacked the resources to freeze out competitors. When it came to the Indian and Asian "country trade," Dutch, English, and French traders played second string to native entrepreneurs.

A limited number of wealthy merchant families—mainly but not exclusively Hindus—dominated commerce flowing between India and other Asian regions. The largest number of cargoes were shipped by traders from the Gujarat region in the northwest, near India's modern border with Pakistan. Bengalis from the region around Calcutta also were active, and some Armenian Christians enjoyed influential contacts at the court of the Mogul emperors.

Trade under the English flag was carried on by East India Company officials acting on their own behalf and for their private profit. At Surat, Madras, and Calcutta, these Company officials were joined after 1700 by a growing colony of Jews, Armenians, and British "interlopers" not affiliated with the East India Company. Some European sea captains owned or co-owned their vessels, while others were employees of East India Company officials or Indian merchant-shipowners.[20]

Whatever their nationality, merchants and shipowners competed in the same markets. Country traders transported some bulk goods, primarily foodstuffs and cotton and dyes for the weaving industry. They also conveyed the same luxury products that the East India Companies exported to Europe. Pepper, spices, sugar, silks, damasks, and porcelain were carried from the Far

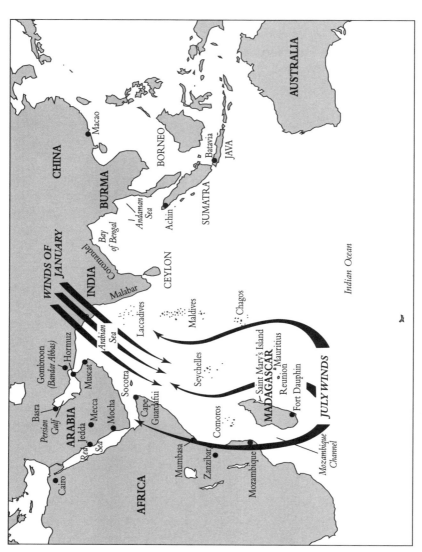

THE PIRATES' HUNTING GROUNDS

East to Surat and beyond to the Ottoman and Persian Empires. On the return voyage from Persia and the Middle East, Indian ships contained equally rich goods. The Middle East provided carpets and rugs, wrought metalwork, and Italian woolens as well as dried fruits and nuts from the Yemen, Persia, and Afghanistan. Some rare products—incense, attar of roses, and Shiraz wine—carried very high prices indeed. Closer to home, ships returning to Surat picked up coffee at Mocha (Al Mukna), dates at Basra, and thoroughbred horses at Gombroon.[21] Opium and other medicinal drugs were widely distributed and were taken as far east as China.

A pirate vessel had no difficulty getting rid of captured rich textiles and spices. During the 1690s, Thomas Tew and other captains received high prices for booty brought back to Rhode Island and New York. Some men stayed at Saint Mary's and trusted Adam Baldridge as a go-between with North American merchants. In May 1697, John Hoar transferred Indian cloth—said to be worth £20,000 ($10 million)—to the merchant ship *Fortune* for sale in New York.[22] At a later stage, when the Saint Mary's men were thoroughly familiar with Indian ports, they found plenty of Indian merchants willing to purchase looted merchandise.

INDIAN MERCHANTMEN PROVIDE RICH PREY

When European marauders arrived in India at the end of the seventeenth century, they found that a few port cities totally dominated maritime commerce. Located on India's northeastern coast slightly south of Gujarat, the city of Surat was the headquarters for commerce coming from the west toward India.[23] Ships from Egypt traveled down the Red Sea to Jedda, where they were transferred to Indian vessels.[24] Jedda also was the port of embarkation for the pilgrim fleet returning from Mecca.

From Jedda, Indian vessels carried passengers and cargo to the mouth of the Red Sea at Mocha, which was gradually surpassing Aden as a commercial port. In addition to Egyptian and Turkish luxuries, the Red Sea ports received valuable merchandise from Italy, Greece, and Syria, including gold, silver, mercury, vermillion, copper, rosewater, woolen cloth, glass beads, and weapons. At Mocha and Aden, Arab traders added opium and fine horses. Heading to the Red Sea to pick up these goods, Surat vessels brought Indian and Indonesian products, such as spices, rare woods, Chinese porcelain, indigo, and above all cotton cloth.[25]

The annual "pilgrim fleet" was an especially rich prize on the return voyage from Mocha to Surat because the ships carried gold and jewels. Each year, large vessels took Indian Muslims to Mocha, where they began the land journey to Mecca. The fleet enjoyed a special status in the Mogul Empire. As an act of religious piety, the emperor sent his own ships with the fleet, so even the poorest Muslim could make his pilgrimage to Mecca. But merchants joined the faithful on the voyage, taking Indian cloth and spices to Mocha and returning with coffee and gold.[26]

The sea lanes between Surat and the Persian Gulf also carried extremely valuable commodities. From Istanbul and eastern Turkey, some goods went overland by caravan through Syria and Mesopotamia to the Ottoman port at Basra, where they began a sea voyage down the Persian Gulf. Wares from Persia itself as well as from Syria and central Asia were transferred to Indian vessels along the Persian or eastern side of the gulf at Gombroon (Bandar Abbas) and the nearby island of Hormuz.[27]

European marauders at first targeted the luxurious booty carried by vessels in the Red and Arabian Seas. Later they headed east after learning that many of these cargoes originally had been brought from southeast Asia to India through the Bay of Bengal. Both Gujarat merchants and Bengalis headed east from Masulipatam to Ceylon, Achin in Sumatra, the Philippines, and southern China.[28]

These major ports lay at some distance from another. From Surat, a vessel heading to Hormuz undertook a voyage of some 1,300 miles; 2,000 miles separated Surat and Mocha. Whether they were owned by Indian, Armenian, or European merchants, luxury goods traveled in large vessels and usually in large, infrequent convoys. To avoid losing their entire fortune to shipwreck or pirates, long-distance traders took part in various types of commerce on several routes, and they split valuable cargoes between several vessels.[29]

The location of ports and the rhythm of navigation were largely determined by the alternation between the northeast and southwest monsoons. For navigation in the Indian Ocean could not be carried on at all seasons as it was in Europe and North America. Outside the proper season, no one ventured to put out to sea.

November to March, during the northeast monsoon, were the months for voyaging from Surat to Mocha in the Red Sea or Hormuz in the Persian Gulf. After March, the winds shifted to the southwest, making travel almost impossible. On one occasion, a dilatory captain did not reach the entrance to the Red Sea until the middle of July. Forced to beat against the southwest monsoon, the ship took forty days to reach Jedda.[30]

Voyagers heading for India also had to take the monsoon into account.

The pilgrimage to Mecca, the Hadj, takes place during the twelfth month of the Muslim year, which moves through the solar calendar each year. After the sacred events were over, pilgrims frequently had to remain at Jedda, waiting on the winds. Marauders could estimate their itinerary with relative accuracy. In 1694, for example, the pilgrim fleet waited out the southwest monsoon, leaving in August[31] to reach Surat by the beginning of September.[32] While the pilgrims tarried, Henry Every's *Fancy* and five other pirate warships gathered at the entrance to the Red Sea, ready for their prey.

Timing was even more difficult in the case of voyages to the East Indies and China. Ships could get down to Malacca and the strait only until April when the southwest monsoon set in. The return voyage from Manila or China called for at least two reverse changes of wind. Surat shipping often to had to take shelter in the Straits of Malacca during the months of contrary wind.[33] As in the Red Sea, pirates could calmly wait for their prey, knowing that the latter had to follow a fixed rhythm.

THE ROUTE TO THE EAST

The rhythm of the monsoons also influenced voyages between Europe and Asia. The various East India companies ordered captains to leave Europe for India by the beginning of March at the very latest. By departing in the early spring, ships could make it south to the Cape of Good Hope and cross into the Indian Ocean by May, when the southwest monsoon begins to blow. This schedule took them to the west coast of India in October or November.[34]

From Europe, ships took the northeast trade winds down the coast of Africa as far south as the Cape Verde Islands. Once across the equator, however, the trade winds in the Atlantic come from the southeast, making it impossible to continue directly south. Vessels headed far to the west, sometimes as far as the coast of Brazil, before turning south to tack against the southeast trades.

Having arrived at the Indian Ocean, European vessels followed one of three main routes. British merchant vessels frequently used the "inner passage," the sea lanes taken by the Portuguese fleet under Vasco da Gama in 1498. After leaving the Cape of Good Hope, this route followed the African coast through the Mozambique Channel between Madagascar and Africa. Ships bound for Surat or the Malabar coast crossed the equator at about 54° east. From that point, they steered directly east for Indian ports.

Another inner route lay between Madagascar's eastern coast and the Seychelles group. Both of these passages could be used from April through

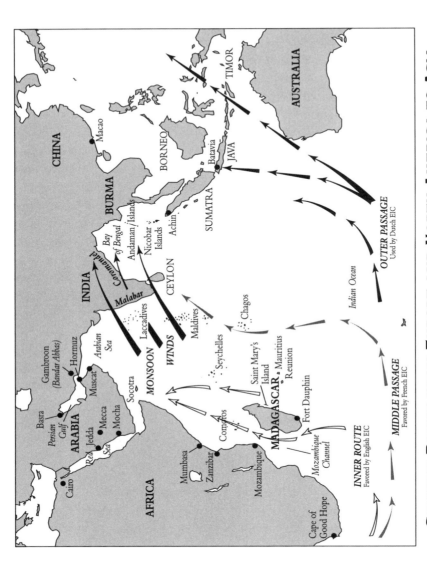

SUMMER ROUTE FROM EUROPE AND NORTH AMERICA TO ASIA

September, during the southwest monsoon. The choice between the two depended on the exact timing of a ship's arrival at the Cape.[35]

Vessels taking the "middle passage" turned north at about 65 or 70 degrees of longitude. French naval and merchant vessels often followed this route and stopped at Réunion or Mauritius on the way to the French trading stations at Pondicherry. The "outer route" was less commonly used. Vessels making this passage went even farther east before turning north between 80° and 95°. Some Dutch ships, on their way to the Sunda Strait, avoided India altogether. These vessels sailed northeast from the Cape of Good Hope, traveling more than 4,400 nautical miles across the entire width of the southern Indian Ocean.[36]

Just as the outward voyage from Europe had to be made at set seasons, the return from Asia also followed fixed schedules. Ideally, ships departed from Indonesia by the first of December and left India by Christmas.[37] It was essential to pass around the Cape of Good Hope before the end of May to avoid the strong gales and rough seas of the Southern winter. On the voyage to Europe, most vessels took one of the routes east of Madagascar. It was too risky to spend time in the Mozambique Channel or in the southern Indian Ocean between December and April, the season of cyclones.

The complexities engendered by the various wind systems were summed up in a letter sent to the Board of Trade in September 1698 by William Dampier, an expert navigator.[38]

> The Council of Trade yesterday asked me. (1) How long a ship might be running from England to Madagascar at this time of year. I answered that to the best of my judgement it might be done in three months and a half. (2) How long a ship might be in passing from Madagascar to the Red Sea? . . . [Since] on the coast of Madagascar the winds are at N.E. and N.N.E. from the end of January to the end of May (which is right against them) the voyage could not be performed in less than two months. (3) How long a ship might be in passing from the Red Sea to Cape Comorin. This depends upon the setting in of the western monsoon. . . . thus if a ship leave England in November, she may reach Madagascar by the middle of February and the Red Sea about the Middle of April. She must then wait about a month for the monsoon, and about the middle of June she will reach Cape Comorin, a week or two sooner or later according to setting in of monsoon.

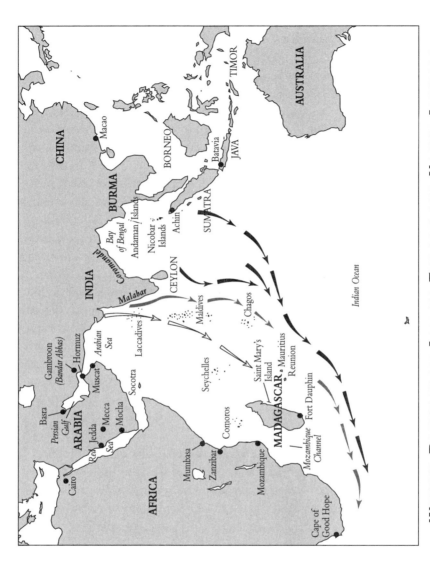

WINTER ROUTE FROM ASIA TO EUROPE AND NORTH AMERICA

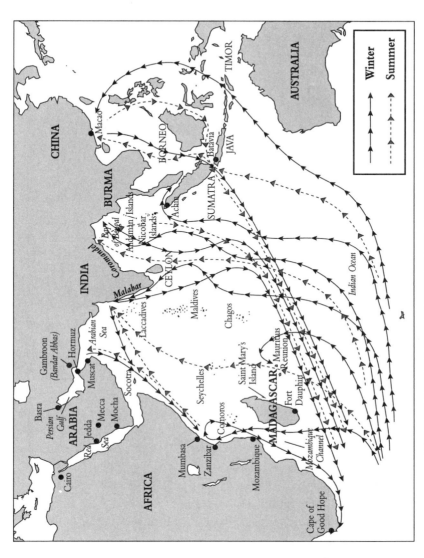

EIGHTEENTH-CENTURY NAVIGATION ROUTES

Legend:
Winter
Summer

Labels on map:
CHINA
Macao
BURMA
BORNEO
Batavia
JAVA
SUMATRA
Achin
TIMOR
AUSTRALIA
Bay of Bengal
Andaman Islands
Nicobar Islands
Coromandel
INDIA
CEYLON
Malabar
Maldives
Chagos
Indian Ocean
Gambroon (Bandar Abbas)
Hormuz
Muscat
Arabian Sea
Basra
Persian Gulf
Jedda
Mecca
Mocha
Socotra
ARABIA
Red Sea
Cairo
Laccadives
Seychelles
Saint Mary's Island
Mauritius
Réunion
MADAGASCAR
Fort Dauphin
Comoros
Mumbasa
Zanzibar
Mozambique
Mozambique Channel
AFRICA
Cape of Good Hope

CHAPTER THREE

Madagascar Is Invaded by Polynesians, Arabs, Africans, and Europeans

Madagascar is one of the world's great islands. Nearly a thousand miles long and three hundred fifty miles wide, it is about as large as California and more than twice the size of Great Britain. The variety of vegetation and the diversity of human settlers is astounding.

The entire eastern coast presents a straight line of unbroken sand dunes. Immediately inland is a narrow coastal plain hemmed in by an escarpment. The land quickly rises to a high inland plateau, with elevations of nearly six thousand feet occurring within sixty miles of the coast. This upland plateau is a disorderly jumble of hills with occasional majestic outcrops of granite and scattered volcanic cones. Rivers flowing east to the Indian Ocean must cross this mountain barrier, creating spectacular waterfalls. Traveling west from the high plateau, the land drops off more gradually. Rivers fall in regular valleys and broaden out into large alluvial estuaries. Wide plains run along much of the western and southern coasts.

The mountains of the high plateau divide Madagascar into two main climatic regions—a narrow "windward" area along the Indian Ocean and a wider "leeward" region facing the Mozambique Channel. Blowing throughout the year across the vast expanse of the Indian Ocean, the southeast trade winds deposit their rains mainly on Madagascar's northeastern coast. Tamatave, somewhat south of Saint Mary's, receives on average 120 inches a year, with rain falling on two out of every three days.[1]

During the seventeenth century, this eastern coastal plain was almost entirely covered by a dense tropical forest. In many sections, this has been

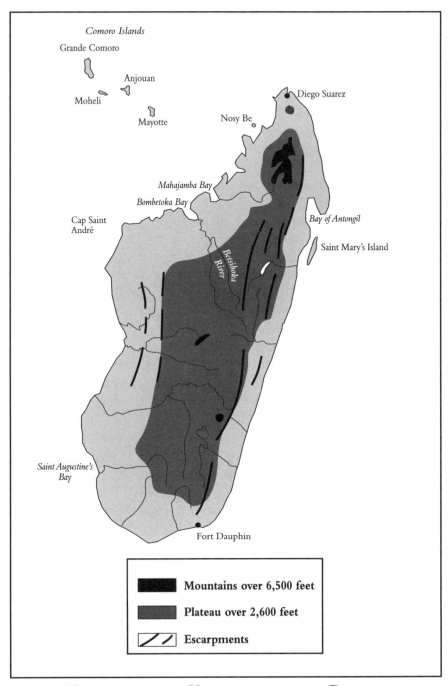

Comoro Islands

Grande Comoro

Anjouan

Moheli

Mayotte

Diego Suarez

Nosy Be

Mahajamba Bay

Bombetoka Bay

Cap Saint
André

Bay of Antongil

Saint Mary's Island

Betsiboka River

Saint Augustine's
Bay

Fort Dauphin

Mountains over 6,500 feet

Plateau over 2,600 feet

Escarpments

MADAGASCAR: MOUNTAINS AND PLAINS

replaced by the *sàvoka,* a degraded secondary foliage characterized by the fan-shaped travelers tree (*ravenala*). Ferns and scattered tufts of grass barely cover and fail to protect the soil.

On the high plateau, the climate is more temperate. The original forest has been destroyed nearly everywhere. Here even the *sàvoka* gives way to steppes covered by a coarse grass known as *bòzaka.* The barren, eroded hills are interspersed with terraced rice cultivation in the valleys.

The moisture-laden southeast trade winds fail to cross the high plateau and reach the western regions. The climate is hot but drier and more continental, with a marked dry season between May and November. Rainfall diminishes rapidly as one moves towards the southwest. On the southeastern coast, Fort Dauphin still receives about fifty inches a year. But across the island in the southwest, Saint Augustine's Bay is semidesert, with fewer than fourteen inches of rain a year.[2]

Before the Malagasy arrived, a less dense but still tropical forest originally covered parts of Madagascar's western coast. But here, too, the forest was quickly destroyed in this region of a long dry season. Already during the 1600s, arid plains or savanna covered by coarse grass and scattered palm trees covered much of the southwest. The region largely was given over to cattle. Although not especially favorable for raising cows, the land is even less suitable for growing crops. Around Saint Augustine's Bay in the southwest, the soil supports only a thorny scrub punctuated by the grotesque shapes of the baobab trees.

The mountainous nature of the country and the impermeable granite watershed at the central core of the island made inland travel extremely difficult. Crossing the island from east to west over the high plateau was virtually impossible. Nor are the rivers naturally navigable. Indeed, the width of rivers along the west coast forms another considerable travel barrier to the north or to the south.

THE MALAGASY: POLYNESIANS IN AFRICA

The buccaneers were only one group in a long line of immigrants to Madagasgar who arrived by sea. Whether in the seventeenth century or today, Europeans and Americans might well expect Madagascar to be inhabited by a Negro population with African customs. The island is separated from Eastern Africa only by the Mozambique Channel, a mere 250 miles of water. Indeed, both pirates and government officials commonly referred to all Malagasy as Africans or Negroes (*noirs* in French).[3]

In fact, several distinct racial types coexist today—and the contrasts were even stronger during the seventeenth century. Some individuals appear to be of Malay or Indochinese origin, with long, straight hair, pale-brown skins, and a slight bone structure. Others closely resemble the Bantu of southern Africa: They are much darker in color, and have crinkly hair, thick lips, and flat noses. Most inhabitants fall somewhere in between and combine the extreme Indonesia and African physical types. Generally the peoples living along the northeastern coast and on the central plateau most nearly resemble Indonesians, while those along the west coast appear closer to black Africans.

Whatever their appearance, Madagascar's peoples speak a common language, also known as Malagasy. This language is nothing like the idioms on the African mainland and belongs to the Indonesian branch of the Malayan/Polynesian linguistic group. Despite regional variations, the island's peoples also share many habits and institutions. Like their language, this common culture seems to owe more to Indonesian than to African influences.[4] Still, because overland travel in Madagascar is so difficult, the island's inhabitants have not coalesced into one common nationality. Although they all speak a common language, the Malagasy remain ethnically diverse.

Madagascar was uninhabited until the first millennium A.D. The first arrivals were Polynesian peoples who came from Indonesia in outrigger canoes, much as other Polynesian navigators sailed east, populating islands as far away as Hawaii and Easter Island. These early settlers may have voyaged due west from Java, following the trade winds and the equatorial east-west current. Or they may have taken a more northern route and settled first along the coast of eastern Africa before making for Madagascar.

Polynesian seamen were followed by Arabic-speaking traders moving down Africa's east coast from the north. By the ninth century, their dhows had reached the Comoro Islands, and they went on to establish commercial links with Madagascar. Over time, "Arab" merchants built trading posts all along the northwest coast, which were still flourishing when Europeans arrived in the sixteenth and seventeenth centuries.

These Arab-speaking peoples mingled and intermarried with the Bantu tribes. They also added to the island's genetic mix by carrying African slaves in both directions between Madagascar and the mainland. For hundreds of years, until the French conquerors abolished slavery in 1896, there was a continuous trade in black African slaves. The Malagasy imported slaves from Africa and also enslaved Africans captured in continuous intertribal wars. By mating with their female concubines, Malagasy slave owners contributed to the blurring of the races.[5]

"WHITE KINGS" OF MADAGASCAR

As in the Garden of Eden, the human population of Madagascar created its own terrors. When Europeans arrived during the sixteenth century, the Malagasy were fragmented into numerous clans and tribes. Along both coasts, many hundreds of chieftains ruled tiny principalities. These chiefs continuously warred with one another to obtain loot and slaves without attempting to expand their territories. As the Reverend John Ovington described the situation,

> Madagascar is governed by many kings, independent from one from another, who often make war, each one trying to encroach upon his neighbors. . . . Their wealth consists . . . in the great number of their slaves, and all their wars have no other end but to take prisoners and reduce them into slaves.

Beginning in the late 1600s, chiefs of the Sakalava tribes in the south and southwest grew more ambitious. Claiming divine authority, they deliberately sought to create larger political groupings. Internecine warfare and slave raids grew even more vicious. Chiefs and kings welcomed Europeans with firearms, rewarding their help with up to half the enslaved prisoners.[6] It is possible that the arrival of white slavers accelerated both tribal wars and the consolidation of kingdoms. The exchange of muskets for slaves created a vicious cycle that increased royal absolutism. Muskets facilitated slave raids which were carried out to obtain muskets.

The origins of Malagasy dynasties are unclear. Most kings claimed to be descended from "white men." This term did not imply a European origin. It suggests only that the dynasty's founder may have been Arab-speaking or possibly from a family that had retained its Indonesian racial appearance. Nevertheless, by the time Europeans came to Madagascar, the Malagasy were accustomed to a racially mixed society in which lighter-skinned kings and nobles governed darker-skinned slaves.

THE PEACEABLE KINGDOM OF THE BETSIMISARAKA

There were real similarities between the two groups that facilitated their intercourse and made it easier for the pirates to integrate themselves into

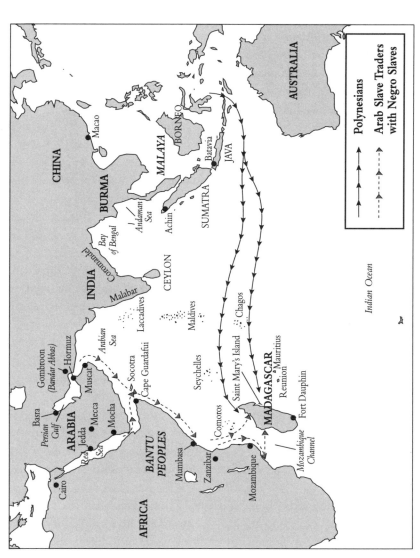

MIGRATIONS TO MADAGASCAR

Malagasy society. Compared to hierarchical settler societies, the native and mariner communities were democratic and egalitarian, and both highly prized cohesion and cooperation within the group. While they were on the island, moreover, the mariners—like the Malagasy—mainly sought to enjoy a peaceful and pleasant life.

From Antongil Bay south to Mananiary, the coastal strip was inhabited by the Betsimisaraka, the second largest ethnic group on the island. Further south along the coast lived smaller groups such as the Antaifasy and Antaimoro. All were Malayo-Polynesian in ethnicity. While there had been some Arabic influence, there had been no African penetration.

Some customs were the same throughout Madagascar. But the details of everyday life were very different among the various peoples separated by large distances and geographical barriers. African influences were strongest among the Sakalava on the Madagascar's west coast. Along the northeast coast the houses built on stilts, the tools, the fruit trees and edible plants—all were similar to those in East Asia. Rice was the main food and was served accompanied by a variety of spicy dishes.

This narrow coastal strip is split into small segments by numerous rivers rushing down from the eastern escarpment. Particularly in the northeast, tropical rain forests occupy the region. This further isolated village communities—even those at a relatively short distance from the Indian Ocean coast. Unlike the Sakalava along the western coast, the eastern peoples had not yet coalesced into kingdoms, and the village was still the highest political unit. Even today, the modern name for these peoples—*Betsimisaraka*, meaning "the many inseparable"—remains more of a political slogan than a fact.

Despite their divisions, the inhabitants of the region shared a common culture and beliefs. The Betsimisaraka believed in the immortality of the soul and life after death. They recognized one totally good supreme creator (known to them as Zanahary) but believed that this high god had little to do with their daily life. The spirits dwelling in the forest had more influence, as did a devil who harms men unless placated with offerings. Many places and activities were considered *taboo,* or forbidden.[7]

But it was their veneration of ancestors that had the greatest influence on the life of the Betsimisaraka. Like all Malagasy, they believed that the dead and the living form a single society in constant contact. Although the dead have disappeared from this world, they lead a new existence in the next. The ancestors remain in touch with their descendants, judging their

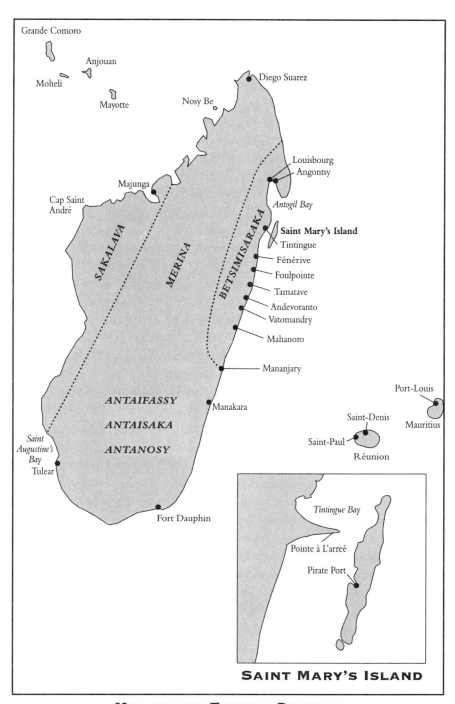

Grande Comoro

Anjouan

Moheli

Mayotte

Nosy Be

Diego Suarez

Majunga

Cap Saint
André

SAKALAVA

MERINA

BETSIMISARAKA

Louisbourg
Angontsy

Antogil Bay

Saint Mary's Island

Tintingue

Fénérive

Foulpointe

Tamatave

Andevoranto

Vatomandry

Mahanoro

Mananjary

Manakara

ANTAIFASSY

ANTAISAKA

ANTANOSY

*Saint
Augustine's
Bay*
Tulear

Fort Dauphin

Port-Louis

Saint-Denis

Saint-Paul

Mauritius

Réunion

Tintingue Bay

Pointe à L'arreé

Pirate Port

SAINT MARY'S ISLAND

MALAGASY ETHNIC GROUPS

obedience to tradition and giving them advice in dreams. They punish serious violations of taboo by visiting sickness and death on malefactors.

Many societies have believed that the dead can bring good or bad fortune to their descendants. On Madagascar these beliefs influenced every
aspect of life. The Malagasy sough to live out their lives in peace and to
continue the family through their children. They highly prized harmony
with the other members—both living and dead—of their family and clan.
The family was the essential political and social unit, and it served as the
model for other social alliances. Two or more men from different clans
would thus create an artificial family tie through blood brotherhood.

The descendants of one living ancestor formed an extended family.
Several large families with the same dead ancestors made up a clan. Its
members invoked their honored dead through prayers and sacrifices. They
shared the same family tomb, which was held in great veneration. Exclusion
from the ancestral tomb was a severe punishment, reserved for the most
serious crimes.[8]

Some families and clans were thought to be of noble ancestry. Nobles
had particular religious duties and privileges, but their material way of life
was much the same as that of commoners. The two castes lived in similar
types of houses and shared comparable economic conditions. Both owned
slaves, a group made up of prisoners of war, descendants of slaves, and
members of the clan who had committed serious crimes.

Village governments followed democratic practices. Before resolving
any important matter, the chief was expected to call a council or assembly
of the heads of families. Decisions were made, and criminal judgments were
rendered, only after consulting the living and dead members of the clan.[9]

Within this framework of kinship networks, men and women were relatively equal in rights and duties. Marriage was contracted with limited cer-
emony and mainly involved a payment to the bride's parents. Affluent men
often had several wives, and either partner could leave if dissatisfied.[10]
Although they did different kinds of work than men, women enjoyed considerable power. They directed the home, influencing and sometimes controlling their husbands. They were free to come and go as they pleased and
expressed their opinions at public assemblies.

Despite their emphasis on family ties, the Malagasy did not unduly
restrict sexual activities. Boys and girls enjoyed complete liberty, and there
was no stigma of immorality attached to promiscuity even after marriage.
When friends stayed overnight, fathers offered them their daughters, and

husbands loaned them their wives. Among the Betsimisaraka, wives were free to initiate sexual liaisons on their own—especially at clan feasts, which featured generous amounts of alcoholic beverages.[11]

Although it did not restrict sexual activities, the emphasis on ancestry did lead to considerable color prejudice. For centuries the Malagasy had imported Nergo slaves. Nobles tended to be whiter than commoners, and black skin was associated with servile status. Parents did not want their children to marry Africans, whereas they accepted and encouraged marriages to Europeans. A light color was considered attractive, and the extended family absorbed children of mixed blood without difficulty.

EGYPTIAN PHARAOHS AND ROMAN EMPERORS
By the time the buccaneers showed up in the 1690s, many other Europeans already had stopped at Madagascar, but none of the others stayed on. It is one of the island's many oddities that white mariners had come to the island thousands of years before the Polynesian settlers arrived. For centuries, Mediterranean mariners sailed down the Red Sea to the Indian Ocean. Some made for India, while others headed south along the African coast. But they had come to trade for luxury goods and did not stay long on the uninhabited island of Madagascar.

Egyptian expeditions to the "land of Punt" began as early as 2,800 B.C. and continued for two thousand years. According to the Jewish scriptures, the Phoenicians built a navy for King Solomon, sailed it to "Ophir," and brought back gold and sandalwood.[12] Phoenician voyages in the Indian Ocean continued for at least another four centuries. About 600 B.C., under Pharaoh Necho II, the Greek historian Herodotus says,[13] another Phoenician expedition successfully circled the entire continent of Africa. Leaving from the Red Sea, the Phoenician fleet returned to Egypt through the straits of Gibraltar and the Mediterranean.

In 510 B.C., Herodotus also relates, Persian fleet traveled from the Indus River to the Gulf of Suez.[14] Greco-Egyptian navigators continued to visit the Indian Ocean for centuries after Egypt was conquered first by the Ptolemies (who ruled from 305 to 30 B.C.) and later by the Roman Emperors. During the first century A.D., a sea captain wrote the *Periplus Maris Erythraei,* describing Indian Ocean commerce and sea routes. Since one sea route went down the coast of Africa as far as Zanzibar, Greek mariners probably landed on Madagascar at some point.

The rise of Islam during the seventh century A.D. ended European voyages to the east. Individual travelers might take the caravan route across Arabia and as far east as China. Marco Polo, one of these explorers, described a large island off Africa named Madagascar. But the Muslim dynasties ruling Egypt and Persia denied Europeans access to the Indian Ocean for almost eight centuries.

Europeans returned in the early 1500s, looking to seize the lucrative trade in Oriental spices from Muslim merchants.[15] Portuguese fleets were the first to arrive after rounding the Cape of Good Hope. Vasco da Gama, who led the first fleet to India in 1498, knew there was a large island opposite Mozambique.[16] However, da Gama kept close to the African coast both going to and returning from India.

The first recorded landing on Madagascar by Europeans took place by accident during a storm in 1500. But the Portuguese had little interest in a land without gold, silver, or spices. Portuguese fleets continued to hug the coast of the mainland, where they built fortified way stations. They returned to Madagascar solely to attack their Arab competitors in the spice trade. As part of their war against the Muslims, Tristan da Cunha in 1506 and Alfonso d'Albuquerque in 1507 savagely destroyed the Arab trading settlements along Madagascar's northwestern coast.

The Portuguese kept their monopoly of the spice trade for almost a century. When the Dutch rebelled against Spain (united with Portugal since 1580), Amsterdam merchants leapfrogged over their competitors by sailing beyond India to the source of spices in Indonesia. By 1602 the Dutch had seized Bantam in Jakarta. The Dutch East India Company then moved its headquarters to Jakarta in 1619, seized Malacca in 1641, and took over the entire island of Ceylon in 1658.

The East India Company needed a post where seamen could break the long journey from the Netherlands to Java. The first Dutch expedition to Sumatra and Java in 1595, commanded by Cornelius van Houtman, stopped for supplies at Saint Augustine's Bay. Houtman treated the local people with great brutality. When he stopped over again in 1599, the Malagasy fled into the bush with their cattle. Hundreds of sailors and soldiers died of scurvy and dysentery.

The East India Company next tried to settle a small, uninhabited island east of Madagascar, which they renamed Mauritius after Prince Maurice of Nassau. However, both Mauritius and Madagascar were abandoned following the success of the Dutch settlement at the Cape of Good Hope, founded in 1652. There, taking advantage of the subtropical climate and the absence of strong native tribes, the Dutch East India Company finally established a permanent settlement along the route to Asia.

THE MALAGASY DRIVE OUT ENGLISH SETTLERS

As did their Dutch and Portuguese counterparts, English and French rulers also coveted the profits from commerce in Oriental spices, luxury silks, and gems. However, both came rather late to the scene. English mariners initially searched for a northwest passage to India across northern Canada and then turned to ravishing Spain's Caribbean possessions. The first English ship appeared in the Indian Ocean only in 1580, and this was a pirate coming from the Caribbean, not a merchant vessel from Europe. Sir Francis Drake's *Golden Hind* had crossed from the Atlantic to the Pacific and looted a rich Peruvian treasure ship: now Drake was heading back to England across the Pacific.

The English East India Company, given a royal monopoly in 1600, developed its trade routes slowly and cautiously. A post was founded at Surat in 1613, and Bombay was acquired from the Portuguese in 1661. On India's east coast, Madras saw the beginning of an English fort in 1639.

With the Dutch occupying both Saint Helena (until 1672) and the Cape of Good Hope, English seamen needed their own stepping stone on the route to India. From their first voyages, English East India Company ships normally stopped for provisions at Saint Augustine's Bay on the way east. Madagascar seemed a natural location for a fort and trading post, but the English East India Company was reluctant to sink money into permanent settlements. In 1635 King Charles I chartered a second company empowered to trade in the East and "to settle factories and to plant colonies after the Dutch manner." Three ships finally reached Saint Augustine's Bay in March 1645, carrying 140 settlers. Sixty survivors would flee Madagascar a year later.

The climate at Saint Augustine's Bay is hot and arid, and the soil is thin. Their crops soon perished, and many settlers died of dysentery and fever. Above all, they failed to establish good relations with the Malagasy, whose cattle provided their only food. The expedition's leaders forgot to bring the bright-red carnelian beads that the Malagasy preferred, and the colonists and natives began to steal each other's cattle. The Englishmen were better armed but few in number, and efforts to intimidate local chiefs brought devastating reprisals. By May 1646, the Malagasy and English settlers were openly at war, and the latter pulled out and fled to India.

THE FRENCH COLONY AT FORT DAUPHIN IS DESTROYED

Unlike the English, French settlers at Fort Dauphin managed to hang on for thirty years. But they also made enemies of the Malagasy, and ultimately they, too, would be driven out. With the encouragement of Cardinal Richelieu, a French Society of the East received a monopoly of trade with Madagascar. Under the direction of a man named Pronis, small groups of colonists arrived in 1642 and 1643 and settled on a peninsula at the island's southeastern tip. There they erected Fort Dauphin, named in honor of the future Louis XIV. On the way, Pronis took possession of Mascarin (later Bourbon, now Réunion Island), the Bay of Antongil, and Saint Mary's Island.[17]

Pronis chose a better site than had the English at Saint Augustine's Bay. Fort Dauphin is far enough south to enjoy a period of cool weather, and it receives breezes from both east and south. There is no really good harbor, but a wide bay provides a shallow anchorage and some protection from the winds. The local people, the Antanosy, initially welcomed the settlers. Europeans already had visited the region, and some of the Antanosy were themselves descendants of shipwrecked Portuguese sailors. As a child, the chief ruler had spent three years in Goa and been baptized a Roman Catholic.

Pronis sought to cement this friendship by formally marrying the chief's niece, with whom he was living. But relations soon soured. In 1646, the colonists mutinied and chained up Pronis, who was released six months later by the captain of a newly arrived vessel. Pronis exiled his French captors to uninhabited Réunion Island, and he murdered a Malagasy chief who had comforted Pronis's wife during his imprisonment. He also rewarded the captain who had freed him by giving him seventy-three Malagasy captives, enticed to the fort by promises of meat; they were then sold as slaves to the Dutch.[18] From then on, the Antanosy avoided Fort Dauphin as much as possible.

Informed of these troubles, the Company replaced Pronis with one of their own members, Etienne de Flacourt. The new governor was a good manager as well as a man of learning.[19] But the colony's situation was hopeless. With France locked in civil war, the Company sent no more ships for five years. Lacking any European goods to trade for food, Flacourt indulged in cattle raiding. The Antanosy attacked with thousands of men, who were dispersed by the fort's cannon. Flacourt retaliated by destroying their main village.

Flacourt and his followers resorted to a cruel military domination of the Malagasy, exacting tribute and pillaging the countryside.[20] In 1664, the French government set up a new East India Company, which took over the rights of the earlier settlers. Over the next few years, the new company sent out thousands of settlers and soldiers. It extended control over a wider area in the south and established trading posts on Saint Mary's Island and other points in the northeast. But the company lost money on these efforts. After five years, it gave up on Madagascar and concentrated its efforts in India.

The French East India Company's rights reverted to Louis XIV, who sent out Admiral Blanquet de la Haye as viceroy. When de la Haye returned from India in 1671, he decided to abandon Fort Dauphin, and he removed many colonists to Réunion Island. In August 1674, Malagasy warriors surprised and massacred half the remaining settlers. After spiking the fort's cannon and burning their remaining supplies, the sixty-three survivors left for Réunion off on a recently arrived ship.

Despite substantial investments in money and lives, the French settlement failed because it lacked a consistent policy. The two East India Companies could not decide whether to set up a trading post or to found a plantation settlement growing tropical crops. The colony failed as a trading post because the island lacked products of intrinsic value. Although France's Caribbean colonies began to profit from sugar during these same years, settlers on Madagascar also made little effort to plant the crops needed to support a permanent settlement. It was much easier to raid and rob the Malagasy peoples.[21] The buccaneers, in contrast, enriched the native peoples by bringing their booty to Saint Mary's. Treating the island as a rest and recuperation base, they appreciated the easygoing Malagasy way of life and sought to learn from rather than to despoil their hosts.

CHAPTER FOUR

LIFE AT SAINT MARY'S—
THE WHITE MALAGASY

Oh, the palms grew high in Avès, and fruits that shone like gold,
And the colibris and parrots they were gorgeous to behold;
And the negro maids to Avès from bondage fast did flee,
To welcome gallant sailors, a-sweeping in from sea.

Oh, sweet it was in Avès to hear the landward break,
A-swing with good tobacco in a net between the trees,
With a negro lass to fan you, while you listened to the roar
Of the breakers on the reef outside, that never touched the shore.
　　—Charles Kingsley, "The Last Buccaneer" (1857)

Throughout the ages, pirates have congregated at certain havens. Ancient pirates sought the coasts of southern Turkey, while medieval sea rovers frequented Wales and the west coast of England. During much of the seventeenth century, Caribbean buccaneers flocked to Tortuga Island and Port Royal, Jamaica. At all times, marauders went where trading ships converged or where the main trade routes were close at hand. In addition, since they needed the assistance of merchants to fence their booty and provide supplies, pirates always have looked for havens where the government encouraged or tolerated their operations.

Chance also played a role in the development of great pirate havens. In the Mediterranean, Muslim pirates were welcome at both Algiers and Tunis; Algiers had the larger community because it had been conquered and occupied first. In the same way, once Saint Mary's was flourishing, there was little likelihood that an alternative resort would come into existence. Everything needed was at Saint Mary's.

Mariners came to Saint Mary's for a variety of reasons. It was the preferred harbor to pick up supplies and water after crossing the Cape of Good Hope as well as to wait out the change of monsoon winds. Through Adam Baldridge and later Edward Welch, captured Indian goods could be traded for European products. After it was firmly established as the main haven in the Indian Ocean, Saint Mary's also functioned as a hiring hall and a center for communications and financial transactions. Ultimately, some mariners stayed at Saint Mary's just because they preferred the easygoing Malagasy way of life to the rigid social hierarchies of New York, Massachusetts, or Barbados.

Saint Mary's and neighboring Antongil Bay are superbly located anchorages for European vessels cruising the Indian Ocean. (The French navy recognized this as well as the pirates: Saint Mary's Island was the first place the French sought to occupy when they returned to Madagascar during the 1750s.) Saint Mary's location on Madagascar's northeast coast also fits in well with the seasonal schedule of the winds. Additionally, the island provides an excellent supply depot for ships returning from India, and it is a convenient starting point for ships looking to catch the southwest monsoon to the Red Sea and India.

Saint Mary's was ideally located as a rest stop for ships making the long journey east from Europe or North America. The entire journey from England or Europe to India generally lasted some seven or eight months, and a ship that left England in March aimed to arrive at Surat in November. But every long sailing voyage presented different challenges. French archives record when ships left Europe and the date they arrived at Réunion Island, some 500 miles due east of Madagascar. On average, the trip took about four months. But one ship made it in an extraordinarily fast 82 days, while a less fortunate vessel needed 183 days.[1]

Few mariners tried to go so great a distance without stopping. By the time they reached India, the ship would have run out of food and water, and the crew would have collapsed from scurvy. By the 1680s, merchant ships followed established routes, at least in peace time. Most vessels visited the Cape Verde Islands, a Portuguese possession, and then went on to the Dutch colony of Capetown at the tip of Africa. English vessels generally made an intermediate stop at Saint Helena. But pirates were unwelcome at both Saint Helena and Capetown and had to sail directly from the Cape Verdes around the Cape of Good Hope—a distance of some 8,000 miles.

Madagascar was the first good landing after the cape. Beginning with the first voyages to India, Europeans stopped at Madagascar to recuperate from the long voyage. The island provided them with ample fresh water, beef, and fruits that cured scurvy—even tropical diseases were less virulent than in Africa.

Unfortunately, Madagascar does not welcome travelers approaching from the sea. Despite its long coastline, the island offers few harbors suitable for large ships. The east coast, for most of its length, is almost a straight line of sand dunes that offer no protection against the trade winds and the powerful swell that surges against the narrow beaches and blocks the estuaries with sandbars. Saint Mary's Island provided one of the few good harbors. Other anchorages were found at Fénérive and at Fort Dauphin in the far south.[2]

Although it is more irregularly shaped, the western coast also offers few welcoming harbors. Seamen coming from Europe frequently stopped at Saint Augustine's Bay (Tuléar). Going north up the coast came Bombetoka Bay (Majunga), Mahajamaba Bay, and Nosy Be. In the far north, Diego Suarez forms one of the world's great natural harbors. However, an uninhabited mountain massif, rising to almost 9,500 feet, separates the port from the rest of the island; even today, Diego Suarez sees little commercial shipping and serves mainly as a naval base.

The smaller pirate vessels, displacing on average only one hundred fifty to two hundred tons, could find shelter in numerous inlets. However, few of these housed a friendly population that could offer needed food and other provisions. Along the western coast, powerful and capricious kings of the Sakalava tribes were as likely to enslave as to trade with white men. The peoples in the southeast initially had been less hostile, but those living around Fort Dauphin still had bitter memories of the French colonists they had thrown out in 1674. Pirates sometimes took on food and water on Madagascar's west coast as well as at Fort Dauphin—but Saint Mary's was their preferred destination.

LIFE IS SWEET ON SAINT MARY'S

A large island thirty-five miles long and ten miles wide, Saint Mary's lies twelve to fifteen miles from mainland Madagascar and runs from the northeast to the southwest. In the seventeenth century, it was occupied by a tropical rain forest that provided lumber for repairs; white sand beaches were excellent for careening ships.[3] At the southwestern end of Saint Mary's Island is a circular lagoon entered through a narrow and easily fortified passage. The anchorage is guarded by the body of the island, which blocks the ocean currents and the southeast trade winds. (Because, for example, Saint

Mary's Island protects the mainland coast immediately to the west, the rivers there have built up a peninsula of alluvial soil at Point-à-Larré.)

The Malagasy expression *mamy ny àina* ("life is sweet") is especially valid on Madagascar's northeastern coast, with its warm climate and abundant vegetation. While lacking spectacular scenery, Saint Mary's is one of the loveliest spots on Madagascar and rivals the Pacific islands in tropical charm. Perhaps the rainfall is a little too frequent and heavy. But the island's natural fertility and the friendliness of the inhabitants assured the pirates a wide variety of provisions.

Pigs, chicken, fish, turtles, yams, bananas, pineapples, coconuts, rice, taro, oranges, lemons, honey, sugar—all were abundant, and cattle were present, albeit in smaller numbers. One of the first white men to see Marosy Island in Antongil Bay named it "the mountain of fruits," because of its superabundance of oranges, lemons, bananas, and sugar cane.[4] The inhabitants grew rice and obtained more by trading with tribes on the mainland. By fermenting honey and sugar, they brewed a potent alcoholic beverage called *toke*.[5] Only salt was lacking, and many captains took on this necessity at the Cape Verde Islands.[6]

It is not surprising that many gave up any thought of returning to North America or Europe. Heterosexual pirates delighted in the unspoiled charms of Malagasy women, and they copied native chiefs in assembling large harems. Lying in a hammock on the veranda of a strongly built house among bamboo and coconut palms, the prosperous seaman enjoyed unlimited food and potent home-brewed alcohol. Surrounded by affectionate wives, he surely felt himself in paradise.

In the face of this natural abundance, mariners nevertheless wanted the European products they were used to. Fortunately for them, Adam Baldridge proved highly successful as a trader and fence after building the island's first fort in 1691. Later the same year, Baldridge arranged a partnership with Frederick Philipse, an international trader in New York. In September 1691, Baldridge wrote to Philipse that he could supply him with a shipload of two hundred slaves at a cost of 30 shillings each (about $750), a price well below that of slaves purchased from the natives of West Africa. In addition, he could provide pieces of eight, Indian goods, and a ready market for wares that Philipse might wish to sell on the island.[7]

The trip to Saint Mary's was long and expensive, and Philipse was relatively slow to accept Baldridge's suggestion. Philipse's trading and slaving vessel, the *Charles,* finally arrived at Saint Mary's in August 1693. Its cargo

MERCHANT SHIPS
AT SAINT MARY'S, 1693–1697

Ship	*Charles*	*Katharyn*	*Charming Mary*	*Margaret*
Captain	James Thurber	Thomas Mostyn	Richard Glover	Samuel Burgess
Owner	Frederick Philipse	Frederick Philipse	Governor, and others, Barbados	Frederick Philipse
1693	Arrives Saint Mary's, August 7			
1694				
1695		Leaves New York, February; Saint Mary's, August	Seized by pirates at Saint Mary's, August	Leaves New York, December
1696				
1697				Returns to New York, May

included merchandise for which Baldridge gave the captain 1,100 pieces of eight (about $125,000) and 34 slaves as well as some cattle and iron bars.

The type of goods Baldridge had ordered provides insight into life on Saint Mary's. The consignment mainly consisted of European clothing and hand tools that would be useful either on Saint Mary's or aboard a ship. Some of the men apparently had told Baldridge that they wanted to learn how to read, since the cargo also includes "books, Catechisms, primers and horne books, [and] two Bibles."[8]

The *Charles's* cargo offered refreshment for the body as well as the soul with "5 Barrells of Rum, four Quarter Caskes of Madera Wine, [and] ten Cases of Spirits." Pirate fiction and films insist that the men constantly were drunk on rum. But there were seldom more than one or two supply ships a year. Split among hundreds of men, their cargoes of alcoholic beverages would have lasted barely a week. If the men on Saint Mary's wanted to get drunk, they either had to capture a ship carrying European spirts or consume the local toke.

During the next four years, until the Malagasy drove Baldridge from the island in 1697, a dozen more merchant vessels came to Saint Mary's to trade European goods for slaves and Indian booty. Although Baldridge has been described as Philipse's employee, he remained throughout a free agent and also dealt with other merchants from North America and the Caribbean.[9] By 1696 or earlier, Baldridge had taken Lawrence Johnston as partner.[10] Said to be a former pirate, Johnston was killed during the rebellion against Baldridge in July 1697.

Subsequent supply ships brought cargoes similar to that carried by the *Charles* in 1693. Carrying Philipse's last shipment to Saint Mary's, the *Margaret* left New York in June 1698 with salt, gunpowder, beer, wine, and rum as well as guns, pistols, muskets, knives, flints, cloth, looking glasses, thimbles, scissors, ivory combs, buttons, cotton for candlewicks, thread, three thousand needles, tobacco pipes, hats, and shoes.[11]

The substantial sales enjoyed by Adam Baldrige are evidence that Saint Mary's supported a large mariner population. When reporting the loss of their ship and cargo, sea captains naturally exaggerated the number of their attackers, and some speak of several thousand marauders on Saint Mary's. In November 1697, Commodore Thomas Warren (who had not been to Saint Mary's) told the Board of Trade that fifteen hundred men sailed out of the harbor, which was guarded by forty to fifty guns.[12] In contrast, seamen who visited the island during the 1690s testified to a permanent population of

MERCHANT SHIPS AT SAINT MARY'S, 1697–1699

Ship	Amity	Fortune	New York Merchant	Swift	Unknown Ship	Nassau	Margaret
Captain	Richard Glover	Thomas Mostyn	Cornelius Jacobs	Andrew Knott	Captain Coster	Giles Shelley	Samuel Burgess
Owner	Gov. and others, Barbados	Owner unknown	Frederick Philipse	John Johnston	New York owner	Stephen Delancy	Frederick Philipse
1697	Arrives Saint Mary's, May; plundered by crew of *Resolution*, June	Arrives Saint Mary's, June	Arrives Saint Mary's, June	Arrives Saint Mary's, July		Leaves New York for Saint Mary's, June	Leaves New York for Saint Mary"s, June 7
1698	Arrives New York with 14 former pirates, June		Arrives New York, cargo transferred to ship bound for Hamburg, Germany, April		Arrives Saint Mary's while Captain Kidd is present		Reaches Madagascar, June; Ship seized at Cape of Good Hope with 18 to 24 pirate passengers (some are Kidd's men), Dec. 11
1699						Returns, bringing home 75 former pirates	

two hundred or less.[13] However, these witnesses apparently did not count the men on their own vessels. At any given time, Adam Baldridge and dozens of other permanent residents were joined by perhaps a hundred men present between voyages. When several warships were docked at once, Saint Mary's pirate population swelled to five or six hundred.

Saint Mary's offered more than a safe harbor and abundant supplies. With everyone flocking to the island, it was an excellent place to do business. Recent arrivals brought the latest maritime news. (It is remarkable how rapidly the men acquired important information in an age without telephones or the Internet. They often learned of distant events sooner than seems possible.)

The development of Saint Mary's into the one major haven in the Indian Ocean also facilitated a sense of community. As men changed from ship to ship throughout their careers, they were likely to encounter fellow crewmen of bygone voyages and talk over their subsequent experiences. When Captain Kidd reached Saint Mary's in 1698, he ran into Robert Culliford, whom he had last seen nine years before. They two men immediately repaired to Kidd's ship to drink rum and talk over old times.

At Saint Mary's, captains could recruit crews, and seamen could switch ships. A man leaving on an extended sea voyage literally put his life in the hands of the ship's officers and his fellow crewmen. Before enlisting, he closely questioned friends about the competence of the ship's company. Nevertheless, incompatibilities sometimes showed up only during the voyage. After crossing the Atlantic and rounding the Cape of Good Hope, men left or were thrown off their vessels at Saint Mary's. About 1693 or 1694, according to Sarah Birch, her husband John sailed from Carolina to Saint Mary's with William Griffin and Daniel Smith. John Birch stayed with the ship he arrived in, while Griffin and Smith switched to another vessel. Eventually all three men returned to Saint Mary's. John Birch apparently died, since Griffin and Smith confessed that they were obligated to pay his booty to Sarah.[14]

Sarah Birch's efforts to retrieve her husband's money points up another value of a long-established rendezvous such as Saint Mary's. Some men had no desire to go back to the cold climates they had left. But a number intended to return to their wives and families and arranged to send them money in the meantime. When Gabriel Loffe and Martin Skines received their shares from Captain Kidd, they entrusted bales of fine cloth to a New York ship trading at Saint Mary's. The men also trusted their shipmates to carry out the terms of their wills. Robert Culliford wrote to a crewman's widow, informing her that he was sending all her husband's possessions with Captain Giles Shelley of the *Nassau*.

LIVING THE SIMPLE LIFE

Thousands of Europeans came to Saint Mary's, where some ultimately were buried. Since the pirates mainly built out of wood, there are no physical remains of their settlements, which are known only from literary sources.[15] Adam Baldridge settled on a small island in the middle of the lagoon, which is still called Pirate's Island. There he built a house, storerooms, and a log fortress armed with the "six great guns" he had purchased from the *Batchelor's Delight* in 1693. Baldridge erected a second fortification near the harbor, which also included as many as twenty-two cannon.[16]

Following the 1697 Malagasy rebellion, Baldridge's place as chief factor or trader was taken by Edward Welch, who had lived on Saint Mary's for some years.[17] Baldridge's buildings were destroyed during the uprising, so Welch erected a new fortress with Baldridge's six guns about four miles from the harbor.[18] Edward Davis, who returned to New York with Captain Kidd, testified that he "went to a place ashore called the Hill, about four miles from where Kidd's ship lay." To attract the attention of a vessel anchored nearby, Davis fired one of the "greate guns" on the hill.[19] Since naval cannons at that time could not hit a target four miles away, these guns must mainly have been used, as in this case, for signaling.

The men lived in encampments near the pirate's lagoon, although those who took Malagasy wives sometimes moved near the village of their head wife. Mariners temporarily staying on the island bedded down as paying guests with Baldrige and Welch or in a home owned by a shipmate. Several houses often were erected in the middle of a miniature fort, surrounded by a wall made of large logs pierced by loopholes and sometimes holding small cannon.

Adopting the Malagasy style of housing, mariners constructed one or more rooms on platforms elevated on stilts and entered by climbing a ladder. The walls were made of wood or often of bamboo, and the roof was covered with banana or ravenala leaves.[20] Servants quarters and store rooms had plank flooring; the better homes were endowed with fine, smooth floors of tropical hardwoods such as ebony. These homes perfectly suited the warm damp climate. Air could circulate beneath the raised platform, which also provided a kind of balcony. The walls woven from flattened laths of bamboo allowed air to pass through, while the more tightly woven roof kept out the frequent rain and insulated the rooms from heat.

Some mariners brought in cabinets or chests they had taken from prizes. Otherwise, little furniture was needed. The inhabitants slept on raffia or reed mats, rolled up during the day, and sat on smaller mats to eat and talk. In 1717, the hero of *Robert Drury's Journal* visited the home of John Pro, a former pirate turned slaver who

> lived in a very handsome manner. His house was furnished with pewter dishes, &c., a standing bed with curtains, and other things of that nature except chairs, but a chest or two suited for that use well enough. He had one house on purpose for his cook-room and cook-slave's lodging, storehouse and summer-house; all these enclosed in a palisade.[21]

The Malagasy wove cloth out of cotton, silk, and raffia (a fabric made from the stripped membranes of the raffia palm). However, the mariners retained a taste for European clothing for as long as they could get it. Many had been buccaneers in the Caribbean and continued to wear the buccaneer's preferred outfit—a loose, billowing shirt and loose pants cut off just below the knee. Some wore "petticoat trousers": Very full and open at the bottom, these resembled a divided knee-length skirt or the modern women's shorts known as culottes. Although seamen went barefoot while at work aboard ship, shoes sometimes were worn on land.[22]

Mariners could make do with plain sailcloth pants, but they preferred cotton dyed cheerful colors, such as scarlet and sky blue. Shirts tended to be more or less white with "speckles" or with small colored squares. In this climate, the embroidered coats of the era were worn only to impress the natives.[23] Contrary to nineteenth-century fables for children—later elaborated on by Hollywood—European pirates did not wear earrings or tattoos either in the Caribbean or in the Indian Ocean.[24]

THE PIRATES AND THE MALAGASY

With rare exceptions, the mariner community lived in peace with the native peoples for half a century.[25] This racial harmony is especially remarkable given the Malagasy hatred of other Europeans sojourning on the island. During the seventeenth century, the Malagasy violently threw out English and French settlers attempting to colonize the island. With modern military technology, the French finally conquered the islanders during the nine-teenth century—but only after suppressing stubborn resistance.

The differing fates of the colonists and the pirates reflect their divergent attitudes toward the native peoples. The would-be colonists condemned the Malagasy as indolent savages; they wanted to convert them into slaves on European-style plantations.[26] To the contrary, most pirates accepted the Malagasy as they were. Indeed, they adopted the Malagasy way of life as much as they could.

There were real similarities between the two groups that facilitated their intercourse and made it easier for the pirates to integrate themselves into Malagasy society. Compared to the hierarchical settler societies, the native and pirate communities were democratic and egalitarian, and both highly prized cohesion and cooperation within the group. While they were on the island, moreover, the mariners—like the Malagasy—mainly sought to enjoy a peaceful and pleasant life.

For their part, the Malagasy fled to the relative peace of the European settlements to escape wars on mainland Madagascar. There they accepted pirate "kings" as the counterpart of their own native rulers and slave own-ers. The arrangement must have seemed more familiar because of the mixed racial background of some pirate crewmen, who were partly of African or of American Indian origin.

The easygoing, untroubled sexuality of the Malagasy surprised and delighted Europeans, and numerous men took wives by paying their fathers a bride price.[27] Defoe's *The General History of the Pyrates* and other fictionalized accounts describe the pirates as "stealing away and ravishing the wives of the natives."[28] But there was no reason for them to seize by force what the Malagasy were happy to sell. The Betsimisaraka—the tribes along the coast—favored white skin, which was considered a sign of nobil-ity.[29] They willingly collected a high bride price from fair-complected seamen.

Both mariners and Malagasy gained from these marriages. The hus-bands enjoyed attractive and sexually uninhibited wives who kept their houses, cooked their meals, and bossed their slaves. For their part, the wives gained a virile partner and a more luxurious way of life. When ships of the Royal Navy visited Antongil Bay in 1722, Clarence Downing ran into John Plantain, who had shared in John Taylor's rich booty. Many crewmen had gone back to the Caribbean with Taylor, but Plantain had stayed behind, accompanied by James Adair and Hans Burgen. The three men lived in large houses in a fortified encampment. Burgen's wives were dressed in the richest silks and flaunted jewels and diamond necklaces.[30]

The settlements of the pirates and their marriages with Malagasy women helped more than just a few individuals; the entire Betsimisaraka nation benefited. The wife's extended family gained the assistance of an experienced fighter in their wars. The white men helped them take slaves from other tribes, and some of these prisoners might be sold to passing slavers.[31] But the Saint Mary's community learned from Adam Baldridge's debacle and did not again make the mistake of selling the tribesmen among whom they lived.

Furthermore, Malagasy widows of pirates, being on the spot when their husbands died, inherited considerable pirate booty, and the trade with merchants and slavers brought in additional wealth as well as firearms. Before the Europeans arrived, the disunited clans of the Betsimisaraka had been easy prey for Sakalava warriors from the west, raiding for slaves. However, from the late 1600s, the Betsimisaraka first repelled the Sakalava and then carried these slave wars into Sakalava territory. The wealth of the region between Tamatave and Antongil Bay, based on trade and marriage with the pirates, became the envy of tribes to the south and west.

During the Baldridge era, colonial governors did not molest mariners returning from the Indian Ocean, and several warships made a series of round-trip voyages to Saint Mary's. The turning point came in 1699. Vessels of the English navy visited Saint Mary's and offered its residents a royal pardon. But back in London, the Admiralty Court took advantage of legalistic technicalities and refused to honor the pardons. From that time on, the men naturally refused to trust English justice and remained at Saint Mary's.

During the 1700s, several hundred men left for nearby Réunion Island, whose French governors were eager to pardon former pirates. However, at all times, a considerable number of men remained among the Malagasy rather than returning to any European society. In December 1706, Captain Thomas White visited Réunion while returning from India loaded with booty. A dozen men or more stayed at the French colony. However, White and the vast majority of crewmen went on to Saint Mary's, and one settler from Réunion took off with them. Even though they had enough money to secure a warm welcome, some two hundred men preferred not to live at an established colony.

The climate and material way of life at Réunion were much like that at Saint Mary's, and settlers at Réunion had easier access to French wines and other European goods. The pirates' motives for preferring Madagascar were primarily sentimental. Some may have chosen not to abandon their Malagasy wives and mixed-race children—or at least preferred native women to the French and colored females available at Réunion. Perhaps some favored, as had Robert Culliford, the company of men. (However, Réunion was a tolerant place, unlike Dutch colonies, which routinely strangled men or drowned them in the ocean for committing "sodomy."[32]) For whatever reason, even when they could leave, men wanted the unrivaled freedom of the pirate republic.

This tendency to go native was not, of course, unique either to pirates or to the Indian Ocean. Throughout the centuries, men and women in North America were captured by Indians, and many came to prefer their new life with their captors. On the Pennsylvania-Ohio frontier in 1764, at the end of the Indian war known as Pontiac's Rebellion, the British-American victors demanded that the Shawnee and Delaware deliver up all their white captives. But to the shock of the colonials, the great majority of whites refused to come home.

Some had been kidnapped as children and grew up with their native "family," knowing no other life. But not every white Indian started out as a captive. From the beginning of the colonial era, joining the Indians had a powerful appeal for those who chafed under the rules and expectations of European civilization. William Penn, remarking on the allure of Indian life for some in his Quaker colony, noted that Europeans "sweated and toil" for their daily bread, while Indians appeared to live only for pleasure, passing their days "Hunting, Fishing and Fowling."

Frontier whites in frequent contact with the Indians observed the advantages of this life and slipped into it easily, abandoning homesteads for an unfettered existence in the wilds. The same Puritan divines—including Cotton Mather—who excoriated pirates also abominated the moral degeneracy of whites who joined the heathen natives. Still the defections continued, and French colonists adapted to Indian life as easily as their English counterparts. As late as 1782, Hector de Crèvecoeur noted with astonishment that "thousands of Europeans are Indians, and we have no examples of even one of those aborigines having from choice become Europeans!"[33] Modern observers will not be surprised that black and mulatto slaves also ran away and adopted Indian languages and culture.[34]

The white men on Saint Mary's already had rejected the rigidities and hardships of European society by turning pirate. Some simply could not bear to return to civilization, even with a pardon they trusted. Those without much booty enjoyed a more abundant life on Saint Mary's compared to their opportunities in chilly New York or Pennsylvania. And even men wealthy in gold sometimes wanted to live among the Malagasy, with their strong sense of community, social equality, and freedom from the grotesque complexities of European sexual customs. Whatever the attraction was, hundreds of men were captivated enough to turn their backs on civilization and become white Malagasy.

ABRAHAM SAMUEL, KING OF FORT DAUPHIN

On Madagascar, real escapades often seem more fantastic than even the most flamboyant pirate fiction. Among the most successful in adopting the Malagasy way of life was Abraham Samuel, a colorful rogue as well as a man of ability and ambition. Samuel had been born to a black slave and a French planter on the island of Martinique. One way or another, he joined Captain John Hoar's crew while it was cruising in the Caribbean and remained on board when the *John and Rebecca* headed for the Indian Ocean in 1695. After raiding in the Arabian Sea and the Persian Gulf, Hoar's men captured an Indian prize near Surat and went back to Saint Mary's in February 1697.[35]

While in the Indian Ocean, the men took an extraordinary step by electing Samuel quartermaster. Except during battle, the quartermaster had as much responsibility and authority as the captain. Ships from the Caribbean and New York often contained black and mulatto mariners, but Samuel was the only black elected to this most important office. While the pirates were remarkably democratic, they also held the racial prejudices of their era. Only a man of talent would have inspired the confidence the crew placed in Samuel when they named him quartermaster.

While the *John and Rebecca* was moored at Saint Mary's, the Malagasy rebelled against Adam Baldridge. Captain Hoar and many crewmen were slaughtered during the uprising, but some got safely away, with Abraham Samuel in command. Heading for New York, the ship got no farther than the abandoned French settlement at Fort Dauphin before it hit a reef and sank.

The Malagasy chief had died, and his widow ruled the area. One day, while watching the shipwrecked seamen bathing in the ocean, she was struck by some marks on Samuel's body. These were identical to those of a child she had borne to a Frenchman, taken away by his father when the French fled Madagascar in 1674. The woman claimed Samuel as her son and made him the region's chief. A cynic might suspect that she only pretended to recognize Samuel as a way of retaining control of local affairs. However, since the Malagasy trusted in signs and portents, she may have believed her own story. Perhaps fearing the woman might change her mind, Samuel took care to retain the friendship of his shipmates.[36]

For a brief time, Fort Dauphin rivaled Saint Mary's in importance, as slavers and pirates arrived to trade with Samuel. In November 1699, he charged an American slaving ship £100 for a trading license. Attached to the license was a wax seal bearing the Lamb of God and the Cross, plunder from some unfortunate Portuguese vessel. The following year, Captain Littleton of the Royal Navy entertained Samuel and two of his queens and reported that he was loved by his people.[37]

When the governor of New York clamped down on traders bringing supplies to Saint Mary's, the pirates increasingly acquired their ships by stealing them from slavers. At Port Dauphin, Abraham Samuel seems to have played the same trick. In July 1699, a visiting captain heard the rumor that Samuel had seized a Dutch ship six months earlier and murdered its crew. In September, Captain Evan Jones pulled into port and looted an American slave ship. He gave the ship itself to Samuel, who in turn sold it to four pirates for 1,100 pieces of eight ($120,000). The sale was recorded in a document signed by Abraham Samuel, "King of Fort Dauphin, Tollannare, Farrawe, Fanquest, and Fownzahira."[38]

When news spread of King Abraham's duplicity, ships stopped going to Port Dauphin. Thus we cannot say how long King Samuel reigned in splendor. He was already gone when a Dutch slaver put in at Port Dauphin in December 1706. The captain found a fort built by Samuel in ruins. A Malagasy chief named Demarrasive declared himself Samuel's successor but was very vague about his fate. Perhaps he went back to pirating, or he may have been murdered by a rival for the throne of Fort Dauphin.[39]

CHAPTER FIVE

THOMAS TEW AND THE
RHODE ISLAND QUAKERS

After he became governor of New York, the earl of Bellomont spent much of his time investigating and attacking his predecessor, Colonel Benjamin Fletcher. Bellomont arrived in New York in April 1698, sent Colonel Fletcher home under a heavy bond, and began a thorough search into his delinquencies. For the next three years until his sudden death in March 1701, Bellomont deluged the Board of Trade with tirades concerning Fletcher's alleged crimes—especially his collusion with the Red Sea pirates. After a preliminary hearing, however, the Board decided there were no legal grounds for proceeding against the former governor. The Lords of Trade ruled that Fletcher might not be totally innocent, but there was insufficient evidence for conviction.[1]

In his own day, Lord Bellomont failed to persuade the Board of Trade that Fletcher's New York was the center of North American piracy. Despite this, some historians subsequently have accepted Bellomont's charges at face value.[2] In fact, during the 1690s, mariners sailing for Madagascar preferred to outfit their vessels in Rhode Island. At Newport, pirates had little to fear from the colony's government and openly admitted their profession. They worked together in obtaining ships and supplies and consorted together on cruises.

Among the Newport captains, Thomas Tew stands out. A Rhode Island mariner of good family, pleasant manner, and considerable boldness, Tew was a natural leader.[3] It was Tew's success that made seamen fully aware of the riches available in the East. He was not the first to maraud in the Indian Ocean, but he made it look easy to take extraordinary amounts of booty.

During the middle 1680s, Tew lived in Jamaica and may have gone buccaneering.[4] About 1692, he arrived in Bermuda and purchased a share in the *Amity,* a seventy-ton sloop. Outfitted as a warship and carrying eight cannon, the *Amity* was owned by a syndicate of Bermuda merchants and government officials.[5] Toward the end of 1692, Isaac Rigier, Bermuda's lieutenant-governor, granted Tew a commission to attack French slave trading stations on Africa's west coast.

Tew was the first pirate to become well-known in England. In his *General History of the Pyrates,* Daniel Defoe begins his stories about Madagascar and Saint Mary's Island with Tew's voyage. Writing thirty years later, Defoe had few facts to work with, and he embellished Tew's biography with fictional anecdotes. Defoe went so far as to insert Tew (who really lived) into stories about Captain Misson (a totally fictional character).

Tew's *Amity,* the *General History* asserts, sailed from Bermuda in the company of another sloop but lost her consort during a storm. It was only at this point, according to Defoe, that Tew decided to turn pirate. Calling his men together, he told them that it would be better to risk their lives to make themselves rich rather than to enrich the English slave traders competing with the French. "One bold Push would do their Business, and they might return home, not only without Danger, but with Reputation." Persuaded by Tew's speech, the men "cry'd out, one and all, *A gold Chain, or a wooden Leg, we'll stand by you.*"[6]

The *Amity* was small and overcrowded to undertake a long voyage into the storms of the South Atlantic. Yet Tew's undertaking turned out to be exceedingly profitable. The *Amity* presumably left Bermuda soon after the crew and the owners signed the ship's articles on January 8, 1693. Only nine months later, on October 19, the *Amity* reached Saint Mary's filled with gold and ready to return to North America.

On the way back to Bermuda, the *Amity* sprang her mast and could only sail with the wind. After trying for two weeks to reach the island, Tew brought his booty to Rhode Island. He hastened, however, to send word to his partners that he had something for them.

Tew arrived in Rhode Island with as much as £100,000 (about $50 million today).[7] Each crewman received £1,200 ($600,000),[8] and Tew is said to have kept £8,000 ($4 million) for himself.[9] The owners also received large sums—perhaps as much as £5,000 in all (some $2.5 million).[10] Several used their profits to purchase large tracts of land on Bermuda.[11]

No firsthand evidence survives describing how Tew took this great plunder. In his *General History,* Daniel Defoe describes a battle with a tall warship manned by three hundred soldiers in addition to her seamen. Defoe attributes the pirates' success to their "Skill and Courage." But his account closely tracks and probably was copied from his description a few pages later of Henry Every's 1695 battle with the *Gunsway.*[12]

TEW LEADS A SQUADRON OF PIRATE WARSHIPS TO THE INDIAN OCEAN

Although he might well have settled in Rhode Island with his booty, Thomas Tew decided to make another plunder voyage. He remained in Newport for only a few months before sailing in January 1695. During his short stay, Tew organized a squadron for a rendezvous in the East. As Edward Randolph reported to the Board of Trade, three other vessels joined Tew's *Amity.*[13] These were the *Dolphin,* the *Portsmouth Adventure,* and the *Susana,* all relatively small vessels to undertake a long voyage with limited opportunities to take on fresh supplies. Each of the three captains was an associate of Tew. On two of the vessels, an officer (and probably several of the crewmen) had marauded on the *Batchelor's Delight* during its cruise in the Indian Ocean from 1688 to 1692.

William Want commanded the *Dolphin,* a Spanish brigantine with six cannons and sixty men outfitted near Philadelphia.[14] A former buccaneer, Want had been on the *Batchelor's Delight* when that warship was wrecked off the Carolina coast in 1692.[15] Although married and settled in South Carolina, Want nevertheless joined Tew's 1693 voyage to the East as first mate on the *Amity.*[16]

A fifty-ton bark built in Newport, the *Portsmouth Adventure* was equipped with six guns but carried only twenty men. The *Adventure's* intended captain was John Banks, a Rhode Islander, who also had taken part in Tew's first voyage. At the last minute, however, Joseph Farrell took Banks's place as captain.[17] Dirk Chivers, a Dutchman from New York and another veteran of the *Batchelor's Delight,* was the *Adventure's* first mate.[18] Thomas Wake, the captain of the *Susana,* also was a former buccaneer; he had taken a pardon during the brief reign of James II.[19]

Want, Banks, and Wake all received privateering commissions authorizing them to attack French shipping off the Canadian coast. The governor of Rhode Island later denied granting them commissions.[20] This was technically true but fundamentally dishonest: the commissions instead had

PIRATE WARSHIPS
AT SAINT MARY'S, 1695–1696

Ship	Amity	Pearl	Dolphin	Susana	Portsmouth Adventure	Fancy
Captain	Thomas Tew	William May	William Want	Thomas Wake	Joseph Farrell	Henry Every
1695	Leaves Rhode Island, Jan. Gunsway, Aug. Arrives at Saint Mary's, exchange Amity for Charming Mary, Dec.	Leaves Rhode Island, Jan. Gunsway, Aug.	Leaves Rhode Island, Jan. Burned as chases Gunsway Crew transfers to Fancy, Aug.	Leaves Rhode Island, Jan. Gunsway, Aug. Arrives at Saint Mary's, Dec.	Leaves Rhode Island, Jan. Gunsway, Aug. Wrecked Comoro Islands; some men join Henry Every at Réunion	Leaves Spain, May Gunsway, Aug. Stops at Réunion Island, Nov.
1696		Plunders several Indian vessels. Returns to New York early in 1696.		Crew dies of disease, April		Arrives at Bahamas, April

been granted by the governor's deputy, Jack Greene.[21] Rhode Island's governors did not personally sign such documents; as Quakers, they publicly opposed acts of war. In any case, Tew himself went to New York, where he obtained a commission from Governor Benjamin Fletcher authorizing the *Amity* to attack French Canada.[22] Tew gave Fletcher a bond or promissory note for £3,000 as security against improper actions.[23]

Since he went to considerable effort to obtain one, Tew presumably believed that a privateer's commission might offer some protection if the *Amity* were stopped by a warship or visited an English port.[24] Caribbean buccaneers also had considered commissions desirable and had gone to some lengths to acquire them. In practice, however, these documents were of limited usefulness, since they allowed the holder to plunder only the king's enemies. During the Nine Years War, that meant only the subjects of the king of France. England's allies included the Netherlands and Spain, while Portugal was neutral.

Moreover, Fletcher's commission to Tew authorized him to cruise solely near Canada. Had he instead returned with silks from India, his commission by itself would not have made his cargo "good prize." He could have sold his booty only if the governor had been willing to ignore the laws. But dishonest governors tolerated pirates whether or not they had a privateer's commission. In practice, a privateer's commission was merely a talisman and did not serve as effective protection against prosecution.[25]

THE BATTLE FOR THE *GUNSWAY*

Sailing from Newport in January 1695, the four vessels in Thomas Tew's squadron arrived at the mouth of the Red Sea in July 1695. There they entered into consort with Henry Every and the much larger *Fancy* to attack the pilgrim's fleet coming south from Mocha. The men knew that the pilgrim fleet had to follow the rhythm of the monsoons. While they patiently waited for their prey, they were joined by yet another private vessel, the *Pearl,* commanded by William May.[26]

The *Pearl* also had been outfitted in Rhode Island. But it did not form part of Tew's squadron, having left North America in July 1693 before Tew had returned from his first cruise in India. Unlike the other pirates, May had managed to obtain a commission from the governor of Rhode Island rather than his deputy.[27] This empowered May to attack French slave stations in Africa. Instead, the *Pearl* arrived at Saint Mary's in January 1694 and then meandered along the coast of India with little success. The *Pearl* put in at Mangalore, India, in October 1694 and later departed without Robert Culliford, the quartermaster. The following year, May took the *Pearl* to the Red Sea and joined Henry Every in stalking the pilgrim fleet.

After the pirates had waited several weeks, the Muslim vessels came into view. As detailed in Chapter Six, Every and the *Fancy* seized rich booty from two ships, *Fateh Mohammed* and the *Gang-i-Saway* (*Gunsway*). But the outcome was less agreeable for most of the Rhode Island pirates. The *Fancy*'s crew shared only a small part of their plunder with their companions. Thomas Tew and several others died during the battle. Moreover, although some crewmen did make it home, none of the five ships that attacked the *Gunsway* in August 1695 returned to Europe or North America. The *Dolphin* was abandoned and burned during the chase after the *Gunsway*. The *Fancy, Portsmouth Adventure,* and *Pearl* were wrecked at sea. The *Susana* was left derelict when her crew died at Saint Mary's. Thomas Tew's *Amity,* flagship of the Rhode Island pirates, was severely damaged during the battle, and her crew eventually abandoned her at Saint Mary's.

The *Dolphin* was the first to be lost. As the pirate squadron chased after the Muslim vessels, the *Dolphin* fell farther and farther behind. Finally burning their vessel, her crew went aboard the *Fancy.* The men had taken part in the battle for the *Gunsway*, so they received the same share as the *Fancy*'s own crew. Captain Want and his company remained on the *Fancy* until it reached the Bahamas, and they then went home on other vessels.[28]

The *Portsmouth Adventure* and *Susana* also fell behind, and their crews thus had no share in the battle or the booty from the *Gunsway*. After the engagement, the *Portsmouth Adventure* was wrecked on Mayotte in the Comoro Islands. Captain Farrell and some of the others made it to Réunion Island, where they were picked up by Every and the *Fancy* in November 1695. Farrell commanded the sloop that took Every from the Bahamas to Ireland, and Every gave him the vessel in payment.[29]

Perhaps the *Susana* had the worst luck of the five vessels consorting with Henry Every. The ship reached Saint Mary's in December 1695, and her crew settled down to wait for the monsoon to shift to the southwest so they could return to India. In April 1696, a tropical fever suddenly struck down Captain Wake and most of the men.[30]

The men of the *Pearl* did not fare much better. Since they had joined in taking the *Gunsway*, they received part of the booty. But they lost their shares when they attempted to cheat the crew of the *Fancy* after the battle.[31] Captain May took the *Pearl* to Ethiopia and then went back to India. East India Company records credit him with the plunder of several "rich Moors

Howard Pyle's portrait of the imaginary "Captain Keitt" for The Ruby of Kishmoor *(1908). See page xii.*

*The Panama Isthmus lies between the Caribbean (here called the "North Sea")
and the Pacific (the "South Sea"). During the 1680s, Bartholomew Sharp and
other buccaneers crossed to the Pacific by the southern or Darien route passing near
Santa Maria. Peruvian silver was carried from the city of Panama ("Old Panama") through Venta de Cruces to Nombre de Dios or (after 1595) to Portobelo.
From Lionel Wafer,* New Voyage *(1699). See pages 5, 169, 228.*

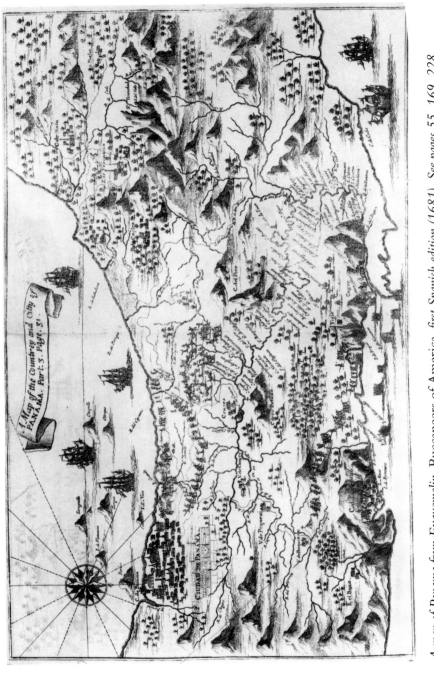

A map of Panama from Exquemelin, Buccaneers of America, first Spanish edition (1681). See pages 55, 169, 228.

Fortifications at Muscat on the southeast Arabian coast (and now the capital of Oman). Originally built by the Portuguese government, these forts were captured by Persian troops in 1648. From The Oriental Annual (1836). See pages 98–99.

Northeast monsoon storms arrive at Madras. From The Oriental Annual (1834). See page 22.

Spanish or Portuguese galleon. From Jurien de la Gravière, Les corsaires
barbaresques *(1887). See pages 26–27, 214.*

Tropical tree with orchids growing on the trunk and branches. Part of the rain forest located along Madagascar's northeastern coast. From William Ellis, Three Visits to Madagascar *(1859). See pages 40, 57.*

Village near Tamatave on Madagascar's northeastern coast. The scene shows female slaves pounding rice (left) and filling bamboos with water from the well. From William Ellis, Three Visits to Madagascar *(1859). See pages 46–48.*

Traditional dwellings at Tamatave on Madagascar's northeastern coast. From William Ellis, Three Visits to Madagascar *(1859). See pages 46, 62–63.*

A mother and child of the Betsimisaraka people (left) and a woman of the Hova people (right)—sketches made during the 1850s. From William Ellis, Three Visits to Madagascar *(1859). See pages 48–49.*

ships" early in 1696.[32] After this, the *Pearl* disappears from the seas and probably was stranded or wrecked in the East.[33] However, some of her men survived to join the burgeoning pirate community at Saint Mary's Island. In January 1699, while the crew waited in the Red Sea for the pilgrim ships returning to India, William May was elected commander of the *Charming Mary*. This was the warship that had offered refuge to the men of the *Amity* following the death of Thomas Tew in August 1695.

CAPTAIN TEW'S MEN STEAL THE *CHARMING MARY*

Thomas Tew died and the *Amity* was crippled during the battle. A ball from one of the *Gunsway*'s enormous cannon struck the ship, killing Tew and several others.[34] In Daniel Defoe's version of the incident, "a Shot carry'd away the Rim of *Tew*'s Belly, who held his Bowels with his hands some small Space; when he dropp'd, it struck such a Terror in his Men, that they suffered themselves to be taken."[35]

In fact, the *Amity* was on the winning side, although it was in poor condition on returning to Saint Mary's the following December. There Adam Baldridge told the crew about the *Charming Mary,* a well-armed two hundred-ton slave ship from New York that recently had visited the island. The pirates immediately chased after and seized the *Charming Mary* at Port Dauphin. In exchange, they gave the *Amity* to her captain, a mariner named Richard Glover.[36] (Richard Glover was not related to Robert Glover, the pirate captain.)

The theft of the *Charming Mary* marks a radical change. Until this time, raiders in the Indian Ocean had been careful to stay on good terms with their fellow Americans. They rewarded owners for the use of their ships and paid generous "fees" to royal officials. The *Charming Mary* belonged to the governor of Barbados and a New York merchant.[37] Stealing the ship would suggest that the men of the *Amity* no longer thought of the North American colonies as their primary base. Some indeed returned to America after they retired from buccaneering. However, they now considered Saint Mary's Island their chief haven while actively cruising for booty.[38]

After taking the *Charming Mary*, the men elected a new captain named Bobbington. According to the East India Company representative at Gombroon, Bobbington came from New England. His ethnic background was thoroughly mixed. This Bobbington says that "He is an Irishman, says his father was Dutch and his mother English, confesses that they are of all sorts [nations] in the ship, but says that she comes from the King of England's dominions."[39]

In September 1696, the *Mary* reached Rajapur on India's west coast and captured a Muslim vessel despite fierce resistance. By December 1696, the *Mary* was in the Persian Gulf, where a party went ashore to search for provisions. They ran into a small group of Persian soldiers, who killed three men and took Captain Bobbington and the rest prisoners.

Deserting their comrades without trying to rescue them, the men of the *Charming Mary* determined to try new cruising grounds and sailed south and east to the waters around Sumatra and the Strait of Malacca. After the double loses of Tew and Bobbington, the crew also voted to manage without a captain. Day-to-day command was shared by John Yarland, the sailing master, and Henry Smith, the quartermaster.

CHARMING MARY CONSORTS WITH THE *MOCHA*

The *Charming Mary* reached Mergui on the Burmese coast toward the end of January 1697. In the harbor, the *Mary* encountered the *Mocha,* an East Indiaman that had been taken over by a mutinous crew the previous June. Although the seas are wide, sea raiders tended to hunt in the same waters, and they frequently ran into old acquaintances. Many men on both the *Mary* and *Mocha* would have known each other from sojourns at Saint Mary's and at other pirate haunts. Although the *Mocha* was larger and more heavily armed, the two crews agreed to sail together for equal shares.[40]

Sailing west toward India, the pirate warships enjoyed some success during the next three months. Several European and Indian vessels were captured, although none carried an especially valuable cargo. In May 1697, both vessels careened in the Maldives Islands. While they were there, the two crews quarreled and separated.

The southwest monsoon made it impossible to return to the hunting groups west and north of India. So after a brief stop at Saint Mary's Island, the *Charming Mary* crossed around the Cape of Good Hope, crossed the Atlantic, and reached Barbados in October 1697.[41] The booty was divided into shares of some £700 (about $350,000). For the original crewmen, who had sailed with Thomas Tew in January 1695, their shares represented the reward for almost three years at sea. While this was much more than they would have received as ordinary seaman on a merchant vessel, other Saint Mary's men took much richer plunder. The following year, some of the men took the *Mary* back to Saint Mary's, where her crew now chose William May as captain.

Part Two

SAINT MARY'S HEYDAY, 1695–1699

CHAPTER SIX

HENRY EVERY, KING OF SAINT MARY'S

Come, all you brave boys, whose courage is bold,
Will you venture with me? I'll glut you with gold.
Make haste unto Corona: a Ship you will find,
That's called the Fancy, *will pleasure your mind.*

Captain Every is in her, and calls her his own;
He will box her about, boys, before he has done.
French, Spaniard, and Portuguese, the heathen likewise,
He has made a war with them until that he dies.
—"A Copy of Verses, Composed by Captain Henry Every" (1696)

In his own time, Henry Every was famous throughout Europe and the Americas, achieving a renown that was seldom equaled by any other pirate. Every became an international celebrity in August 1695. Overcoming determined resistance, his pirate crew looted immense wealth in gold, silver, and gems from two Indian treasure ships, the *Fateh Mohammed* and the *Gang-i-Sawai* (*Gunsway*).

Every's plunder raid made Saint Mary's notorious, as the island became the subject of stories, songs, and plays. These painted a fascinating, if inaccurate, portrait of the pirate haven. Americans and Englishmen—even most European governments—were convinced that Every had created a vast pirate kingdom based at Saint Mary's. There he was said to rule more than fifteen thousand men and forty ships of war.

For years afterward, Every's legend continued to grow. About 1709, a little book appeared in London with the intriguing title *The Life and Adventures of Captain John Avery, now in Possession of Madagascar*. From this book,

Daniel Defoe borrowed the name John Avery, a usage copied by some subsequent writers. However, his signature reads Henry Every, and this also is his name in government documents of the time. "Henry Every" could, of course, be a pseudonym. Several records use the nickname Long Ben. Perhaps "Benjamin Bridgeman," which the captain adopted when he went into hiding, really was his original name.

Attributed to a fictitious Dutchman, a Captain Van Broeck, *The Life and Adventures* portrays Every as a tender lover as well as a powerful king. In Van Broeck's account, Every seizes both the Indian emperor's treasure and his beautiful granddaughter. The pirates kill many women on board the *Gunsway.* But Captain Every falls deeply in love with the Indian princess, protects her, and marries her according to her own religion.

Fleeing with his treasure and his bride, Every reaches Saint Mary's Island, lush but uninhabited. A local chieftain sells the island to the pirates. They meet in constitutional assembly, write laws for their new kingdom, and choose Every as their ruler. At Saint Mary's, he lives in opulent luxury with his Indian queen, "who soon forgot the Pleasures of her Grandfather's court in the Joys of her own."

Happily satiated himself, Every wants all of his subjects to enjoy sexual bliss. Ships sent to Africa supply each pirate with as many "dusky" brides as he wishes to purchase. From every nation, mariners flock to so blessed an island paradise. There they build great cities and impregnable forts.

For all their romancing, seventeenth-century stories, such as Van Broeck's *Life and Adventures,* took piracy seriously. Unlike some recent movies and novels, seventeenth-century authors seldom portrayed pirates as cavorting idiots. As described by Van Broeck, Every's crewmen work as hard and act as intelligently as nonpirates. But it is Every himself who is the main force behind the rise of the kingdom of Saint Mary's. Every owes this unparalleled success to his drive for power. Daring and good-humored when his rule is accepted, Van Broeck says, Every turns "insolent, uneasy, and unforgiving to the last Degree, if at any Time imposed upon."[1]

Four years later, in 1713, Every was the hero of *The Successful Pirate,* a combination of farce and tragedy that played at London's Drury Lane Theatre. Even more than in Van Broeck and other earlier versions of Every's life, the play emphasized his power over his crew. Throughout, Every's is the will that drives them to build harbors, roads, and forts. They willingly give their very lives to create his kingdom.

With me they made a Circle round this World,
Disclaim'd Relation, Country, Friendship, Fame.
They toil'd, they bled, they burnt, they froze, they starv'd,
Each Element, and all Mankind their Foe,
Familiar to their Eyes saw horrid Death,
In every Climate, and in every Shape,
When, in this Isle, our shatter'd Barks found Rest,
With Universal Voice, they call'd me King.[2]

To readers today, Every's story seems like a typical buccaneer Romance. In the early 1700s, however, this combination of derring-do, pirate tyrant, and sexual innuendo was bold and new. And precisely because it was new, this astonishing Romance was believed. It is a fact that European rulers received adventurers pretending to be Every's ambassadors sent from Saint Mary's. It is a fact that English and Scottish officials at the highest level gave serious attention to the proposals of these "pirate diplomats." It is a fact that Peter the Great of Russia tried to hire the Saint Mary's pirates to help build a Russian colony on Madagascar.[3]

These tales about Every show how much fantasy is contained in the stories about pirates that circulated during their own lifetimes. Every did not create Saint Mary's. The island already was a flourishing pirate haven when he visited it in 1695. If anything, Every's plunder of the *Gunsway* had the effect of weakening the Saint Mary's community by cutting off the flow of new recruits from Europe and the Americas.

During the years before Every reached the Red Sea in 1695, pirates from Saint Mary's looted dozens of ships, some with very rich cargoes. Except for the pirates' friends in North America, however, no one took much notice. Since none of the Saint Mary's raiders were caught, there were no trials to gain the public's attention. Those that did know about Saint Mary's were not bothered by raids on Indian or other foreign vessels. And few Englishmen had much sympathy for the hated East India Company.

Every's one plunder raid attracted more attention than all the preceding pirate cruises. He took incredibly valuable booty—captured in shining gold and sparkling jewels. Most important, Every had plundered a ship belonging to the emperor of India and carrying cargo owned by powerful officials at the emperor's court. The Indians were convinced that all Englishmen either were pirates or at least colluded with pirates. In retaliation to the raid, they imprisoned the East India Company's traders, and the emperor threat-

ened to throw the Company entirely out of India. To save England's trade
with the East, the Company promised to protect Indian shipping in the
Red Sea. Meanwhile, the English government cracked down on the pirates'
friends in North America.

After considerable hue and cry, the government also managed to arrest
a few of Every's crew—but not Every himself. Six men were sentenced to
death after a much publicized series of London trials. State trials and public
hangings were a major source of entertainment for the London mob. Pamphlets and songs produced to sell on the day of hanging provided the basic
elements that grew into the Every and Saint Mary's legends.

Expressing their authors' monarchical beliefs, seventeenth-century stories portray Every as lusting for power, as a tyrant ruthlessly driving his
men. In fact, Every led by example and not by intimidation. An excellent
navigator and seaman, he carefully planned his voyages and personally commanded in battle. Above all, he was highly persuasive and enjoyed a charismatic rapport with his followers. Time and again, both novice seamen and
experienced captains chose him as their chief. Every was in real life a near-
perfect pirate leader. He deserves his fame—even if pirate legends do exaggerate his power.

Contemporary stories and plays provided Every with a fanciful biography, crammed with conventional and unconvincing cliches. He suddenly
enters history in May 1694. Leading a mutiny, he took over the *Charles II,*
a forty-six-gun warship docked at La Coruña in northwestern Spain. He
renamed her the *Fancy* and headed for Saint Mary's and the treasure ships
plying the Red Sea.

Along with the *James,* the *Charles II* was among the private warships
assembled for a raid on the French West Indies. Since 1689, England, Spain,
Holland and several other nations had been at war with France. Late in
1692, the Spanish began to hire English and Dutch men-of-war under
"privateering" contracts, whereby private individuals provided the ships and
crew. In return, the government allowed the owners and crewmen to divide
up whatever booty they seized. Under these terms, the *Charles II* and *James*
had been sent to Spain by Sir James Houblon, alderman of London and a
director of the Bank of England.

Every had been hired as master and first mate of the *Charles.* This was
a highly responsible position, and the ship's owners presumably were convinced that Every was an effective navigator and commander. He was all of
that—and much more, as events proved.

Unfortunately for their crews, the two warships spent months at La Coruña, waiting for the expedition to sail. One of the rules of privateering (as of piracy) was "no purchase, no pay." Unless and until they took booty, the men received no wages. Tired of inactivity and hungry for their wages, some of the sailors aboard the *James* and *Charles II* laid plans for a mutiny. According to the evidence when they came to trial, the discontented mariners chose Every as their leader.[4] On May 7 (the 17th according to our modern calendar), the rebels seized the *Charles*. They allowed some twenty men to row ashore, including the captain, who was sick with a fever; only the ship's doctor was compelled to remain against his will.

Seventy or eighty men voluntarily stayed on board and were joined by another twenty-five from the *James*. All joined in unanimously electing Every as their captain. He may already have had a reputation as a pirate. During the mutiny, one rebel boasted that Every and several others were "true Cocks of the Game and old Sportsman."[5]

Once in control of the ship (now renamed the *Fancy*), Every made for Saint Mary's. He and his followers clearly were aware of the rich pickings in the Red Sea. But this knowledge provides no clue to his origins, since mariners from throughout North America and England made the voyage to Saint Mary's. Every needed supplies and crewmen before taking the *Fancy* into the Red Sea. Although more than enough to sail the ship, the men on board might prove too few to man the cannon during battle. On the way south, the *Fancy* hugged the coast of Africa, looking for provisions and recruits.

Always a persuasive leader, Every easily convinced seamen to join his band. When it finally reached the Red Sea, the *Fancy* was packed with mariners from many nations, including men whose countries were at war. At the Cape Verde Islands, nine men joined up from three small English vessels. At Principe Island, farther south, the marauders seized two Danish ships, and a dozen or more from their crews enlisted.[6]

Rounding the Cape of Good Hope, the *Fancy* stopped for a time at Saint Mary's, where Every recruited several dozen of the pirates present on the island. He also packed the ship with water, wood, and cattle and generally got everything ready for the battles he expected in the Red Sea. By now, the *Fancy* was heavily manned.

Somewhere along the way, the *Fancy*'s crew had picked up the fevers that killed so many visitors to Africa. The crowded ship had no room for sick and dying men. Planning to put his casualties ashore with friendly natives, Every stopped at Johanna (Anjouan) Island in the Comoros chain, northwest of Madagascar. The second day in port, three East Indiamen suddenly appeared in the harbor. The *Fancy* just made it to sea, stopping at Patta Island, near modern-day Kenya.[7]

Several men from the *Fancy* were left at Johanna, including William May. Captain Leonard Edgcumbe, who commanded one of the three East Indiamen, was a notorious bully. He went ashore and badgered May and the other sick men, threatening to make them dance at the end of a hangman's noose.

While he lay in feverish despair, May was approached by a dark-skinned native, who addressed him in slangy seaman's English. After recovering from his shock, May learned that the man had lived for a time in Bethnal Green, a London suburb, and had fond memories of English mariners. His black friend fed and cared for May, saving his life, and also protecting him from Captain Edgcumbe's bullying.[8]

After some weeks, Every returned to Johanna Island to make last-minute preparations for the long voyage still ahead. The *Fancy* was as ready for battle as possible. Before departing, Every left a curious letter with a native chief, asking him to deliver it to the first English ship that came into port. On the missive, after identifying himself and the *Fancy,* Every promised that the pirates would not attack English or Dutch vessels. Any English ship could obtain his protection by flying its flags in an unusual arrangement that would identify them as Every's friends.

> Riding here at this instant in the Ship *Fancy* Man of War, formerly the *Charles* of the Spanish expedition, who departed from Croniae the 7th of May 1694 Being (and am now) in a Ship of 46 Guns, 150 men, and bound to seek our Fortunes. I have never as yet wronged any English or Dutch, nor ever intend whilst I am Commander.[9]

Every was lying, since he had looted English ships in the Cape Verde Islands. In writing the letter, he apparently shared the common belief that he would escape punishment as long as he only stole from "Moors."

The *Fancy*'s intended target was the pilgrim fleet that sailed between Surat in India and Mocha at the tip of the Arabian Peninsula. Now on its way back to Surat, the fleet was the richest prize in Asia, perhaps in the world. At the southern end of the Red Sea, the pilgrim fleet had to pass through the narrow strait of Bab al Mandab. Every anchored at waterless Perim Island, at the strait's most constricted point, to wait for the pilgrim fleet. As the *Fancy* got into position for the attack, Every discovered that other marauders had the same goal.

In all, five smaller craft joined the *Fancy* at Perim Island. William Want commanded the *Dolphin*. William May was captain of the brigantine *Pearl*. (This was another William May and not the sick crewman Every had left at Johanna Island.) Thomas Wake had charge of the *Susana*. Joseph Farrell commanded the *Portsmouth Adventure;* Thomas Tew captained the sloop *Amity*. These vessels were stationed at Saint Mary's, where their captains had learned of Every's plans.

As they lay in wait at Perim, the experienced Saint Mary's men on these five vessels joined Every in a consort partnership. Captains and crews agreed to cooperate throughout the attack on the pilgrim fleet; those taking part in the battle would share in the spoils. As another sign of Every's repute with his fellow marauders, they agreed that Every would command the combined fleet. All swore their oath to obey his orders during battle.[10]

While the pirates lurked off Perim for four or five weeks until August 1696, a merchant vessel took notice and warned the pilgrim fleet. The entire fleet, twenty-five ships in all, managed to sneak by at night and almost escaped. Fortunately for the raiders, Every caught a straggler the next morning, and the chase was on. For five days, Every pressed across the Arabian Sea toward Surat, the fleet's home port. Only the *Pearl* and the *Portsmouth Adventure* kept up. Indeed, the *Dolphin* was such a poor sailor that her crew burned her and transferred to the *Fancy*.[11]

Finally, approaching Cape Guardafui, the hunters caught up with their first victim. The unarmed *Fateh Mohammed* belonged to Abd-ul Ghafur, the richest and most influential Indian trader of the day.[12] Without a struggle, Ghafur lost his ship carrying gold and silver said to be worth £50,000 to £60,000 (about $30 million today).

Leaving some men aboard the *Fateh,* Every sailed on to the east. That afternoon, the *Fancy* and the *Pearl* came upon the *Gunsway* at anchor. With at least forty great guns, this immense and heavily armed vessel was the pride of the Indian emperor's navy. In addition to her crew, the *Gunsway* carried four hundred musketeers plus other soldiers.[13] The *Gunsway* was much larger than the two pirate vessels, and she carried more and bigger cannon. The Indian soldiers and sailors outnumbered their attackers at least four or five to one. It took either courage or stupidity to attack.

Every's good luck continued to hold. As soon as the *Gunsway* opened fire, one of her huge cannon blew up. As deadly fragments sprayed the deck, the defenders fled in confusion. Soon after, a shot from the *Fancy* smashed the mainmast, leaving the enormous vessel unmaneuverable. Despite this, the Indians held out for two or three hours, and a dozen or more of the invaders were killed. Finally the pirates came alongside, drew their swords, and climbed up the side of the great ship.

The *Gunsway*'s captain fled below as the marauders boarded his ship. Khafi Khan, an Indian historian, describes the taking of the *Gunsway;* he wrote soon after the incident but lived far from the battle. In desperation, Khafi Khan reports, the captain armed dozens of slave girls and sent them into battle.[14] If so, the pirates quickly overcame these amazons.

Soon after, all fighting ceased. The pirates towed the *Fateh* and the *Gunsway* to nearby Socotra Island. There they plundered them for two days before allowing them to go on to Surat. Since the *Gunsway* was considered the safest ship in the pilgrim fleet, its six hundred passengers included many at the Mogul's court. Some Indian stories say Every's men fiendishly tortured the crew and passengers and raped Indian women of high rank. Khafi Khan, never a friend of Englishmen, claims the men fell into an extraordinary and unparalleled sexual dementia, ravishing every woman in sight, whether pretty or repulsive.

When they had laden their ship, they brought the royal ship to shore near one of their settlements, and busied themselves for a week searching for plunder, stripping the men, and dishonouring the women, both old and young. They then left the ship, carrying off the men. Several honourable women, when they found an opportunity, threw themselves into the sea, to preserve their chastity, and some others killed themselves with knives and daggers.[15]

East India Company officials at Bombay related these rumors to London. So frenzied were the pirates' lusts, they reported, that they assaulted even very old women.

There happened to be a Great Umbraws Wife (as Wee hear) related to the King, returning from her Pilgrimage to Mecha, in her old age. She they abused very much, and forced severall other Women, which Caused one person of Quality, his Wife, and his Nurse, to kill themselves to prevent the Husbands seing them (and their being) ravished.[16]

Other tales told how Every had captured the emperor's own grand-daughter. Proving to be more durable than the rumors of rape, these stories served as the basis for Every's marriage to the Mogul princess in the *Life and Adventures* and other Romances. Ordinary Englishmen were determined to think well of Captain Every. As the years passed, the Indian charges of gang rape were forgotten. The world remembered only the idyllic life on Saint Mary's shared by Henry Every and the Mogul princess.[17]

Some twenty-five years after the battle for the *Gunsway*, Daniel Defoe described the attack in *The King of Pirates*. In this fictional biography, contrary to his usual practice, Defoe removed both rape and romance from the story. Every does storm into the princess's magnificent cabin—but only to get her money. When he enters her cabin, Every tells us, the queen was "frighted and crying." He quickly reassures her: "I, like a true pirate, soon let her see that I had more mind to the jewels than to the lady."[18]

The prosaic version in *The King of Pirates* is truest to the evidence given by the men that turned informer against their comrades. The prosecution's witnesses reported that the attackers' one goal was plunder. They admitted that some captives may have been tortured—but solely to make them tell where they had hidden their gold.[19] Some men did look for sex, but only after they had thoroughly searched the two ships. Even if one assumes that Every joined in dallying with the captive women, there is no evidence that he took a princess with him when he returned to the *Fancy*.

Whether or not they committed torture and rape, there is no question that Every's men took an extraordinary plunder from the two Indian vessels. The owners of the cargo later estimated their loses at £600,000 and demanded compensation from the English East India Company. The Company's president (who wanted to pay as little as possible) claimed the pirates had taken goods worth £325,000—equivalent to $200 million today.[20]

If one accepts the lower estimate, only two or three times in history did criminals take more valuable loot. And the *Gunsway* carried the best form of plunder—light in weight, untraceable, and in great demand among the natives of Saint Mary's as well as in Europe and North America. In addition to gold and silver bars and coins, the pirates carried away bags of loose gems plus a saddle studded with hundreds of rubies, intended as a present to the emperor.[21]

As soon as the Indian vessels left for Surat, the crewmen split their booty as best they could. Each adult man with a full share got jewels and cash worth about £1,000. Contrary to the stories of Every's vast riches, he was awarded only two shares. The *Portsmouth Adventure* had not taken part in the battle, so only the men of the *Fancy* and the *Pearl* shared in the loot. As the money was being distributed, the *Pearl's* crew cheated those on the *Fancy* in exchanging gold for silver. When they examined the gold coins, Every's men discovered that their edges had been clipped, reducing their value. They immediately repossessed the silver at gunpoint, leaving the *Pearl* only 2,000 pieces of eight ($225,000) to purchase provisions.[22]

The *Pearl*, *Amity*, and *Portsmouth Adventure* headed back to Saint Mary's. On the way, the *Adventure* was wrecked in the Comoros. Captain Wake's *Susana* hunted in the Persian Gulf before reaching Saint Mary's in December. Having taken and kept most of the plunder, the men of the *Fancy* were free to retire wherever they chose.

Every wanted to sail directly to the Bahamas. But the men mutinied and forced Every to stop at the French colony on Réunion Island in November 1695.[23] About half the crew—most of the foreigners but also many Englishmen—got off at Réunion.[24] Some later went to Europe on French ships, while others preferred to remain on Réunion.[25]

INDIAN RULERS PLUNDER THE EAST INDIA COMPANY

Meanwhile, as Every began the voyage back to the Americas, the forlorn *Fateh Mohammed* and *Gunsway* finally limped into port at Surat, plundered down to the keel. Rumors quickly spread throughout the city, detailing the killing of holy pilgrims and the fiendish rape of women. Angry crowds turned violent and besieged the staff of the English East India Company in their compound. For a Muslim, the capture of the imperial pilgrim ship was more than a crime; it was a direct act of sacrilege against God. The taking of the *Gunsway* fanned to the fiercest heat the fires of hatred against the company's "factory"—its walled compound of living quarters and warehouses.

Surat's governor sent troops, who barely prevented the murder of the Englishmen. Samuel Annesley, president of the Surat factory, and more than sixty other Company employees were put under house arrest while the governor awaited the emperor's orders. To prevent their escape, they were imprisoned for a time in heavy iron chains. Nevertheless, Annesley praised the governor, who had risked his own life to protect the Englishmen.[26]

News of the *Gunsway* soon reached Emperor Aurangzib. The pious ruler took a special interest in religious questions. When he heard of the infamous attack on the pilgrim fleet, the enraged emperor denounced the English as criminals and infidels. He sent a great army to attack the English at Bombay, and he ordered the seizure of the East India Company's officials and goods throughout India.

After the emperor's rage had abated, the prime minister managed to get these harsh orders canceled. But more than sixty men at Surat remained under house arrest (and sometimes back in chains) for almost a year until June 1696. All trade was forbidden until the Company both agreed to reimburse the losses on the *Gunsway* and also promised to protect future pilgrim fleets.[27]

Indian officials similarly pressured the French and Dutch trading companies, which also agreed to protect Indian shipping. However, only English traders were arrested and imprisoned. Indian officials were convinced that all pirates were Englishmen. They also believed that the East India Company conspired with the marauders to rob the company's competitors. The letter Every posted at Anjouan before attacking the pilgrim fleet naturally was seen as proof of this collusion.

There was some justification for both charges. The largest number of Saint Mary's men came from England or North America. English was the common language on the island, spoken more or less fluently by all the pirates. East India Company officials hated pirates, who also pillaged the Company's vessels. However, some Saint Mary's men had worked for the Company before they turned pirate, and employees at Company stations sometimes did purchase pirate plunder.

To demonstrate its innocence and protect its trading rights, the East India Company desperately needed to capture and hang the *Gunsway*'s despoilers. The Company officers bombarded the London government with desperate appeals. In July 1696, the privy council issued a proclamation condemning Henry Every and the *Fancy*'s crew. The council ordered colonial governors to seize them as pirates and offered a reward of £500 for their apprehension, which the Company agreed to pay.[28]

EVERY GETS AWAY WITH ALL HIS BOOTY

Every and his men wanted to reach the Americas ahead of news about their crimes. Stopping only at the Portuguese island of São Tomé (Saint Thomas) in the Gulf of Guinea, the pirates headed directly for the Bahamas. In April

1696, the *Fancy* anchored off New Providence Island. Every offered Governor Nicholas Trott a generous bribe—the *Fancy* and all her gear as well as a considerable amount in gold. Governor Trott welcomed the pirates to Nassau and entertained Every and the other officers in his own home.[29] (In defense of his actions, Governor Trott later declared that he could not arrest men on mere suspicion and without evidence. Moreover, there were only about sixty men on the island at this time, whereas the *Fancy* held 113 men "plus negroes."[30])

The Bahamas were a private colony. Since he represented their owners and not the crown, Governor Trott could not grant a royal pardon. The governor of Jamaica later claimed that he turned down Every's offer of £20,000 ($10 million) for a pardon.[31] Footloose now, the crew of the *Fancy* broke up and scattered. Some remained on Providence, where Governor Trott and his successors are said to have fleeced them.[32] Other men fled to the North American colonies and found it easy to escape justice. They arrived with large amounts of cash, confirming the reports that the *Gunsway* carried a very rich cargo.[33]

Two groups purchased sloops and sailed for England. Every, using the alias Benjamin Bridgeman, took one sloop to Ireland.[34] With about twenty others, he reached Ireland's north coast in June 1696. In landing their booty, they aroused suspicions; and one man, Philip Middleton, was caught. Another crewman, John Dann, made it safely to shore and crossed to England. He was arrested when a maid found more than £1,000 in heavy gold coins "quilted up in his jacket."[35]

Henry Every got completely away. But an additional six men were caught during the next months and were brought to trial in October 1696. Both Dann and Middleton turned informer and testified against the other six. The East India Company did everything it could to aid the prosecution, even buying new clothes for Middleton and paying his mother a pension.

The government assembled the most famous judges in the land, and Dann and Middleton were young and attractive witnesses. Nevertheless, the jury brought in a verdict of not guilty. The Company's leaders, present to witness the trial, were mortified. They needed a conviction to convince the Mogul that they detested pirates. The six men were retried two weeks later. Under great pressure from the court, the second jury found them guilty, and the death sentence was pronounced with great solemnity.[36]

The verdict actually did little to help the Company's men in India. What the East India Company really needed was to wipe out the pirate base at Saint Mary's. Instead, the entire *Gunsway* incident actually protected Saint Mary's by making the pirates appear to be even stronger than they were. Given the government's failure to find Captain Every, the public chose to believe that he had stayed at Saint Mary's, where he ruled in splendid grandeur.

DANIEL DEFOE DENIGRATES EVERY'S DEEDS

In his *General History of the Pyrates,* Daniel Defoe invented a fictional history that has been believed up to our own time. Defoe gave some pirates— Blackbeard, for example—everlasting fame. Others, including Henry Every and the men at Saint Mary's, he demoted for his own literary rather than historical reasons.

Defoe wrote two books about Every and Saint Mary's. In 1719, he produced *The King of Pirates: Being an Account of the Famous Enterprises of Captain Avery, the Mock King of Madagascar.* This work was almost totally based on the 1709 *Life and Adventures.* But *The King of Pirates* amends the legends in many serious ways. Perhaps simply through carelessness, Defoe moved the pirate haven from Saint Mary's to Madagascar. Every's motives became very much less noble than in earlier accounts. And *The King of Pirates* totally dismisses the earlier stories about Every the great lover.

In *The King of Pirates,* Every begins his crimes in the Caribbean, sailing under the psychopathic Captain Redpath. When a canonball tears off Redpath's head, Every is elected captain. In Defoe's mordant view, Every succeeds as a leader solely because he focuses on the task of making money. Other captains make mistakes because they are distracted by their lusts or their vanity; Every never forgets that stealing gold is what piracy is all about.

Every's crewmen discover that they cannot trust each other. If they return to civilization, one of the men may betray the others. They decide to live at Madagascar because the climate is good, and the people there are easily terrified. Reaching Madagascar in April 1693, the pirates establish a colony on the island's northeastern coast. Every returns from a visit to England and easily captures the *Gunsway.* In this tale, however, since money is Every's first love, he neither rapes nor marries the emperor's granddaughter.

If *The King of Pirates* made Every less than heroic, Defoe totally destroyed Every's reputation in volume one of the *General History,* published in 1724. The *General History* describes a pirate kingdom at Madagascar. However, for his own literary reasons, Defoe transfers leadership of the Madagascar marauders from Henry Every to a fictitious Captain Mission.

In the *General History,* Defoe deliberately strips Every of any ability, courage, or even capacity for real evil. In this version, Every is a mutineer "of more Cunning, than Courage" who steals the *Charles* while her captain is drunk. At Madagascar, Every joins forces with other pirates in a small sloop. The two vessels accidentally blunder onto the *Gunsway.* While Every cowardly bombards the *Gunsway* from a distance, the men in the sloop storm the ship. Every robs the sloop's crew, and steals their plunder, then makes it to England. But he dies in poverty, cheated by the merchants to whom he sold the Indian jewels.[37]

The compelling mixture of fact and fantasy in Defoe's *General History* made it the standard textbook of piracy for centuries. Thus the public forgot both Every's victory over the *Gunsway* as well as the pirates of Saint Mary's. Yet Saint Mary's Island deserves to be remembered, and Every played an important role in its history. In his own time, Every's attack on the *Gunsway* made the island famous throughout the world. Ironically, over the longer term, his voyage actually weakened the pirate island. By firing the pirates' friends—men such as Governor Trott of the Bahamas—the English crown ended the constant stream of new recruits from North America.

Meanwhile, the Saint Mary's men that joined in attacking the *Gunsway* probably did not care what the London mob thought of their exploits. In the short term, the raid increased the island's prosperity and the happiness of its inhabitants. Many of those on the *Fancy* took their Indian gold and gems back to their island paradise. Although not quite accurate, the many legends of Every and the Indian princess enclose a kernel of truth. The *Fancy's* crew did not need to steal Indian wives. Once they had the *Gunsway's* gold, Malagasy princesses were delighted to become their brides.

CHAPTER SEVEN

"PIRATES FROM ALL PARTS"

In October 1696, the head of the East India Company factory at Bombay wrote to London that:

> Horrible clamours are occasioned by the pirates from all parts, which are unanimously reputed to be English. Besides the *Gunsway*, the Mogul's own ships were robbed last year near Surat and barbarously used. Abdul Gophow has since had one robbed of a great sum in the Gulf of Persia, and this day we have news from Mocha of two ships belonging to the Company's merchants being taken . . . . If care be not taken to suppress pirates in India, and to empower the Company's servants to punish them according to their deserts . . ., the said servants fear it is probable that their throats will all be cut by malefactors and by the natives of the country in revenge for frequent losses, and, moreover the trade in India will be wholly lost.[1]

Pressured by the Indian government, English authorities took Every's adventure more seriously than other piracies. But London worked slowly, and its efforts often were in vain. The East India Company demanded that a naval squadron be sent east, but a long war with France had exhausted English funds. The warships did not leave for India until January 1699.

In the short run, government antipiracy campaigns increased the population of the pirate encampments. Whereas Thomas Tew had gone back to North America after each season of marauding, Tew's successors planned to spend several years at Saint Mary's before retiring from piracy. Some came to like the place so much that they stayed for good.

By now, moreover, Saint Mary's was a flourishing permanent settlement that continued to thrive even when cut off from North America and Europe. London removed Governor Benjamin Fletcher in April 1698, but New York merchants continued to visit Saint Mary's until the end of the following year. When the government finally cracked down, the pirates turned to Arab and Indian suppliers. As their old ships wore out, they simply captured new ones at sea. Since vessels in the Red Sea now traveled in guarded convoys, raiders headed far to the east, into the Persian Gulf, the Malacca Straits, and the South China Sea.

Each year from 1695 to 1699, large warships sailed from Saint Mary's, often marauding in consort. Among the most successful were two vessels commanded by outstanding captains—the *Mocha* under Robert Culliford and Dirk Chivers's *Soldado*. The men of the *Charming Mary*, in contrast, followed their democratic principles to a logical conclusion and chose to sail without a captain.

More and more, the men were old-timers, who remained at Saint Mary's and transferred from ship to ship. Beginning in 1696, however, they made use of a new fleet of warships. The *John and Rebecca* and the *Resolution* were brought over from Rhode Island. The *Charming Mary* was a merchantman seized by the crew of the *Amity*, whose own vessel had been severely damaged battling the *Gunsway*. The *Mocha*, the largest of the warships, was snatched from the East India Company by Saint Mary's men who had recently escaped from Indian imprisonment.

RESOLUTION AND *JOHN AND REBECCA* AUGMENT THE PIRATE FLEET

Only two more warships crossed the Atlantic to Saint Mary's during the 1690s. Both captains came from Rhode Island but were not part of Thomas Tew's clique. John Hoar was master of the *John and Rebecca*. Robert Glover, who had married a sister of Hoar, owned and commanded the *Resolution*. Both men had gone to Newport from the Caribbean island of Antigua, where they had operated profitably as privateers during the early years of King William's War with France. In the summer of 1694, the two brothers-in-law went north to Canada—although not together. There each captain captured a substantial French warship, which allowed them to recruit crews and head east to the Indian Ocean.

After briefly hunting in consort in the Red Sea, the *Resolution* and the *John and Rebecca* separated. Nevertheless, Captains Glover and Hoar suffered

PIRATE WARSHIPS
AT SAINT MARY'S, 1695–1697

Ship	John and Rebecca	Resolution / Soldado	Charming Mary	Mocha	Adventure Galley
Captain	John Hoar	Robert Glover, Dirk Chivers	Captain Bobbington	Ralph Stout, Robert Culliford	William Kidd
1695	Leaves Boston (Rhode Island-based), December	Leaves New England, mid-1695?; At Comoro Islands, picks up Dirk Chivers, crew of *Portsmouth Adventure*, late 1695	Seized by *Amity* crew, December		
1696	Arrives Saint Mary's; consorts with *Resolution*, April At Red Sea, takes *Ruparell and Calicut* (not in consort), August Captures Indian ship with cloth	At Saint Mary's consorts with *John and Rebecca*, April; Red Sea, then Indian Coast, August Glover deposed, Chivers is captain, September Holds Calcutta for ransom, Nov. 23–26 Glover reaches Saint Mary's, Dec.	Leaves Saint Mary's, May Western India, Sept. Bobbington killed in Persian Gulf, Nov. or Dec.	Seized in mutiny, June 16 Goes to Burma, rescues Robert Culliford	Leaves London, Feb. Leaves New York, Sept. 16; Madeira, Oct. 8; Canary Islands, Oct. 19; Cape Verde, Oct. 24
1697	Arrives Saint Mary's, February Hoar and many of crew killed in native uprising, July *John and Rebecca* stranded at Port Dauphin	Leaves India for Saint Mary's, April Caught in a hurricane at Antongil Bay, June Leaves Saint Mary's, September	Reaches Burma, late Jan.; consorts with *Mocha* until April Reaches Bahamas, October	Consorts with *Charming Mary* until April Take *Satisfaction* (Portugese vessel), Jan., Feb. Stout killed, Culliford becomes captain, May 30; battle with Dorrill, June Leaves Malacca Straits, Dec.	Talear near Saint Augustines, Jan. 29 Johanna, Mehila, March, April Mouth of Red Sea, mid-July to mid-Aug. Chased off by English warship; Malabar Coast, Sept.; Maldives, Oct.; meets Loyal *Captain*, takes *Rouparelle*, Nov.

The warships *Pelican* and *Speaker* were also at Saint Mary's during this time.

the same fate. Both ships eventually returned to Saint Mary's. Their captains were killed, along with many from their crews, during a native uprising at the end of the summer in 1697.

Robert Glover was the first to leave for Madagascar, toward the middle of 1695. Glover had arrived in Rhode Island at the end of 1694, having captured a warship in a battle with privateers. Her French owners had themselves taken the *Algerine Pirate* (or *Algerine Galley*)[2] from Barbary corsairs and brought it to the Americas. There the ship again changed hands in battle and was renamed the *Resolution* by Captain Glover.[3]

Three years earlier, in 1691, Glover and his sloop *Dragon* had been granted a privateer's commission by Christopher Codrington, governor of the Leeward Islands. During the next few years, Glover proved himself an excellent sea raider, but he also gained a reputation for dishonesty. He captured about twenty French vessels and sold them without paying the fees owed to the crown.[4]

In February 1694, Glover left Saint Thomas in the Virgin Islands and headed to Newport, Rhode Island, in consort with the *Dolphin,* commanded by Erasmus Harrison. Cruising off Canada throughout the summer, Glover's sloop and the *Dolphin* captured several vessels from French privateers. One of these was kept by Glover and renamed the *Resolution.*

Glover continued to play fast and loose with privateering customs. Although the two crews had signed a consort agreement and promised to divide their spoils equally, Glover refused to split the substantial booty from a French merchantman with the men of the *Dolphin.*[5] The argument led to extended litigation, as almost everyone on board both vessels went to court.[6] (At Saint Mary's, in contrast, the principle of equal shares generally prevailed without dispute, and arguments about booty were rare.)

Captain John Hoar also was operating off Canada during the summer of 1694, carrying a commission from the governor of Jamaica. As Glover had done, Hoar captured a substantial French warship.[7] Toward the end of 1694, Hoar brought his prize to Rhode Island, where the governor's council confirmed his ownership of the vessel. Since Rhode Island had no Admiralty Court, the legislature in February 1694 had assigned maritime matters to the council.[8]

Hoar and Glover both outfitted their vessels in Rhode Island.[9] However, following Thomas Tew's example, they traveled to New York to recruit additional members of their crews. Both men also purchased a privateer's commission from Governor Fletcher, empowering them to seize French vessels off Canada.[10]

Glover and the *Resolution* left Rhode Island about the middle of 1695 and took the middle passage between Africa and Madagascar. Toward the end of 1695, Glover reached the Comoro Islands, where he augmented his crew by taking aboard Dirk Chivers and other men from the wrecked *Portsmouth Adventure*.[11] The *Resolution* apparently cruised unsuccessfully in the Red Sea; but the ship was at Saint Mary's by April 1696, when John Hoar showed up with the *John and Rebecca*.[12] Hoar had left Boston in December 1695 and picked up additional men at Jamaica before crossing to the Indian Ocean.[13]

CAPTAIN HOAR BURNS TWO EAST INDIA COMPANY VESSELS AT ADEN

The two brothers-in-law agreed to hunt in consort, and sailed together to the Bab al Mandab at the mouth of the Red Sea. However, the *John and Rebecca* was alone on August 14 and 15, when it captured the *Ruparell* and *Calicut,* two merchantmen belonging to the East India Company and bound for Bombay.[14] As was true of most of the Company's coastal traders, the crews were Indian, but the officers were European. Henry Watson, the ship's surgeon, wrote a detailed report about the incident for the company.

Hoar and his men plundered the ship from end to end and slapped around the Indian pursers to make them reveal their hiding places. All together, the two merchantmen carried only £7,500 in cash ($3.75 million)—a small sum to split among more than 120 men.[15] However, Hoar believed the company would pay a ransom for the return of the vessels, which were crammed with eighty tons of fresh coffee.[16] He ordered their captains to take the two ships to Aden and promised to release them in return for £7,000, considerably less than the value of their cargo.[17]

There was no English settlement at Aden, and no one on board was acquainted with the native merchants in the city. After four days, a shot was fired as a signal that the ransom would not be paid. The pirates looted the captured vessels of anything usable, put the Indian crewmen ashore, and took the English officers on board. They made a point of running up the English flag on both vessels before setting them on fire close to shore and in full view of the people of Aden.

Someone made up a colorful story about the incident, which has been repeated to demonstrate the cruelty of the Saint Mary's pirates. Alexander Hamilton, a merchant at Surat, tells the story as it circulated among the English community in India. According to Hamilton, one of the captured captains named Sawbridge

began to expostulate with them about their Way of Life. They
ordered him to hold his Tongue, but he continuing his Discourse,
they took a Sail-needle and Twine, sewed his Lips together, and so
kept him several Hours, with his Hands tied behind him. At length
they unloosed both his Hands and Lips, and carried him on board
their Ship, and, after they had plundered *Sawbridge*'s Ship, they set her
on Fire, and burned her and the Horses together. *Sawbridge* and his
people were set ashore near *Aden,* where he died presently after.[18]

The story is amusing as well as heartless, but there is no truth to it.
Doctor Henry Watson was captured at Mocha and imprisoned aboard the
John and Rebecca for six weeks. Watson never mentioned the supposed atrocity. Instead, Watson said that the pirates treated him with consideration during his stay in their company.

DIRK CHIVERS LEADS A MUTINY ON THE *RESOLUTION*

Following the burning of the *Ruparell* and the *Calicut,* the two warships split
up, although with the intention of reuniting at a later time.[19] Hoar took the
John and Rebecca north to the Persian Gulf, while Glover and the *Resolution*
sailed south to India's west coast. The *Resolution* finally took a prize in the
harbor at Rajapur, a few miles south of Bombay. But the captive turned out
to be an Indian vessel from Muscat carrying dates and rice—a cargo of little use to sea-raiders.

The *Resolution* now had been at sea for more than a year without much
success. Glover and most of the crew disagreed strongly about their next
step. Glover wanted to return to Saint Mary's, but a faction led by Dirk
Chivers was convinced the *Resolution* would have better luck if it headed
east toward China. According to documents back in Rhode Island, Glover
represented the owners of the *Resolution*. By 1696, however, legal ownership carried little weight on warships operating out of Saint Mary's. Except
during battle, democracy was practiced, and decisions were made by a
majority vote.

The crew dismissed Robert Glover as captain. In his place the men
elected Dirk Chivers, who had been their comrade for about a year. Hoping
to change their luck, the crew gave the *Resolution* a new name, rebaptizing
it the *Soldado*. The crew gave Glover and his twenty-four followers the
Indian prize. Although a vessel of decent size armed with twelve guns, it was
in poor condition and did not reach Saint Mary's until December 1696.[20]

Originally from New York's Dutch community, Chivers was by now more at home at Saint Mary's and in the Indian Ocean than in New York City and the Atlantic. Chivers had cruised on the *Batchelor's Delight* from 1688 to 1692. In January 1695, he joined Thomas Tew's flotilla as first mate of the *Portsmouth Adventure*. Later the same year, the *Adventure* had been wrecked in the Comoro Islands. Some of the crew caught a ride on a merchantman to the French colony at Réunion Island. Chivers wanted no part of the regulated life in a plantation colony, preferring to live among the natives on Mayotte until he enlisted on the *Resolution* late in 1695. Now another year had passed with only very poor booty. Confident that he could do better, Chivers helped convince the crew to dismiss Glover as captain.

Meanwhile, Captain Hoar had taken the *John and Rebecca* east to the Persian Gulf, intending to raid near the prosperous port city of Gombroon (Bandar Abbas) across from Hormuz. However, when he learned that numerous European warships were in the area, Hoar stayed well offshore. In November, the *John and Rebecca* finally took a rich prize, an Indian vessel from Surat loaded with high-quality cloth.[21]

It was time to go back to Saint Mary's Island. The crew had been continually at sea for many months and had run out of food. While Doctor Watson was their captive, the *Rebecca* stopped at one island in the Persian Gulf. The men killed many wild antelope, but soon became tired of their strong-tasting meat. A small fishing village provided dates and salted fish. Otherwise, there was nothing to eat except "stinking beef and dough boys (that is dough made into a lump and boiled)."[22]

The *John and Rebecca* reached Saint Mary's Island in February 1697. Soon after, the merchantman *Fortune* came into port with supplies for Adam Baldridge and the pirate community. With Baldridge's assistance, Hoar consigned the captured Indian calicos for sale in New York. Fourteen men also returned to North America on the *Fortune* and escaped to with their plunder.[23] Robert Monday had served as surgeon on board the *John and Rebecca*; Monday and George Cutler, another of the ship's officers, were each said to have gotten away with £1,400 or £1,500 in gold and silver (about $725,000).[24]

Captain Hoar and the rest of the crew remained at Saint Mary's and prepared for another season of plunder. They were still there the following September, when the Malagasy on Saint Mary's unexpectedly rose in rebellion, incensed at Adam Baldridge's trickery. Baldridge himself escaped harm; but Glover, Hoar, and some of the men men were murdered. Others escaped and took the *John and Rebecca* to Port Dauphin. Although the shorthanded crew wrecked the ship, the men made it ashore and later enlisted on other vessels.[25]

CAPTAIN DIRK CHIVERS OF THE *SOLDADO* HOLDS CALICUT CAPTIVE

Leaving Saint Mary's during the summer of 1696, Dirk Chivers initially copied Hoar's ploy of holding East India Company vessels for ransom. The trick had failed at Aden because the East India Company did not have an office in that port. So Chivers sailed to India's west coast and boldly entered the harbor at Calicut on November 23, 1696. Without warning, the *Soldado* fired a broadside into the outermost ship, throwing the entire port into panic. In the confusion, men from the *Soldado* seized the ship. Swarming into longboats, they easily captured three more vessels—including one belonging to the East India Company and one of the Mogul's hired merchant vessels. They then cut the anchor cables of five other ships in port, sending them onto the beach.

Indian shipowners and merchants were outraged and attacked the local representatives of the East India Company. Rightly or wrongly, they identified all pirates as English and believed Company officials were their partners in crime. According to one Company official, the governor and Indian merchants were so exasperated that "had not some soldiers and others stood by the English and protected their factor, the country-people [Indians] would have destroyed the Company's servants; for they were all reporting that the pirate was an English ship and belonged to the Company."[26] The city's governor put guards around the Company's buildings, both protecting the Englishmen and effectively placing them under arrest.

Under pressure from the governor, the Company sent out a Englishman identified only as "Captain Mason" to negotiate.[27] He reported Chivers' ultimatum: Pay £10,000 pounds or the invaders would burn all the ships in the harbor. The Indian governor considered this an outrageous amount, as did the Company's representatives. From their resources on hand, they decided to offer no more than £5,000 (about $2.5 million).

During the night the pirates moved their four prizes to deeper water so they could not be recaptured. Captain Mason rowed out to the *Resolution* to bargain for a smaller ransom. Mason told the pirate crew about the governor's threats against the East India Company. He asked them to take pity on their countrymen on shore, with their business at a halt and their leaders in jail.

Chivers retorted with a resounding declaration that pirates were out-laws owing allegiance only to themselves. As Mason reported it, Chivers boasted that the men of the *Soldado* "acknowledged no countrymen, that they had sold their country and were sure to be hanged if taken, and that they would take no quarter, but do all they mischief they could."[28]

Captain Chivers continued to demand the full £10,000. When it failed to arrive by four P.M., the *Soldado* hoisted "bloody colors"—a red flag sig-naling "no mercy"—and her crew set one of their prizes afire. Soon after, Chivers agreed to take 40,000 rupees ($3 million) to release the remaining three vessels. However, when Mason still did not bring the money, Chivers burned a second ship the following day.

Captain Mason kept shuttling back and forth from the shore to the *Soldado*. The city's governor was playing a double game. While pretending to negotiate, he had sent messages to a band of native Indian pirates. On the third night, ten "grabs" (native warships) anchored in port. The next morn-ing, the *Soldado* hoisted all sails and fled with the Indian pirates in pursuit.

THE *SOLDADO* RIDES OUT A HURRICANE AT SAINT MARY'S

Chivers returned to India's west coast with the intention of trying for the Persian Gulf. By the end of April 1697, however, the *Soldado's* bottom was thoroughly worm-eaten and leaking badly. This was season of the change-over from the northeast to the southwest monsoon—the worst time of the year to head southwest toward Madagascar. Nevertheless, Chivers and his crew decided that Saint Mary's was only place where they could careen and repair the *Soldado* in total safety.

Careening a warship of three hundred tons, such as the *Soldado*, was no easy task. The ship had to be run aground gently and then hauled over on one side so that the bottom was exposed. To do this, the crew first made the vessel lighter by removing the yards and top masts, cannon, and other heavy gear. After her bottom was scraped clean and dressed with tallow and sulphur, all this heavy equipment had to be put back on board. In the case of a large vessel, the entire process might take several weeks. While she was careened, the ship could not use her guns and was in a completely helpless state. At an Indian port, even when those on shore were hospitable, a careened vessel was easy prey to any passing warship. At Saint Mary's in contrast, the cannon at Baldridge's fort offered protection and kept enemy warships from entering the harbor.

Despite the season, the *Soldado* almost reached Saint Mary's. Near Antongil, she encountered a severe storm—perhaps a cyclone. Chivers just made it to the safety of Antongil Bay. But the storm had torn off the ship's masts, and the local timber could not be used to replace them. When the crew went to Saint Mary's in their long boats, they thus were delighted to learn that the *Amity*, Thomas Tew's old warship, was back in port, reincarnated as a slaver.

Richard Glover, the *Amity*'s captain, now lost his ship at Saint Mary's for a second time. In December 1695, the crew of the *Amity* had taken the *Charming Mary* from Glover, and they had given him the half-wrecked *Amity* in exchange. Glover somehow made it to back to Barbados. The *Charming Mary*'s owners had repaired the *Amity*, completely remasted her as a brigantine, and sent Glover to buy slaves at Madagascar. Now the men of the *Soldado* returned in force to Saint Mary's, took over the *Amity* and brought her up to Antongil Bay to cannibalize her for the *Soldado.* There they stripped the vessel of masts, sails, rigging, and water casks; the empty hull was set adrift to founder on the rocks at the entrance to the bay.[29]

Once again seaworthy—at the *Amity*'s expense—the *Soldado* left Saint Mary's in September 1697. The next months were spent cruising with little success at the southern tip of India. Toward the end of March 1698, the *Soldado* captured the *Sedgwick,* an East India Company vessel carrying pepper from western India to Cuddalore on the east coast. Chivers decided not to take the *Sedgwick*'s cargo and removed only sails, ropes, and other naval stores. Some of the crew thought the *Sedgwick* would make an excellent pirate cruiser. However, Chivers and the other officers finally released the ship, her captain having "put them into good humor with sundry bowls of punch."[30]

The *Soldado* continued to hunt for prey along India's eastern coast. In June, she appeared at the Portuguese trading post at Saint Thomas, a little to the south of Madras.[31] Chivers kept out of sight while the ship's doctor and purser went ashore. The *Soldado* apparently had captured a ship carrying sugar, some of which they sought to trade for saltpeter, used in making gunpowder. They also offered to sell thirty brass cannon, presumably taken from the *Amity* and other prizes. East India Company officials learned that the *Soldado* was at Saint Thomas. They sent two armed vessels to intercept her, but the *Soldado* already had left before these arrived at Saint Thomas.[32]

To escape his enemies, Chivers crossed over to India's west coast. About the middle of August, the *Soldado* ran into Robert Culliford and the *Mocha,* which had left Saint Mary's in June. Agreeing to cruise as consorts, the two vessels headed north. Off Surat in September 1698, the pirates jointly captured the *Great Mahomet* carrying some £130,000 in cash (about $65 million). Chivers and his crew transferred to their prize, renamed the *New Soldado,* and the two warships returned to Saint Mary's.

STOUT AND KELLEY OVERTHROW CAPTAIN EDGCUMBE OF THE *MOCHA*

During the summer of 1695, as the *Fancy* headed toward the Red Sea, Henry Every stopped in the Comoros group to buy provisions and to put ashore some ailing crewmen. When three East Indiamen suddenly arrived, Every sailed off without William May and the other men recuperating on the island. At his trial sixteen months later, May still remembered with evident hatred Captain Leonard Edgcumbe, the commander of one of the three vessels. May testified that Edgcumbe bullied the sick men until they were rescued by Comoro natives.

Other seamen corroborate May's description of Edgcumbe as both a tyrant and a coward. John Leckie was the physician aboard the vessel that stopped at Johanna in 1695. When the ship arrived in Bombay, Leckie denounced Edgcumbe to the East India Company. During the voyage from England, the two men had apparently quarreled. Convinced that Leckie had poisoned him, Edgcumbe beat the doctor with the flat of his cutlass. While they were anchored at the Comoros, Edgcumbe even ordered that Leckie suffer the cruel ordeal of keelhauling, during which the victim was dragged by ropes under a vessel's barnacle-encrusted hull. But the deranged captain had to back down when the ship's officers and men refused to carry out the cruel punishment.[33]

When the ship arrived at Bombay, many crewmen deserted. In June 1696, Edgcumbe was ordered to take the East Indiaman *Mocha* on a trading voyage to China. The East India Company forced some deserters to return to duty despite their justifiable hatred of Edgcumbe.[34] But the ship was still undermanned, and Edgcumbe hired any men he could find in port. Among these were Ralph Stout, James Kelley, and other pirates recently arrived in Bombay. Though warned about their antecedents, Captain Edgcumbe prided himself on his ability to impose discipline.

Given Edgcumbe's well-deserved reputation for cruelty, Stout and Kelley found it easy to incite the *Mocha*'s sullen crew to mutiny. As they neared Sumatra on June 16, 1696, the men rose up and took the ship.[35] It was time that Captain Edgcumbe paid for his brutality, although there are varying stories about the method of his execution. Reports reaching Bombay at the time said that Edgcumbe had been shot.[36] Lord Bellomont asserted that Kelley had strangled Edgcumbe while he was asleep.[37] Others say the crew pelted the hated captain with broken bottles and then threw his bleeding body to the sharks.[38]

Only Captain Edgcumbe was murdered; the mutineers did not molest the ship's officers or seventeen crewmen who would not join the rebellion. These were set adrift in a small boat and reached safety at the Sumatran city of Achin (Banda Aceh).[39] Having taken control, the men agreed to cruise for booty and elected Ralph Stout captain. The office of quartermaster went to James Kelley, who took over the guarding of 150,000 rupees (about $7 million) found on the ship.[40]

JAMES KELLEY'S FIFTEEN-YEAR CRUISE

Both Captain Stout and Quartermaster Kelley had recently escaped after five years in Indian prisons. During their captivity, the head of the East India Company at Surat had refused to help the men in any way. They finally succeeded in stealing a small boat, in which they reached Bombay determined to show no mercy toward the Company.

When they were arrested in January 1691, Stout and Kelley had been officers aboard the *Unity*. The two men had been taken—along with some twenty others—when the *Unity* stopped for water at Mangrol in northwestern India. Mangrol's citizens were angry because the *Batchelor's Delight* recently had left without paying for supplies. According to rumors, the Nawab of Mangrol offered the men lavish entertainment, and they were collared while intoxicated.[41]

In addition to working them mercilessly, the Nawab converted the captives to the Muslim faith. Several men died while being circumcised, though Ralph Stout and James Kelley survived. However, the marks of the operation provided a foolproof method for identifying Kelley when he eventually returned to Boston and was arrested in 1699.[42] (Except among Jews, male circumcision was rare in Europe at that time.)

In January 1691, when the Indians seized Kelley and Stout, the men of the *Batchelor's Delight* had just taken over the *Unity*. As their captain, the *Unity*'s newly formed company had chosen Kelley, an experienced mariner who had visited most of the world's oceans. James Kelley was one of the serious, sensible seamen who kept ships running during lengthy voyages. Since he repeatedly was elected quartermaster and captain, Kelley clearly enjoyed the respect of his comrades. However, he also was an unlucky man, who had little to show for fifteen years of piracy when he was elected quartermaster of the *Mocha* in 1696.

While serving on a slave ship in 1680, Kelley had been captured by a Dutch buccaneer and joined his company. Some years later, he helped rescue John Cook and Edward Davis, who had been marooned by their mates. In 1684, when Cook and Davis sailed around the tip of South America, Kelley was aboard the *Batchelor's Delight*. He stayed with the *Delight* throughout its four-year cruise in the Pacific and was still aboard when the ship returned to Jamaica in 1688.[43]

Kelley got back on the *Delight* when it left for Madagascar in 1688. On transferring to the *Unity* in 1691, Kelley received his share of booty taken by the *Batchelor's Delight*. Everything was lost, however, when he and Stout were imprisoned by the Indians. When Kelley became the *Mocha's* quartermaster in June of 1696, he literally was penniless.

THE *MOCHA* RESCUES ROBERT CULLIFORD

Under her new captain and quartermaster, the *Mocha* went to Burma's southwest coast to take on water and other supplies. While the *Mocha* lay at Mergui, a merchant vessel entered the harbor. On board were Robert Culliford and another sailor, held captive by the ship's captain. Stout freed the two men, who immediately enlisted on the *Mocha*.

Like James Kelley and many others, Robert Culliford was a Caribbean buccaneer who had found better hunting grounds in the Indian Ocean. Culliford was among those who had stolen the *Blessed William* from Captain Kidd in 1690, sailed to New York, and then taken the *Jacob* to Madagascar. Quarrels plagued the *Jacob* throughout the voyage. At the end of 1691, Culliford and about twenty others left the vessel at Mangalore in western India.[44]

Hired by the East India Company as a gunner, Culliford served without incident until 1696. In June of that year, he was aboard the *Josiah,* one of the Company's coastal trading vessels. At about the same time mutineers were seizing the *Mocha,* Culliford and other crewmen took over the *Josiah* as it traveled from Bombay to Madras.[45] Culliford was elected captain and went to the Nicobar Islands to careen and refit the ship.

Exactly what happened next is not certain. Perhaps Culliford quarreled with his new crew; perhaps another ship took the *Josiah* away from the pirates. In any case, as the merchantman *Elizabeth* passed through the Nicobar Islands, Culliford and two other men approached in a canoe and were picked up. The *Elizabeth's* captain did not believe their stories and imprisoned them until the ship reached Mergui, where they were rescued by the *Mocha*.[46]

MOCHA MENACES THE STRAITS OF MALACCA

Now crowded with a hundred Europeans and an unknown number of blacks, the *Mocha* had been turned into a large and heavily armed warship. In addition to at least eight cannons on each side of the gun deck, two mortars and ten larger pedreros were mounted in the forecastle.[47] Toward the end of January 1696, the *Charming Mary* also arrived at Mergui, having crossed over from India's western coast.

The *Mary* and the *Mocha* entered into consort, and the two vessels headed west, back toward India.[48] Near Ceylon on January 14, 1697, they seized the *Satisfaction,* an East India Company coastal vessel commanded by William Willock. No one on the *Mocha* was familiar with the waters east of India. Stout thus brought Captain Willock on board as pilot, stripped the *Satisfaction* of her cargo and rigging, and sank her.

Early in February, the *Mocha* and her consort ran across three Portuguese merchantmen bound for Macao. Flying French flags to confuse their prey, the pirates' warships seized one of the Portuguese vessels, loaded "with at least 100lb. weight of gold and 2,300 pieces of silk, besides great store of provisions."[49] A week later, the *Mocha* and the *Charming Mary* took the Indian merchantman *Alamshay*. In addition to looting her of money and cargo, the pirates also removed her serviceable cannon to replace their own shattered guns. Unlike most merchant vessels, this ship put up a stubborn fight, and three men were killed on the *Mocha*. Despite these losses, their comrades released the *Alamshay* without harming her Indian crew.

The *Mocha* and *Charming Mary* careened in the Maldive Islands for several weeks. With time on their hands, the two crews quarreled, and the *Mocha* went on alone toward the Straits of Malacca. After further stops in the Laccadive and Andaman Islands, the Malayan coast was reached on May 30. While they were ashore looking for water, the local tribesmen attacked and killed Captain Stout and most of those with him.

The survivors elected Robert Culliford as captain, his bellicose spirit having favorably impressed his mates on the *Mocha*. Although he was an excellent leader in battle, Culliford was a mediocre pilot and did not attempt the difficult passage though the Straits of Malacca. Captain Willock

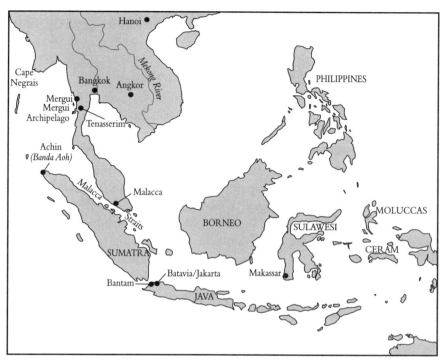

THE PIRATES' CRUISING GROUNDS
AT THE MALACCA STRAITS

was still their prisoner, but the crew could not force him to pilot the ship, which circled just outside the entrance to the Straits.

THE *DORRILL* CHASES AWAY THE *MOCHA*

At the beginning of July 1697, the *Mocha* encountered the *Dorrill,* a large and heavily armed East Indiaman, bound for China with gold coins and other valuable cargo. The ensuing battle shows the disadvantages of pirate democracy. For two days the *Mocha* followed after the *Dorrill* while the crew debated whether to attack. The men were split into several groups and kept changing their minds. "Hell was never in greater confusion than was then aboard." Because so many refused to follow him into battle, Culliford resigned as captain.[50]

At length, those who were for attacking won the argument, and Culliford resumed command. The *Mocha* sailed close to the *Dorrill,* and Culliford called over to her, "Gentlemen, we want nott your ship, but onlie your monie." "That's well," the *Dorrill's* crew responded, "Come and take it."[51]

Naval cannon of that era were extraordinarily inaccurate. (In fact, this is the origin of the slang expression "a long shot," still used to describe a bet or anything else apt to be lost.) Like two wrestlers, the *Mocha* and *Dorrill* circled each other for more than three hours, continuously firing their guns at close range. The captain of the *Dorrill* finally got off two solid broadsides, which damaged a mast. Pugnacious as ever, Culliford called for the crew to continue fighting. But the *Mocha's* crew gave up, afraid their fine warship might be sunk. "Says one, 'You may put her about yours an you will, for I'll fight no more,' one man yelled. 'Nor I,' says another, which then became the general cry."[52] The *Mocha* dropped its sails, allowing the *Dorrill* to escape with several dead and wounded men.

The *Mocha* continued to cruise at the mouth of the Malacca Straits. Looking for easier prey, the men seized several Indian brigantines coming from Java with arrack, an alcoholic beverage distilled from fermented rice. At the end of August, they also took another European vessel to which they transferred Captain Willock and their other European prisoners. Willock led the *Mocha* to Cape Negrais in Burma, where a Portuguese ship, the *Loretta* was plundered of gold and silk worth £12,000 (about $6 million).[53]

At the end of December 1697, the *Mocha* released her prisoners and left the Straits, arriving at Saint Mary's sometime in March or April 1698. Not long afterwards, the warship *Adventure Galley* sailed into the port. As the ship entered the northern channel into the pirate's harbor, a canoe approached, filled with well-armed and raffish-looking Europeans. The men climbed aboard and greeted the *Adventure Galley*'s captain, William Kidd. Some of them already knew Kidd from their voyages together in the Caribbean, and he quickly reassured the *Mocha*'s crew that "he was as bad as they." They took Kidd with them to the *Mocha* to inform Robert Culliford of his friendly intentions.

At first, each was wary of the other. Culliford was concerned that Kidd might still harbor a grudge because of the theft of the *Blessed William* nine years earlier. Through seamen's gossip, Culliford also was aware that Kidd had sailed with a commission to capture pirates. Kidd, in turn, was afraid that Culliford, having a much more powerful vessel, might attack and take away his booty and prizes.

According to witnesses at his trial, William Kidd promised Robert Culliford that he would do nothing to harm him. Persuaded that Captain Kidd posed no threat, Culliford returned with him to the *Adventure Galley* and piloted the ship into the small harbor. After the *Galley* was docked, Kidd and Culliford reminisced about their maritime careers and toasted their reencounter with *bumboo*, a punch made with rum, warm water, sugar, and nutmeg. Kidd became emotional and swore that he would have his soul "fry in Hell-fire" before he would do anything against his old comrade and newfound companion.[54]

CHAPTER EIGHT

THE NEW YORK AND LONDON CONNECTIONS

Saint Mary's Island may be compared to a Caribbean colony, such as Jamaica. On both tropical islands, a small number of white men lived with hundreds of dark-skinned slaves and fathered numerous mulatto children. To pay for the European goods they consumed, Jamaican planters exported sugar, while the pirates sold the loot from Indian vessels. There is one striking difference between the colony ruled by English governors and the pirate republic at Saint Mary's: The pirates lived together in greater tranquility than did the Caribbean planters.

A FACTIOUS PEOPLE: NEW YORK CITY'S POLITICS

During the late seventeenth and early eighteenth centuries. New York City was an especially contentious place—even in comparison to other English colonies. Ethnic and religious differences exacerbated the disagreements among ambitious men eager to harvest the riches of a still unpopulated continent. Political disputes were characterized by animosity, and personal quarrels led to civil wars. These quarrels and rebellions influenced the fortunes of the pirates in far-off Madagascar. They also have distorted understanding of the pirate colony, with politician's fibs having been accepted as true.

New York came under English rule in 1664, when a military expedition ended the administration of Peter Stuyvesant and the Dutch West India Company. The settlement became a proprietary colony owned by James, Duke of York, who assumed the throne as King James II in 1685. In 1688, New York and New Jersey were combined as the Dominion of New England under Governor Edmund Andrus.

In April 1689, news reached New England that James II had been over-thrown and replaced by William and Mary. Bostonians arose, imprisoned Governor Andrus, and declared the Dominion defunct. In New York City, Jacob Leisler, a leading merchant and a militia captain, seized power in June 1689. Leisler declared himself commander in chief of the entire province two months later, but his forces did not take control of Albany until March of the following year. Leisler, a dedicated Calvinist, enjoyed support among Dutch New Yorkers as well as among those who had failed to gain high rank under the previous regime. However, as Leisler became increasingly domi-neering and demagogic, his coalition of supporters broke up, and his oppo-nents flooded London with petitions criticizing his government.[1]

Ignoring Leisler's seizure of power, King William named Henry Slough-ter as governor in January 1690, although Sloughter did not reach New York City until March 16, 1691. On his arrival, Sloughter arrested Leisler, who was convicted of treason and murder and executed in May.[2] Sloughter him-self died soon afterwards, during the summer of 1691, and was temporarily succeeded by Richard Ingoldesby.

Colonel Benjamin Fletcher, the new governor, landed in New York in August 1692. Although Fletcher became enmeshed in New York politics, he was appointed primarily to protect the province from French invasion. During the wars with France (1689–1697 and 1702–1713), New York was the most vulnerable of the English colonies and the most impoverished by defense appropriations. The war in North America had begun disastrously for the English colonists, as France's Indian allies attacked and destroyed the English settlements in New York.

Fletcher was a professional soldier who had distinguished himself (and lost his personal fortune) during William III's recent campaigns in Ireland. He was the king's own choice to direct the war against the French and Indi-ans in New York. He was simultaneously named governor of Pennsylvania for a two-year period and given command of the militias in Connecticut, Rhode Island, and New Jersey. As it turned out, there was relatively little fighting on the frontier with Canada. With too few soldiers and inadequate supplies, Fletcher could not launch a serious attack. Massachusetts, Penn-sylvania, and Connecticut failed to furnish their quotas of men, and the troops sent from England were badly paid and quick to desert.[3]

Governor Fletcher sided strongly with the anti-Leislerian party and looked for allies among the New York merchant community. Fletcher retained the members of Sloughter's executive council, including Nicholas

Baird, Stephen van Cortlandt, William Nicoll, and Frederick Philipse. Fletcher ingratiated himself with their faction by giving out great chunks of valuable land, and he granted new manors with semifeudal rights. In 1693, the holdings of Philipse, the richest man in the province of New York, were consolidated and erected into the Philipse Manor, with its center at Yonkers. In 1697, the Cortlandt manor was created in the Croton valley on the east side of the Hudson.[4]

North American politics became entangled with those in the mother country. Although King William III still retained considerable authority, the era witnessed increasing conflict between two political factions, the Tories and the Whigs. Benjamin Fletcher had been appointed governor under a Tory government; in 1694, officials from Whig party took power in London, weakening Fletcher's influence at court. Meanwhile, government officials in Pennsylvania, Connecticut, and Massachusetts criticized Fletcher's efforts to recruit their militias for service against the French. These officials made common cause with Leislerians in New York, enraged because Fletcher had removed them from power. William Penn, lord proprietor of Pennsylvania, thus sent a letter to the Board of Trade signed by Peter Delanoy, a prominent follower of Leisler. Although Delanoy was Fletcher's political enemy, this letter has often been cited to prove that Fletcher worked hand in glove with the Red Sea pirates.[5]

By the summer of 1695, the Whig faction was replacing the Tories. With King William away directing the war effort in the Netherlands, the crown's powers were in the hands of seven Lords Justices, six of whom were Whigs. Prominent Whig politicians were looking for lucrative posts throughout England and the empire. Among those determined to make their way was the earl of Bellomont, a leading Whig who was being officially mentioned as New York's next governor.

Richard Coote, first earl of Bellomont in Ireland, was both a longtime supporter of King William and financially impoverished. In early 1695 Lord Bellomont's friends had won him appointment as governor of Massachusetts.[6] Unfortunately, the provincial assembly in Massachusetts was extremely niggardly in its payments to royal governors. To make up the shortfall, it was suggested that Bellomont also be appointed governor of New York, where a larger salary had been established.[7] But Benjamin Fletcher, New York's current governor, still had some patrons in London. To get rid of him, the Board of Trade had to be convinced that Fletcher had misused his office.

LIVINGSTON AND KIDD: INNOCENTS ABROAD

Into this swamp of political double-dealing stepped Robert Livingston and William Kidd, two provincials who had come to London in 1695 for their own purposes. The two men ended up making a deal with Lord Bellomont and other Whig politicians. Under this arrangement, Bellomont and his partners provided Captain Kidd with a warship. Kidd promised to sail to Saint Mary's island, defeat its residents, and turn over their booty to Bellomont at New York. In exchange for his patronage, Bellomont would keep an astonishing 60 percent of the profits, with Kidd and the crew sharing the remainder.

Why Kidd agreed to so one-sided a bargain will never be known. It is clear that both Bellomont and Kidd were living in their own fantasies and had no understanding of the situation in the Indian Ocean. The absurd scheme required Kidd to defeat one or more heavily armed warships. Kidd's poorly paid crewmen then would bring vast treasures to North America without demanding a cut for themselves. Needless to say, the plan failed, and Kidd was forever branded a pirate. To divert attention from his own schemes, Bellomont devoted much of his time as governor of New York and Massachusetts to blackening the reputation of Benjamin Fletcher, his predecessor at New York.

Political parties in New York resembled those in England like an image in a cloudy mirror. Whatever was the case in London, financial self-interest and personal relationships influenced party allegiances in New York; political ideology played little part. Certainly this was true of Robert Livingston, a rising entrepreneur and statesman. Livingston began on the best of terms with the Tory and anti-Leislerian group, gradually drifted away, and dramatically joined the Whigs in 1695.

Livingston had served as the commissary, responsible for feeding British troops in New York and Albany. In connection with his office, Livingston claimed he had lent the provincial government £4,000 (including interest), and he demanded payment. Governor Fletcher instead diverted all available funds to military purposes. Fletcher took the view that Livingston, a rich man, could afford to wait for his money until the war ended. Deciding to appeal over Fletcher's head, Livingston sailed for London in December 1694. Along the way, a storm knocked off the ship's rudder, and the vessel drifted aimlessly for four harrowing months before hitting a beach in Portugal.[8]

When he finally reached London in July 1695, Livingston was quick to see that the Whig faction had seized power from the Tories. Livingston devoted his time to making contacts with influential Whig officials. Among his new Whig acquaintances was the earl of Bellomont, who at that time was still scheming to be named governor of New York.

Bellomont and Livingston joined forces to blacken the reputation of New York's current governor, Colonel Benjamin Fletcher. Bellomont's motives are obvious: If Fletcher were doing a good job in wartime, why send Bellomont to replace him? For his part, Livingston wanted the Board of Trade to issue orders requiring immediate payment of his claims. To justify this request, he charged that Fletcher was using New York's revenues not for frontier defense but to line his own pockets. When he appeared before the Lords of Trade on August 28, 1695, Livingston presented witnesses to substantiate his charges against Fletcher. At this time, his enemies accused Fletcher of financial malfeasance and interference with elections. His supposed collusion with pirates was not brought up until later.[9]

Among the witnesses against Fletcher was Livingston's friend and political associate, William Kidd. Like Livingston, Kidd had gone to London to gain patrons at the heart of England's empire. In June 1645, Kidd took his ship *Antegoa* (*Antigua*) on a trading voyage to England, which went much more smoothly than Livingston's. The two men found each other in London, and Kidd helped Livingston in his court battle by testifying that Governor Fletcher tried to intimidate New York's voters.[10]

CAPTAIN WILLIAM KIDD, REFORMED PIRATE

William Kidd probably was about fifty years old when he testified against Fletcher.[11] Although nothing can be asserted with certainty about his childhood or youth, by the 1680s he had joined up with Caribbean buccaneers. During King William's War, Kidd became a useful citizen, serving as a registered privateer and distinguishing himself during a naval battle in January 1690. Christopher Codrington, governor of the Leeward Islands, reported that Kidd "behaved himself well." His commanding officer during the battle, Captain Hewetson of the *Lion,* was even more impressed. Later, during Kidd's trial for piracy in 1701, Hewetson appeared as a character witness. Eleven years after the event, Hewetson still recalled Kidd as a "mighty man in the West Indies" who "fought as well as any man I ever saw."[12]

Unfortunately for Kidd, the *Blessed William*'s buccaneer crew was not as enthusiastic as Hewetson about their captain's daring attacks on French warships. Shortly after the battle, they made off with the vessel and all its contents, including £2,000 (about $1 million) in booty belonging to Kidd.

Kidd somehow acquired another captured French vessel, renamed it the *Antegoa*,[13] and chased after the *Blessed William*. He followed the ship's trail to New York but arrived after its crew had transferred to the *Jacob* and set out for the Indian Ocean.

Kidd did arrive in time to take sides in the civil war raging in New York City. Jacob Leisler had seized power when William and Mary overthrew James II. Ignoring Leisler, the new rulers sent over Colonel Henry Sloughter as governor. Sloughter's ship ran aground on Bermuda, and he arrived in New York in March 1691, a full two months after the troops sent with him on other ships. Their leader, Colonel Richard Ingoldesby, asked Leisler to surrender. Leisler instead rallied his adherents and took over Fort James, at the tip of Manhattan. Ingoldesby's troops blockaded the fort, and there was an exchange of fire on March 17, causing a number of dead and wounded.[14]

Captain Kidd supported the new government and used the *Antegoa* to carry guns and ammunition for Ingoldesby, who was preparing to assault Fort James.[15] The very next day, Governor Sloughter's ship finally entered the harbor. Kidd and the *Antegoa* carried a delegation that alerted the new governor to the situation. Sloughter was grateful for Kidd's assistance and rewarded him generously. Kidd received £150 (in New York currency) for his aid in bringing about Leisler's downfall.[16] He also profited from a court case involving a French ship taken by Leisler's privateers. Sloughter confiscated the vessel and sold it to Frederick Philipse. A few months later, Philipse became a fence and supplier for the Saint Mary's pirates.[17]

William Kidd thus had influential friends in New York, where he also found an attractive and wealthy bride. On May 16, 1691, he married Sarah Bradley Oort, just days after the death of her husband, John Oort.[18] Thanks to inheritances from her first two husbands, the new Mrs. Kidd owned substantial amounts of property.[19] Kidd also continued to cruise as a privateer against French shipping and brought in at least one and possibly several prizes.[20]

The Kidd family prospered. They moved into a fine house situated on the East River at 119–121 Pearl Street, a little north of the heart of New York's business area.[21] They also purchased a pew in and supported Trinity Church, the first Anglican parish in New York City. Kidd kept on good terms with local political leaders, and he was close to Robert Livingston. In 1693, Livingston bought a property from Kidd to build a new private dock. The following year, Kidd was foreman of a grand jury that refused to indict Livingston for trading with the French enemy during wartime.[22]

LORD BELLOMONT STRIKES A HARD BARGAIN WITH LIVINGSTON AND KIDD

A favorable recommendation by the Lords of Trade ultimately rewarded Livingston's incessant pleadings. While he was awaiting their decision, Livingston spent a great deal of time during October 1695 arranging a privately financed expedition against the Saint Mary's pirates. The royal navy was too occupied with the war against France to send a squadron to India. Instead, a strong warship operating as a privateer would do the navy's job by seizing pirate ships in the Red Sea and elsewhere. To pay for the expedition, all booty found on board captured vessels would be kept and not returned to its original owners.

In October 1695, Kidd, Bellomont, and Livingston signed a contract. Bellomont promised to secure royal orders empowering Kidd as a privateer and authorizing him to attack both French and pirate vessels. Bellomont also agreed to put up four-fifths of the cost of outfitting an appropriate warship, with the first payment of £1,600 due in one month. Kidd would command the expedition, and he promised to hire a crew of about one hundred men, sailing on a "no purchase, no pay" basis. All prizes and booty were to be brought to Boston, where Bellomont planned to be governor. Bellomont would receive 60 percent of all booty taken, the crew would get 25 percent, and Livingston and Kidd would share the remaining 15 percent. If he captured prizes worth more than £100,000, Kidd would get to keep the warship provided for the cruise.

Bellomont was determined not to be cheated. If Kidd did not capture at least £100,000 in lawful prizes before March 25, 1697, then he and Livingston were obliged to return Bellomont's investment in the expedition. Bellomont was additionally protected by performance bonds, obligating Livingston for £20,000 ($10 million today) and Kidd for £10,000 ($5 million) if Kidd failed to return with booty.[23]

Bellomont was as broke as usual. Through separate secret agreements, he split his shares with four partners holding some of the highest political offices in England. These sponsors would advance the majority of the funds. They also would keep most of the loot, although King William III was promised 10 percent. Their influence in the judiciary and admiralty would ensure that Kidd received the powers needed to carry out the scheme.

The most active of the sponsors was Sir Edward Harrison, a wealthy investor who helped Kidd pick out a ship and crew. Because they were personally involved in manipulating the judicial bureaucracy, the other sponsors concealed their involvement. Attorney General Sir John Somers was also Lord Keeper of the Great Seal; in the latter capacity he controlled judicial appointment. In addition, Somers simultaneously served as one of the seven Lords Justices to whom the administration of the realm was entrusted while the king was in the Netherlands. Charles Talbot, Duke of Shrewsbury, was Secretary of State and another of the seven Lords Justices. Edward Russell, Earl of Orford, had served as both Admiral of the Fleet and Treasurer of the Navy. Henry Sidney, Earl of Romney, was a longtime adherent and friend of King William.

Some months were needed to make the deal official with three commissions. On December 11, 1695, the Admiralty issued a standard privateering letter, which allowed Kidd to plunder Frenchmen while the war lasted.[24] The next step was more complicated because the Admiralty was reluctant to grant a commission to seize pirates and their goods. So Kidd's noble partners obtained a patent under the king's Great Seal, the same seal used to grant the Lords of the Admiralty their authority and powers. Issued on January 26, 1696, it referred to the piracies committed by various Red Sea pirates. "Captain Thomas Too, John Ireland, Captain Thomas Wake, Captain William Maze or Mace, And other our Subjects, Native or Inhabitants of New England, New York, and elsewhere in our Plantations in America do . . ., against the Laws of Nations, daily commit many great Piracies. . . ." To bring them to justice, Kidd was authorized to seize the persons and property of all "Pirates, Freebooters, and Sea Rovers" anywhere in the world, even if they were not English subjects.[25]

One further document was required. Under normal law, a merchant or other legitimate owner could sue to recover stolen property seized by Kidd. On April 30, 1696, King William granted Kidd a third commission. This was directed to all royal officials anywhere in the world. It gave Lord Bellomont and his partners the right to keep all ships and booty taken by Kidd. The partners gained ownership without going through the normal legal procedures and without paying the normal fees to the Admiralty.[26]

While their partners shepherded the paperwork through the judicial and naval bureaucracy, Kidd and Edward Harrison arranged for a ship and crew. The partners purchased the *Adventure Galley,* a vessel under construction that was launched in December 1695. At the time it was registered, it was described as a ship of 287 tons equipped with thirty-four guns. The *Adventure Galley* was a hybrid vessel; it carried sails, but it also could be propelled at about three miles per hour by forty-six oars, twenty-three on each side.[27]

The *Adventure Galley* was well suited for the task of hunting pirates. It was large enough to carry one hundred to one hundred fifty men but still small enough to be careened on a beach. (A much larger ship would have needed a dockyard—something not readily available in the Indian Ocean.) The combination of oars and sails provided speed and mobility in virtually any kind of weather as well as in tight quarters. Unfortunately, the *Adventure Galley* proved to be poorly built, as it fell apart at the end of only three and a half years.

By this time in the war with France, experienced mariners were in short supply. Kidd's commission allowed him to enlist just seventy men, only half of whom could be experienced seamen. Since this was fewer than would be needed to man the ship's guns, Kidd undoubtedly planned from the beginning to stop in New York and fill up the vacancies in his crew.

A STRANGE ADVENTURE FATED TO FAILURE

In later years, after this bizarre scheme ended in disaster, Kidd and Bellomont each claimed that the other man had invented it. At his trial, Kidd said that Livingston and Bellomont initiated the scheme and asked him to accept command of the vessel. Kidd asserted that he at first rejected Bellomont's offer. But Bellomont insisted and threatened to seize Kidd's ship, the *Antegoa,* and keep it in London if he refused to take part.[28] Bellomont, for his part, placed the blame squarely on Kidd. He claimed that Kidd had concocted the plan and convinced Livingston of its viability. Livingston then presented it to Bellomont with assurances of Kidd's good behavior.[29]

Although we cannot know for certain who first thought of Kidd's expedition, Robert Livingston is the most likely culprit. Outside of the East India Company's offices, few in England recognized the extent of Indian Ocean and Red Sea piracy. It was Henry Every's looting of the *Gunsway* that first caught the attention of the English public. But Livingston began advocating the scheme early in August 1695.[30] He thus was pushing it even before Every's attack on the *Gunsway* (and probably before he ran into Kidd in London.) Moreover, the final draft of the Bellomont-Kidd-Livingston agreement was signed on October 10, 1695, long before anyone in England could have known about Every's depredations.[31] There could not have been any connection between the scandal over Every's crimes and the launching of Kidd's expedition.[32]

As New York merchants, Livingston and Kidd knew much more about Indian Ocean piracy than anyone in England. Moreover, the king's commission allowing Kidd to attack pirates specifically mentions New York as the pirate haven, and it lists only pirates associated with New York. Although based in Rhode Island, Thomas Tew had visited New York in the fall of 1694 and publicly courted Governor Fletcher to obtain a privateering commission. Thomas Wake was one of the captains in Tew's squadron. The William Maze referred to in the royal commission almost certainly is William Mason, who stole the *Blessed William* from Kidd in 1689. Mason had gone to New York, transferred to the *Jacob,* and made for Madagascar. When the *Jacob* returned in July 1693, the crew was flush with gold and apparently flaunted their riches.[33]

On the face of it, the scheme could have brought in a substantial profit if Kidd had managed to capture one or more pirate ships like the *Jacob.* Moreover, commissioning a private pirate catcher was not unprecedented. Sir Robert Holmes had received a special commission to hunt pirates in the Caribbean and off North America in 1687. Had he caught any, however, Holmes only had to carry them to a nearby English port. Kidd's commission obligated him to carry all prizes, wherever taken, to Boston.[34]

Kidd accepted ridiculously onerous terms in his October 10 agreement with Bellomont. Kidd had to put up one-fifth of the expedition's cost, perhaps as much as £400 ($200,000), and he had to promise to turn over sixty percent of any booty taken. In addition, he legally obligated himself to pay over the extraordinary sum of £20,000 ($10 million) if he failed to deliver.

Had Kidd wanted to go pirating, he could have stayed in New York and obtained much better terms from Governor Fletcher. Since New York in 1695 was a small town filled with gossip, Kidd surely knew that Fletcher charged less for a privateering commission than Bellomont was demanding. Given that the men on the *Jacob* had stolen his own vessel, Kidd presumably paid attention when they returned in 1693. He must have heard that Fletcher granted the *Jacob*'s crew safe conduct in return for the ship, worth £800. In contrast, Bellomont demanded a full 60 percent of all booty, a cut which might amount to many thousands of pounds.

CAPTAIN KIDD REFUSES TO SALUTE NAVAL VESSELS

By late February 1696, Kidd was ready to leave England. On the 26th, he received sailing orders from Lord Bellomont. Without directing Kidd to cruise in any specific location, Bellomont's letter recited their agreement over the disposition of prizes. Unless Kidd by chance fell in with a fleet bound for England, he again was ordered to bring his booty to Bellomont in Boston.[35]

An incident soon after Kidd sailed provides insight into his character. Kidd believed that his privateering commission under the great seal made him the equal of any officer in the Royal Navy. Thus he refused to lower his flag or fire a salute to show deference when passing a ship of the Royal Navy, as law and custom demanded. As it went by Greenwich on the way down the Thames, the *Adventure Galley* did not dip its flag to a royal vessel. When the ship fired a shot at the *Galley,* the sailors on her yards expressed their derision with a traditional gesture of contempt.

> [Kidd considered] his authority was as ample as any King's com-
> mander, and therefore he should pay no respect to the King's
> colours, wherever he met them. A captain of a yacht . . . was not
> on board when Kidd passed him, and Kidd having a front wind,
> did as he said, showed no respect. But being shot, believing the
> yacht out of danger of call, Kidd's men in the tops turned up and
> slapped their backsides, in derision.[36]

Kidd also refused to salute a second royal ship shortly afterward. Perhaps in response, a warship stopped the *Galley* and impressed all or most of the crew into the Royal Navy. Kidd appealed to Admiral Edward Russell, one of his financial backers. Russell arranged for an order forcing the royal warship to hand the men back. However, its captain did not restore all the original crew but replaced some of the *Galley*'s mariners with less-experienced seamen.[37]

RECRUITING SAILORS IN NEW YORK

From England, Kidd sailed due west to New York City, capturing a French fishing ship along the way. (A New York Admiralty Court condemned the prize; the proceeds of the sale were used to buy provisions for the *Galley*.)[38] Kidd reached New York about July 4, 1696, presented his royal commission to Governor Fletcher, and set about raising a crew.[39] The admiralty had allowed him to recruit only seventy sailors in England, and he needed at least twice as many to sail the ship and man its guns.[40]

To attract men, Kidd wrote new ship's articles, which offered more liberal terms than had been envisioned in England. The provisions for dividing profits were similar to those that had become customary among pirates during the past fifty years. Any booty would first be used to pay for provisions, medical expenses, and compensation to those losing an arm, leg, finger, or toe. Whatever remained was divided into equal shares. The sailing master took two parts; other adult crewman received one share. The articles allowed Captain Kidd five shares for himself and thirty-five for supplying the ship. Forty shares might amount to as little as 20 percent of the total take. That was considerably less than the 65 percent Kidd had promised Bellomont and his partners in the contract signed on October 1695.[41]

These more generous terms allowed Kidd to recruit another 90 crewmen for a total of 152. Because of a nasty comment by Governor Benjamin Fletcher, these men traditionally have been condemned as former pirates. Writing to the Board of Trade after Kidd had sailed, Fletcher suggested that Kidd would have trouble controlling his crew. If he failed to take booty, the men, desperate for money, would turn pirate.

> Many flockt to him from all parts, men of desperate fortunes and necessitous in expectation of getting vast treasure. He sailed from hence with 150 men. . . . It is generally believed here, they will have money *per fas aut nefas* [legally or illegally, "by fair means or foul"], and that if he miss of the design intended for which he has commission, "twill not be in Kidd's power to govern such a hord of men under no pay."[42]

Fletcher may have been misled or he may have disliked Captain Kidd.[43] In any case, his description of the men is not apt. Some were not even mariners. They were skilled artisans working at crafts such as those of carpenter, vintner, shoemaker, gunsmith, and cordwainer.[44] Benjamin Franks was a jeweler and a member of a prosperous family of Jewish merchants. Franks's own ventures had failed, and he signed on only until the ship reached India, where he planned to reenter the jewelry trade and reestablish his fortune.[45]

Only one man is known to have been a pirate before sailing on the *Adventure Galley.* John Browne had been aboard the *Blessed William* when the crew stole the ship from Kidd in 1690. Browne had taken the *William* to New York, cruised in the Red Sea on the *Jacob,* and had received a full share of £400 to £500 when the *Jacob* returned in 1693. He had retired but now returned to the sea. Even though he had helped to steal the *Blessed*

William, Kidd accepted Browne because of his experiences in India. As far
as is known, no one else sailing on the *Galley* in September 1696 had ever
been to the Indian Ocean or the Red Sea.

Indeed, on all counts, this was an extraordinarily unsuitable crew for a
pirate-hunting warship. In this kind of expedition, the seamanship and fighting abilities of the crewmen were at least as important as the ship. The entire
purpose of the exercise was to capture ships and take their booty. Attacking
and sinking them with cannon fire would defeat that goal. Instead the crew
would have to chase and catch up with an enemy vessel, swarm aboard, and
overcome their opponents in hand-to-hand combat. The venture called for
seasoned mariners who were also hard men willing to fight.

Few aboard were qualified for the mission. Those who had been to sea
before had worked only on colonial freighters. With the exception of John
Browne, few had gone any farther than the island of Jamaica. One man
transferred to the *Galley* from a Dutch privateer in New York Harbor. No
one is known to have served on a warship, and no soldiers were listed
among the landsmen making the voyage.

One wonders why Browne was the only marauder to enlist on the
Adventure Galley. There was no lack of possible candidates. Royal officials
in the colonies complained that pirates avoided arrest and walked the streets
with impunity. When Thomas Tew had sailed from Rhode Island in January 1695, Red Sea men flocked to his venture from as far away as South
Carolina. Pirates wanted their captains to be men with a habit of good luck,
and they expected them to govern the ship in a democratic fashion. Experienced adventurers may have believed that Kidd's quixotic mission was
doomed to failure. Perhaps more important, Kidd also had a reputation as a
conceited and arbitrary captain, whose crews deserted when they could.

Himself a former buccaneer, Captain Kidd was aware that his crew was
woefully untrained and inexperienced compared to men who made a profession of piracy. During the preceding years, numerous pirate vessels had
sailed from Rhode Island and New York to the Indian Ocean. As we have
seen, pirate crews tended to stick together. While new men joined the ship
for each voyage, the crew always included a cadre of experienced mariners
and combatants.

How could Kidd have expected to carry out his mission? Under the
terms of the royal commission and his agreement with Bellomont, Kidd was
expected to capture pirates and their vessels and bring them to Bellomont.
What did he expect to happen if the pirates resisted arrest? Kidd apparently

assumed his crew could learn seamanship and naval gunnery during the months needed to reach the Indian Ocean. Even so, hardly any of the men had been in any kind of battle. How could Kidd have expected them to overcome and capture men familiar with every trick of warfare at sea?

Kidd's biographers have not considered his career within the context of Madagascar piracy. Thus they have not noticed just how unusual and even bizarre his mission was. At a time when colonial governors sold privateering commission for a few hundred pounds, Kidd made a legally binding commitment to turn over 60 percent of his booty to Bellomont. When he arrived in New York, he signed a second contract promising as much to the ship's crew. Finally, he sailed for Madagascar with an inexperienced and untrained crew.

It is difficult to understand why Kidd agreed to Bellomont's proposal. It is impossible to understand how he expected to succeed. If he did manage to capture pirate ships and take them to Boston, the proceeds were promised twice over, and he would get nothing. For three centuries, Kidd was portrayed as a ruthless and brilliant fiend. More recently, he has been described as an innocent gentleman savaged by an unjust trial. There is another possibility: He may well have been held captive by some kind of mental delusion. Assuming he was sane, he ought to have known that Bellomont's pirate-catching scheme could only end in disaster.

CHAPTER NINE

CAPTAIN KIDD GOES TO
SAINT MARY'S ISLAND

My name is Captain Kid, who has sail'd
My name is Captain Kid, who has sail'd;
        My name is Captain Kid,
        What the laws did still forbid
Unluckily I did while I sail'd.

Upon the ocean wide, when I sail'd
Upon the ocean wide, when I sail'd
        Upon the ocean wide
        I robbed on every side,
With most ambitious pride, when I sail'd. . . .

Many long leagues from shore when I sail'd
Many long leagues form shore when I sail'd
        Many long leagues from shore
        I murdered William More,
And laid him in his gore, when I sail'd. . . .

Farewel, the ocean main, we must die,
Farewel, the ocean main, we must die;
        Farewel the ocean main:
        The coast of France or Spain
We ne'er shall see again; we must die.[1]

After three months at New York, the *Adventure Galley* was as ready as it
could be made, and Captain William Kidd sailed in September 1696.
Kidd steered the course that had become customary for North Americans
heading to India; this route took advantage of the winds and weather sys-

tems prevailing in the fall of the year. From New York, the *Galley* followed the westerlies to the Madeira Islands and then sailed south to the Cape Verde Islands. At about the latitude of Sierra Leone, Kidd turned west and south, heading toward Brazil to find the Trade Winds for the trip to the Cape of Good Hope. Out of sight of land for two months, the men had little to do beyond trimming the sails to catch the winds that increasingly blew from the west. Then, in the middle of the South Atlantic on December 12, they suddenly encountered five vessels of the British Royal Navy commanded by Commodore Thomas Warren.

Following the depredations of Henry Every and other Saint Mary's marauders, Warren's squadron had been ordered to escort the 1696 East India Company fleet on its outbound voyage. However, when scurvy appeared among their crews, the Company vessels had gone on alone, leaving behind the slower warships. Warren demanded that Kidd hand over thirty men, so Kidd ordered the *Galley*'s crew to row away during a period of light wind.[2] Frustrated at losing much-needed recruits, Commodore Warren and his officers spread the rumor that Kidd was a pirate.[3]

After months at sea, the crew of the *Adventure Galley* also was suffering from scurvy. Knowing that Warren would put in there, Kidd avoided the Dutch colony at Capetown and headed straight for the southern coast of Madagascar. On January 29, five months after leaving New York, the *Galley* anchored at Tulear, slightly north of Saint Augustine's Bay.

The *Adventure Galley* stayed at Tulear for about a month and then sailed north through the Mozambique channel to Johanna (modern Anjouan) in the Comoro Islands. Some three thousand miles beyond the Cape of Good Hope, the Comoros group was a popular stopping point for English captains heading for India. Fresh fruits and vegetables were abundant on Johanna, and the inhabitants were hospitable. The Comoros thus provided a convenient place to wait until the southwest monsoon asserted itself sometime in April, allowing vessels to proceed to India.

On the way to Johanna, the *Adventure Galley* ran into two East Indiamen, and two more came into the harbor during the *Galley*'s brief stay. John Clerke, captain of one vessel, reported that Kidd flew the royal ensign and tried to force a merchantman to lower its flag in deference. Kidd told the officers of the East Indiamen that he intended to go to Saint Mary's to hunt pirates. However, as the various crews mingled ashore and gossiped, rumors spread that Kidd hoped to catch one of the East Indiamen alone. He desperately needed sails and supplies and planned to take them by force.

[Kidd] invited us all on board his ship and said he was bound to
Port St Mary to hunt for pirates, but for all his pretences, his men
confess'd that they expected to find only one East Indiaman in
Johanna. The people ashore told us that Kidd had given the King
of Johanna a bill on the King of England for his provisions, which
was not accepted. Kidd not liking our company, filled up with
water and sailed away.[4]

Before going on, it was imperative to careen the *Adventure Galley* and
scrap her clean of worms and barnacles. Kidd went on to the nearby island
of Mehila, which provided a convenient sandy beach for this arduous task.
By the time the job was done, five weeks later, many men had fallen sick of
some disease or plague. As many as fifty died, and others were struck down
for weeks.[5]

Returning to Johanna, Kidd enlisted French and English seamen,
some of whom loaned Kidd money to "mend his ship."[6] The number
taken aboard is not known, but they surely were too few to make up for
the deaths from disease at Mehila. There also is no evidence whether any
of these new recruits were marauders from Saint Mary's. After helping loot
the *Gunsway*, Dirk Chivers's *Portsmouth Adventure* was wrecked at the
Comoro Islands in 1695, and other pirates got off there, separating from
shipmates they no longer trusted. But honest mariners also came ashore at
Johanna.

It was the end of April before Kidd finished careening and resupplying
the *Galley*. The southwest monsoon had begun, carrying ships north from
the Comoros into the Arabian Sea. It now was more than a year since Kidd
had left England in February 1696. One-third of the crew was dead, and
the ship had captured only a fishing boat worth £800. Under the terms of
Kidd's agreement with Lord Bellomont, he had to bring back booty by the
end of March 1697 or forfeit £10,000. He already had missed the deadline,
and he could not return to New York empty-handed without facing financial ruin and the wrath of Bellomont, by now installed as governor.

Given these pressures to perform, Kidd undoubtedly had some plan of
action in mind when he left Johanna Island. However, he never tried to
explain what this plan was after he returned to North America and was
arrested.[7] Had he intended to fulfill his mission as a pirate catcher, Kidd
would have circled around Madagascar and visited Saint Mary's Island. Kidd
lived in Manhattan and was amiably acquainted with Frederick Philipse,

one of the pirates' chief suppliers. Moreover, at least one member of Kidd's crew had visited Saint Mary's. Kidd surely knew that Saint Mary's was the one place in the vast spaces of the Indian Ocean where he was certain to find pirates and their loot. And the island was especially well supplied with booty at this time. In February, Captain John Hoar and the *John and Rebecca* had brought in a three hundred-ton prize carrying goods worth £20,000 ($10 million). Dirk Chivers arrived with the *Soldado* in June.

But Captain Kidd also knew that the pirate's port at Saint Mary's was approached through a narrow and guarded passage. Perhaps he believed an attack with his woefully undermanned vessel would be suicidal.[8] If Saint Mary's was ruled out, that left two other ways to seize booty. Kidd either could capture a French vessel, or he could turn pirate.

Kidd was empowered to loot French merchantmen, but these would be difficult to find. Piracy was more likely to succeed, but it posed greater dangers. A few years earlier, colonial governors had ignored raids on Moorish vessels. Thomas Tew and others had found a safe haven in Rhode Island, and Governor Fletcher of New York had sold amnesty to the *Pearl* in 1693. But times had changed. The hue and cry over Henry Every's raid was at a peak by the time Kidd had left New York in September 1696.

KIDD ATTACKS THE MOCHA FLEET

His course after he left the Comoros indicates that Kidd opted for piracy. The *Adventure Galley* ran north along the coast of East Africa, rounded the Horn of Africa, and turned due west for the strait of Bab al Mandab at the mouth of the Red Sea. All southbound shipping passed through the narrow channel, making it an ideal place for pirates—Henry Every, among others—to wait for Indian vessels. During Kidd's trial, a hostile witness testified that he intended to "make his voyage" at Mocha. Another quoted him as saying "Come boys, I will make money enough out of that fleet."[9] Kidd might have answered his accusers by responding that he went to the strait to look for pirate vessels awaiting the pilgrim fleet. In fact, he said nothing about the incident.

When he arrived at the strait, Kidd anchored on the south side of Perim Island. Sent to spy on the harbor at Mocha fifty miles to the north, the *Galley's* quartermaster reported that fourteen or fifteen ships were preparing to leave. Men were posted on a hill at the harbor's west end and ordered to signal the fleet's arrival by waving flags.[10] Bunched together to avoid attack, the Indian merchantmen slipped past the Bab during the night of August 14. As the sun rose the morning of the 15th, they found the *Adventure Galley* sailing in their midst.

This time, however, the merchantmen were accompanied by three heavily armed vessels, two Dutch and one English. As a direct result of Henry Every's attack on the *Gunsway* in 1695, Emperor Aurangzib had told the various European East India Companies to protect the pilgrim fleet. The *Sceptre*, a thirty-six-gun East Indiaman, was commanded by Edward Barlow, who kept a detailed journal of his voyages. Barlow reports that the *Adventure Galley* flew the blood-red pendant used by pirates intending to attack. As the *Galley* sailed past at some distance, Barlow fired his cannon and raised the East India Company's banner. Kidd ignored the *Sceptre* and fired at one of the Indian vessels, which steered away from the intruder.

Throughout the day, the winds were weak and fitful. Barlow lowered his ship's boats, which towed the *Sceptre* toward the *Adventure Galley*. Long before it was in range, Barlow fired his guns and sent his men into the rigging to shout threats and curses. As this bellicose vessel approached, Kidd raised his sails and ordered the men to lower oars and row away. He thought the *Sceptre* was a navy warship, and it carried more and heavier guns than the *Adventure Galley*.[11] Twice more, Barlow pulled toward the *Galley*, with cannon firing and men yelling. In the late afternoon, Kidd gave up and sailed away from the pilgrim fleet.[12]

From the Red Sea, Kidd took the *Galley* west to Carwar on the Indian coast. So far, he had not committed piracy. Although the *Galley* had fired at several ships, none had been boarded and robbed. Kidd crossed the line on the way to Carwar when he stopped a small Indian vessel. At Kidd's orders, his men seized some of the Indian crewmen, tied their hands behind their backs, and hoisted them aloft with ropes. The prisoners were beaten with the flat side of cutlasses to make them tell where money was hidden. Before leaving, Kidd seized some coffee and sugar and perhaps one hundred pieces of eight. He also kidnapped the ship's English captain, Thomas Parker, and a Portuguese officer, named Antonio, planning to use them as pilot and translator.[13]

News of Parker's and Don Antonio's kidnapping had reached Carwar by the time the *Adventure Galley* arrived on September 3. But Kidd denied holding them captive and kept them locked in the hold while the ship took on wood and water. By now the East India Company was convinced that Kidd was a pirate. So were some of the crew. Benjamin Franks left the *Adventure Galley* at Carwar, and several seamen deserted as well. They confirmed the Company's suspicions that Kidd held Thomas Parker captive.[14] In addition, the Company had Captain John Clerke's report on Kidd's meeting with Company vessels at Johanna Island. By the end of September, Captain Barlow of the *Sceptre* was back in Surat and told of Kidd's apparent attack on the pilgrim fleet.[15]

On September 22, 1697, Kidd was confronted by two Portuguese warships sent out by the viceroy of Goa to arrest him.[16] As the smaller of the two vessels chased the *Galley*, she left her slower companion behind. Kidd suddenly turned and pounded his pursuer with cannon fire until the larger Portuguese ship arrived.[17] He then made his escape.

After purchasing supplies at Calicut, Kidd turned away from the coast and stopped at the Maldive Islands, southwest of India, to careen and repair the *Galley*. The crew forced the islanders to work for free, used their boats for firewood, and raped several women. When one crewman went ashore alone, the natives surrounded him and slit his throat. To avenge his murder, Kidd burned the islanders' houses and had several killed.[18]

In late October or early November, Kidd ran into the East India Company ship *Loyal Captain* close to the tip of India.[19] Although her captain swore that the ship contained nothing but sugar, her passengers included Armenian and Greek merchants carrying jewels. Most of the *Galley*'s crew voted to loot the prize, but Kidd bullied and cajoled them into letting the ship go. According to Hugh Parrot, a seaman aboard the *Galley*, when Kidd refused to order an attack, the mutineers threatened to use the ship's boat to take the *Loyal Captain*. Kidd swore he would run them down with the *Adventure Galley*. "If you desert my ship you shall never come aboard again, and I will force you into Bombay, and I will carry you before some of the council there."[20]

KIDD MURDERS WILLIAM MOORE

About two weeks later, the *Adventure Galley* sailed close to a Dutch vessel. Again, some of the men wanted to attack the other ship, among them William Moore, the ship's gunner. Moore was on deck, grinding a chisel and chatting with a few others about ways of taking the nearby vessel. Kidd came out of his cabin and confronted Moore, who suggested ways they might seize the Dutch ship without anyone finding out.[21] Kidd became enraged and denounced Moore, calling him a "lousy dog." To which Moore replied, "If I am a lousy dog, you have made me so; you have brought me to ruin and many more." Upon his saying this, Captain Kidd cried, "Have I ruined you, ye dog?" and took a bucket bound with iron hoops, and struck him on the right side of the head, of which he died the next day."[22]

Emotions clearly ran high among the crew of the *Adventure Galley*. Under their "no purchase, no pay" arrangement, they had cruised for more than a year with nothing to show for their pains or the hardships they had suffered. Since leaving the Comoros, they had robbed Captain Parker's vessel and badly smashed a Portuguese warship. Kidd apparently felt he could explain away these crimes as long as he avoided plundering English vessels. In contrast, men like William Moore correctly assumed that the East India Company already had condemned them as pirates. Since they had crossed the line into criminality, they might as well take as much loot as possible.

Kidd pinned his hopes on legal technicalities. Both privateers and merchant captains played a game of fake ownership. Merchant captains carried multiple sets of flags and passports. If they were chased by a warship, they would hoist a flag and get out papers identifying them as a friend of the pursuer. Privateers knew about this game and often sailed under a false flag until a merchantman was lured close by. At the last minute, the aggressor revealed his true colors. By that time, the merchantman's captain had falsely identified himself as the enemy and was promptly snatched up by the privateer.[23]

At the end of November, Kidd used this ruse to seize the *Rouparelle*, a Dutch vessel with an Indian crew and some Dutch officers.[24] The *Adventure Galley* approached, flying the French flag. When Captain Michael Dickers came aboard, he was confronted by one of the Frenchmen from Johanna, a Monsieur Le Roy, playing at captain. Hoping to save his ship, Captain Dickers presented a French pass (passport). As soon as he did, Kidd cried out, "By God have I catched you? You are a free prize."[25]

Kidd took possession of the *Rouparelle*, which was renamed the *November*. Dickers and two other white men enlisted on the *Adventure Galley*; the Indian crewman were allowed to go ashore in the *Rouparelle*'s longboat.[26] The *Galley* and *November* were taken to Quilon, just north of Anjengo on the Indian coast. There Kidd sold her cargo of two horses and eleven bales of cloth to a renegade East India Company employee who fenced pirate goods.[27] Back on board, Kidd gave the crew its share of the money received. Assembling the men, "he called every man by the list, and they came with their hats in their hands, and he gave them their money, and they swept it up and went away."[28]

Continuing to cruise off India's southwestern coast, the *Adventure Galley* seized two small prizes. Kidd did not play games with false flags, as he

had with the *Rouparelle*. In both cases, the ships were simply stopped and
stripped. Then near Calicut, the crew took a small Moorish ketch carrying
candy, tobacco, sugar, and myrrh. Rather than trying to sell this poor cargo,
the goods were "shared between the men in messes, seven men to a mess,
for their own spending."[29] Some weeks later, a Portuguese vessel was looted
near Anjengo. Two chests of opium were sold on shore; the rest of the
booty was again divided among the crew.

KIDD CAPTURES THE *QUEDAH MERCHANT*

At the end of January 1698, Kidd took his only rich prize off Cochin, not
far north of the tip of India. A vessel of four hundred to five hundred tons
owned by Surat merchants, the *Quedah Merchant* was returning from Bengal with cloth, opium, sugar, iron, and saltpeter;[30] much of the cloth was
owned by an official at the Mogul's court.[31] Flying French flags, the *Adventure Galley* and the *November* intercepted the *Quedah*. Hoisting his own
French ensign, the *Quedah*'s English captain came aboard the *Galley* and
showed a French pass (just as Captain Michael Dickers had done, hoping to
save the *Rouparelle*).

Kidd took over the *Quedah*, which was towed by the *Adventure Galley*.
Some of the cargo was sold at Quilon, and the proceeds again were shared
out with the crew. According to witnesses, goods worth between £7,000
and £12,000 were sold at this time, but Kidd kept a significant amount of
fine cloth.[32] Continuing south, the *Galley* looted a small Portuguese vessel
and unsuccessfully pursued the *Dorrill* and the *Sedgwick*, two East India
Company ships.[33] (Robert Culliford had been defeated in a gun battle with
the *Dorrill* the previous June; Dirk Chivers captured the *Sedgwick* two
months later.)

By now it was late February. In a few weeks, the monsoon would
reverse and blow continuously from the southwest. Unless Kidd left now,
he would be stranded on the Indian coast until October. It was imperative
to get to a safe harbor because the *Adventure Galley* literally was falling apart.
Water seeped in constantly, and the captured Indian seamen worked the
pumps day and night to keep her afloat. To help hold the ship together,
Kidd had cables tied around the hull.[34]

Kidd's little squadron took one more prize, a small Indian ketch that
was stripped of food and water. Several of Kidd's European prisoners were
put aboard the ketch, including the captain of the *Quedah Merchant* and the
unfortunate Captain Thomas Parker, kidnapped six months earlier near

Carwar. Michael Dickers, the captured captain of the *Rouparelle/November*, resumed command of that ship for the voyage across the Indian Ocean. The *Adventure Galley*'s mate, George Bullen, took over the *Quedah Merchant*.[35] Heading south and then west, the three vessels sailed for Saint Mary's Island, where drama of a different sort awaited Captain William Kidd.

WAS CAPTAIN KIDD A PIRATE?

For many years after his death, popular legends condemned Kidd as the most fiendish pirate that ever ravaged the seven seas. At the beginning of the twentieth century, his reputation suddenly improved, as Kidd acquired biographers who argued that he was an innocent man condemned in a unfair trial. Kidd's defenders placed a great deal of emphasis on the mysterious disappearance of the French passes taken from the *Rouparelle* and the *Quedah Merchant*.

After six months at Saint Mary's Island, Kidd left for North America in November 1698, sailing in the *Quedah Merchant*, renamed the *Adventure Prize*. Meanwhile, East India Company officials in London had learned of his crimes. He was branded a pirate and omitted by name from a general pardon issued in 1698. In November 1698, the government ordered colonial governors to conduct an all-out manhunt. Kidd learned the bad news when the *Adventure Prize* reached the Caribbean island of Anguilla in April 1699. After the Danish governor of Saint Thomas refused to grant protection, Kidd went to Mona Island and Savona Bay in Hispaniola. British traders bought cloth from Kidd, and one sold him a sloop. After he left, the *Adventure Prize* was looted and burned.

With stops at New Jersey and Long Island, Kidd headed for Boston, where Governor Bellomont arrested him in July 1699. The imprisoned Kidd reached London in April 1700 where his case became embroiled in British politics. The opposition party tried to impeach the sponsors of his voyage, and Kidd testified before the House of Commons in March 1701. Although the impeachment motion narrowly failed, only Kidd's execution would remove him as a dangerous witness.

In May 1701, Kidd was convicted of murdering William Moore and robbing the *Quedah Merchant* and other ships. He argued that the *Rouparelle* and *Merchant* were legal prizes because they carried French passes. (The war already had ended when Kidd seized these ships, but the peace treaty applied south of the equator only after March 1698.) After Kidd had reached Boston, a lawyer acting on his behalf turned the passes over to Lord

Bellomont. The latter sent the passes and other papers to London accompanying a letter of July 26, 1699.[36]

In London, the Admiralty took charge of Kidd's papers but temporarily loaned them to a committee of the House of Commons. The French passes were among the items received by the Commons, which printed copies in its Journal.[37] When the committee returned the papers, it instructed the Admiralty to give Kidd anything he needed for his defense.

However, the passes subsequently disappeared and could not be found in time for Kidd's trial. In his defense, Kidd insisted that the passes would prove his right to seize the *Rouparelle* and *Quedah Merchant*. The prosecution and judges disbelieved and even ridiculed this claim, arguing that the passes never existed.

After Kidd was hanged, it generally was assumed that the passes were fictitious. In 1911, however, Ralph Paine found the original of the pass issued for the *Quedah Merchant* and printed it in *The Book of Buried Treasure*.[38] Following this discovery, several authors came to Kidd's defense. Since the passes really did exist, then Kidd must have been innocent, as he claimed.

A panel of six eminent judges scrupulously conducted Kidd's trial, following the legal practices of 1701. Those procedures were less rigorous in protecting a defendant than those that subsequently have evolved. However, Kidd was not treated any differently than any other eighteenth-century prisoner. It is unfortunate that the French passes were not returned to him, but they would not, in themselves, have proved his innocence.

In determining whether a privateer had seized a valid prize, the test was not the pass or passes carried aboard. The nationality or domicile of the owners (and not that of the captain) defined a ship's nationality. The passes provided Kidd with a valid defense only if he reasonably believed that the *Rouparelle* and *Quedah Merchant* were the property of French subjects or of persons domiciled in French dominions. But the two vessels carried passes from many nations, and Kidd knew full well that both were Indian ships belonging to Indian owners. Robert Bradinham and Joseph Palmer testified to that effect, and their statements are corroborated by the depositions (taken in Boston) of Hugh Parrot, William Jenkins, Barlycorn, and Richard Lamely, who were present when Kidd plundered the two vessels.[39]

Had he produced the French passes during the trial, any reasonable jury would still have found Kidd guilty of piracy against the *Rouparelle* and the *Quedah Merchant*. Moreover, the juries in separate trials also convicted him of piracy against three other vessels; in these incidents Kidd never suggested that any French passes had existed. Kidd's defenders contend that because his trial was "unfair," he must have been innocent. But the two issues are not connected. Even if Kidd had been acquitted, the evidence shows that he did, in fact, commit piracy against at least six vessels.

After studying the record, Lord Birkenhead (a former chancellor of England) concluded that

> There can be no doubt of [Kidd's] guilt. The facts alleged were hardly disputed. It is idle to say that the evidence was only that of two of the gang. In such cases the evidence of accomplices must be taken. Nowadays the court requires corroboration, but the necessary corroboration was certainly available. Besides, Kidd did not deny the facts. He merely said that the ships were lawfully captured, and the other men either made no defence on the merits, or claimed that they had obeyed his orders. . . . He thoroughly earned the hangman's rope.[40]

CHAPTER TEN

CAPTAIN KIDD, ROBERT CULLIFORD, AND THE PIRATE DEMOCRACY AT SAINT MARY'S

Despite the ship's abysmal condition, Kidd managed to bring the *Adventure Galley* to Saint Mary's Island. The *Galley* and the *November* arrived in April 1698; the *Quedah Merchant* showed up sometime in May. The *Galley* and the *November* were destroyed soon after, and Kidd transferred to the *Quedah,* which he renamed the *Adventure Prize.* Toward the end of May, all the officers and most of the crew deserted Kidd. Some elected to stay at Saint Mary's, while many enlisted with Robert Culliford's *Mocha.*[1]

Kidd lingered at Saint Mary's Island for six months until mid-November 1698. During this time, he salvaged some of the iron fittings and gear from the *Galley* and the *Rouparelle* and traded these items and part of the cargo for gold and silver.[2] To fill out his depleted crew, he recruited pirates on the island who wished to travel to North America. Among those joining him were Edward Davis and James Kelley, both of whom had served as quartermaster or captain of several pirate companies.

Thanks to the *Quedah Merchant's* slow speed as well as his long sojourn at Saint Mary's, Kidd did not make it back to New York until June 1699, almost exactly three years after departing for Madagascar. This long delay is one of the mysteries surrounding Kidd's voyage. Kidd had to know that procrastination only increased the likelihood that he would be arrested upon returning. If Kidd intended to return to North America at all, then the sooner he left, the better. While he waited, the evidence against him was accumulating without any response from his side.

For months, East India Company officials in India had been bombarding London with complaints about Kidd's suspicious activities in the Red Sea and at Carwar. News of Captain Kidd's theft of the *Quedah Merchant* in March 1698 reached London the following August in a letter from Samuel Annesley, president of the Company's "factory" (trading post), located at Surat. Soon after, a report came through that Kidd was at Saint Mary's; he planned to go to the West Indies to refit, the story went, before returning for more piracies in the Indian Ocean. On November 18, the Company wrote to the Lords Justices, definitely accusing Kidd of piracy.[3]

It has been suggested that Kidd stayed at Saint Mary's while he waited for the monsoon to reverse from southwest to northeast. However, monsoon winds seldom reach as far south as Madagascar, where the southeast Trades are more influential. Storms do occur more frequently during the summer, but waiting until November did not ensure the journey's safety. The *Quedah Merchant* was a large, lumbering vessel, built to carry heavy loads of cargo in the Indian Ocean's relatively gentle seas. At any time of year, it was a risky gamble to take so clumsy a vessel around the Cape of Good Hope and across the South Atlantic.

Something other than weather concerns prompted Kidd's sojourn at Saint Mary's. It is entirely possible that he considered settling at Saint Mary's and then changed his mind. He had a history of wandering and had lived in Manhattan for only five years before leaving for London in 1695. The deceitful account he prepared for Lord Bellomont shows that Kidd expected to be accused of piracy. The booty he was taking to New York would be split six ways among his noble sponsors. They might well think their shares inadequate payment for defending a notorious pirate.

The full story never will be known. Among those joining up with Culliford's *Mocha* were Robert Bradinham and Joseph Palmer. The government's two chief witnesses at Kidd's trial thus knew nothing about his conduct after the *Mocha* sailed in June. Kidd's own version of events was misleading and disingenuous. He had had more than a year to prepare his story before he returned and was arrested by Lord Bellomont. The ship's log having disappeared, Kidd wrote a narrative of the voyage for Bellomont. This self-serving document devotes more words to events on Saint Mary's than to any other episode.[4] Kidd foresaw the obvious question asked by a judge at his trial: "You have produced letters patents that empowered you to take pirates; why did you not take [Robert] Culliford?"[5]

Immediately upon arriving, Bradinham and Palmer testified, Kidd sought cordial relations with Culliford and the other pirates on Saint Mary's.

"He took a cup of Bumboe, and swore to be true to them," Bradinham says, and he also claimed that Kidd gave Culliford four cannon and an anchor.[6] The *Adventure Galley* had become so unsound and leaky that Kidd ordered the men to burn her after removing everything of use or value. The *November* also was stripped and then was scuttled in Saint Mary's harbor.

When the *Quedah* arrived, Kidd held a formal share out of the spoils. Some money and goods already had been distributed in India. Now the bales of silks and muslins and other merchandise were counted and divided into 160 shares, each share being represented by three or four bales and an assortment of other goods. Kidd kept forty for himself, Bradinham and Palmer testified, and he divided the rest among the crewmen.[7]

KIDD BLAMES CULLIFORD'S ESCAPE ON HIS MUTINOUS CREW

Kidd alleged an entirely different version of events in his *Narrative*. When the *Galley* arrived at Saint Mary's, he says, Culliford and his men fled into the woods, leaving the *Mocha* empty-handed. The crew of the *Adventure Galley* mutinied, Kidd reported, refusing his order to seize the deserted ship.[8] Only thirteen men remained loyal while ninety-seven enlisted with Culliford.[9]

According to Kidd, the mutineers burned the *Rouparelle* sometime afterward.[10] In his absence, they shared out the *Quedah*'s cargo and then stripped it and the *Adventure Galley* of anything useful.[11] The deserters also took away the captive Indians manning the *Galley*'s pumps, causing the ship to sink. To hide the evidence of their crimes, Kidd claims, the mutineers stole his journal and other papers and even threatened to kill him.

[The said deserters] threatened several times to murder the Narrator, as he was informed, and advised to take care of himself; which they designed in the Night to effect; but was prevented by him locking himself in his Cabin at night, and securing himself with barricading the same with Bales of Goods; and, having about Forty small Arms, besides Pistols ready charged, kept them out; Their Wickedness was so great, after they had plundered and ransacked sufficiently, went Four Miles off to one Edward Welche's House, where his the Narrator's Chest was lodged, and broke it open; and took out Ten Ounces of Gold, 40 Pound of Plate, 370 Pieces of Eight, the Narrator's Journal, and a great many Papers that belonged to him, and the People of New York that fitted him out.[12]

Kidd's story is implausible. Had they made a concerted attempt to do so, the mutineers could easily have killed him; Kidd says that they outnumbered his defenders ninety-seven to thirteen. Whether or not he was present when the booty was divided, Kidd did receive the forty shares promised him by the ship's articles. Upon reaching the West Indies, he deserted the *Quedah Merchant* and most of its cargo, purchased a sloop, and made for New York. Lord Bellomont arrested Kidd and diligently rounded up gold, silver, jewels, and fine cloth worth some £14,000 (about $7 million).[13] The mutineers had hardly stripped him bare.

KIDD IS DEFEATED BY HIS OVERBEARING AND BRUTAL STYLE OF COMMAND

Whether or not they literally committed mutiny, there is no question that the officers and crew deserted Kidd at Saint Mary's. Kidd was universally disliked. He had commanded the *Adventure Galley* when piracy was committed, but his methods and manners were not those that pirates expected of a captain. By the 1690s, pirates elected their officers and insisted they follow the ship's rules. Except during battle, officers were expected to consult the men before deciding important matters. Kidd, in contrast, was a martinet who demanded deference from men of inferior rank. With a privateer's commission from King William III, Kidd believed he was equal in status to a commander in the Royal Navy. On the way down the Thames to the sea, he had refused to salute naval vessels, and he had expected to receive full honors from the captains of East Indiamen.

Since Kidd considered himself superior to captains in the Royal Navy, it is not surprising that he exacted unquestioning obedience from the seamen and apprentices on the *Adventure Galley*. Instead of consulting the men, he expected them to follow orders, and he maintained discipline with frequent physical punishments. When Kidd stopped at Carwar in September 1697, the East India Company's representative described the atmosphere on board the *Adventure Galley*:

> This captain is very severe to his people, by reason of his commission, and carries a very different form from what other Pirates use to do [that is, he acts differently than other pirate captains], this commission procuring him awe and respect from his men, and to this is added his own strength, being a very lusty man often calling for his pistols and threatening any that durst speak to the contrary

of what he desireth, to knock out their brains which causeth them to be very desirous of putting off his yoke. . . . They are a very distracted company, continually quarreling and fighting amongst themselves, so it is likely they will in a short time destroy one another, or starve, having only sufficient provision to keep the sea for a month more.[14]

In his bullying cruelty, Kidd resembles Captain Edgcumbe of the *Mocha*—whose crew mutinied in June 1696, led by Ralph Stout and James Kelley. Like Edgcumbe, Kidd was unpopular with mariners, and especially with those attracted to freebooting. In 1689, the crew absconded with the *Blessed William* while Kidd was away on shore. Relatively few experienced seamen were willing to enlist on the *Adventure Galley* when it reached New York. Kidd killed William Moore in a fit of enraged anger. But he also may have acted because he felt that the men would not obey an order to arrest Moore.

If they hated Kidd, why did not the crew mutiny earlier? The men were at sea in foreign waters, far away from home, and in a foul and leaking vessel. To rebel successfully, they needed to find a leader who could sail the *Adventure Galley* and also command the crew's loyalty. The crew did not include anyone with the requisite skills who was willing to confront Kidd's volatile temperament.

After leaving New York, the *Adventure Galley* stopped only at Madagascar and the Comoro Islands. In September 1697, the ship reached Carwar on the Malabar Coast, the first port where a European might find safety and employment. While they were at Carwar, Benjamin Franks bribed Kidd for permission to leave. Several others, who tried to desert on a ship's boat, were captured, returned to the *Galley,* and whipped. About nine men did manage to escape and carried their complaints to the East India Company and the Portuguese viceroy at Goa.[15]

At Carwar, in addition to running away, the crew also tried to find another commander to replace Kidd. The East India Company sent out two captains to negotiate with Kidd. One was the same Captain Mason who also bargained with Robert Chivers when he attacked Calicut in November 1696.[16] Some of the sailors took Mason aside while he was aboard the *Adventure Galley* and tried to persuade him to take command.

Although the voyage was not an outstanding success, the men nonetheless ended up with significant booty. Leaving aside the smaller prizes, the

Quedah Merchant and its cargo were a valuable catch, by some estimates worth as much as £45,000 (roughly $23 million).[17] A full share must have amounted to more than £350 (about $175,000). At least four former crewmen went back to New York on the *Margaret,* commanded by Samuel Burgess. Along with the *Margaret* and all its passengers, they were arrested at the Cape of Good Hope; three men had £400 or £500, one carried £1,100.[18]

Other captains did much worse without losing the crew's loyalty. In contrast, virtually everyone fled from Kidd at Saint Mary's; some men enlisted with Culliford, while others remained on the island. By the time they arrived at Saint Mary's, the men who had joined in New York had been at sea for nineteen months, and the original crew was two years out of London. Many men may have wanted to return home, but they waited for another ship rather than spend more months at sea with Captain Kidd.

Kidd exhibited a rigid sense of social status. He functioned well in New York and London, both deferential societies where he and others knew their place. He showed due respect to superiors such as Frederick Philipse, Robert Livingston, and Lord Bellomont. He was a stern master to the servants he had acquired by marrying Sarah Bradley Oort. But seamen and especially pirates were thoroughly egalitarian and refused to pay the customary respect to social rank and status.

Whether or not Kidd wanted to return to New York, there was no place for him on Saint Mary's Island. His days as a captain were over, and no other ship's company would have accepted him as an officer. He may have considered setting up as a trader in competition with Baldridge and Welsh, but he was unwelcome even in that capacity. There is no question that Kidd committed piracy, but it also is clear that he failed as a leader of men. Given his authoritarian personality, Kidd totally lacked the political skills needed to function in a society as radically democratic as Saint Mary's.

Kidd's experiences are further evidence that Saint Mary's was a remarkably civilized place. The men hated Kidd, but they did him no harm. They even let him keep forty shares of the booty. Given that most captains took only one or two shares, this was a generous gesture. Since the men had signed ship's articles promising Kidd forty shares, they kept their word. The one thing they would not do is let Kidd live among them in the pirate republic of Libertalia.

ROBERT CULLIFORD PLUNDERS THE *GREAT MAHOMET*

Robert Culliford was as popular as Kidd was detested. In 1689, Culliford had helped lead the mutiny that made off with Captain Kidd's *Blessed William.* Ten years later, in April 1699, the two men met up again at Saint Mary's. Kidd's crew left him—some for Culliford's *Mocha,* which had reached Saint Mary's just before the *Adventure Galley.* They did not change ship because Culliford was extraordinarily successful. The *Mocha* came to Saint Mary's having taken only two mediocre prizes during a ten-month cruise. Those with full shares got £100 each (about $50,000), considerably less than the £300 or more Kidd distributed on the *Adventure Galley.*[19]

Men elected Robert Culliford as captain and continued to follow him on land because he exemplified the qualities they prized in a leader. Culliford was a man of some education, skilled in gunnery and seamanship.[20] He was spirited and belligerent in combat, as he showed during the battle with the *Dorrill.* Above all, men believed they could trust him. They counted on him both to keep his word and to follow the customs of Saint Mary's. He respected the men's democratic convictions, leading by exhortation rather than, as Kidd did, by curses, whippings, and blows.

With its new crew, the *Mocha* left Saint Mary's in June 1698. Culliford went first to Johanna, where he took £2,000 in gold (about $1 million) from a French vessel.[21] Turning west toward the Indian coast, the *Mocha* ran into Dirk Chivers and the *Soldado.* The two crews agreed to cruise as consorts and headed north. Not far from Surat on September 23, 1698, the pirate warships came upon the *Great Mahomet,* returning from Jiddah loaded with gold from sales at the annual pilgrimage fair. The vessel had been part of a convoy accompanied by an East India Company warship, but her captain had left the convoy to make a faster passage.

By now, the *Soldado* was totally unseaworthy. The two warships took their prize to the coast and put the Indian captives ashore. The crew of the *Soldado* transferred their cannon and stores to the *Great Mahomet* (renamed the *New Soldado*) and then sank their own vessel.[22] Before heading back to Saint Mary's, the two crews—250 men in all—shared out their booty. According to some testimony, the gold coins and ingots on the *Mahomet* amounted to £100,000 or more, and each man received a share worth £700 to £800 (about $375,000).[23] The Admiralty Court in London estimated the plunder at £30,000,[24] but even this was an enormous sum (worth about $15 million today).

Pirate Warships at Saint Mary's, 1698–1701

Ship	Resolution/Soldado	Mocha	Adventure Galley	Pelican	Speaker
Captain	Robert Glover, Dirk Chivers	Ralph Stout, Robert Culliford	William Kidd		
1698	Takes *Sedgwick*, March; Consorts with *Mocha*, Aug.; Take *Great Mahomet*, Sept.; Returns to Saint Mary's, Dec.	At Saint Mary's, March or April till June; Consorts with *Soldado*, Aug.; Take *Great Mahomet*, Sept.; Returns to Saint Mary's, Dec.	Takes *Quedah Merchant*, Feb. 1; At Saint Mary's from April 1; Leaves Saint Mary's for New York, Nov. 15	Arrives after *Great Mahomet* is captured, Sept.; Takes Portuguese ship, sells wine to *Mocha*; Docked at Saint Mary's, Dec.	
1699			Anguilla, Saint Thomas, April; At Hispaniola, abandons *Quedah Merchant*, early May; New York, June 10; Boston, June 28; Arrested, July 6		George Booth seizes; John Bowen is QM
1700			Arrives at London, April 14		Takes two Surat ships
1701			Trial, May 8–9; Hanged, May 22		Loots *Borneo*, Oct. 1701; Returning, crashes at Mauritius

Soon after the gun duel with the *Great Mahomet*, the *Pelican* showed up. Since the *Pelican* had not taken part in the engagement, the men of the *Mocha* and the *Soldado* refused to share their booty. Four days later, while they were at Rajapur (see map on page 28), the *Pelican* again appeared, this time towing a Portuguese merchantman filled with cloth and wine. An unlikely tale has the thirsty men on the *Mocha* purchasing two hogsheads of wine for 100,000 pieces of eight (about $11 million).[25]

Still trailed by the *Pelican*, the *New Soldado* and the *Mocha* returned to Saint Mary's late in December 1698. With the rich booty looted from the *Great Mahomet*, their crews would not have to go out again for many months or even years. The great majority decided to stay on at Saint Mary's.[26] Only a few wanted to return to North America—and only if they could avoid arrest. Through the mariner's grapevine, they were aware that colonial governments were under attack for not paying attention to returning pirates.

Their fears were reasonable and prescient. A few months later, a naval vessel showed up at Saint Mary's, and its captain offered a free pardon to anyone willing to give up piracy. Robert Culliford led a group that accepted the pardon and sought to return to North America. However, when they reached North America, the government reneged on its promise. Interpreting its terms in a narrow and inaccurate manner, the courts denied the validity of the king's proclamation and sentenced half a dozen men to death. At the news of this judicial murder, its citizens became even more determined to stay and enjoy the freedom of the pirate republic at Saint Mary's Island.

THE EAST INDIA COMPANY IS PUNISHED FOR THE THEFT OF THE *GREAT MAHOMET*

At the end of 1698, East India Company traders and officials in Surat were physically attacked by local mobs and also faced the wrath of India's imperial government. It was Dirk Chivers's and Robert Culliford's theft of the *Great Mahomet* in September 1698 that brought Indian rage down upon the Company. Kidd's robbery of the *Quedah Merchant* the previous March had caused a stir at the mogul's court, but Emperor Aurangzib held back from punishing the English. Much of the *Quedah*'s cargo belonged to Muklis Khan, a nobleman of high rank; and the ship's native captain had seen Kidd's royal commission. Convinced that the English traders were cooperating with the pirates, Muklis Khan wanted the East India Company to compensate him for his losses. But none of the dire consequences feared in

Surat followed, perhaps because Surat's governor was heavily bribed to defend the Company's interests at the imperial court. Emperor Aurangzib also may have waited because European warships were just then guarding the annual pilgrim fleet, returning from Mocha.[27]

In contrast, when news of the *Great Mahomet* reached Surat in November 1698, the response was swift. Robert Culliford and others on board the *Mocha* and *Soldado* testified that the capture went smoothly, and only a few Indians were killed during the battle for the ship.[28] However, when he got back home, Hussein Hamidan, the *Mahomet*'s owner, told the customary, hackneyed story of pirate brutality. Khan declared that the raiders had savagely tortured Indian merchants to make them reveal their hiding places. They then tossed hundreds of prisoners overboard or set them adrift in boats without oars or water. Sixty women were kept on board to satisfy the unrelenting lusts typical of Europeans.

Samuel Annesley, who headed the East India Company factory at Surat, reported Khan's tales to his superiors.

> The town at newes of this was presently in great disorder, it was reported the villaines turned adrift in the ships boats, without Oars, sail or Provisions, 150 of the pilgrims, whom the Tide carryed to Bassen. The women passengers, about 60 were kept aboard, and inhumanely abused to avoid wch indignity five stabbed themselves.[29]

Enraged mobs filled the streets, besieging the English factory and shouting curses at the inmates trapped within. Amanat Khan, recently named governor of Surat, placed the English traders under house arrest. The men of Surat petitioned Emperor Aurangzib, complaining that "ye infidells had robbed killed etc. the true believers, and they would forbear all publick worship in their Musteels, till the King would order them satisfaction."[30]

In December 1698, the emperor once again commanded that the European companies compensate the victims of piracy and guarantee the safety of Muslim trade. Amanat Khan, Surat's governor, promulgated the imperial edict on January 1, 1699, and threatened to enforce it unless he received huge bribes. He demanded that the English traders pay their annual customs dues immediately, sent soldiers to guard the English factory, and horsewhipped their Muslim brokers. Preceded by beating drums, town criers announced that the Mogul's subjects could no longer have any dealings with Europeans or even sell them food.[31]

The heads of the French and Dutch companies soon came to terms. Both paid bribes to the governor and signed guarantees to protect the safety of ships sailing to Mocha and the Persian Gulf. Samuel Annesley was in charge of the factory at Surat. He pleaded with Sir John Gayer, his superior at Bombay, for permission to make a deal with Amanat Khan. Gayer not only refused but rushed to Surat to forestall any compromise by Annesley. Sitting safely aboard a ship at Swally Hole away from the city, Gayer commended patience to those trapped in the English factory.

The English procrastination enraged Amanat Khan, and he had Indian brokers and servants working for the English arrested, publicly whipped, and imprisoned. Several hundred soldiers blockaded the factory, threatening the inmates with scourging and death. On January 25, Annesley gave in, paid off the governor, and promised to convoy ships from Surat to as far east as Sumatra and Java.

CHAPTER ELEVEN

ENGLISH WARSHIPS FAIL TO CLOSE
DOWN SAINT MARY'S

*Whilst I was in the hands of the Pirates nothing was heard from these
rascals the whole time but swearing, damning and blaspheming to the
last degree imaginable saying they would have no dealings with Acts of
Grace, by which to be sent to hang a sundrying at Hope Point as were
the companies of Kidd and Bradish trepanned under lying promises. If
they were attacked by too strong a force they would blow up their ship
and all go merrily to hell.*

—Captain Carey (April 1720)

Kidd's theft of the *Quedah Merchant* and Culliford's plunder of the *Great
Mahomet* caused a great clamor. London ordered colonial governors to
put a halt to voyages bringing supplies from North America to Saint Mary's.
In New York, however, despite Lord Bellomont's best efforts, Frederick
Philipse managed to send out another vessel. Commanded by Samuel
Burgess, the *Margaret* left New York in June 1697 and reached Saint Mary's
in January 1698.[1]

Burgess stayed in port for about ten weeks. He sold liquor and other
supplies for gold, careened the *Margaret,* and then took on water and food.
He also collected nineteen passengers for Barbados and New York, each
man agreeing to pay one hundred pieces of eight (about $1,100) and to
provide his own food for the voyage. Captain Burgess had served alongside
Robert Culliford on the *Blessed William,* and he also had sojourned at Saint
Mary's in 1692 with the *Pearl.* Burgess's criminal past and the dubious legal-

ity of his current voyage apparently encouraged the men to trust him and buy passage on the *Margaret*. But the decision to leave Saint Mary's turned out to be a terrible mistake.

During an especially rough passage around Africa's southern tip, the ship's provisions were ruined, forcing an emergency stop at the Cape of Good Hope in December 1699. Burgess fired three guns to salute the Dutch fort but failed to pay the same honors to the East India Company ship *Loyal Merchant,* commanded by Matthew Lowth. Lowth carried a privateer's commission, and the *Loyal Merchant* flew the king's jack and pennant.

Outraged that Burgess had gone past without honoring the flag, Captain Lowth sent over a boat to inspect the *Margaret*. The ship carried a legal cargo of some one hundred black slaves purchased on mainland Madagascar. But Lowth also found a large number of white passengers, some dressed in East India Company clothing. He swooped down, seizing the *Margaret* and its cargo. Six passengers and two crewmen escaped ashore. Lowth arrested all the others and accused them of piracy.[2] The prisoners were carried to India, where some died in the Bombay jail; the survivors did not reach England until August 1701.[3]

After sailing from Saint Mary's, Burgess had left some of his pirate passengers at Saint Augustine's Bay while he was off buying slaves. During his absence, an English man–of–war arrived carrying copies of a royal pardon for those engaged in piracy. Burgess later testified that "the passengers seemed . . . to be very joyfull of the said Proclamation of Pardon and very ready to embrace it."[4]

THOMAS WARREN THE YOUNGER OFFERS THE PIRATES A ROYAL PARDON

News that an English squadron was in the area was received with greater skepticism at Saint Mary's. The men prepared to defend themselves, and the crews of the *Mocha* and *New Soldado* sacrificed their ships to ensure the safety of the pirate's port. Thirty or more cannon were removed to the palisades overlooking the anchorage. The two large warships then were sunk across the entrance to the bottlenecked harbor, leaving only a narrow passage. The other ships at Saint Mary's either were run high ashore or burnt.[5] The unlucky *Pelican* was among those destroyed at this time; a seaman living at Saint Mary's later described her as "leaky" and a "poor sailor."[6]

The proclamation finally arrived at Saint Mary's in August 1699. It was carried not by a warship but by the *Vine Pink,*[7] and it was brought by

Thomas Warren Junior, son of the squadron's commander. Robert Culliford continued to act as the men's captain and leader on land as on sea. As soon as the *Vine* dropped anchor, Warren reported, Culliford rowed out in a boat manned by "several Negro servants," and asked to hear the precise terms of King William's proclamation of pardon. Warren read the proclamation and then endorsed it with the date and Culliford's name.

The act offered a full pardon to all mariners "eastward of the Cape of Good Hope, who shall surrender themselves for piracies or robberies committed by them upon the sea or land." However, it carried several conditions that later proved significant. The pardon did not cover crimes committed after July 31, 1699. Those seeking to benefit from the pardon had to surrender to Thomas Warren Senior, assisted by three other commissioners named in the act.[8]

Culliford promised to discuss the pardon with the residents of Saint Mary's. For his part, Warren exhibited the proxy deputizing him to act in his father's place. He also promised to see to it that an exception was made, even though it now was some days past the cutoff date.

Either Warren was persuasive, or Culliford eventually decided he wanted to go home. On September 18, seventeen pirates delivered a petition to Warren, accepting the terms of the pardon and asking for passage on the *Vine*. Culliford and five other men signed their names; John Swann, Culliford's longtime male lover, and ten others could only make a mark.[9] After further stops at Port Dauphin and Saint Augustine's Bay, the *Vine* reached the Cape of Good Hope on the night of December 20, 1699.

The men on the *Vine* recognized Samuel Burgess's ship, the *Margaret*, which was still docked in the harbor. Eager to share the good news of the king's pardon with their friends, Culliford and his companions rowed over to the *Margaret*. But they instead found the ship guarded by men from Captain Lowth's *Loyal Merchant*. Lowth's men tried to arrest the pirates, eliciting a noisy brawl. Dutch troops boarded the *Margaret*, quelled the riot, and took possession of the *Vine*.[10]

The next day, Captain Warren explained to the Dutch governor, Willem van der Stel, that his passengers had a royal pardon. So van der Stel had to free the prisoners and let the *Vine* go on. Captain Warren stopped at Barbados, where nine men got off. After some delay, the Barbados government recognized the validity of their pardon.[11] Less fortunate, Culliford and another man went on to England and were arrested. Although Culliford managed to escape, he was recaptured in September 1700. While he languished in jail for two years, his share of the *Great Mahomet's* treasure disappeared.[12]

Ultimately Robert Culliford was pardoned after cooperating with royal officials in the prosecution of Samuel Burgess. Five other men were convicted despite proof they had accepted the pardon. They had heard of the pardon after returning to North America and surrendered to Governor Jeremiah Basse of New Jersey. But the Admiralty and its legal officers ruled that the proclamation had to be defined literally and narrowly. Three of those pleading the pardon were tried twice for piracy, both on the *Quedah Merchant* with Kidd and on the *Great Mahomet* with Culliford. During the former trial, Judge Edward Ward insisted on a strict construction of the pardon. "Now there are four commissioners named that you ought to surrender to; but you have not surrendered to any one of these, but to Colonel Bass, and there is no such man mentioned in this proclamation."[13]

THE WARREN EXPEDITION IS SENT OUT AFTER A LONG DELAY

Had he made it to Saint Mary's, the older Thomas Warren, commander of the vessels carrying the pardon, would have been familiar to some of the island's residents. It was Warren who had intercepted Captain Kidd as he traveled to Madagascar in September 1696. Invited on board the flagship, Kidd became truculent as he drank Captain Warren's wine, boasting of the feats he was planning and the wealth he would amass. Warren suspected that Kidd would turn pirate, and his apprehension increased when the *Adventure Galley* rowed away from the squadron at night.[14]

Warren had led the first English warships to visit the east. Sent out as a direct result of Henry Every's crimes, Warren was ordered to inspect the harbors and watering places used by East Indiamen as far as the Cape of Good Hope. After he returned to England late in 1697, Warren was, perhaps unwisely, treated as an expert on Indian Ocean piracy.

About the time Warren returned home, the East India Company in London received letters—many written long before—reporting pirate crimes during the preceding eighteen months. In apocalyptic language, these told how John Hoar had burned two Company ships near Mocha, described Dirk Chivers's attack on Calicut, and lamented the mutinies aboard the *Mocha* and *Josiah*.[15] Company officials in London were even more alarmed by Captain Warren's letter reporting on the men and ships at Saint Mary's—which Warren never visited.

There is a small island called Santa Maria at the north-east part of Madagascar, where the pirates have a very commodious harbour to which they resort and clean their ships. Here they have built a regular fortification of forty or fifty guns. They have about 1,500 men, with seventeen sail of vessels, sloops and ships, some of which carry forty guns. They are furnished from New York, New England and the West Indies with stores and other necessaries. I was informed that if they could obtain pardons they would leave that villainous way of life.[16]

King William took seriously England's lucrative trade with the East. At the end of December, Secretary of State James Vernon forwarded the letters from India to the Board of Trade and asked for suggestions.[17] The Board responded with alacrity, its members as appalled as the king by the pirates' exploits. The brigands at Saint Mary's were molesting the East India trade and endangering English privileges in India. Moreover, the thriving trade in East Indian goods between Saint Mary's and North America took business away from England's woolen industry.[18]

The Board began planning an attack on Saint Mary's in January 1698. The governor of the East India Company was asked to address the Board's January 4 meeting. Six days later, Captain Warren presented his views on East Indies piracy.[19] Both returned during the next several months, and captains of merchant ships also appeared to tell about the situation in the Indian Ocean.[20]

The East India Company's policy was simple and consistent: Pirates and their accomplices should be "extirpated"—rooted out, exterminated, and wholly destroyed. The Board preferred Captain Warren's suggestion: Lure the pirates home by granting them a pardon. Extirpation might require many ships and men. Even though the war with France had ended in September 1697, money remained tight.

The Board of Trade sent the king its recommendation on January 13. To take the fort at Saint Mary's, guarded by as many as seventeen relatively small vessels, the Board asked for three swift cruisers. These might set sail as early as March 1698 with the annual fleet of the East India Company. The commander would go to Saint Mary's and offer a pardon to those willing to give up piracy. Pirates refusing to submit would be attacked and killed at Saint Mary's or wherever else they might be found.[21]

While the Board's plan ultimately was followed, the naval squadron missed the March 1698 deadline and did not finally set out until January 1699, almost a year later. After the Board repeated its recommendation, the king approved the plan on February 28, and he named Warren to lead the expedition in May.[22] But preparations continued at an agonizingly slow pace. By the end of July, the Board was exasperated by the delays and reminded the Lords Justices that it had made several reports on the matter. It wanted another vessel added to the squadron and the four ships dispatched speedily.[23]

The project was further stalled as the Board prepared drafts of the pardon and the instructions for Warren and the other commissioners who would try the pirates.[24] As drafts of these documents passed back and forth, King William added a provision that the pardon must be accepted before a specific date.[25] The relevant papers finally were ready at the end of September.

Although all government agencies move with extreme slowness, the nine months' delay seems excessive—especially since the king enthusiastically backed the project. Several officials held up approval because they felt the East India Company rather than the government should pay for the expedition.[26] Moreover, three of those involved in approving the plan were among Captain Kidd's sponsors. It is tempting to believe that they deliberately dawdled to give Kidd a free hand in the Indian Ocean.[27]

Because of the long delay, the expedition failed to achieve its goal of ending piracy at Saint Mary's and Madagascar. Commodore Warren and the Board of Trade originally proposed that the ships go directly to Saint Mary's. However, by the time of sailing, the expedition had taken on new tasks that instead took it to India. News of Captain Kidd's theft of the *Quedah Merchant* in March 1698 reached London in August; to mollify the East India Company, Captain Warren was ordered to "pursue and seize Kidd, if he continue still in those parts."[28] Warren also was charged with conveying to India England's first royal ambassador to that country.

THE KING CHARTERS A NEW EAST INDIA COMPANY

The East India Company had come under attack at home as well as in India. In September 1698, the crown chartered a new East India Company, replacing the organization that had existed for more than a century. Representing the new company, Sir William Norris was sent to ask the Indian emperor for privileges at least equal to those enjoyed by the former company.

Given the value of English trading rights, Ambassador Norris deserved an impressive escort, and Captain Warren's squadron was available.[29] Moreover, news that the Malagasy had attacked the settlement at Saint Mary's in July 1697 finally reached London fourteen months later, in September 1698. Royal officials believed that the natives had totally wiped out the pirates. They thus felt that Warren no longer needed to make Madagascar his first stop.[30]

Following William and Mary's accession in 1689, the East India Company's monopoly of the highly profitable Indian trade had come under sustained assault.[31] Through a combination of forceful lobbying and generous bribes, the Company secured the renewal of its charter in 1693. But its foes continued their activities in the House of Commons. In January 1694, a resolution was passed declaring that "all subjects of *England* have equal right to trade to the *East-Indies,* unless prohibited by Act of Parliament."[32] During the next five years, revelations of East India Company bribery began to scandalize even the most cynical members of parliament. At the same time, the Whigs sought to force King William to repeal the charter by blocking parliamentary approval of Company loans to the monarch.

Because of his war with France, King William found himself desperately short of money, and he effectively auctioned off a monopoly over English trade with Asia. In 1698, the government announced that it needed £2,000,000 and would regard favorably requests by those providing the money. The existing East India Company offered £700,000 at 4 percent a year, while its opponents promised £2,000,000 at 8 percent interest.

Despite the higher interest rate, the cash-starved king accepted the latter offer. On September 5, 1698, a new company was incorporated as the English East India Company Trading to the East Indies. It was granted a monopoly of eastern trade, but the old company won the right to continue in existence. It remained a powerful and resourceful foe both in parliament and in India, and the two East India Companies merged in 1709.[33]

THE ROYAL NAVY VISITS INDIA BUT FAILS TO ATTACK SAINT MARY'S

On January 21, 1698, Commodore Warren left England commanding the *Harwich* and accompanied by the smaller *Anglesey, Hastings,* and *Lizard.*[34] Warren had been ordered to take Ambassador Norris to India and only then to cruise, looking for Kidd and other pirates. Following the traditional route, Warren's squadron stopped at Madeira and the Cape Verde Islands and arrived at the Cape of Good Hope on June 5.[35]

While he was at the Cape, the Dutch governor passed along the erroneous news that Captain Kidd was trapped at Saint Augustine's Bay on Madagascar's west coast. An English skipper had told the Dutch governor that Kidd had beached his worn-out vessel in the river and was waiting for an opportunity to get away. Warren immediately made for Saint Augustine's but found that Kidd had left long before for the Caribbean and North America.[36]

Commander Warren went on the Comoro Islands and then to India, docking at Masulipatam on September 20, 1699.[37] Soon afterward Warren died and was buried in India.[38] At some point, probably while the squadron was at Johanna Island in early August, he gave his son Thomas Junior command of the *Vine Pink* and authorized him to grant the pardon to repentant pirates. The younger Warren went on to Saint Mary's Island, where he collected Robert Culliford and sixteen others.[39]

In India, James Littleton succeeded to Warren's command. The squadron spent some time convoying English merchantmen and carrying goods for pay. Two of the ships helped to guard the Mogul's annual fleet to Mecca. In March or April 1700, just before the monsoon switched from northeast to southwest, Littleton left India with Warren's three smaller vessels.[40] (The largest vessel, the *Harwich,* was in China, protecting a ship owned by the New East India Company.) Littleton claimed that his squadron had cruised along the Madagascar coast and captured two pirate ships. He took a few raiders to London, but others had escaped on shore.[41]

However, rumors reaching India at the time tell a different story. Littleton remained off Madagascar for nine months without firing a shot. When his ships first reached Saint Mary's, the pirates greeted them with a salute of nine guns, to which they responded with five. Littleton and the other officers were in close and daily conversation with the men at Saint Mary's, who paid generously for naval protection. The captain of the *Hastings* assisted the pirates so freely that Littleton arrested him, fearing that he would turn his vessel over to the brigands. Alexander Hamilton, a sea captain and trader at Surat, says the naval squadron even helped the pirates careen their ships.

> It was reported in *India,* that Commodore *Littleton* had some of that Gang on board the *Anglesey* at *Madagascar,* but, for some valuable Reasons, he let them go again; and because they found Difficulty in

cleaning the Bottoms of their large Ships, he generously assisted them with large Blocks and Tackle-falls for careening them.[42]

Although they may be exaggerated, these rumors of collusion are believable. Plundering and mistreating "Moors" was considered a venial offense.[43] Moreover, English naval officers of the late seventeenth century did not practice a high standard of professionalism. During King William's War, naval captains took bribes and smuggled gold into England. Some embezzled goods and demanded bribes from merchant vessels, often without having a valid reason to stop the ship in the first place.[44] Almost all officers traded on their own account. It would not be surprising if Littleton's squadron took bribes from pirates and transported goods and slaves between ports. Littleton and the other English officers demonstrated their lack of scruples, when, after leaving Madagascar, they stopped at Mauritius. While staying at the small Dutch colony, they physically abused civilians, stole cattle, and refused to pay for the provisions they consumed.[45]

The four warships sent to the Indian Ocean in January 1699 failed to achieve their goal—either to exterminate the Saint Mary's colony or to convince the pirates to accept a pardon and cease their activities. Only a few accepted the pardon and returned home with the younger Warren. Commander Littleton spent considerable time off the Madagascar coast, but he did not try to invade other pirate havens.

Several hundred men remained at Saint Mary's and continued to practice their craft for another two decades. Embittered by the treachery involving the pardon sent by Warren, they avoided surrendering to English officials. Those that left Saint Mary's were careful to retire from the sea at ports with more trustworthy governors, such as the French colony at Réunion Island. Even twenty years later, pirates remained skeptical about all Acts of Grace. As late as April 1720, Bartholomew Roberts captured a ship commanded by a Captain Carey, who described the pirates continuing bitterness about dishonest pardons.[46]

Part Three

THE PIRATE NATION OF LIBERTALIA, 1700–1725

CHAPTER TWELVE

WHO WOULD BE A PIRATE?

That sail which is rapidly overhauling us may be an ordinary enemy: a Don or a Frenchman. The ordinary enemy may easily be made just as lethal as the pirate. At the moment when she runs up the Jolly Roger, what exactly does this do to the imagination? It means, I grant you, that if we are beaten there will be no quarter. But that could be contrived without piracy. It is not the mere increase of danger that does the trick. It is the whole image of the utterly lawless enemy, the men who have cut adrift from all human society and become, as it were, a species of their own—men strangely clad, dark men with ear-rings, men with a history which they know and we don't, lords of unspecified treasure buried in undiscovered islands. They are, in fact, to the young reader almost as mythological as the giants. It does not cross his mind that a man—a mere man like the rest of us—might be a pirate at one time of his life and not at another. . . .

 —C. S. Lewis, *Essays Presented to Charles Williams* (1947)

The Saint Mary's raiders do not fit into any of the pirate stereotypes that fiction and films have conditioned us to expect. They were neither foul fiends, noble heroes, nor cackling madmen. On the surface, they were like most other men living at the time. They were ordinary men—but they did extraordinary things.

Because pirates were normal men, it is not easy to find out anything about their private lives.[1] Even outstanding captains are notorious only for their professional activities. Naval forces never captured a pirate vessel on the high seas. The only pirates brought to justice were those—such as Kidd,

Robert Culliford, and Samuel Burgess—who voluntarily surrendered to the authorities. When these men went to trial, the Admiralty Court cared only about proving specific incidents of piracy; court records pass over in silence the defendant's early years and private affairs. The many tales about the youthful adventures of Captain Kidd and Henry Every were made up after the fact.

Of one thing, however, we can be certain. Pirate captains were neither degenerate brutes nor madmen. Most were expert mariners, distinguished from other sea captains by an outgoing personality and a charismatic style of leadership. Lord Bellomont, Benjamin Fletcher's successor as New York's governor, savagely attacked Fletcher for inviting Thomas Tew to his home. These charges seem unjust. How could Fletcher have known that Tew was a pirate? Tew was related to a reputable family in Newport, and he was well regarded by Rhode Island and Bermuda officials. In physical appearance and everyday demeanor, Tew no doubt resembled other colonial merchants and captains at Fletcher's soirees.

There was one major difference: Governor Fletcher found Thomas Tew an unusually interesting and a pleasant companion. After Fletcher was removed from office, he tried to explain the relationship to the Board of Trade in London. Fletcher believably argued that he never took bribes from Tew. He simply enjoyed Tew's company more than that of most men with whom he had to deal in colonial New York.

> This Tew appeared to me not only a man of courage and activity, but of the greatest sence and remembrance of what he had seen, of any seamen I had mett. He was allso what they call a very pleasant man; soe that at some times when the labours of my day were over it was some divertisment as well as information to me, to heare him talke. I wish'd in my mind to make him a sober man, and in particular to reclaime him from a vile habit of swearing. I gave him a booke to that purpose; and to gaine the more upon him, I gave him a gunn of some value. In returne hereof he made me also a present which was a curiosity and in value not much. . . .[2]

Captains active during the 1690s previously had served on colonial merchantmen. Some moved back and forth between merchant vessels and pirate warships. Samuel Burgess is said to have come from a seafaring family of good repute. After returning from Saint Mary's in 1693, he went to work for Frederick Philipse, a shrewd New York merchant. This tells us little about Burgess's personal life, but it does imply that there was nothing freakish about his demeanor.

Before heading for Saint Mary's in 1695, John Hoar had commanded private warships and plundered the French during King William's War. Again, one has to sympathize with Governor Benjamin Fletcher, much put upon for granting Hoar a privateering commission. As Fletcher told the Board of Trade, the captain had done his duty all the other times he went out against the French. How could Fletcher have known that this time he would turn pirate?[3]

The governors of Rhode Island and Massachusetts might have given the same excuse after John Halsey took the *Charles* to Saint Mary's in 1705. Halsey had successfully commanded privateers in the past, and he had been given the *Charles* by a consortium of shrewd Puritan merchants. When told that colonial governors were intimate with "pirates," a modern reader may think of Captain Hook or some other odd fictional creature. In fact, pirates were normal in appearance and mien. They stand out because they were willing to sail thousands of miles and take extraordinary risks in the hope, often fulfilled, of making their fortune.

Even more so than captains, we usually hear about crewmen only when they were practicing their profession of piracy. Exceptionally, the records provide a glimpse into the private lives of former pirates settling on Réunion Island.[4] By the 1700s, Réunion was the favorite refuge for pirates who did not want to remain on Madagascar. After the English courts reneged on an offer of pardon in 1699, the men were leery of English colonies. French officials on Réunion, in contrast, were eager to accept pirate settlers as long as they ceased from robbery and recognized the Roman Catholic faith.

Life on Réunion was much like that on Madagascar. Men were expected to grow food and tropical products for export. But most pirates retired with substantial booty, allowing them to purchase black servants and slaves to do the hardest work. With its brief history and limited population, Réunion had not yet developed the rigid social hierarchy found in Europe and North America. Sexual mores were only slightly less permissive than among the Malagasy, as the government left it up to each family to police its members' behavior. Since illegitimacy was common, it seems likely than many men and women did not interfere with their spouses' promiscuity.

A pirate taking his loot to Réunion found plenty of companions. Between 1667 and 1714, government censuses counted a total of 121 male

heads of families living on Réunion. No fewer than forty-four, or one
third, were former pirates.[5] Twenty-two landed in 1686, six of whom
became permanent settlers. Seventy pirates, loaded with gold, got off the
warship commanded by Henry Every in 1695. Some took the next ship for
Europe stopping at Réunion, but thirteen settled for good.[6] At least two
more men arrived in 1699, and John Bowen dropped off four or more during a visit in 1701. Bowen himself and forty crewmen took refuge at Réunion in 1704—though some again continued on to Europe.[7] At least
fourteen others landed with Captain Thomas White two years later.[8]

There is no reason to think these men were significantly different from
the thousands of others marauding from Madagascar. Not everyone going
to Réunion was French and Catholic. The island's governors required
merely that Protestants—whatever their nationality—sign a formal statement abjuring heretical beliefs. That taken care of, no one asked about a
man's beliefs or insisted that he attend Mass. Their decision to go to Réunion is the greatest difference between these men and those that lived out
their lives among the Malagasy. And this choice was a matter of personal
taste, not of social origins.

PIRACY: A TEMPORARY CAREER FOR YOUNG MEN ON THE MAKE

Piracy was a young man's game. On average, the men were about thirty
years old as they retired on Réunion Island.[9] One was just seventeen, nineteen were in their twenties, and fifteen were thirty-something; only two
were in their forties. When they purchased slaves and land on Réunion,
most former pirates had large amounts of gold, so they may have been at sea
for some years and probably enlisted in their early twenties. Significantly,
pirates tended to be all much the same age. The range was wider on merchant vessels, which employed both a larger number of older men and more
cabin boys under nineteen.[10] In 1722, instead of continuing on to Madagascar, some mariners unwisely decided to remain off the African coast
with Captain Bartholomew Rogers. Fifty-two of these men were captured
and hanged; they were only twenty-four years old on average.[11]

The pirates' relative youth is significant. The Saint Mary's raiders could
endure months at sea—always without creature comforts and often without
adequate food—because they were at the height of their physical powers
and stamina. Their comparative youth also helps to explain why they took
off on multiyear cruises without hesitation. A man in his early twenties

probably was not married and had relatively few ties at home. Once aboard ship, he and his comrades formed an independent society. Perhaps the best comparison is to today's collegiate and professional athletic squads. Under the leadership of a charismatic older captain, relationships were characterized by tight male bonding. The men lived, worked, and suffered as a team. They also celebrated their shared triumphs with boisterous parties.

At least in the Indian Ocean, pirates were not the scum of the earth, as often is assumed. Although most probably were seamen, a significant minority had had careers on land before they turned sea raiders. Believing Guy Dumesnil's story that he was the noble lord of Darentières (now in Belgium), the governor of French India acted as godfather to Dumesnil's son.[12] Five others were skilled craftsmen, including a clockmaker and an engraver. Half of all the men retiring at Réunion could read and write. Jacques de Lattre was a remarkable linguist, fluent and also literate in six or seven European languages plus Malagasy. Only three had been soldiers, perhaps because most military forts were located inland.[13]

In order to become a pirate, a man first had to find a ship heading for the Indian Ocean. Sea rovers came from many nations and every social level—but almost always from a seafaring community. Some were born in pirate ports, from which their families had marauded for generations. In any coastal town, everyone was involved one way or another with water-borne commerce. Landowners and craftsmen were aware of both the rewards and the dangers of the sea to a degree unknown to men born far inland.[14] Most pirates were born in Atlantic ports in Europe and the American colonies. Several are known to have resided on Caribbean islands before heading for the Indian Ocean.

Grants of amnesty by Réunion's governors were illegal. In fact, French law even prohibited islanders from selling provisions to pirates. But the governors all came to tolerate trading with pirates and accepted them as settlers. Réunion desperately needed manpower. The French East India Company did not try to recruit settlers, and the passengers on vessels stopping at Réunion preferred to continue on to India, where there was a higher probability of prosperity.

Réunion's policy of toleration was based on more than expediency. Experience had proved that former marauders made excellent settlers. Most invested in land and were more or less successful as planters. Only a few joined the island's other drunks, who impregnated their own daughters and lay around in the streets calling out obscene curses at passers by.[15]

Réunion's governors could ignore idleness and incest. It was more important to them that former pirates were less likely than other colonists to commit crimes of violence against their neighbors. No doubt, their experiences aboard overcrowded vessels had taught them how to get along without quarrels. The democracy of pirate communities similarly instilled habits of toleration and respect for other members of the community.

Far from seeing them as violent criminals, Réunion's governors treated retired pirates as naive men who might easily become victims. Understanding the people he governed, Governor Joseph Beauvollier de Courchant's primary concern was protecting former pirates from the greed of the island's inhabitants. On January 10, 1721, the governor issued a decree regulating how much islanders could charge the new settlers for food and housing. In return for a payment of fifteen piasters a month, each man was guaranteed a dwelling without leaks as well as a sturdy mattress, a pillow, and a blanket. Except on fast days, his host was ordered to furnish soup and boiled or roast meat as well as half a bottle of the local brew.[16]

The only critics were missionaries of the Lazarist religious order, who complained that the pirates were enjoying the fruits of sin. However, the authorities in Paris were enraged by and wholly rejected the Lazarists' protests. Marriage, the East India Company told Réunion's governor, undoubtedly provided the best means of taming the pirates and preventing them from taking up their old profession. The Lazarists were nothing but troublemakers; to stop their whining, the governor was ordered to exclude them from the island's political council.[17]

IN NORTH AMERICA, FORMER PIRATES MELT INTO THE CROWD, ESCAPING PUNISHMENT

Réunion's experience with former pirates is especially well documented. But other localities where pirates retired to enjoy their hard-earned booty experienced equally few difficulties. During the 1690s, many men returned to North America or Europe after a successful voyage. They soon were reabsorbed into the population.

English officials collecting revenues in the colonies wrote letter after letter, becoming almost hysterical in their criticism of colonial governors said to tolerate former pirates. Edward Randolph, surveyor of customs, sent a long report to the Board of Trade in August 1696, complaining that pirates were accepted in one colony after another.

Carolina.—Abut three years ago seventy pirates . . . came to Charleston with a vast quantity of gold from the Red Sea. They were entertained and had liberty to stay or go to any place. . . . *Pennsylvania.*—William Markham, a very infirm man, is Governor. . . . Several known pirates are allowed to live and trade there. *Rhode Island.*—Caleb Carr, an illiterate person, was lately Governor. It is now a free port for pirates. . . .[18]

Governor Markham of Pennsylvania came under attack almost as harshly as Fletcher of New York. Markham, it was said, not only gave sanctuary to Henry Every's men; he even allowed his daughter to marry one of Every's crew.

Five or six vessels (as is reported) are come from the Red Sea; some are gone southward towards Carolina and Providence. I doubt not to hear later that some of them have touched at Pennsylvania, where Mr. Markham continues their steady friend. He entertained and countenanced some of Every's men; he had the Lords Justices' proclamation against them but after that let two of them go to Carolina, and the other two are in the province. One of them, Claus, a Dane, keeps a shop in Philadelphia; I saw him every day. Another of them, James Brown, is married to Markham's daughter, and lives near Newcastle if he be not dead.[19]

Taken at face value, these complaints seem to prove the governors were corrupt. Perhaps so. But they also are evidence that—on land, at least—pirates tended to be indistinguishable from their neighbors. Even the East India Company, a fierce foe of piracy, sometimes hired former pirates for its stations in India. In 1691, while the *Jacob* was cruising along India's west coast, the majority of the crew fired William Mason and elected a new captain. Mason and eighteen others left the ship at Mangalore and went to work for the East India Company. They proved to be as law-abiding as other Company employees.[20]

This is not to deny that pirates were a special breed of men. During an era when few men and women traveled more than a few miles from their native villages, Saint Mary's men left their homes for many months, even years. Luxuries were rare on pirate cruisers. Both the crewmen and officers put up with crowded ships, sleeping on hammocks or on deck. They endured limited food supplies that often ran out on the way to Saint Mary's.

With deft skill and arduous labor, the men survived storms, avoided shoals, and escaped warships. At sea, they formed a close-knit community, whose members relied on each other for their lives. Despite their democratic ways, the pirates ran a tight ship. The myth that they were lazy and drunken louts is debunked by the reports of those taken prisoner. Captives were struck by the cleanliness and good order of pirate vessels as well as by the crew's constant practice with weapons.[21]

Having reached their hunting area, marauders tried to take their prey by surprise and without fighting. Pirates were not soldiers trying to kill an enemy; they merely wanted to make money, something a dead man cannot enjoy. Cannon and other long-distance weapons rarely were used, since these might sink the prey. Pirates instead tried to board and frighten defenders into surrender through a show of fierce savagery.

Hard as they tried, though, pirates could not always avoid fighting. On several occasions, these men—who were not professional soldiers—took over larger and more heavily armed vessels. Henry Every, Dirk Chivers, and Ralph Stout attacked and vanquished ships armed with large cannon and defended by Indian troops. At that time, Europeans considered it only natural that a few Englishmen would crush hundreds of Indians. In fact, the Indian emperor's armies were manned by well-trained solders, including many fierce warriors form Afghanistan. In any case, pirate vessels also took on and defeated ships of the English East India Company.

Sea rovers have come to be stereotyped as either heartless fiends or drooling idiots. But their history is much more interesting than a record of deviates. Pirates were normal men. They achieved ambitious and extraordinary goals by exceeding the normal limits men usually impose on themselves.

CHAPTER THIRTEEN

THE PEACEFUL DEMOCRACY OF LIBERTALIA

A sailing ship's company might be isolated at sea for months at a time. The men on board formed a natural community, an independent society with its individual system of rules and regulations. The Madagascar marauders shared many customs with other mariners. They stand out because they imposed democracy upon themselves both while at sea and at Saint Mary's. Moreover, their democratic system maintained good order at Saint Mary's for more than three decades.

The Saint Mary's pirates lived in harmony with the Malagasy, and they kept on good terms with colonial governors both in North America and in the Indian Ocean. They also got along remarkably well with each other. With thousands of young, physically active men passing through for more than thirty years, altercations and quarrels were inevitable, but there is no evidence of internecine violence. Men did come to dislike each other, but they worked out their difficulties, partly through the ritualized duels prescribed by ships' articles.

Perhaps the pirates lived in peace with each other because life on Saint Mary's was pleasant. Those with a liking for brawls also were aware that their opponents were likely to be armed, and they may have remembered that they had to live on a small island together with their fellows. For whatever reason, the criminals on Saint Mary's did not commit crimes against each other.

In the twenty-first century, when one-man, one-vote is a universal religion, it is important to understand how radical this form of government was in 1700.[1] Everyone who encountered the pirates was struck by the democratic way in which they governed themselves. Mauritius was among the places where the men sold their loot. The island's governor reported that "Every man had as much say as the captain, and each man carried his own weapons in a blanket."[2] An entire community governed by consensus would be unusual today. The pirates' fierce independence seemed fantastic to visitors from the hierarchical societies in Europe and North America.

The pirates created a way of life totally unlike anything back home or on other vessels. Richard Lazenby was captured by John Taylor's *Victory*. Used to the East India Company's despotic rules, Lazenby writes with amazement of men who openly debated their plans. Captured by Taylor at a later date, the Dutchman Jacob de Bucquoy was equally astonished by a ship in which crewmen elected and could fire their officers at any time, even while the ship was at sea.[3]

Seventeenth- and eighteenth-century merchant ships were as authoritarian as naval vessels. Officers lived apart from common seamen, treated them as inferiors, and literally drove them with whips. Ships were one-man dictatorships, with all power flowing down from the captain. Mates, gunners, boatswains, surgeons—each had a specific authority inherent in their formal roles, and these inferior officers exercised considerable power over the men. But even the chief mate was perpetually under the captain's control. The situation was no different aboard the private warships known as privateers. Captain Woodes Rogers was a successful privateer captain and later governor of the Bahamas. Rogers was considered unusual because he followed a policy of consulting with his senior officers.[4]

Because captains had absolute power over the officers and seamen of their ships, they could make life as tolerable or unbearable as they wished. Their authority was guaranteed by law, upheld in the Admiralty Courts, and embodied in the wage contract signed by each seaman.[5] Some compared the captain to a king, but the captain's authority was in fact greater than that of the English monarch, who by now shared power with Parliament. The captain's authority was just as absolute on vessels of other nations. In Dutch colonies, a sailor striking an officer was flogged and sentenced to many years of hard labor while bearing heavy chains.[6]

Conditions on board merchant vessels may have been less harsh and dictatorial during the Middle Ages. By the 1680s, however, captains routinely imposed their tyranny through intimidation, calculated viciousness, and physical torture. Many literally got away with murder, when seamen died of inadequate food and overwork. When all else failed, officers beat crewmen with their fists, canes, ropes, belts, sticks, and whatever else came to hand.

Some captains copied the Royal Navy and held formal floggings with the cruel cat-o'-nine-tails. The East India Company maintained such severe discipline that the quarterdeck (where floggings were administered) sometimes ran red with so much blood that it resembled a slaughter house.[7]

There supposedly were limits to a captain's power to assault his men, and the Admiralty Court sometimes punished excessively brutal masters. But with ships away from England for years at a time, men were long dead before they could file charges before the court. Rebellion and mutiny were the only effective check on a captain's powers. The crews of several ships claimed that they turned pirate to escape unbearable hazings and brutal floggings. The evidence suggests that they were telling the truth.

Saint Mary's men were fiercely independent even compared to earlier pirates. Among the Caribbean buccaneers, captains still treated crewmen as subordinates. They kept some of the booty to pay for the use of their vessels and also took a larger cut for themselves. At Saint Mary's, everything was divided into shares of equal value, and the officers received only a little more than the men.

To limit the captain's influence, some of his powers were transferred to the quartermaster. Only the quartermaster could punish a crewman (after a vote by the crew), and he also guarded the plunder and supervised the final share out. If the pirates kept a captured ship, the quartermaster usually became its captain. This system of dual command was unique to the pirates. It was deliberately intended, they told captives, to keep any one man from gaining too much power.

This trend toward absolute democracy began during the 1680s, as the Caribbean buccaneers undertook multiyear voyages to South America's Pacific coast. With every port inhabited by their enemies, crews could not tolerate incompetent officers. Making decisions by consensus became a habit that grew even stronger at Saint Mary's where the pirates themselves formed the only government for Europeans.

SHIP'S ARTICLES: BLUEPRINT FOR LIBERTY

The Saint Mary's rules of governance were enshrined in the ship's articles, which had become virtually miniature constitutions by the 1720s. Before beginning a new cruise or expedition, the entire ship's company came together. Each man swore a solemn oath to obey the rules, usually with his hand on a Bible. He then signed or, if illiterate, made his mark. The meeting frequently turned festive, with men pledging the company and each other in multiple bowls of native toke or rum punch. A man enlisting with the company during the voyage also signed the existing articles, but a new set of articles was prepared if men broke away and joined a different vessel.

The Madagascar marauders used the institutions they inherited, modifying them to meet their special needs. Articles were an ancient device, which originally were mainly concerned with money matters. At the end of the seventeenth century, English merchant seamen generally signed a wage contract. This specified the nature and length of the voyage and the wages offered. In addition, the contract usually contained a formal promise of obedience to the captain's commands.

The English government allowed pillage by private warships under certain conditions, and the men aboard these "privateers" also signed agreements. Under the principle of "no purchase, no pay," they received no wages but instead took some of whatever booty was brought home. But the crew's share was only a small fraction of the take. The government demanded twenty-five to thirty percent off the top, and the fees of the Admiralty Court swallowed up as much as another twenty-five percent.[8] Then half to two-thirds of the remainder was taken by those owning and supplying the ship. The crew divided what was left, but officers received four to ten times as much as seamen.

Between 1708 and 1711, Woodes Rogers commanded a triumphant privateering squadron that captured one of the fabled Manila Galleons—the first English ships to do so since 1587. The voyage was atypical for another reason as well: Instead of Captain Rogers imposing his own will, all major decisions were made by a committee of officers. (As usual, however, ordinary seamen had no voice.) But the ship's rich booty was distributed in standard ways. The owners of the vessels took two-thirds after taxes; one-third, split into carefully apportioned shares, went to the officers and crew.[9] Moreover, Rogers also imposed new limits on the custom of "plunder," which permitted crewmen to keep everything found on the main deck or above. Under Rogers's regulations, the senior officers decided what was plunder; the goods were split among the crews of both ships in the same proportions as their shares.[10]

ALL PROFITS ARE DIVIDED EQUALLY AMONG THE MEN
By the end of the Saint Mary's era, the pirates had overthrown totally this hierarchical system of pay. With only rare exceptions, everyone belonging to the ship's company received the same amount. The first steps toward

equal shares came in the 1650s and 1660s among the Caribbean buccaneers, according to Exquemelin, a Dutch surgeon who served with them. Before sailing, Exquemelin says, the buccaneers signed an agreement, primarily dealing with compensation. The ship's owners did not impose this contract; the seamen drew it up themselves "by common vote." Before dividing up the spoils, they took set amounts off the top and gave these to the wounded; a man who lost a right arm, for example, received six hundred pieces of eight (about $70,000) or six slaves. The captain then took two shares for himself and several more for the use of his ship.[11]

In 1670, Sir Henry Morgan assembled the English and French buccaneers for a plunder raid on Panama City. It is noteworthy that the captains imposed their rules on Morgan. Even though this was a privateering raid licensed by the governor of Jamaica, the booty was split up in the more democratic fashion followed by the buccaneers. After compensating the wounded, captains took eight shares for the use of their ships and two for themselves; everyone else received one share. However, only officers signed these articles and took part in the war council that decided where and when to attack.[12]

The buccaneers followed similar rules both when they invaded the Pacific during the 1680s and later when they moved east to Saint Mary's. Obviously only coins or gold bars could be divided with rigid equality. When possible, other cargo was sold to fences, such as Adam Baldridge, and the proceeds split up. To prevent arguments, crews sometimes auctioned off merchandise of imprecise value. In 1687, after an assault on Qualaquil, Ecuador, captured goods were auctioned after the cash money had been shared out.[13] At other times, rough guesses had to be made. In 1721, raiders commanded by Edward Taylor and Oliver La Buse captured a Portuguese vessel carrying diamonds worth £500,000. Daniel Defoe says one man felt cheated because he received only one large diamond instead of forty small ones.[14]

The earliest extant articles to mention an oath upon the Bible were signed by the men of a slave ship that had mutinied near the Caribbean island of Nevis. These articles called for equal shares except for the captain (two and a half shares) and the sailing master and physician (one and a half each). The articles based their authority on the men's voluntary agreement. They promised "severe punishment" to anyone turning on the other men because all of "you have taken your corporall oath upon the holy Evangelists to stand one by the other as long as life shall last."[15]

Since the earliest raiders to visit Saint Mary's were Caribbean buccaneers, it is not surprising that their articles resemble those described by Exquemelin. As had the buccaneers' compacts, these early articles devoted the most attention to compensation and pay. One of the first to head for the Indian Ocean, Thomas Tew left Bermuda early in 1693. Tew's articles promised a share to each crewman after deducting expenses, including the customary payments to men who became maimed. Nine shares went to the ship's owners, two and a half to the captain, and one and half to the sailing master.[16]

Tew was an able and charismatic captain, who easily attracted followers. His authority was greater than was later the case, when the quartermaster became the captain's equal. Before sailing from New York in June 1696, Captain William Kidd's crewmen signed articles indicating the quartermaster's increasingly important role. Called "the company's quartermaster" throughout the document, he was elected by the crewmen to represent their interests. Perhaps they felt they needed a spokesman because of Kidd's dictatorial ways during the voyage from London to New York.

Consisting of fifteen numbered sentences, the articles were presented as an agreement between Captain Kidd and the crew's quartermaster. Nine deal with the men's pay. As usual, the food, medical supplies, and compensation to the disabled were taken off the top. The remainder was to be split into equal shares with Kidd having forty shares for himself and the use of his ship.[17]

Forty shares was an overgenerous one-fourth or more of all potential booty. Kidd had been a buccaneer in the Caribbean, where captains received six to eight shares for the use of their ship. Tew's articles gave the owners nine shares. Because his demands were so far out of line, Kidd could not find enough experienced mariners to man his ship. He ultimately filled the company with unemployed landsmen who had never before been to sea.[18]

Kidd's articles also are among the earliest to specify punishments for dereliction of duty. On merchant vessels, a captain could do as he pleased. Precisely because they had a say in running the ship, Caribbean buccaneers generally did not spell out a crewman's obligations at sea. In this case, since they did not trust Kidd, the articles specified which actions would be punishable.

A coward during battle lost his share, and anyone stealing anything worth half a piece of eight or more (about $60) would be marooned on an uninhabited island. In other cases—desertion, mutiny, drunkenness, and refusal to board the enemy—the miscreant "shall suffer what punishment ye

"Captain Avery captures the Great Mogul's Grand-daughter." An illustration for a modern edition of Daniel Defoe's novel The King of Pirates *(1903–04). See page 91.*

Safely back in London, Henry Every sells jewels looted from an Indian ship in the Red Sea.

Illustration by Howard Pyle in Harper's Monthly Magazine, September 1887. See page 90.

Captain William Kidd. Illustration by Howard Pyle in Harper's Monthly Magazine, *December 1902. See pages 129–132.*

Charles Laughton catches Randolph Scott rifling his cabin in the 1945 movie Captain Kidd. *See pages 129–130.*

Captain Kidd buries his treasure on Gardiner's Island, New York, in this imaginary scene by Howard Pyle for Harper's Monthly Magazine, *November 1894. See pages 137–138.*

Thomas Tew (left) entertaining New York Governor Benjamin Fletcher at the governor's home about 1694. Fletcher later described Captain Tew as "agreeable and companionable." Illustration by Howard Pyle in Harper's Monthly Magazine, *November 1894. See page 158.*

Errol Flynn and Maureen O'Hara in Against All Flags *(1952), a movie supposedly set at Diego Suarez in Madagascar. In fact, the movie's plot very loosely refers to Thomas Warren's visit to Saint Mary's Island in 1699. See pages 170–173.*

"And So the Treasure was Divided." Illustration by Howard Pyle in Harper's Monthly Magazine, *December 1905. See pages 168–169.*

"Marooned." Illustration by Howard Pyle in Harper's Monthly Magazine, *December 1905. See page 172.*

Bartholomew Roberts. In the background are his Royal Fortune and Ranger and the eleven merchantmen Roberts captured off the African coast in January 1722. Each of Roberts' vessels displays a different flag, contrary to the myth that all pirates flew the Jolly Roger. From the second edition of the General History of the Pyrates (1725) by Daniel Defoe. See page 229.

Capt. and ye company Quarter-Master shall think fitt, and shall have no share."[19] During the voyage, Kidd proved to be even more despotic than the crew had feared; he punished men harshly—even murdering one seaman— and without consulting the quartermaster. Because of Kidd's overbearing tyranny, almost a hundred men deserted him when the ship reach Saint Mary's Island.

Kidd's articles were transitional. In later years, articles became more detailed and thus more diverse. However, they uniformly insisted that every major decision must be made by a majority vote of all crewmen. The captain had no more say than any other man. Everyone had to abide by the crew's decisions about where to cruise, whether to attack a vessel, and when to break up the company.

More than anything else, the men wanted to overturn the dictatorship of naval and merchant captains. It was not enough to empower the quartermaster as a counterweight to the captain. Every man was to have a voice. It is safe to assume that this principle was more honored on smaller vessels; on those with crews of several hundred, some men inevitably were more influential than others. Nevertheless, the ship's articles proposed equality as their fundamental principle.

Equality brought responsibilities. Even if he disagreed with them, anyone signing the articles had to accept the majority's decisions. The ship's company was a voluntary association formed by an oath that imposed indelible obligations. No one could be forced to join. But having taken the oath, no one could leave before the voyage's conclusion without the permission of the other men.

The oath itself was a crucial part of the entire procedure. Men at that time attached an enormous importance to oaths, particularly those sworn on the Bible or, in Catholic countries, on the relics of a saint or other sacred talisman. There was a sense, now lost, that a man who broke his word was beneath contempt. While on earth, an oath breaker put himself outside the law and could be killed on sight. After death, because he had profaned the holy things to which he had pledged loyalty, he was eternally damned.[20]

In signing the ship's articles, every man pledged to obey the rules they contained. Over time, the articles became lengthier, as they increasingly forbade behavior that would endanger the other men. Since the crew and not the captain made the important decisions, the men felt free to restrict their own behavior. The number of such rules increased to the point that some articles resembled miniature constitutions.

Although their intentions are similar, the surviving articles differ in details. These differences are proof of the importance attached to a ship's articles. The men did not simply copy the articles used on prior voyages. They discussed the usefulness of various provisions, adding and deleting as seemed best to the company. Every agreement insists that important matters must be settled by a vote of the entire crew. However, even though booty was divided equally in practice, some contracts did not include a provision specifically mandating equal shares. Equal division may have been taken for granted. Under democratic rules, moreover, the men could vote someone an extra share whenever this seemed right to the majority.

The pirates intended their articles to be secret, and the contents are known by accident. Raiders sometimes, for example, carried away educated men who later described their captors' way of life. In 1721, John Taylor and Oliver La Buse took extraordinarily rich plunder at the Comoros and Réunion Islands. Learning that an English naval squadron was on its way to Saint Mary's, the two vessels went to Mozambique and occupied a Dutch fort at Delagoa Bay. When he went back to Madagascar, Taylor took with him Jacob de Bucquoy, a Dutch engineer who remained his prisoner for several months. Taylor was himself an educated man, and he often had long talks with his captive.[21]

The code of the *Victory,* Taylor's warship, begins by emphasizing that a man's only family and homeland are his comrades in the ship's company. Everyone outside the association is an enemy to be plundered; those resisting should be killed. Other articles placed restrictions on the men in their dealings with each other and with their victims. These were designed, Bucquoy says, to maintain peace aboard ship and to stir up courage against the enemy—an apt summary of all such codes.

When a ship is taken, the *Victory*'s articles continue, those surrendering are guaranteed their lives; anyone killing or wounding them should be put to death. Without exception, everything found aboard the prize must be turned over the quartermaster. No man should be forced to join their group, and the rape of a woman is punished by death. Captured ships should be scuttled, but only after putting ashore the crew and especially any women. (Keeping women off the ship helped to prevent jealousy and quarrels, but it also reflected a real dislike of rape, which was considered abhorrent at that time.)

Furthermore, under pain of death, a man must keep the faith and assist his comrades. A slow death is prescribed for deserters, those leaving the company without permission. After their noses and ears are cut, they are to be abandoned totally naked on a deserted island. To limit altercations, discussions about religion and gambling for money are prohibited.

The quartermaster was responsible for enforcing these rules. When a crime was committed or suspected, the quartermaster assembled a jury of twelve men, half of them chosen by the defendant. The quartermaster imposed the jury's sentence, without partiality toward his own friends. When a serious quarrel arose, the captain and the quartermaster presided at a duel to the death.[22]

Captain Taylor and many of men began their cruise in the Bahamas, but it is pointless to ask whether the men drew up these articles at Nassau or at Saint Mary's. The articles of Caribbean pirates during the 1720s resemble those aboard the *Victory* with some variations. Those of Edward Low permit gambling but punish cheaters, and they forbid "snapping" guns in the ship's hold.[23] Bartholomew Roberts's articles also sought to prevent fires by mandating that all lights and candles be extinguished at eight o'clock; after that hour, moreover, drinking was allowed only on deck. To limit fights, Roberts's articles prohibited keeping young boys as well as women aboard ship.[23] The articles of Low and Roberts leave punishments to a majority of the crew; the provision for jury trials in Taylor's articles is uncommon.

Instead of death or marooning, the articles drawn up in 1727 by Captain Dulaïen's corsairs contain a fittingly symbolic punishment for crimes endangering the entire crew. A man guilty of quarreling, stupefying drunkenness, theft, and sleeping while on watch was tied down to a canon while everyone else on board gave him one lash with a rope's end.[25] (If the crew were numerous, this might well have been a punishment worse than death.)

THE IMMORTAL PIRATE CAPTAINS

Pirate fiction and films are mischievously misleading about the nature and exploits of marauders. But the legends are right about one thing: Piracy is a story of outstanding captains. Captains also take pride of place in firsthand accounts by raiders and their captives. In stressing the captain's actions, these historical documents reflect the realities of life at sea. Since decisions must be made rapidly, there must be one recognized authority aboard any ship. Pirate vessels also needed discipline, even though they were governed in radically democratic ways.

Perversely, the very social equality aboard pirate ships actually made captains stand out more sharply from their followers. Governments appointed naval commanders; the captains of merchantmen were hired by the ships' owners. In both cases, second-rate men could survive by whipping the crew into obedience. A pirate captain, in contrast, stayed in business only if men freely volunteered to join his cruise. At sea, he maintained order by persuading and motivating his crew. Merely to survive in office, a captain had to have a strong, assertive, and commanding personality.

Given the nature of a pirate's occupation, navigational skills probably were less important than mastery of naval combat and the ability to inspire the men. So long as one takes into account the timing of a monsoon, the Indian Ocean is a comparatively gentle and forgiving sea. Although none was the equal in seamanship of the most talented buccaneers or Barbary corsairs, some East Indies captains were skilled mariners. Others, recognizing their deficiencies, named a sailing master from among the crew or employed a master kidnapped from one of their prizes.

The men marauding in the Indian Ocean were aware that they needed an authority figure who could unite the crew and lead it to victory. Few thought of doing away with the office of captain. During the Saint Mary's era, only the *Charming Mary*'s crew tried the experiment of operating without a captain.[26] But the men were adamant in wanting to limit the captain's power to abuse and cheat them.

To restrain would-be dictators, the pirates created a system of dual command, taking away some of the captain's authority and giving it to the quartermaster. And they insisted that a majority of the crew could override decisions by both the captain or the quartermaster. As a final resort, the crew could fire any officer, including the captain, at any time during the cruise. These policies first evolved during the raids on South America in the 1680s. They were universally adopted at Saint Mary's by the buccaneers who had made the long journey east. Highly democratic practices were then carried back to North America and adopted aboard the warships marauding from the Bahamas in 1716 and 1717.[27]

The Caribbean buccaneers already had taken steps to prevent captains assuming airs as if they were superior to the men. These egalitarian habits increased after the pirates set up camp at Madagascar. Observers used to vessels of the Royal Navy and East India Company found it astounding that the pirates gave captains no special privileges. Captain Snelgrave, himself a merchant captain, noted with displeasure that the officers slept on deck with the men, "the Captain himself not being allowed a Bed."[28] When food ran short, supplies were put under the care of the quartermaster, who discharges all things with an Equality to them all, every Man and Boy faring alike; and even their Captain, or any other Officer, is allowed no more than another Man; nay, the Captain cannot keep his own Cabin to himself, for their Bulk-heads are all down, and every Man stands to his Quarters, where they lie and mess.[29]

There is no evidence that the early Caribbean buccaneers ever took the final step in asserting the crew's authority by firing a captain. Cruises in the Caribbean rarely lasted for more than a few months; men dissatisfied with their current captain could afford to wait and leave the ship when it returned to Port Royal or Tortuga. The change came during the 1680s. Successive waves of buccaneers either walked across the Isthmus of Panama or sailed around Cape Horn to attack South America's Pacific coast. Either route was dangerous and best attempted only by a group. A seaman returning to the Caribbean might have to wait months until another expedition departed. From the beginning, therefore, the raiders insisted that *they* elected the captain, and they could replace him to ensure the expedition's success.

The first company to cross Panama to the Pacific set out early in 1680, leaving their ships behind. John Coxon became captain of the unified force through election, as John Ayre makes clear in his 1684 history of the expedition.

Gold was the bait that tempted a pack of merry boys of us, near three hundred in number, being all soldiers of fortune, under command (by our own election) of Captain John Coxon, to list ourselves in the service of one of the richest West Indian monarchs, the Emperor of Darien.[30]

The raiders reached Panama City but were too few to take the city by force. When dissidents accused Coxon of cowardice, he resigned as captain and went back to the Caribbean. Another captain was chosen but then killed leading an attack.

John Sharp was elected as the expedition's third leader and went south along the Pacific coast in a captured vessel. In January 1681, Sharp reached the Juan Fernandez Islands, intending to go back to the Caribbean via Cape Horn. But many had lost their booty at cards and dice. To guarantee that the cruise would continue, the crew turned Sharp out and elected another man as captain.[31] The men apparently feared that Sharp, his voyage "made," would lack ardor for future assaults. Given that the goal was booty, fervor in battle was the captain's first responsibility.

CREWMEN HIRED AND FIRED THEIR CAPTAINS

Throughout their stay at Saint Mary's, the pirates continued to assert their right to fire unsatisfactory captains, but they did not take this step lightly. Captains were ousted for crimes prohibited in the articles they had signed. Perceived cowardice and refusal to attack likely prey were a compelling justification for removal. Captains also left and were deposed when there were disagreements over fundamental matters, such as whether to continue a cruise. On one occasion, Captain Robert Culliford resigned because he was eager to attack an East Indiaman, but the men thought the challenge too daunting.[32]

As Sharp had been, Robert Glover was ousted because he wanted to end the cruise prematurely. Glover brought the *Resolution* from Rhode Island in 1695 and cruised for a year with little success. At the end of 1696, the *Resolution* reached northwestern India. The ship was in poor shape, and Captain Glover decided to ride the northeast monsoon back to Saint Mary's. Dirk Chivers and others instead wanted to continue on south and then turn east toward China. After Chivers's group won the vote and dismissed Glover, the men allowed him to go back to Saint Mary's in a captured Indian vessel.[33]

Captain Edward England also was treated relatively gently. After a bitter debate, England convinced the crew to release the captured captain of the *Cassandra*—contrary to the ship's articles, which imposed the death penalty on those resisting capture. The captain got home, took command of a naval squadron, and began to chase his erstwhile captors. Blaming England for all their troubles, the men fired him and set him down either at the Mauritius Island or on Madagascar's northeastern coast.[34]

Sometimes a captain was accused of cowardice when he was right to be careful. Cruising in the Red Sea in 1707, John Halsey met with a much larger Dutch vessel coming from Mocha. The crew thought it was a merchantman; Halsey was sure it was a heavily armed warship. After tailing the Dutch ship for a week, the men deposed Halsey. Just then, the Dutchman fired a broadside. Realizing that he had judged the situation accurately, the crew reelected Halsey by acclamation.[35]

Desertion from the company naturally led to dismissal. John Taylor and Oliver La Buse were off the Mozambique coast in the *Cassandra* and *Nostra*

Senhora de Cabo. The crews of the two vessels formed one company, the *Cassandra* and *Cabo* being but their most recent conquests. La Buse and some of his officers plotted to slip away and take the *Cabo* to the West Indies. When the plot was discovered, all the men were called together and deprived La Buse of his office. He and the other conspirators were flogged at the main mast and lost their shares of the booty.[36] The ship's articles actually called for an even harsher punishment—marooning on an uninhabited island.

Dishonesty in sharing out the booty was grounds for severe punishment. In 1691, Samuel Burgess was left behind at Saint Augustine's Bay because the crew believed he had cheated them as quartermaster.[37] The company had not yet taken a prize, but the crew apparently believed that a man who was deceitful about provisions would also cheat them in distributing booty.

In addition, the unlettered salts among the crew also may have been suspicious of Burgess because of his relatively greater education.[38] Captain Snelgrave, who was captured off West Africa in 1719, relates the story of seamen mislead by an unscrupulous but apparently lettered captain. Repenting of their actions, they marooned the captain and some others in an open boat while at sea. They then elected Thomas Cocklyn as captain precisely because of "his Brutality and Ignorance; having resolved never to have again a Gentleman-like Commander."[39]

THE QUARTERMASTER'S EXTRAORDINARY POWERS

Firing the captain was an extreme step, one that might lead to disaster if he were the only navigator aboard a ship. To prevent a captain from misusing his authority and cheating the men, the Madagascar pirates delegated countervailing powers to the quartermaster, who had the final say in his own areas of command. On most vessels, the captain had unlimited authority during battles, but he was subject to the quartermaster in many routine matters. In this way, as Walter Kennedy explained at his trial, pirate crews avoided putting too much power in one man's hands.[40]

As was the captain, the quartermaster was elected by the crew and received an extra share when the booty was divided. If the pirates kept a captured ship, the quartermaster often took over as its captain. He protected the seamen against each other by maintaining order, settling quarrels, and distributing food and other essentials. The quartermaster had responsibility for maintaining all supplies, which could be taken only with his permission.[41] Serious crimes were tried by jury, but the quartermaster could punish minor offenses.

The quartermaster took part in all battles and often led boarding-party attacks. If the pirates won, he decided what loot to take. He was required to seize gold, silver, and jewels. But he took more bulky cargo at his discretion, depending on storage space and distance from markets. He guarded the plunder until it was distributed, and he supervised the final share-out of goods at the masthead.[42]

The quartermaster also protected the men against a cunning captain who might take advantage of his office. In matters under the quartermaster's control, the captain obeyed him just like any other member of the company. Captain Snelgrave describes an incident during his captivity. Among his possessions were three secondhand waistcoats, embroidered with colorful designs. "As they were going on Shore amongst the Negroe-Ladies," the three pirate captains took the coats to impress their mistresses. Snelgrave says this angered all the crew, who greatly feared

> If they suffered such things, the Captains would for the future assume a Power, to take whatever they liked for themselves." So, upon their returning on board next Morning, the Coats were taken from them, and put into the common Chest, to be sold at the Mast.[43]

The pirates at Madagascar perfected if they did not invent this system of divided command. On merchant or naval ships, the quartermaster was not even an officer. The post was given to an experienced seaman who received an additional shilling or two per month to assist the mates. He provided an extra hand in storing supplies, coiling cables, and steering the vessel.[44]

The Caribbean buccaneers did not give the quartermaster special powers or extra shares of booty, according to A. O. Exquemelin, who wrote in the early 1670s. The quartermaster rose in status during the raids on South America's Pacific coast. In 1681, John Cook was considered second-in-command as quartermaster and had first claim on any captured ship.[45] At about this time, the crewmen elected the quartermaster when they elected the captain. While the captain saw to navigation and commanded in battle, the quartermaster devoted himself especially to representing the interests of the men in dealings with the captain and owners. Captain Kidd's articles in June 1696 were presented as a contract between Kidd and "the company's quartermaster."

Although this represented a large step in elevating the office, the quartermaster had not yet become the captain's equal. The final step—making the quartermaster supreme in certain things—was taken at Saint Mary's during the 1690s. Samuel Burgess had charge of all provisions and booty in 1693. Similarly, when the crew took over the East Indian *Mocha,* James Kelley was elected quartermaster and given control of 150,000 rupees (about $7 million) found on the ship.[46]

This new concept spread rapidly because the Madagascar pirates were surprisingly well informed about events on other vessels. Ships often hunted in packs, and they docked at havens like Saint Mary's, where men freely left one company and enlisted with another. The greater prestige and increased powers were retained by quartermasters operating from the Bahamas in 1716 and 1717. However, the system was still not well known to the outside world as late as the 1720s. Captive mariners—well-informed men such as Snelgrave and Bucquoy—commented on the quartermaster's role as something unique to the pirates. They took pains to describe his powers at length, treating them as a new and unheard of phenomenon.[47]

The order and tranquility at Saint Mary's did not pass unnoticed. Most commentators have been dumbfounded by this peaceful pirate state precisely because its existence contradicts the standard mythology about pirates. According to legend, these enemies of humanity were psychopathic monsters who rejected every rule of decency and wallowed in brutish depravity. How then did they live in happy peace with royal governors and native kings as well as with each other?

At the time, observers found it relatively easy to explain away toleration of former pirates by English governors. North American officials simply attributed this to the shameless greed of their political enemies. Their European contemporaries also had no difficulty in understanding why the pirates were on good terms with the Malagasy. For nonpirate Europeans, the latter were heathen savages almost as immoral as the pirates.

MARAUDER AND MALAGASY CONTRIBUTIONS TO THE RISE OF A PIRATE NATION

But why were the pirates able to govern themselves efficiently and without the violent tumults found in other English-speaking lands? Those who remain convinced that pirates were stupid brutes also believe that they could not have invented a tranquil democracy on their own—that they must have borrowed or copied their rules from some nonpiratical source.

The pirate's communitarian tradition commonly is attributed to the tradition of Protestant dissent in England. The dissenting denominations operated apart from the established state or "Anglican" church. From the 1630s, the dissenters had tried to impose their views by force, leading to the English Revolution. In 1645, military leaders cut off the head of King Charles I, and Oliver Cromwell ruled England until his death in 1658.

When the monarchy was reestablished in 1660, restoration governments repressed political agitators, but they did not try to impose religious uniformity. Along with Jews, Roman Catholics, and nonbelievers, Protestant dissenters were excluded from Parliament, local governments, and the universities; but their private religious services were tolerated. In England and her colonies, these religious groups are said to have preserved a tradition of democratic governance. And it is this tradition that ostensibly was copied by the pirates.

"In adopting a command structure based on mutual concurrence," Professor Barry Burg writes,

> pirates were again employing ideas and practices that were a part of their accumulated class experience. In the south of England and in colonial towns where future captains were raised, dissenters from the Church of England had been using egalitarian methods to govern their parish churches for almost one hundred years. . . .
>
> Dissenters chose their own ministers, ignored legally constituted ecclesiastical authority, gave legitimacy to their churches by founding them with the consent of the membership, and usually subscribed to a covenant, a set of written articles in which all agreed to worship together and observe the regulations and practices specified by their own elected elders.[48]

Radical dissent was common in English colonies in the Caribbean. Following the 1660 Restoration, English radicals who could not conform emigrated to the West Indies, especially to Barbados. When they were squeezed off that tiny island, some—including Sir Henry Morgan—went to Jamaica. There they joined the buccaneers, who were patronized by Jamaica's rulers, all former Cromwellians. A new set of governors turned against the pirates in the 1680s, so they moved to North America and from there to Madagascar.[49]

But there are many difficulties with this theory attributing pirate democracy to the men's Protestant upbringing. One problem is the fact that French Roman Catholic pirates were just as democratic as Protestant Englishmen. Exquemelin, the pirate surgeon, served with French and not English crews during the 1660s; his famous autobiography describes French practices. In 1709, a governor of Saint Dominique (modern Haiti) wanted to revive the buccaneer tradition and turn it against England and France's other enemies in wartime. To encourage recruits, he restored the principle of equal shares among the men—*à compagnon bon lot*—with the ship's suppliers receiving one-eighth or less of the total booty.[50] The pirates at Saint Mary's included a large minority of Frenchmen, almost all Roman Catholics. Of thirty French subjects retiring at Réunion Island, only three were Huguenots (French Calvinists).[51]

Most pirates probably were not motivated primarily by religious concerns—although they may have been comforted by the thought that most of their victims were not Christians of any kind. It is true that a religious upbringing in youth has a powerful influence on adult opinions. But in the case of pirates at Saint Mary's, Protestants and Catholics seems to have shared the same beliefs, whatever their education.

The problem is that such speculation assumes we know all about the pirates' families and childhood.[52] It is very rare to find, as we do at Réunion Island, information about the men's private lives. Certainly no testimony relates which books of the Bible were a pirate's preferred reading. However, we do know that both Protestants and Catholics considered the Old Testament as authoritative as the Gospels. And the Old Testament is hardly about democracy. Through Maccabees, the Old Testament is a record of chieftains, prophets, and kings leading warrior bands into battle—very much as their captains, a type of elected king, took pirate bands into combat.

Daniel Defoe, who was educated to be a Dissenting minister, took kings very seriously. His political writings espouse the rule of a charismatic warrior king, who would redeem English and European Protestantism.[53] The *General History of the Pyrates* and his other works about pirates are monarchist in their assumptions.[54] Defoe apparently could not imagine a group of men peacefully ruling themselves in an egalitarian fashion. He was convinced that every nation needs a ruler of genius to bring order into its affairs. In other words, every group needs a ruler, whose talents show that he was elected by God before he was elected by the people.[55]

In *The King of Pirates,* written in 1719, Henry Every is the king who establishes the pirate state at Saint Mary's. By the time Defoe wrote the *General History*'s second book in 1728, he had turned against Every. Here he attributes the founding of Saint Mary's to a wholly fictional Captain Misson, a Frenchman belonging to a French and English crew.

Father Caraccioli, a renegade priest, converts Misson and the other men to his ideology of rationality and human freedom. The poor live in "the most pinching Necessity" solely because of the avarice and ambition of the rich. Rebellion is the only manly answer, since rulers destroy "the People's Rights and Liberties." The crew agrees to make war on the whole world, asserting that liberty which God and Nature gave them.[56]

Elected captain, Misson leads the men during adventures in the West Indies and in Africa. Prisoners that surrender are courteously treated, and captured slaves are liberated and encouraged to join the crew, on equal terms. Misson and his men finally found a settlement on Madagascar, which they call Libertalia. The booty and cattle are divided equally among them all, and Misson's just laws ensure economic, political, and racial equality.

A native uprising destroys Captain Misson's Libertalia before its communist theories can be tested in practice. Later on in the *General History*, Defoe creates another perfect Utopia. From 1704, Captain North's crew settled for some years on Madagascar, where they were "strictly just both among themselves and in composing differences of the neighboring natives." All quarrels were tried by the Captain, assisted by judges chosen by lot. The men grew "continent and sober. . . . It's true they were all Polygamists."[57]

In real life, the pirate republic of Libertalia was not founded by Defoe's philosopher kings. It represents a natural extension of common mariner practices. There is something inherently communitarian about a small ship, whose members relied on each other for their lives. On larger vessels, men were divided into hierarchies of power and skill. However, tasks often were communal, and some could only be accomplished by many men. Even common seamen understood the purpose and rudiments of a specialist's tasks. An experienced sailor knew whether his ship was operated correctly, even if he could not navigate it himself.

Mariners shared certain traits, growing out of their unique way of life, and pirates resembled other sailors at the time they lived. Indeed, pirate crews often seem to exaggerate and even flaunt the "lifestyle" they shared with other mariners. They thought of their ship's company as separate from and generally superior to landsmen. They tended to be independent and plain-spoken (and sometimes foulmouthed). Although they had little respect for titles, they formed close bonds with individuals they trusted.

Pirates possessed these common nautical traits to an unusual degree. At sea, they were more isolated than other mariners, who could visit with passing vessels and dock at any port. This sense of alienation was expressed by Dirk Chivers when he attacked Calicut in November 1696. When asked not to destroy his fellow Englishmen, Chivers responded that the men of the *Soldado* were outside the law and owed allegiance only to themselves and their mates. They "acknowledged no countrymen, . . . they had sold their country and were sure to be hanged if taken, and that they would take no quarter, but do all they mischief they could."[58]

The pirates' isolation from other white men—both real and psychological—radically increased after 1699, when the English government cut off trade between North America and Saint Mary's. This left the island without a regular source of necessities such as gunpowder and sails. The men could trade booty for some types of naval supplies at plenty of ports in India. But the safety of these ports was transitory, and they could not be turned into permanent havens. Once back at Saint Mary's, the men depended solely upon themselves and their fellows.

Their distrust of men outside their circle was confirmed when English courts refused to honor an offer of pardon signed by the king himself. Obviously no one thought to surrender afterwards, since it was believed that any man falling into English hands would be hanged. And the men also were infuriated that a bunch of landlubberly lawyers had tricked and made fools of their comrades. Captured captains testify that the men became enraged at the mere mention of English pardon.

Under the circumstances, it is not surprising that the men clung together for support, exaggerating the democratic forms of governance inherited from the Caribbean pirates. As we have seen, communitarian and even communist practices had been widespread among the buccaneers. One of these was the relationship between two *matelots*, who shared their lives and their goods with their "messmate." Matelots pooled their possessions, fought side by side in battle, and nursed each other when ill. French missionaries wrote that matelots formed a family, just like a man and wife, but without fussing or quarreling.

Matelotage involved a voluntary relationship between two men, whereas Libertalia was inhabited by dozens and, at times, by hundreds of men. But the same egalitarian impulse engendered both.[59] Moreover, something like the democracy of Libertalia prevailed among the log cutters of Campeche and Honduras, who also were former buccaneers. A visitor in 1714 and 1715 wrote that the Baymen were hard drinkers and very quarrelsome, but that neighbors lived in common under two elected governors, much as the Red Sea pirates elected both a captain and a quartermaster.

Their short compendium of laws was—like the pirates' articles—"very severe against theft and Encroachments."[60]

Their shared life with the Betsimisaraka may also have influenced the democratic institutions of Libertalia. In contrast to the folk along Madagascar's western coast, the Betsimisaraka practiced a kind of democracy. Village chiefs were more or less hereditary, but they deliberated with those affected before taking action. To facilitate negotiations with their pirate sons-in-law, village chiefs would no doubt have wanted to deal with their counterparts among the mariners. The men met this need by electing a captain on land much as they did at sea.[61] Defoe's stories of founder kings may be colorful, but kings were not needed to invent the pirate system of governance. True to its egalitarian nature, Libertalia was created and maintained by hundreds of men over the course of more than three decades.

CHAPTER FOURTEEN

GOING IT ALONE

Despite the dispatch of battleships in 1699 and 1700, several hundred men continued to cruise from Saint Mary's and settlements on the nearby coast of Madagascar. A European government could have stopped them only by permanently stationing a naval squadron at Madagascar.

Officials in London did succeed in preventing voyages from North America to Saint Mary's. Those already at Madagascar could purchase supplies from Arab traders, European slave ships, and vessels that came from India to purchase their plunder. But seamen no longer flocked to the island from North America. From 1699 to 1719, the pirate fleet added only one American vessel, John Halsey's *Charles,* carrying fewer than one hundred men. Without new recruits, plunder raids gradually ceased as the crew of each ship decided to retire with their plunder.

Despite their isolation, the marauders managed to carry out profitable cruises prior to Halsey's arrival in 1707. When warships stopped arriving from North America, they made do by seizing merchantmen and slavers. Between 1697 and 1705, at least six slave ships were taken over while they were anchored at Saint Mary's or another port. One after another, their captains anchored near a pirate community only to lose their vessel and sometimes their lives. The profits from trading with the Madagascar marauders must have been extraordinarily high to justify taking so large a risk. In each case, the crew aboard the ship put up little resistance or even helped the pirates seize the ship. Seamen clearly considered piracy preferable to a berth on a slaver.

Because English justice had reneged on the crown's offer of pardon in 1699, few men returned to North America or Europe when they had made their fortune. Some joined trading posts in India, and a few retreated to the Dutch island of Mauritius. The largest number settled at Réunion Island,

PIRATE WARSHIPS AT SAINT MARY'S, 1699–1708

Ship	Speaker	Speedy Return	Prosperous	Defiance	Unnamed vessel	Charles	Neptune
Captain	George Booth, John Bowen	John Bowen	Thomas Howard	Nathaniel North	Thomas White	John Halsey	Samuel Burgess
1699	Slave ship *Speaker* captured						
1700	Takes Indian vessel; Bowen is captain						
1701	Plunders *Borneo*, Oct.; *Speaker* wrecked at Mauritius						
1702		Bowen's band seizes slaver *Speedy Return* at Saint Mary's; In consort with *Prosperous*	Howard seizes slaver *Prosperous*, May; goes to Saint Mary's; In consort with *Speedy Return*				
1703		Plunders *Pembroke*, March; Seize and transfer to *Defiance*	Plunders *Pembroke*, March; Seize and transfer to *Defiance*				
1704		Bowen retires at Réunion, April	Howard retires in India	Nathaniel North takes *Defiance* to Madagascar			
1705				Fate of *Defiance* not known	White seizes unspecified slaver	Leaves Rhode Island	
1706					Takes Portuguese galleon (?), *Dorothy*, *Forgiveness*; Settle at Saint Mary's or Foulpointe	Saint Augustine's Bay; Takes *Buffalo* and *Calicutt* near Malaysia, Sept.; Goes to Madagascar, picks up White's crew	
1707						Takes *Essex* and *Rising Eagle* in Red Sea, Aug.; Transfers & returns in *Eagle*	
1708					*Dorothy* sunk in storm, Jan.	*Rising Eagle* sunk in storm, Jan.	Pirates seize *Neptune*, Feb.; her subsequent fate unknown

which had no qualms about accepting former pirates. Many stayed on in small encampments among the Betsimisaraka peoples on Madagascar's northeastern coast.

CAPTAIN JOHN BOWEN LEADS THE MEN TO RICH BOOTY

During 1697, a ship came from Martinique to barter liquor and goods for slaves. At Fénérive across from Saint Mary's, ten Englishmen, led by George Booth, took over the vessel and recruited its crew. Julien Forget, the ship's incompetent captain, was left behind but managed to make it to the French colony on Réunion Island by September 1697.[1]

With George Booth as captain, the men used the French ship until they seized the *Speaker,* another, larger slave ship at the end of 1699. However, John Bowen and not Booth commanded the *Speaker* the following year when it captured an Indian vessel.[2] Defoe says that Booth captured the *Speaker* at Mathelage (now called Majunga) on Madagascar's northwest coast and took it to Zanzibar for supplies. In a quarrel with Arab soldiers, Booth and twenty men were killed, and John Bowen was elected in his place.[3]

There is no question that Bowen was in charge by late 1700. In addition to several Indian vessels, the *Speaker* plundered the English ship *Borneo* in October 1702. The men had no difficulty fencing their booty to Indian and European merchants along the Malabar coast.[4] Because they dealt with several purchasers, they may have gotten a better price than those who had relied solely on Adam Baldridge during the 1690s.

On the way back to Saint Mary's in 1701, Bowen wrecked the *Speaker* on a reef near Mauritius Island. Since Mauritius was not on the direct route to Saint Mary's, it is likely that Bowen was deliberately making for the small Dutch island. Like the inhabitants of French Réunion, the settlers on Mauritius welcomed visits from marauders and eagerly took them in when they retired from an active career as pirates.

The castaways got ashore and were welcomed by Mauritius's governor, Roelof Deodati. They had managed to save at least some of their booty and paid generously for assistance. Bowen later boasted of their warm reception to a captured English captain, and the records of the Dutch settlers confirm his tale. Bowen said that after taking their prizes,

Then [they] left the Coast, and sailed for the island [of] Madagascar, but in the way was lost on the island of Maritiyus, on St. Thomas's Reef, where they were most courteously received and feasted, their sick carried into their fort and cured by their doctor, and a new sloop sold them. And [they were] supplied with all sorts of necessaries for their cutting her [the sloop] and making her a brigantine, which they performed by the middle of March [1702], and took their leave of the Governor, giving him 2,500 pieces of eight. . . . And being invited to make it [Mauritius] a place of refreshment, sailed for the island of Madagascar, where at a place on the east side, called Maritan [St Mary's Island], the captain with a gang settled themselves.[5]

When it was wrecked, the *Speaker* was jammed full with 170 seamen and thirty Indian captives. Although the men increased the size of the sloop as much as possible, they had to leave behind twelve Englishmen as well as all the Indians.[6] After leaving Mauritius, Bowen stopped at Réunion Island. Several French pirates got off with their share of the booty, but at least two of the settlers at Réunion joined the crew and went on to Saint Mary's.[7]

Early in 1702, two relatively small Scottish vessels docked at the pirate's port. The *Speedy Return* and the *Content* had left Glasgow in May 1701 to buy slaves on the African coast.[8] Both instead went on to Saint Mary's, where they were seized by Bowen and his followers. Most of the two dozen crewmen aboard each vessel joined up with Bowen's band. Their captains, Robert Drummond of the *Speedy Return* and Captain Stewart of the *Content,* were left behind at Saint Mary's. Drummond was still living on Madagascar two years later, and both men apparently died on the island.[9]

The disappearance of the *Speedy Return* led to a spectacular miscarriage of justice. The attack was erroneously attributed to Captain Thomas Green and the crew of the Scottish ship *Worcester,* which traded along the Malabar Coast in 1702 and 1703. Returning to Scotland, Green and seventeen of his comrades were convicted of massacring the *Speedy Return's* crew. Green and two others were hanged in 1705; the rest later were pardoned and released.[10]

THOMAS HOWARD COMMANDS THE WELL-NAMED *PROSPEROUS*

About the time John Bowen took the *Speedy Return,* a separate band or company was living at Saint Augustine's Bay. In May 1702, yet another slaver, the *Prosperous,* arrived from England. Once again, as had happened on the ships seized by Booth and Bowen, the *Prosperous* was captured with the connivance of most of the crewmen. The mutineers killed Captain

Hilliard, and twenty-eight men were left on shore.[11] Thomas Howard was elected captain.[12] Howard took the *Prosperous* to Saint Mary's, where he met up with Bowen and the *Speedy Return*.

Agreeing to sail in consort, Bowen and Howard took the two former slave ships to Mayotte in the Comoros. After about two months, the East India Company ship *Pembroke* came into the harbor; by mistake her captain anchored where the bay became dry when the tide ebbed. Men from the *Speedy Return* and *Prosperous* rowed over and explained the problem, and Captain Whaley just managed to save the *Pembroke*.

The boats returned the next day, March 10, 1703, and the strangers asked to come aboard. This time their intentions were less than honorable. Unlike many other crews, however, the men of the *Pembroke* remained loyal and tried to fight off the invaders.

> Captain Weoley answered one of them might come only. Yet they both came rowing on and when they came under our quarter all their men at once started up with their arms guarded [ready to fire] swearing if any of us fired a shot they would give no quarter, but if we did not fire they would do us no harm nor take anything from us. Captain Weoley ordered everyone to fire, which we did, and they at us. . . . But we were not able to keep up with them, they firing six shot to our one. . . . So we called for quarters which they gave, disarming every man and turning them into the head.[13]

After ransacking the *Pembroke,* the pirate crews voted not to burn their prize, even though four of their men had been killed during the attack. They let the ship go but kept Captain Whaley with them as a pilot until the following October.[14]

Whaley reports that Bowen and Howard went to Mathelage, returned to the Comoros, and then sailed to the Highland of Saint Johns. They captured two Indian ships returning to Surat from Mocha. One was taken by the *Prosperous* and left adrift off Daman without anchor or cable; the *Speedy Return* captured a larger vessel and carried it to Rajapur. There the two crews burned their own ships and transferred to Bowen's Indian prize, which they armed with fifty-six guns and renamed the *Defiance*. Captain Whaley says the combined crew consisted of 164 fighting men, including fifty Frenchmen and forty-three Englishmen, the rest being Danes, Dutchmen, and Swedes.[15]

Once again the marauders had no difficulty disposing of their booty. From Rajapur, they sailed south to the Malabar Coast. A little north of Cochin,

> they anchored and fired several guns. But no boat coming off, the Quartermaster [John North] went near the shoar, and had conference by boat with the people, who next day brought off hogs and other refreshments. . . . There came several Dutchmen aboard, and I saw no difference between their treatment of the Pirates and any other ship.[16]

A letter written at that time estimates the take from the two ships at over £200,000 (about $100 million).[17] While this may exaggerate their booty, Bowen, Howard, and some of their comrades felt they had accumulated enough to retire. The *General History of the Pyrates* relates that Howard and about twenty more got off along the coast of India "with what they had, and retired among the Natives, where *Howard* married a Woman of the country, and being a morose ill natur'd Fellow, and using her ill, he was murder'd by her Relations."[18]

If Thomas Howard did retire in India, he made an unusual choice. Buccaneers who left Saint Mary's were more likely to retire at the French colony of Réunion. In this case, Bowen took the *Defiance* both to Mauritius and Réunion in February and April 1704. Six men got off at Mauritius.[19] Bowen and several others, including two Englishmen, were accepted as settlers at Réunion. Five of the men figure in a Réunion list of 1709; they had married, built homes, and prospered.[20] Captain John Bowen died in March 1705. Defoe says he was "taken ill of the dry Belly Ach, . . . and was buried in the Highway, for the Priests would not allow him holy Ground, as he was a Heretick." (This undoubtedly is a fiction, for the priest serving Réunion was a tolerant man.) Since Bowen did not marry, he had no heirs at Reunion, and the East India Company seized his fortune.[21]

However, most of those on the *Defiance* preferred to rejoin the pirate republic at Saint Mary's Island. Some 270 marauders had assaulted the *Pembroke* in March 1703.[22] Witnesses say only about a dozen men stayed at Mauritius and Réunion, while Defoe numbers the retirees at forty. In either case, more than two hundred men went back to Madagascar in 1704.

THE UTOPIA OF NATHANIEL NORTH

With Bowen staying at Réunion it became necessary to elect a new captain, and the *General History of the Pyrates* says the choice fell on the quartermaster, Nathaniel North. North is said to have taken the *Defiance* back to Madagascar to a place called Ambonavoula, probably located across from Saint Mary's somewhere between modern Foulpointe and Fénérive. Here "the men settled themselves among the Negroes, several living in a House; here they lived as Sovereign Princes among the Inhabitants."

With the men safely ashore, North let the Indian prisoners sail off with the *Defiance,* bidding "the Boatswain of the Moors take the Advantage of the land Breeze in the Nighttime, and go off with the Ship and what Goods were left on board."[23] There is no evidence to refute Defoe's tale, which has the advantage of explaining why the *Defiance* never again is mentioned among vessels plying the Indian Ocean.

According to Defoe, North retained the office of captain (though without a ship) and greatly influenced the men for the good. Under his guidance, the pirates were careful never to invade the rights either of their companions or of the Malagasy. In order to attack the clergy of his own country, Defoe portrayed North's settlement as a perfect Utopia. The pirates probably were not as saintly as described, but there is no question that their communities were less troubled than other European colonies. As Defoe wrote,

> Nature, we see, teaches the most Illiterate the necessary Prudence for their Preservation, and Fear works Changes which Religion has lost the Power of doing, since it has been looked upon as a Trade . . . : For these Men whom we term, and not without Reason, the Scandal of human Nature, who were abandoned to all Vice, and lived by Rapine; when they judged it for their Interest . . . were strictly just, both among themselves, and in composing the Differences of the neighboring Natives. . . .[24]

CAPTAIN THOMAS WHITE REFUSES TO STEAL FROM CHILDREN

While Captain North and his companions were living at Ambonavoula in perfect comity, another gang took to the sea under the command of Thomas White. As had Booth, Bowen, and Howard before him, White became captain by stealing a visiting slaver. In 1705, a French vessel came from the Caribbean with a cargo of alcoholic beverages and European clothing. The pirates then in residence at Saint Mary's had little available cash. And the revolt against Adam Baldridge in 1697 had taught them not to sell away from the island the native tribesmen over whom they ruled. So a group sneaked up in a canoe and took over the vessel, which carried thirty cannon. All together, about a hundred men joined the company and elected Thomas White captain. In September, they sailed over to Réunion, traded some of the captured liquor for naval supplies, and recruited at least one settler to their company.[25]

The ship returned to Madagascar, then went on to the Comoro Islands and the Bab-al-Mandab Strait at the mouth of the Red Sea. Captain White enjoyed good hunting. With his much smaller warship, the *General History* says, White captured both a thousand-ton Indian vessel (carrying six hundred men) and also a large Portuguese merchantman. Still in the Red Sea, the gang also captured two smaller English vessels, the *Dorothy* and the *Forgiveness*.[26]

White kept the *Dorothy* for his own use. But he let the *Forgiveness* go without robbing its passengers and even gave them some of the booty taken from other prizes. Among the valuables aboard the *Forgiveness* were

> 500 Dollars, a Silver Mug and two Spoons belonging to a Couple of Children on board, and under the Care of *Stacy* [captain of the *Forgiveness*]. The Children took on for their Loss, and the Captain [White] asking the Reason of their Tears, was answer'd by *Stacy*, that the above Sum and Plate was all the Children had to bring them up.
>
> Captain White made a Speech to his Men, and told em, it was cruel to rob the innocent Children; upon which, by unanimous Consent, all was restor'd them again; besides, they made a Gathering among themselves, and made a Present to *Stacy*'s Mate, and other his inferior Officers, and about 120 Dollars to the Children. . . .[27]

On the way back to Saint Mary's, White and his companions again stopped at Réunion Island, arriving in December 1706. The men now numbered about two hundred, twice as many as had begun the cruise fifteen months earlier.[28] At least fourteen men got off at Réunion.[29] Captain White and most crewmen continued on to Saint Mary's, and at least one settler from Réunion took off with them.[30] Defoe says they shared out at

£1,200 each (about $600,000). They certainly had plenty of money. Some of the pirates staying at Réunion quickly married, purchased land and slaves, and prospered as colonists.[31] Several others just lay around in the tropical heat, drinking up their booty.[32]

Among those who did well was Jacques Boyer. Boyer was a fifteen-year-old cabin boy when George Booth captured the French slaver at Fénérive in 1697. He enlisted and was with Bowen's company when it visited Réunion in 1701 and 1704. This time he apparently felt he had enough money to live in relative comfort. Despite nine years on a pirate ship and a total lack of education, Boyer proved to be a successful settler. He bought at least five separate properties for cash, married a girl eleven years of age, and produced six children before he died in 1719.[33]

CAPTAIN JOHN HALSEY BRINGS THE *CHARLES* FROM RHODE ISLAND

Back in Madagascar, Defoe says, White and his crew settled at Hopeful Point, probably the modern Foulpointe.[34] Unlike North's gang, they did not intend to remain indefinitely ashore but were simply fitting up their ship for the next season. They were almost ready for the sea when John Halsey arrived with the *Charles,* a hundred-ton brigantine carrying six cannon. The *Charles* was more suitable as a warship and in better repair than their own vessel. Although White previously had held the office of captain, he deferred to the group's choice of Halsey, and enlisted under his command.[35]

Aged thirty-four when he arrived at Madagascar in 1706, John Halsey was an experienced seaman from Boston.[36] In November 1704, with a privateer's commission from Rhode Island's Governor Samuel Cranston, Halsey had cruised against French ships on the Newfoundland Banks.[37] Late in 1705, this time commissioned by Governor Joseph Dudley of Massachusetts, he again set out for Newfoundland and the Azores but instead continued on around the Cape of Good Hope to Madagascar.

Halsey was the first captain for several years to travel from North America to Saint Mary's solely and specifically to join up with the marauders. He thus bears a greater resemblance to Thomas Tew and other brigands active in the 1690s than he does to more recent Saint Mary's leaders. As had the captains of the 1690s, Halsey did not have to use a converted slaver or merchantman; he commanded a vessel purposely designed and outfitted as a private warship. The *Charles* was owned by five wealthy and influential Boston merchants. When England and France again went to war in 1702, the ship was sent out with John Quench as second in command. Off Marblehead in August 1703, the crew mutinied, elected Quench commandeer, and threw the original captain overboard.

Sailing down to Brazil, Quench looted gold, silver, and fine cloth from Portuguese vessels, even though England and Portugal were allies. When the *Charles* returned to Marblehead in May 1704, suspicious officials rounded up the crew. The pirates were tried in Boston with the governor presiding, and Quench and five others were hanged on June 30.[38]

Despite her unsavory adventure, the owners took back the *Charles* and gave John Halsey command. Rhode Island authorities granted a privateering commission in November 1704. Halsey spent the next six months in the West Indies, adding eighty more men to his crew while at Port Royal, Jamaica. He enjoyed considerable success, returning to Newport in May 1705 with a prize laden with brandy, wine, sugar, paper, snuff, and oil. Ship and cargo were worth between £4,000 and £5,000 (about $2 to 3 million).

Halsey fell victim to political quarrels between colonial officials in Massachusetts and Rhode Island. The commissions granted to Thomas Tew and other pirates had created a considerable scandal. In January 1704, the Privy Council in London ruled that Rhode Island officials had no authority to erect Admiralty Courts. Citing the royal decree, an Admiralty judge from Massachusetts refused to accept Halsey's commission. But the prize was too valuable to abandon. The owners of the *Charles* induced Rhode Island's legislature to declare that governors could grant privateering commissions despite the royal decree.[39] After considerable wrangling, the Admiralty judge took a £150 bribe and declared the captured vessel a fair prize.

To ensure that he would enjoy his share of any booty, Captain Halsey acquired a second privateer's commission from the governor of Massachusetts. He cruised off Newfoundland and then crossed the Atlantic to the Azores, the Canary Islands, and the Cape Verdes. Along the way, the *Charles* took on much larger Spanish vessels, capturing a ship of twenty-four guns and fighting a bitter battle with a vessel carrying forty cannon.

At the Cape Verde Islands, Halsey decided to turn pirate. He headed south for the Cape of Good Hope, then made for Saint Mary's. It has been suggested that he was embittered by the corrupt practices and petty bickering of colonial Admiralty Courts.[40] He undoubtedly also knew about the rich booty brought into Newport, Boston, and New York a decade earlier by the *Jacob*, the *Pearl*, and Tew's *Amity*. And he may have come to enjoy exercising his considerable talent for maritime warfare.

Defoe's *General History* says Halsey took the *Charles* to Saint Augustine's Bay. From Saint Augustine's, Defoe goes on, Halsey went north to the Red Sea and met with a much larger Dutch vessel coming from Mocha. The crew insisted it was a merchantman; Halsey was sure it was a heavily armed warship. In any case, Halsey had resolved to attack only Indian vessels, which tended to be richer and easier to capture. After tailing the Dutch ship for a week, the crew became restless and removed Halsey as captain. Just then, the Dutchman fired a broadside from its lower tier of guns. Perceiving their mistake, the men sailed off as fast as they could and reinstated Halsey as captain.[41]

If the *Charles* really had been in the Red Sea, then Halsey subsequently made a long journey across the Arabian Sea, around the tip of India, and east to the Nicobar Islands off Malaysia. Near Cape Negrais in September 1706, Halsey caught two coastal traders, the *Buffalo* and the *Calicut*.[42] The two prizes were carried to a harbor near Cape Negrais and kept for about four months.

Without further success, the men became quarrelsome. Some separated and took over the *Buffalo* under a Captain Rowe.[43] Halsey and his followers took the *Charles* east to the Strait of Malacca. Perhaps the fiasco in the Red Sea with the Dutch ship had frightened the men. Failing to come across easy prey, and afraid to attack large European vessels, the crew voted to go back to Madagascar.

The *Charles* stopped for provisions at Réunion Island on May 19, 1707,[44] then went on either to Hopeful Point or Saint Mary's.[45] Already present were the *Buffalo*, which Halsey had taken at Cape Negrais, and the *Dorothy*, captured by Thomas White in August 1706. Men from the other two vessels enlisted on the *Charles* with Halsey, who was judged to have been merely unlucky rather than cowardly or incompetent.[46] Sailing around Madagascar's northern tip, Halsey went to the Red Sea, with a stop for supplies at Johanna Island.

The *Charles* is variously described by different witnesses, but it is clear she was not a large vessel. When the Muslim pilgrim fleet arrived, it came in a convoy of two dozen vessels guarded by Portuguese warships. The hunter became the hunted, and the *Charles* barely escaped by rowing away in a dead calm.

In August 1707, the *Charles* fell in with four English merchantmen going from Mocha to Surat. Three of these were not much larger than the *Charles*. However, Captain Jago's *Bombay Merchant* had been specially armed and manned to protect the other vessels. Showing considerable daring, Halsey sailed in among the four merchantmen and grappled the *Charles* to the *Rising Eagle*. While the two crews were battling, the *Bombay Merchant* closed to join the fight. Suddenly the *Charles* fired a broadside that raked the approaching vessel. Captain Jago turned and ran, leaving the other vessels to their fate. The *Rising Eagle* soon gave in, after which the *Essex* surrendered without a shot being fired. Halsey and his companions are said to have taken £40,000 ($20 million) in cash from the *Essex* and another £10,000 ($5 million) from the *Rising Eagle*.[47]

After losing her treasure, the *Essex* was released and went on to Bombay. With the *Charles* now badly worm-eaten, Captain Halsey gave the ship over to Nathaniel North and took over the *Rising Eagle* for his own use. Halsey and the *Eagle* continued down the coast. Off Calicut they fell in with the *Harriott,* "an East India Company's ship bound for Bengal, which they attempted to terrify into surrender by shewing the Black and Blood Flags together."[48] This time the intended victim resisted, so the *Rising Eagle* caught the monsoon winds to Antanavoula.

Halsey and his gang had treated the passengers on the *Essex* and *Rising Eagle* gently and in a businesslike manner. Early in January 1708, some of them showed up in a small ship named the *Greyhound* and began to barter European goods for the cloth still aboard the *Rising Eagle*. A few days later, the *Neptune* also came into port to trade with the pirates for slaves and gold. Although owned by Scots merchants, the *Neptune*'s captain was English as was the first mate, none other than the former pirate Samuel Burgess. The ship's owners had crammed the hold with a great variety of spirits, including brandy, beer, and wine. They were aware that pirates tended to seize ships to meet their needs but nevertheless hoped to make money on the voyage.

> Captain Miller of Well Close Square [London] is Captain of the *Shoram* Vessaile, and Burgis [Burgess] is gonn his Chief Mate, bound to Madagascar to trade with the Pirats. They carryed from hence about 30 tonns of French brandy, severall chests of Sir John Parsons beer and other liquors, and are to touch at Madera for wine. Yet these people are afraid, if the pirats like the ship, they will keep her, but flatter themselves they will give a good price and another vessaile to bring home the effects, because she was sent on purpose to trade with them. Her name is now the *Neptune Galley of Edinburgh*.[49]

Just then, before the *Neptune* had dropped anchor, a violent storm hit the area. The prizes taken in India—the *Rising Eagle, Buffalo,* and *Dorothy*—all were driven ashore and smashed into pieces. The *Neptune* and *Greyhound* rode out the storm but were in no condition to sail. To avoid being washed ashore, the *Neptune's* captain had cut off the masts at the deck. Since they were preparing to careen their vessel, the crew of the *Greyhound* had transferred their guns, anchors, and stores to the *Dorothy.*

Although they waited for some weeks, the men at Antanavoula ultimately took over the *Greyhound* and the *Neptune* to make up for the loss of their own small fleet. Except for Samuel Burgess, the *Neptune's* officers and passengers transferred to the *Greyhound,* which returned to India.[50] While the men were preparing the *Neptune* for their next cruise, both Thomas White and John Halsey were taken by fevers and died. Daniel Defoe supplies a mock-heroic description of Halsey's funeral.

The Prayers of the Church of England were read over him, Colours were flying, and his Sword and Pistol laid on his Coffin, which was covered with a Ship's Jack; as many Minute Guns fired as he was Years old, *viz.* 46, and three *English* Vollies, and one *French* Volley of small Arms. He was brave in his Person, courteous to all his Prisoners, lived beloved, and died regretted by his own People. His Grave was made in a Garden of Water Melons, and fenced in with Palisades to prevent his being rooted up by wild Hogs, of which there are plenty in those Parts.[51]

In the spring of 1708 at least one hundred Europeans still lived on Madagascar and Saint Mary's. Although not a swift sailer, the two hundred-ton *Neptune* could carry twenty-six cannon. Some of the men determined to take her to the Straits of Malacca on a plunder cruise.[52] Samuel Burgess, the ship's first mate, was known to many of those at Madagascar. He was chosen as captain but soon quarreled with some of the crew.

The *Neptune* was the last vessel used by the marauders until the arrival of Captain Condent in 1720. The ship's fate is uncertain; Defoe says she sank during a storm.[53] By 1709, Nathaniel North had returned to Antanavoula and again led the men as their onshore captain. After taking command of the *Charles* from Captain Halsey in August 1707, North had pointed the ship toward Madagascar. During a storm near the Maldive Islands, the *Charles* lost its anchors and cables, forcing North to run the ship on shore at Saint Mary's.[54] About a year later, he somehow made it to Antanavoula, and was elected captain by those resident there.

Defoe says North continued to treat Europeans with honesty and courtesy. However, he tended toward rashness in his relations with the Malagasy, which led to wars between the natives and the remaining pirates.[55] Defoe's stories exaggerate the scope of these battles; the Malagasy were formidable warriors and could easily have driven out any band of Europeans.[56]

SAMUEL BURGESS: PIRATE, SEA CAPTAIN, MERCHANT, PRIVATEER, SLAVE TRADER

The *General History of the Pyrates* asserts that Samuel Burgess helped the men take over the *Neptune* in March 1707. Defoe's story is plausible, since Burgess had many acquaintances among those living at Madagascar. Burgess had stayed at Saint Mary's in 1691 and 1692 as a crewman aboard the *Jacob;*[57] and he returned in 1696 and 1699 bringing goods to barter for slaves and pirate plunder. On the way home from the second trading voyage, a much larger East Indiaman captured his vessel. Condemned to death for piracy, Burgess was pardoned early in 1703. He was back in 1707, once again selling liquor and other European products. When the men decided they needed his ship as well as his goods, he stayed on at Madagascar—this time for the rest of his life.

Burgess could not keep away from the island, yet he seems to have been unfitted for life in the pirate democracy. Burgess was an expert captain, pilot, and trader. In temperament, however, he was closer to Captain Kidd than to successful leaders such as Robert Culliford. He was deposed as quartermaster of the *Jacob* and temporarily marooned at Saint Augustine's Bay. In 1708, he lasted barely six months as captain of the *Neptune* before he again was ousted by the crew.

When the *Jacob* returned to New York in 1693, Burgess went ashore with booty worth at least £500 ($250,000), a large sum in the New York of that time. Burgess bought a house with a small part of his loot and might have opened a business with the remainder. However, although he had withdrawn from piracy, he was not the sort of man to live quietly on his spoils or to serve as an officer on an ordinary merchantman.

Not long after he landed, Burgess went to work for Frederick Philipse, who owed his success to his willingness to steer close to the edge of the law. Among Philipse's many interests was the Madagascar slave trade, and he was quick to take advantage of Burgess's firsthand knowledge of the island. After sailing one of Philipse's ships to Jamaica and back, Burgess oversaw the building of the *Margaret,* a square-sterned brigantine of eighty tons carrying four cannon and a crew of sixteen, and specifically intended for the Madagascar trade.[58]

With Burgess in command, the *Margaret* left New York in December 1695, carrying a letter from Philipse to Adam Baldridge regarding their business dealings. Burgess called at Saint Mary's in July 1696, sailed up and down the coast buying slaves, and then made a final stop at Saint Mary's. On the way home, the *Margaret* laid over for three months at Saint Helena.[59] While there, Burgess acquired a pass from Captain Thomas Warren—the same naval commander who intercepted Captain Kidd some months later and who sailed for India in 1699 carrying a royal pardon for pirates.

Burgess got home with his cargo of pirate booty and slaves in May 1697. After carrying fish to Lisbon in another of Philipse's vessels, he began preparing for his second trading voyage to Saint Mary's. Meanwhile, the earl of Bellomont took over from New York Governor Benjamin Fletcher, determined to destroy Fletcher and blacken his reputation. In return for evidence about Fletcher's collusion with the *Jacob*'s crew, Bellomont granted Burgess a full pardon, which later saved his life.[60]

In June 1698, Burgess again headed to Madagascar. Bellomont may have grumbled, but there were no laws forbidding either the purchase of slaves or trading with the pirates at Saint Mary's. Philipse and Burgess took pains to stock the *Margaret* with the goods most in demand by the men at Saint Mary's. In addition to guns, pistols, and gunpowder, the ship was crammed full of various wines and spirits and all the items of daily life not easily found in Africa and Asia. Burgess also carried letters to long-absent mariners from wives, relatives, friends, and creditors in North America.

The *Margaret* sailed directly to Saint Mary's, docking in January 1699. Anchored in the harbor were at least two warships, the *Pelican* and the *Resolution*—the latter commanded by Robert Culliford, Burgess's old comrade on the *Jacob*. Burgess found many customers for his goods, which he sold for between eight and ten thousand pieces of eight. However, the purchase of slaves from Malagasy rulers went more slowly, and the *Margaret* did not finally leave for New York until mid-November 1699. In addition to Captain Burgess, a crew of fifteen, and over one hundred slaves, the very crowded vessel carried nineteen former pirates who had paid for passage home.

Bad weather forced the *Margaret* to stop at the Cape of Good Hope in December 1699, where it ran into the East Indiaman *Loyal Merchant*, commanded by Captain Matthew Lowth. Lowth seized the *Margaret*, sold the slaves at the Cape, and carried the ship to Bombay with all its passengers and crewmen.[61]

During the next three years, Samuel Burgess suffered all the terrors of seventeenth-century jails. By the time Lowth left India in January 1701, almost half of his prisoners had died.[62] After a harrowing journey, the *Loyal Merchant* arrived at London in August 1701, and Burgess was committed to Marshalsea Prison as a suspected pirate.

Burgess remained a prisoner for another year, as he became the focus of conflicting demands by the East India Company and the Philipse family. East India Company officials wanted both pirates and their accomplices to be exterminated from the face of the earth. Since marauders could not sail without supplies and gunpower, the Company considered merchants trading with pirates a greater danger than the pirates themselves. The difficulty was proving that Burgess had committed a crime. The law giving the New East India Company a monopoly had taken effect after Burgess left New York in June 1698. He certainly could not be held responsible for the activities of his passengers prior to the day they came aboard his ship. Moreover, the passage money was to be paid to Frederick Philipse, not to Burgess.

In desperation, Admiralty lawyers charged Burgess with piracy during his days on the *Jacob* in the early 1690s, citing a confession he had signed under physical duress while held captive by Captain Lowth. But a confession was not sufficient in itself, and a witness was needed. The East India Companies were especially anxious to make an example of New York merchants trading with Saint Mary's, and they were willing to set free a known pirate in order to win Burgess's conviction. Robert Culliford, who had plundered numerous vessels, was thus offered a pardon if he provided eyewitness corroboration of Burgess's crimes. Culliford wisely refused to admit his own presence on the *Jacob* until he was sure of a pardon. These legal entanglements delayed Burgess's trial until June 1702.

The delay gave the Philipse family time to come to Burgess's defense. The family wanted to be compensated for the property illegally seized at the Cape of Good Hope. According to Captain Lowth, Burgess had a considerable amount of money in his possession, some of which belonged to the Philipses. Altogether, the crew and passengers had carried cash with an estimated value of £11,140, while the *Margaret* and her cargo were worth upwards of £20,000 ($10 million). And this estimate did not even include the value of the slaves Lowth had sold at the Cape or that of other property he had taken for himself.[63]

To their credit, in addition to seeking compensation, the Philipses also did everything they could to help free Burgess. Adolph Philipse, Frederick's oldest son, left New York for London in August 1700, armed with impressive letters of introduction to William Blathwayt, commissioner of trade. The Board of Trade allowed Philipse to examine Governor Bellomont's papers, and he located and made copies of both Burgess's 1698 deposition and Bellomont's letter of pardon.

Tried on July 15, 1702, Burgess was sentenced to death. But Adolph Philipse continued to work on his behalf, arguing that Burgess had been condemned for the same acts already pardoned by Governor Bellomont. It was not clear that Bellomont had the authority to pardon piracy, but Philipse ultimately prevailed.[64] Burgess was released on bail in August 1702 and pardoned by the king in January 1703.

After his release from prison, Burgess enlisted on a privateering expedition bound for the Pacific under William Dampier, a noted author and former buccaneer.[65] Two ships were hired for the voyage, and Burgess joined the *Fame*, perhaps as a lieutenant, under the command of Henry Pullen. Before the ship reached the Canary Islands, Pullen discovered that crewmen were conspiring to seize the *Fame* and go off on their own as pirates. When he captured a French ship, Pullen put the malcontents, including Samuel Burgess, on the prize as crew. "Such a crew of rogues," Pullen later wrote, "were never together in one bottome."[66]

Burgess was captain of the prize by the time it reached Delaware Bay on the way to Rhode Island. There were other prize courts closer to the Canary Islands, and Rhode Island courts were widely considered lax and bribable.[67] An Admiralty Court officer became suspicious and tried to persuade the sheriff to help him arrest the ship, but local officials preferred to trade with the crew rather than capture them.[68] Burgess slipped away in November 1703 and took the prize to New York City, where the goods on the ship were declared lawful prize and valued at £370.[69] Taking his share of the money, Burgess sold his house in New York, and was listed in April 1704 as captain of the *Mary*, bound for London.[70]

Burgess apparently spent the next few years living in London and seeking a berth on a ship bound for Madagascar. Once again, it is striking how easily pirate captains could escape their past; on the surface at least, marauders resembled and were no different than other seamen. Burgess had been employed by the richest merchant in New York. In London, he again associated with wealthy merchants, who appreciated his counsel about the Madagascar trade. Among those seeking Burgess's advice were Thomas Duckett and Thomas Bowery, both prosperous East Indian merchants.[71]

After several ventures failed to be consummated, some Scottish merchants appointed Burgess chief mate on the *Neptune*, which arrived in February 1708 and was confiscated by John Halsey and his men early in March. The *Neptune*'s officers were freed and allowed to leave for India. Burgess voluntarily stayed behind, once again a pirate.

John Halsey died soon after. Defoe says that Halsey made Burgess the executor of his will, trusting him to take some £3,000 ($1,500,000) to Halsey's widow and children. It was jealousy of Halsey's favoritism toward Burgess that supposedly led the men to remove the latter as captain of the *Neptune*. After a few months on Saint Mary's, Burgess moved to Mathelage as the guest of Deaan Toakoffu (Andriantoakafo), known to the English as "long Dick" or "King Dick." At Mathelage, Burgess made his living as a slave trader.

In October 1716, the slave ship *Drake* came into port seeking human cargo. Aboard was Robert Drury, an Englishman shipwrecked in 1702.[72] After fifteen years as a captive of Malagasy rulers, Drury had succeeded in finding refuge aboard the *Drake*, which had stopped at Mathelage on the way back to England. While the captain waited for King Dick, who was away fighting, Drury went up the Betsiboka River to the pleasant and even opulent homes of four former pirates—including Samuel Burgess. One of the four was Nicholas Dove, a cabin boy shipwrecked with Drury. Dove told his old friend that the four men only recently had moved to Mathelage from Saint Mary's and the nearby coast of Madagascar. Grown rich as pirates, they had left the sea and occupied themselves "stealing away and ravishing the wives and daughters of the natives."[73]

The tale in the *General History* differs in some details from the version reported in *Robert Drury's Journal*. In both stories, Samuel Burgess clearly had prospered, free from harassment by the governors, lawyers, judges and other aspects of English society that had bedeviled his life in New York and England.[74] Although not successful as a pirate leader, he seems to have served King Dick well and much as he had served Frederick Philipse in New York, loyal to both because their success served his own interests.

CHAPTER FIFTEEN

DIAMONDS AS BIG AS FISTS

Pirate warships were a constant threat throughout 1719 along the West African coast. Commanded by Captain Condent, a seaman from Plymouth, England, the *Flying Dragon* hunted alone. Also cruising without consorts was Edward England in the *Fancy,* a thirty-six-gun Dutch prize renamed in honor of Henry Every and his warship.[1] Meanwhile, three vessels sailed as a group commanded by Oliver La Buse, John Cocklyn, and Howell Davis, with John Taylor acting as Davis's sailing master.[2] Toward the end of April, the squadron broke up. Cocklyn and Davis stayed in Africa. La Buse and Taylor, now joined by Edward England's *Fancy,* went on to Saint Mary's.

After ten peaceful years, Saint Mary's thus welcomed a second wave of buccaneers in 1720 and 1721. Back in North America, piracy had rapidly increased after 1713, when war again broke out between England and France. The Bahamas briefly became a second Madagascar, as hundreds of men flocked to Nassau on New Providence Island. Dozens of small vessels ravaged the American coast from Florida to Maine.

Less than two hundred miles from the American mainland, Nassau certainly was much closer than Madagascar. But rewards also were much less generous. While those in the East captured treasure ships loaded with gold and gems, the Bahamian pirates had to be content with coastal traders and fishermen.

Nassau's glory days as a pirate haven lasted only for a year or two. In July 1718, Woodes Rogers arrived as royal governor, accompanied by three warships. Though the navy soon departed, Rogers managed to bluff the Nassau raiders into leaving New Providence. Most were caught by naval squadrons. William Teach (Blackbeard) died in battle at North Carolina, and others were arrested and hanged in the West Indies or off the New

England coast. Several pirate ships crossed to West Africa, where they eventually were trapped by a naval squadron.

As in the 1680s, Madagascar proved to be the best haven for pirates chased from the Caribbean. Several crews continued on from West Africa to Saint Mary's, all finding extraordinary success. Near Bombay, Captain Condent's *Flying Dragon* captured a large Arab ship loaded with money, drugs, spices, and silk worth £150,000. Edward England and John Taylor grabbed £75,000 from an East Indiaman in the Comoro Islands. At Réunion Island, Taylor and Oliver La Buse seized a Portuguese carrack carrying booty worth more than £875,000—well over $400 million today—the richest prize ever taken by any pirate.[3]

Even more important than the amount was their success—unlike those who sailed from the Bahamas—in escaping the hangman and living to spend their take. Only Oliver La Buse was captured, and he was taken in 1730 through devious trickery while aboard a French slave ship. Edward England died while living at Saint Mary's or on Madagascar. Taking with them all those wishing to return home, Condent and Taylor went back to Europe and the Caribbean.

Saint Mary's last days as a pirate haven were her greatest days. With their comrades, England and Taylor got away safely despite their willingness to take exactly those risks most pirates avoided. At Johanna in the Comoro Islands in 1721, the vessels commanded by England and Taylor fought a long cannon duel with the East Indiaman *Cassandra*. Pirates almost always ran away from any vessel that strenuously resisted; they were in business to make a living, and dead men cannot spend their plunder. Most pirates were like those aboard Robert Culliford's *Mocha*, which attacked the East Indiaman *Dorrill* in 1697. When the *Dorrill* finally got off two solid broadsides, the men on the *Mocha* immediately stopped fighting and forced Culliford to turn and flee. In April 1721, in contrast, England, Taylor, and their crews ignored their casualties and continued to fight until they won.

This last group of captains stands at the peak whether considered as seaman, as military commanders, or as leaders of men. Why, then, did Condent, England, Taylor, and La Buse receive relatively little attention during their own lifetimes and afterwards? Their relative obscurity shows the power of the communications media—in the eighteenth century as today—to shape and distort the historical record.

For whatever reason, while Henry Every and William Kidd became notorious, the pirate captains of 1720 and 1721 did not catch the fancy of the

British people. Perhaps other scandals diverted their attention, or Britons simply were bored by pirate exploits. And the circumstances and timing of their crimes also helped keep Condent and Taylor out of the limelight. Unlike Captain Kidd, they never were caught, so there was no scandalous trial to arouse public interest. Moreover, although they took much more booty than Kidd, their crimes did not pose as great a threat to British mercantile interests. During the intervening years, the Mogul Empire had lost control of much of India and could no longer shut down the East India Company.

It was Daniel Defoe who created modern pirate mythology, and Defoe's portraits have colored subsequent interpretations. Taking his cue from the British public's lack of interest, Defoe did not do his creative best for the captains of the 1720s. He had depicted Henry Every as the wise ruler of a powerful pirate kingdom. He embroidered the stories that William Kidd murdered crewmen in cold blood. Defoe's biographies of Condent, England, and Taylor are as fanciful as those about Every and Kidd, but they are less interesting.

Defoe's biography of Edward England occurs at the beginning of the first volume of the *General History*. England thus is sandwiched in with Blackbeard, Anne Bonny, Mary Read, and other colorful Bahamian villains. Especially in Volume I, Defoe almost never portrays a pirate as ordinary and humdrum; the captains are presented as extreme types—either as bestial villains or noble heroes. England is the exception: He is described as a relatively decent man with some moral scruples, who was unable to control his crews. England, Defoe alleges,

> had a great deal of good Nature, and did not want for Courage; he was not avaritious, and always averse to the ill Usage Prisoners received: He would have been contented with moderate Plunder, and less mischievous Pranks, could his Companions have been brought to the same Temper, but he was generally over-rul'd, and as he was engaged in that abominable Society, he was obliged to be a Partner in all their vile Actions.[4]

It is the crewmen that commit crimes, while England stands and watches. There even may be some truth in Defoe's description of England as weak-willed; during the course of the voyage, the crew rebelled against his clemency toward dangerous prisoners. However, in exaggerating England's timorousness, Defoe turns him into an easily forgettable nonentity. A weak, decent man like England is less interesting than a forceful monster such as Blackbeard. Less evil, less demented, less sexually depraved, less grotesque in every way, England is colorless and does not measure up to Defoe's best creations.

Defoe invents a Captain Condent almost as brutal though not as depraved as Blackbeard. While Condent was still in the Caribbean, an Indian crewman threatened to blow up the ship. Condent leapt into the hold and shot the obstreperous crewman. "When he was dead," Defoe writes, "the Crew hack'd him to Pieces, and the Gunner ripping up his Belly, tore out his Heart, broiled and eat it." Along the Brazilian coast, on the way to Africa, Condent personally tortured Portuguese prisoners, "cutting off their Ears and Noses."[5]

Cruel though he may be, Defoe's portrait of Condent remains as colorless as that of England. Condent's portrait is never fleshed out, and he does not have the oddities of facial hair, clothing, and behavior that make Defoe's Blackbeard unique. In fact, Defoe simply copied these fables of mutilation and cannibalism from similar tales in Exquemelin's best-selling *Buccaneers of America*.[6] In real life, after taking what he needed or wanted, Condent let captured seamen go free—except for those voluntarily enlisting with his crew. After leaving off from piracy, he was considered a model citizen.

CAPTAIN JOHN TAYLOR, A SUPERB SEAMAN, SOLDIER, AND COMMANDER

Defoe's biography of John Taylor is similarly both uninteresting and exactly opposite the truth. Captain Taylor, according to the *General History,* was merely "a Fellow of a most Barbarous Nature, who was become a great Favourite amongst them, for no other reason than because he was a greater Brute than the rest."[7] Just like Defoe's Edward England, this portrait of Taylor is easily forgotten. And it also is false. Three men were Taylor's captives for relatively long periods of time. They describe him as courageous and intelligent, an excellent seaman, and a charismatic leader. A man of some education and a complicated nature, the actual John Taylor in no way resembled Defoe's brutish savage.

Captain William Snelgrave was held prisoner during the month of April 1719. Snelgrave has nothing but praise for Howell Davis and John Taylor, Davis's sailing Master. He considered Davis a "most generous and humane person." Because his men trusted him, Snelgrave notes, Davis would keep his company in good order without using violence.

Snelgrave had less to do with Taylor than with Davis. But he was awed by Taylor's bravery when a fire broke out that threatened to spread to the gunpowder, thus blowing up the ship and everyone on it. Many men and officers dropped off into the water and swam for shore. But Taylor stood his ground, "as brisk and couragious a Man as ever I saw. . . . This Person, with fifteen more, spared no pains to extinguish the Fire in the Hold; and tho they were scalded in a sad manner by the Flames, yet they never shrunk till it was conquered."[8]

Richard Lazenby became Taylor's prisoner about a year later than Snelgrave, from July 1720 through April 1721. Lazenby's narrative implicitly testifies to Taylor's seamanship. He paints a less flattering description of Taylor's personal qualities than does Snelgrave—perhaps because he was writing for his employers in the East India Company. However, he describes only one incident of physical punishment during ten months, when Captain Taylor caned him at the quartermaster's express request.[9]

The most comprehensive portrait of Taylor is given by Jacob de Bucquoy, a specialist in marine map-making. Taylor captured Bucquoy in Mozambique in April 1722 and kept him until September or October. During that time, Bucquoy slept in a bed in the captain's cabin. Cruel nightmares sometimes awakened Taylor during the night, and he and Bucquoy talked at length.

Bucquoy portrays Taylor as a proud man, driven to dominate those around him. When threatened, he fell into a fierce anger verging on rage. Taylor told Bucquoy that he had been a British naval officer but fell out of favor after a change in government during the reign of Queen Anne. Disappointed in his ambitious plans, Taylor carried a bitter grudge against the English authorities. To gain revenge, he joined a pirate ship in the Gulf of Mexico and was elected captain.

Whether or not this story was true, Taylor was an educated man who mixed as an equal with ships' officers such as Snelgrave and Bucquoy.[10] The latter commented that the pirates chose well when they elected Taylor captain. "Certainly, they could not find a man more capable of commanding a ship than he. Leaving aside the nature of his infamous and hateful profession and his own private vices, Taylor united all that one could hope to find in a seaman, a soldier, and a leader."[11] High praise indeed, considering how many captains Bucquoy served during his career as a designer of oceanic maps.

THE *FLYING DRAGON* PLUNDERS A TREASURE SHIP, AND HER CREW RETIRES IN FRANCE

Captain Condent and his comrades rank among the most successful criminals of all time. The *Flying Dragon* enjoyed extraordinary success during a relatively brief cruise in Indian waters, and the men got away with their crimes. Accepting pardons from the governor of Réunion, Condent and many crewmen then went on to France. Condent used his booty to become a merchant, shipowner, and respected citizen of a town on the Normandy coast.

The ship's good fortune began even before the *Flying Dragon* crossed the Atlantic, when Condent pillaged *La Dauphine* near Rio de Janeiro in Brazil. Then, in late October or early November 1719, the *Georges* was taken off the west coast of Africa. A month of two later, Condent looted the *Prince Eugene* as it sailed below the Cape of Good Hope.[12]

While still off Brazil and Africa, Condent told captive mariners that the *Flying Dragon* was heading for Saint Mary's Island. At Saint Mary's, the men planned to careen the ship and purchase food from a Jamaican half-breed. Married to a daughter of the local chief, the man ruled the nearby area and could obtain whatever supplies were needed by passing ships. Most likely this was John Plantain, a Jamaican who had wed the granddaughter of a Malagasy king.[13]

Condent picked up additional men at Saint Mary's and Antongil Bay before taking the southwest monsoon to the Indian Coast. Near Bombay in August 1720, he captured a ship bound from Surat to Jiddah with gold coins, drugs, spices, and silks said to be worth an astonishing £150,000 (about $375 million). Once again, Condent ordered the men not to abuse their prisoners. In fact, the passengers and crew, who had offered no resistance, were put safely ashore at Malabar Hill near Surat.[14]

Fully satisfied with this one rich prize, the *Dragon*'s crew caught the northeast monsoon back to Saint Mary's, where the booty was shared out. On November 12, 1720, the *Crooker,* a small English ship, dropped anchor off Réunion. Captain Baker, her commander, explained that Condent had sent him to ask for amnesty. While Baker had been at Saint Mary's a little earlier, the *Flying Dragon* and her Indian prize had arrived. Other than taking the *Crooker*'s alcoholic beverages, the pirates did no harm to either crew or ship. Instead, having heard that the French offered a pardon to any pirate giving up his trade, Condent sent Captain Baker to Réunion to verify these rumors on behalf of the pirate leader and 135 crewmen. (The *Dragon* also held some sixty African slaves.)[15]

Governor Joseph Beauvollier de Courchant was delighted to accede to Captain Condent's request for amnesty. Réunion had been taking in pirates for at least three decades,[16] and a royal ordinance had legitimized the island's toleration of sea rovers in 1719. Officials were told to pardon pirates that surrendered; moreover, they also were ordered to make every possible effort to attract pirates and convince them to give up. Beauvollier de Courchant thus convoked the provincial council and wrote an agreement making minimal demands on Condent and his men. They were asked to surrender within four months, to destroy their warships, and to turn over their weapons and ammunition on arriving at Réunion. In return for a small payment, each man could bring along a Negro slave—provided that these were not "warriors" who had fought with the pirates.[17]

In February 1721, thirty-two men from Condent's crew followed him to Réunion; some of those remaining at Saint Mary's enlisted with John Taylor and Oliver La Buse later in the same year. Before leaving, the men burned the *Flying Dragon* and her Indian prize. When a naval squadron stopped at Saint Mary's in April 1722, Clement Downing found "the Ruins of several Ships and their Cargoes piled up in great Heaps, consisting of the richest Spices and Drugs."[18] Perhaps some of this wasted wealth came from the *Flying Dragon* as well as the Portuguese ship subsequently taken by Taylor and La Buse.

Convinced that they would find ways—despite the governor's decrees—of mulcting them, Réunion's inhabitants warmly welcomed Condent and his comrades. However, the former brigands barely had found places to stay when two ships attacked the island, manned by pirates who had not yet given up their trade. The attack started after the *Nostra Senhora de Cabo* limped into the anchorage at Réunion on April 6. The great three-deck East Indiaman had lost its masts in a sudden storm and needed major repairs. Three weeks later, on April 26, as the *Cassandra* and the *Victory* passed by Réunion, their crews noticed the dismasted vessel. They swooped in, swarmed aboard, and captured the ship almost without resistance, taking as prisoners the viceroy of Portuguese India and other passengers of high rank.

During his months on the island, John Condent had earned the trust of Beauvollier de Courchant, who now asked him to negotiate the viceroy's release. After some tense discussions, the invaders released the viceroy and left without harming the islanders. They were immensely grateful to Condent, leading to rumors that he even had married the governor's sister-in-law. While no one from Beauvollier de Courchant's family lived on the island, Condent did enjoy some sort of liaison while at Réunion—the 1734 census mentions a Jean-Baptise "Codnon," aged about twelve years.

Despite their cordial reception on Réunion, some twenty of the thirty-two former pirates went back to Europe in November 1721, and Condent followed them a year later.[19] Arrived in France, Condent settled in Normandy, married, and became a ship owner. Five years later, the local military commander testified that the Condent family lived "with honor and probity."[20]

CAPTAIN SNELGRAVE'S STORY

Early in 1719, three vessels were lurking at the mouth of the Sierra Leone River, under the command of Thomas Cocklyn, Oliver La Buse, and Howell Davis (with John Taylor as Davis's second in command). On April 1, John Snelgrave's *Bird Galley*—an innocent merchantman with cargo from Holland—reached the river and was snapped up without a struggle. Part of the *Bird*'s crew enlisted with the pirates. Captain Snelgrave and the rest remained their prisoners for a month.

An intelligent observer and honest reporter, Snelgrave later wrote a book about Africa which told the story of his captivity. Although he thought all pirates were bad, he realized that some were better than others, and he put down facts that spoke in their favor. Because he told the truth instead of making up grotesque atrocity stories, his book has not enjoyed the popularity of the more fanciful works by Exquemelin and Defoe. Nevertheless, its firsthand testimony about their life makes it one of the most valuable works in the vast bibliography about pirates.

When they captured Snelgrave's *Bird,* Cocklyn and La Buse were sailing under a formal consortship agreement. Howell Davis was cooperating with them but acting on his own. The three captains and crews were not at ease with each other, and Davis considered Cocklyn an ignorant brute. Meanwhile, Taylor was maneuvering to oust Davis as captain.

The three ships had captured other vessels before taking the *Bird,* and they subsequently grabbed the *Saint-Antoine.*[21] Despite good hunting, the men could not agree on a plan. Some wanted to remain on the African coast while another group wanted to take up the old route to Saint Mary's. Like Captain Condent, they had heard of a mulatto trader who could supply their needs.

Howell Davis left first, splitting off by early June.[22] Davis's place in the squadron was taken by Edward England's *Fancy.*[23] John Taylor left Davis's vessel for England's, and the latter acted as admiral of the little fleet, which

PIRATE WARSHIPS AT SAINT MARY'S, 1718–1723

Ship	Flying Dragon	Fancy	Cassandra	Victory	Rising Sun	Unnamed vessel	Unnamed vessel	Nostra Senhora de Cabo
Captain	John Condent	Edward England	Edward England, John Taylor	John Taylor, Oliver La Buse	Thomas Cocklyn	Oliver La Buse	Howell Davis	Oliver La Buse
1718	Takes *La Dauphine* off Brazilian coast							
1719	Takes *Georges* off West African coast, late 1719	Loots *Société*, October		Captured French vessel renamed *Victory* / Loots *Société*, Oct.	Takes *Bird* (Captain Snelgrave), April 1 / Loots *Société*, Oct.	Takes *Bird*, April 1 / Loots *Société*, Oct.	Takes *Bird*, April 1	
1720	Loots *Prince Eugene* off Cape Town, early 1720 / Captures Indian treasure ship near Bombay, Aug. / At Saint Mary's, Nov.	Attacks Dutch vessel off Cape Town, Feb. / Battles and takes *Cassandra*, Aug. 7 / *Fancy* given to Captain Macrae	Edward England transfers to *Cassandra*	Attacks Dutch vessel off Cape Town, Feb. / Battles and takes *Cassandra*, Aug. 7		Wrecks ship at Comoro Islands		
1721	Condent and 32 others accept amnesty at Réunion, Feb.	Saint Mary's, Feb. / John Taylor takes over *Cassandra* / Takes *Cabo*, April 26 / At Saint Mary's, May / Burns *La Duchesse de Noailles*, Dec.	Oliver La Buse takes over *Victory* / Takes *Cabo*, April 26 / At Saint Mary's, May					At Saint Mary's, La Buse burns *Victory*, takes over *Cabo* / Burns *La Duchesse de Noailles*, Dec.
1722	Condent sails for France, Nov.		At Mozambique, April / Taylor sails for West Indies, Oct.					At Mozambique, April / Back to Saint Mary's, Nov.
1723								Cruises off Malabar coast

scoured the coast from Gambia to Ghana.[24] At the end of October, England's squadron plundered the French slaver *Société* in the roadstead of Whydah (Ouidah, now in Benin).[25] Another prize was a French vessel carrying forty-six guns, which was retained as the *Victory*.[26] Some of those on the overcrowded *Fancy* transferred to the prize and elected John Taylor captain.

Soon after, Cocklyn and La Buse went their own ways. La Buse sailed to Madagascar and the Comoro Islands, where he wrecked his ship in 1720.[27] Continuing to cruise in consort, England and Taylor also went on to Madagascar but only after staying for a time along the African coast.

While the men careened their ships at an isolated bay, Defoe relates, "They liv'd there very wantonly for several Weeks, making free with the Negroe Women, and committing such outragious Acts, that they came to an open Rupture with the Natives, several of whom they killed, and one of their Towns they set on fire."[28] In addition to allowing them to rape Negro women, according to Defoe, England also stood by while the men tortured a captive they hated. Tying him fast to the windlass, they "pelted him with Glass Bottles, which cut him in a sad manner; after which they whipp'd him about the Deck, till they were weary."[29]

A FIERCE BATTLE WITH THE *CASSANDRA*

By February 1720, England and Taylor were off Cape Town; they attacked a Dutch ship but gave up when it offered strong resistance.[30] The *Fancy* and the *Victory* were next seen at the Comoro Islands in August of the same year. Their adventures during the intervening seven months are not recorded.[31]

The two pirate vessels arrived at Johanna Island on August 7. In the harbor they found three large English and Dutch merchantmen. The Dutch ship made off, as did Captain Richard Kirby's *Greenwich;* but the third vessel stayed and fought. The *Cassandra* was a new ship of 380 tons on her first voyage. Captain James Macrae enjoyed the support of the crew, and he was determined to destroy the attackers.[32]

Pirates generally avoided combat, and this is the only pitched battle fought in the Indian Ocean during Saint Mary's thirty-year history. The *Cassandra* and the two pirate ships pounded each other with cannon fire with only limited damage. After a time, the *Victory* retreated to sea to stop up leaks. Meanwhile, the men on the *Fancy* tried to row up to and board the *Cassandra,* but a lucky hit shot off their oars.

At the end of three hours, the *Victory* had been repaired and was closing again. Macrae had lost many from his crew and had given up all hope of assistance from Captain Kirby and the *Greenwich*. To save his ship, Macrae ran the *Cassandra* ashore. The *Fancy* followed and beached within pistol shot, with her bow toward the *Cassandra's* broadside. The two grounded ships continued to fire, with heavy casualties on both sides. Thirteen were killed and twenty-four wounded aboard the *Cassandra*, including Macrae himself, struck on the head by a musket ball. When the *Victory* sent three boats full of men to reinforce the *Fancy*, Macrae and the other survivors escaped ashore. They left behind cargo worth some £40,000 (about $20 million), according to the *Cassandra's* invoice.[33]

Macrae hid out for ten days and then took a remarkably daring chance. Hoping that the pirates' anger had cooled, he went aboard the *Victory* and asked for mercy. Because he had resisted capture, some wanted to kill Macrae. But England and several others, who had served under Macrae on various ships, voted to release him. The turning point is said to have come when a man with one wooden leg stomped up, "swearing and vaporing on the Quarter-Deck. . . . *Shew me the Man*, says he, *that offers to hurt Captain* Mackra, *for I'll stand by him.*"[34] (Years later, this one-legged man gained immortality as the inspiration for Long John Silver in Robert Louis Stevenson's *Treasure Island*.)

After a bitter argument with Captain Taylor and many of the men, England persuaded them to let Macrae have the half-ruined *Fancy*. As soon as the pirates had left Johanna Island, Macrae started patching up the *Fancy*, and eventually sailed for Bombay with forty-one survivors of the battle. After a month and a half of terrible suffering, they got to Bombay on October 26.[35]

Taylor retained command of the *Victory*, while England and his crew transferred to the captured *Cassandra*. Richard Lazenby, Macrae's second mate, was taken aboard the *Victory* to serve as pilot. The pirate vessels reached India sometime in October and captured two small ships carrying Arabian horses. At daybreak some days later, the men awoke to find themselves in the midst of a British flotilla, which had come from Bombay to attack native Indian sea rovers. Walter Brown, an East India Company official, had chief command of the squadron, which included at least five warships, some of significant size. Nevertheless, both Brown and the British captains were afraid to open fire, and they sailed off when the land breeze rose.[36]

After visiting the Laccadive Islands, England and Taylor sailed back to India, heading for the Dutch settlement at Cochin. Along the way, they took a small English ship, whose captain was brought aboard very drunk.

He informed them that the warships had been sent out again; this time, they were under Captain Macrae's command and were searching for the pirates.[37] News of Macrae's ingratitude enraged the men, who turned bitterly against England. But for his foolish championship of Macrae, this would not have happened! They now saw that Taylor had been right all along, and they would follow only him in the future. In their rage, they talked at first of hanging England, till more moderate counsel prevailed.[38]

The *Cassandra* and *Victory* sailed south to Cochin, where the men paid lavishly for food, water, arrack, and clothing.[39] On leaving Cochin, they continued to cruise along the coast, taking a small Indian vessel but losing the larger and richer *Saint Louis*.[40] Before long, they ran into Macrae's squadron, which bore down and signaled them to heave to. The two pirate vessels ran to the south and were chased for two days, till by superior sailing they lost their pursuers.

By now it was Christmas, and the men spent their holiday in riotous carousing, according to their captive, Richard Lazenby, a censorious Sabatarian. About the middle of February in 1721, they reached Mauritius. Here or at Saint Mary's Island, Edward England and three others were set on shore. Taylor took over the *Cassandra*, and Oliver La Buse became captain of the *Victory*.[41]

TAYLOR AND LA BUSE MAKE OFF WITH THE RICHEST BOOTY EVER TAKEN

The *Cassandra* and the *Victory* reached Réunion at dawn on the Sunday after Easter. As they approached the northern coast, the men noticed a large vessel without masts lying at anchor.[42] Coming closer, they found *Nostra Senhora de Cabo*, an East Indiaman carrying a crew of 130 and a considerable number of passengers. Among these were the archbishop of Goa and the count of Ericeira, the latter returning to Lisbon after some years as viceroy of Portuguese India. After leaving Goa in January, the great ship had been pummeled by a sudden storm in the middle of the Indian Ocean. The masts were torn off, the rudder was split from top to bottom, and eight of the thirty guns had rolled into the sea.[43] As part of the ongoing repairs, the poop deck had been partly removed at Réunion, and the passengers and many crewmen were housed on shore.[44]

Taylor and La Buse could see that the *Cabo* was deserted and derelict. Without hesitation, they immediately attacked. At the last minute as they reached their prey, both ships struck the English flag, hoisted black banners strewn with "deaths-heads," and opened up with cannon and muskets.[45] After a second volley, the Portuguese aboard the *Cabo* lowered their flag. The attackers crowded into small boats and swarmed aboard their prize without having lost a man. On board the viceroy of Portuguese India was carrying diamonds valued at £500,000 as well as another £375,000 in rare oriental products. Counting earlier plunder, the pirates seized booty worth well over £900,000 (about $450 million). Each man received from one to forty-two diamonds, depending on their size.

In an effort to explain away the surrender of an expensive ship and enormous treasure, the count of Ericeira later claimed he had personally taken command of the *Cabo*'s defense. As the attackers came aboard, thirteen crewmen immediately deserted to the pirates while most of the rest jumped into the sea. But the gallant count, conspicuous in his scarlet coat, made a desperate last stand on the quarterdeck. When his sword was broken in two in hand-to-hand combat, he continued to lash about with his cane until Captain Taylor shouted out an order to give quarter, and the fighting stopped.[46]

Whether he helped defend the *Cabo* or stayed safely on shore (as Taylor claimed), the count was brought aboard the *Cassandra,* while the *Cabo* was towed to a safer anchorage. Taylor and La Buse treated Ericeira with courtesy and even gave him back his sword, its hilt encrusted with gold and diamonds. The same day, the pirates heard that the *Ville de Ostende,* a smaller merchantman, had sought refuge from the same storm on the other side of the island. The *Victory* went to the spot and took the ship without a shot being fired. The crew had mutinied against a hated captain and refused to put up any resistance.[47]

Captain Condent had just retired from piracy with many of his crew. Condent seemed a natural go-between, and the French governor of the island sent him to negotiate with Taylor and La Buse. Richard Lazenby, still held prisoner aboard the *Victory,* says the men argued at great length whether to release Count Ericeira. Some wanted to carry him to Madagascar and hold him for a great ransom, while others thought this would be more trouble than it was worth. In the end, they settled for a ransom of £400, paid over by the French governor.[48] When the cash arrived, his captors rowed the Count ashore in a specially decorated boat to the accompaniment of a viceregal twenty-one-gun salute and mocking cheers.[49]

While the *Cassandra* and *Victory* remained at Réunion for another two days, the men continued to act politely. They went around without weapons and without insulting anyone, and they paid the going price for whatever they wanted. Taylor and La Buse offered the governor a magnificent clock as a parting gift.[50] However, they broke their promise to leave behind at least one vessel to carry away all those who had landed from the viceroy's ship. Apparently some of their prisoners had told them that there were many diamonds hidden in the *Cabo*.[51]

All four vessels sailed during the night, the pirates taking with them the best sailors from their two prizes as well as two hundred slaves from the *Cabo*. The *Ostende* was sent on ahead, and the *Cassandra*, *Victory*, and *Cabo* followed behind. Since there were no suitable trees left on Saint Mary's, the *Ostende* went to Madagascar to cut down new masts for the *Cabo*. When their guards got drunk one night, the prisoners took over the ship and slipped away to Mozambique.[52]

Even without the *Ostende*, Taylor, La Buse, and their comrades took the richest plunder ever captured by any pirate. The *Cabo* was crammed with oriental luxuries—Indian and Chinese silks and textiles, porcelain, and exotic products of all kinds. But what made the *Cabo's* cargo so extraordinarily precious was the enormous consignment of diamonds on board. Hours passed as the men struggled with axes and crowbars to open chest after chest. Watched by their companions, they delivered to the quartermaster whatever they found—glittering gems, coins, solid bars of gold and silver.[53] Piled up before the mainmast, Ericeira's riches must have been an extraordinary and intoxicating sight. The viceroy had obtained the diamonds through private trading. Some were his own property; others had been purchased on behalf of the Portuguese royal family and Lisbon merchants.[54]

The diamonds alone were said to be worth upward of £500,000; the silks, porcelain, and other goods were valued at £375,000. Adding in the value of the *Cassandra* and its cargo brings the total to over £900,000 ($450 million).[55] Assuming there were fewer than five hundred men aboard both vessels,[56] each potentially was owed a share of about £2,000 (about $1 million). Since the bulk of the cargoes aboard the *Cassandra* and *Cabo* never were sold to fences, the men did not gain the full value of their take. However, they did divide up the diamonds and gold, probably at Saint Mary's. With his customary embroidery, Defoe says the pirates shared out

> 42 small Diamonds a Man, or in less Proportion according to their Magnitude. An ignorant, or a merry Fellow, who had only one in his Division, as being judged equal in Value to 42 small, muttered very much at the Lot, and went and broke it in a Morter, swearing

afterwards, he had a better Share than any of them, for he had beat it, he said, into 43 Sparks.[57]

TAYLOR GETS AWAY WITH HIS LOOT, BUT OLIVER LA BUSE IS CAUGHT THROUGH TREACHERY

Nostra Senhora de Cabo was the last valuable prize taken by John Taylor and Oliver La Buse. After an unsuccessful cruise, the company was dissolved and the men split up in December 1722. La Buse and many others stayed at Madagascar. Taylor and 140 men in the *Cassandra* reached the Caribbean in May 1723. In return for the *Cassandra,* still a usable ship, the governor of Panama pardoned its captain and crew.

Immediately after seizing the *Cabo*, Taylor and La Buse went on to Saint Mary's. Some men stayed behind on the island, and a considerable number also died from fever.[58] Those that wanted to continue cruising burned the *Victory* and refitted the other craft. Taylor continued to command the *Cassandra*, while La Buse took over the *Cabo*, now reduced from three decks to two.[59]

The two vessels sailed south and then turned north along Madagascar's west coast. On December 30, 1721, the men captured a French slaver, *La Duchesse de Noailles*.[60] The ship was looted, and several officers were taken captive, including Mister Robert, the ship's supercargo.[61] Up until now Taylor and La Buse had released European ships after they were searched. In this case, they burned the *Duchesse de Noailles*, an act of arson for which La Buse later paid with his life.[62]

The warships commanded by Condent, England, and Taylor were not the only impediments to commerce in the Indian Ocean. Adding to the disarray were the audacious piracies of native Indian captains affiliated with Conajee Angria.[63] As always, the directors of the East India Company wanted pirate settlements entirely rooted out. Four naval warships under Commodore Thomas Matthews left England in February 1721 with orders to rendezvous at Saint Augustine's Bay. Before going on to Bombay, the squadron was told to hunt for pirates at Saint Mary's Island, Réunion, and the mouth of the Red Sea.

Soon after leaving the English Channel, two of the warships lost their masts in a storm and had to put into Lisbon to repair damages. Commodore Matthews' flagship went on to Saint Augustine's Bay. As Matthews could see no suspect vessels in the harbor, he assumed all was well and sailed to Bombay without waiting for the other ships in the squadron. Before leaving, he wrote a letter to their captains, explaining his plans and ordering them to join him at Bombay.

Matthews left this letter with the Malagasy ruler of the area, who dutifully handed it over to Captain Taylor when the *Cassandra* and the *Cabo* showed up. Taylor, who had no idea warships were hunting him, gleefully read the letter to the entire company assembled at the main mast.[64] By the time the rest of Matthews's squadron stopped at Saint Augustine's at the end of June 1722, the *Cassandra* and *Cabo* were long gone.[65]

Deciding that they should get entirely out of the way of naval warships, the company crossed to Africa and occupied a small fort built by the Dutch East India Company at Delagoa Bay (today known as Lourenço Marques Bay) in Mozambique. When they left in August 1722, they took with them a small Dutch ketch of the type known as "hooker."[66] They also kidnaped several Dutch mariners, including Jacob de Bucquoy, who later published the story of his captivity.[67]

The two ships cruised along the African coast without success. Having taken nothing of much value since capturing *Nostra Senhora de Cabo* sixteen months earlier, the men became cranky, and Taylor and La Buse fell into an emotion-laden rivalry. They competed for the support from the crews, with each having his own coterie. At one point, La Buse and some of his officers plotted to desert Taylor and take the *Cabo* to the West Indies. But their plot was discovered, and some of those on the *Cabo* fired a cannon and raised a black flag—the customary signal of distress. An assembly of both crews voted to remove La Buse as captain of the *Cabo*. All the plotters were flogged at the main mast, and their booty was seized for the company's use.[68]

The men degraded and punished La Buse because he wanted to leave without the consent of both crews, contrary to the ships' articles and the consortship agreement. But they also refused to follow Taylor in his grandiose plan to attack the fortified Arab city of Mozambique. Trying to convince the men crowded together before the mast, Taylor made a dramatic speech. Bucquoy, his Dutch captive, asserts that Taylor recalled his many victories and cried out, "If one could attack heaven, I would fire my first shot at God!" He accused the men of cowardice.

> Why did you become pirates? Because you didn't fear danger and wanted to gain booty. Well, at Mozambique, there is rich plunder, but I see that I'm talking to cowards, too weak to take on the work of men.[69]

By now, however, the men were tired of the entire expedition and wanted to return to Madagascar to break up the company. On September 4, they landed on the northwest coast at Bombétouke (near modern Majunga), where they gained the Malagasy king's permission to repair their vessels. The existing sworn association was dissolved. Some of the men stayed on at Bombétouke. Taylor retained command of the *Cassandra* with the intention of returning to the Caribbean. La Buse, degraded only a few weeks before, was again elected captain of the *Cabo* by those wishing to cruise in the Indian Ocean. This group also took over the Dutch hooker captured at Delagoa Bay; they elected a Scotsman named Elk as captain.[70]

In November 1722, as they prepared to go their separate ways, the captains met to say their good-byes. As they drank, the animosity between La Buse and Taylor broke out into a fierce quarrel. In a blind rage, Taylor stormed out, returned to the *Cassandra*, and immediately set sail for the Bahamas.[71]

When the *Cassandra* reached the Caribbean, the governors of the Bahamas and Jamaica both refused to pardon Taylor and his comrades, so they sailed on to the Spanish city of Portobelo, on Panama's Caribbean coast. Portobelo's governor also adamantly opposed an amnesty—until Taylor threatened to attack and burn the town. In return for clemency, the men gave the governor the *Cassandra* and 121 barrels of gold and silver coins. But each man still had his share of Count Ericeira's diamonds secreted on his person.

Jacob de Bucquoy wrote that John Taylor was still alive in 1744. After some years at Portobelo, he went on to Jamaica, married, and fathered four children. When the proceeds from the sale of his diamonds began to run out, he purchased a farm in Cuba and started trading with the neighboring islands using a small ship.[72]

Meanwhile, Oliver La Buse went on to Saint Mary's, sank the *Cabo*, and took command of the Dutch hooker.[73] His company cruised for some time along the Indian coasts, and then retired on Madagascar.[74] In January 1724, John Clayton took a small bark to Réunion and returned valuable liturgical vessels taken with the *Cabo* in 1721. The island's council sent Clayton back to Madagascar with an offer of amnesty. Twenty-three men, most English, accepted and later went back to Europe. But La Buse and his followers were not among their number. Although he was specifically mentioned in the Council's offer of pardon, La Buse did not trust the offer. The inhabitants of Réunion might tolerate the theft of a Portuguese treasure ship; they would be unlikely to forgive the burning of *La Duchesse de Noailles*, which had been carrying much needed supplies to that isolated little island.[75]

As of 1730, Oliver La Buse resided on the small island of Marosy in the middle of Antongil Bay, and he often acted as an intermediary between European slavers and Malagasy chiefs.[76] That year, La Buse joined a Captain Lhermitte in slave trading along Madagascar's coasts. When their expedition neared its end, La Buse was invited aboard Lhermitte's vessel, arrested, and brought in chains to Bourbon. On June 7, 1730, he was hanged for piracy at Réunion, where his grave can still be found.[77]

CHAPTER SIXTEEN

THE LASTING LEGACIES OF THE SAINT MARY'S PIRATES

*Numerous pirates have retired and established themselves on
Madagascar, especially on the East coast, in the province of Managabé
[Antongil], some for ten to twelve years, others for even longer. . . .
Most are petty kings, having each under his domination two or three
villages; they have gained their authority by marrying the leading
negresses [Malagaches], those that have the greatest prestige and that
already were rich through trading with pirates.*

—Le sieur Robert (1730)

Following the capture of the East Indiaman *Cassandra* in 1720, London
sent four men-of-war with orders to hunt for pirates. Commodore
Thomas Matthews's flagship just missed Taylor and La Buse at Saint Augustine's Bay before going on to India.[1] During the summer of 1722,
Matthews took his squadron back to Madagascar. At Saint Mary's, the
wrecks of several large vessels were visible beneath the waves, and the beach
was strewn with drugs, spices, and chinaware from various prizes.[2]

Commodore Matthews did not look very hard for pirates. However, at
Antongil Bay, John Plantain ran up the English flag and hailed the ships,
eager to trade cattle for European liquors. Plantain escaped arrest because
he was guarded by twenty Malagasy warriors. He told the sailors he had
been born at Chocolate Hole, Jamaica. Joining up with Captain England,
he had helped capture both the *Cassandra* and the diamond-rich *Cabo*.

After the loot was divided, Plantain stayed at Antongil Bay with James Adair and Hans Burgen. The three men built a stockaded fort and were accepted as rulers by the natives, whom they provided with firearms during tribal wars. Calling himself the "King of Ranter Bay," Plantain furnished the primitive rooms with oriental treasures. Dressed in exquisite silks embroidered in gold and silver, his beautiful wives wore golden chains, rings, bracelets, and diamonds of great value.[3]

If Matthews had searched more carefully, he would have found dozens of former pirates living in comfortable homes along the Madagascar coast.[4] No one knows how long they survived to enjoy the fruits of their crimes. They had grown accustomed to island food and had acquired some immunity to local diseases. Madagascar offered a better standard of living than Réunion, and Malagasy and European medicine were about on a par at that time. Madagascar's climate was kinder to white men than in Africa or India, and some Europeans lived to a remarkable age. One of the men who retired on Réunion Island was still living there in 1770, aged one hundred and four.

For more than thirty years, visiting and resident Europeans had accepted Malagasy brides. The natives prized light-colored skin,[5] and the pirates' many children were proud of their heritage. By the 1720s, thousands of mixed-blood Malagasy formed a separate clan and were known as the Malata (mulattos) and Zana-Malata (children of the mulattos). Although no longer a cohesive group, their descendants are said to be identifiable by their reddish hair and blue eyes.[6]

During the 1720s, Ratsimilao, son of a princess at Fénérive and a pirate named Tom seized leadership of the Malata. Malagasy legends relate that Tom decided to take his son to London to give him a good education. The boy, aged seventeen, became homesick after three months so his father sent him back with money, weapons, and goods for trading.[7]

At this time, the mainland villages just west of Saint Mary's suffered under a cruel foreign occupation. Contact with the pirates had enriched the region between Tamatave and Antongil Bay, arousing the envy of the peoples immediately to the south. A chief of the Vatomanry region forged an alliance of clans that sent troops north to seize Tamatave, Foulpointe, and Fénérive. The invaders treated the conquered peoples brutally, burning their villages and crops, selling many of them as slaves, and desecrating their tombs.

The last was an unforgivable act to the ancestor-venerating Malagasy. Ratsimilao was able to assemble a force of 10,000 men from several tribes. All swore an oath of blood brotherhood, and Ratsimilao distributed two hundred riffles. Victorious at Fénérive, Ratsimilao was elected king and

changed his name to Ramaromanompo (he that rules over many); his followers called themselves Betsimisaraka (the many who are inseparable).

This Betsimisaraka people, created by the son of an English pirate, has
retained its identity and is considered to be the second largest ethnic group
in Madagascar. However, Ramaromanompo's kingdom began to disinte-
grate soon after his death in 1750. Rather than copying the African style of
divine kingship found on the West Coast, Ramaromanompo chose to rule
in the Polynesian manner as a prime minister of a confederation. His descendants lacked Ramaromanompo's abilities, however, and the French government seized Saint Mary's Island in 1750 and began to expand on the
neighboring mainland.[8]

THE DESCENDANTS OF THE PIRATES TAKE UP
THEIR TRADE

The Malata never forgot their fathers' tales of seafaring adventures. Before
the pirates arrived, the Malagasy had built only small canoes for fishing.
Malata warriors now took to the sea in much larger vessels. With as many
as 500 canoes carrying more than 15,000 warriors, they raided Africa and
the Comoro Islands for slaves and plunder. Even after the last pirates had
died, their buccaneering spirit lived on in their children.

The raids began as slave-catching expeditions. The French East India
Company had turned Réunion and Mauritius into enormous coffee and
sugar plantations which needed continual supplies of food and workers.
Agents for the French paid well for slaves as it became more difficult to
obtain them by raids into the interior of Madagascar.

Malagasy legend has it that men from the Betsimisaraka village of
Angontsy were taken to the Comoro Islands in a pirate ship. There they
helped the victors win a local war. Rewarded with free passage back to
Madagascar, they brought home news of the wealth on the Comoros and
knowledge of how to get there.

The people of An'gon'ci taken to the Comoro Islands on a pirate
ship which had gone there to take on fresh provisions were landed
on Anjouan. It is not known why. They spent a year there and took
part in the war between the inhabitants of the villages of Domoni
and Mutsamudu. Having been trained in warfare by the pirates with
whom they had served, they helped the people of Domoni to victory. Their reward consisted in being sent back to their own country. . . . One of them, called Rassariki, an intelligent, bold man, had

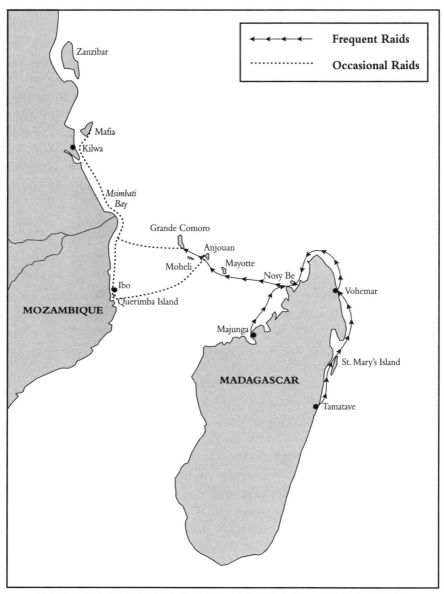

Frequent Raids
Occasional Raids

Zanzibar

Mafia
Kilwa

Msimbati
Bay

Grande Comoro
Anjouan
Moheli   Mayotte

Ibo   Nosy Be
Querimba Island

MOZAMBIQUE   Vohemar

                    Majunga

                        MADAGASCAR   St. Mary's Island

                              Tamatave

RAIDS BY MALAGASY PIRATES, 1765–1820

observed the way in which the sailors of Anjouan managed their boats, noting the route by certain positions of the sun and the stars. When they had arrived in his own country, where slaves were much sought after for trade, he had the idea of going to the Comoro Islands to obtain slaves there. He knew that the people there had not the strength to resist nor to wage war. . . .[9]

Historians of Madagascar do not agree as to when the Zana-Malata expeditions began. If this Malagasy story is accurate, the first raids took place while European pirates still lived on Madagascar or shortly afterwards. However, some historians believe the raids did not start until the 1780s. If so, the legend can be read as a mythical truth thanking the pirates that taught the Malagasy how to navigate the seas.

A millennium earlier, the Polynesian ancestors of the Zana-Malata had crossed thousands of miles of open water to reach Madagascar. But their maritime skills had been forgotten; when the pirates arrived, the east coast peoples knew nothing better than hollowed canoes made out of tree trunks. Their European fathers taught the Malata how to construct larger canoes—up to 45 feet long and 12 feet wide—from planks bolted together with wooden pegs or sewn with raffia fibers. These craft probably gained stability from outriggers, but they were still at the mercy of the winds. The return journey back to Madagascar could only be made during the monsoon season around the beginning of the year.

The raiders normally set out in October and returned early the following year, their vessels loaded with booty and slaves. Between 400 and 500 canoes, carrying 15,000 to 18,000 warriors, took part in a grand raid about every five years. In the intervening years, only fifty canoes would be sent, allowing the battered Comorans to rebuild their farms. In addition to sacking all the Comoro Islands, the Malagasy also plundered along the entire Mozambique coast, attacking African, Arab, and Portuguese settlements. The pirates easily captured several European merchantmen, and they destroyed a Portuguese naval warship sent to punish them. Living in terror, the unhappy Comorans appealed in vain to the Sultan of Zanzibar as well as to the kings of Portugal, England, and France. The slaving expeditions ceased entirely only after the Merina king of Tananarive extended his rule over the north of Madagascar.

Throughout the years, the people of Antongil Bay opposite Saint Mary's took the leading role in these expeditions. Sylvain Roux was the

French agent at Tamatave during the early 1800s. He speaks of the men of
Antongil as

> the bravest soldiers and the boldest sailors on the whole island.
> Every seagoing expedition made against Anjouan, the Comoros
> and other places in the south of Madagascar always is led by these
> people, who alone provide two thirds of the men and vessels.[10]

Five hundred canoes, surging together across the sea, must have been an
extraordinary and fearsome sight. An English historian was reminded of the
ninth century, "when the high-prowed ships of the Norsemen crossed the
North Sea every spring to ravage the coasts and estuaries of Britain."[11] And,
indeed, Norse blood did flow in the veins of the Zana-Malata—descended
in part from Norman seamen who had set up camp at Saint Mary's and
mingled their genes with those of earlier invaders.

UNDER THE BLACK FLAG

The men on Saint Mary's transformed their profession as well as their off-
spring. If their sons on Madagascar inherited their buccaneering ways, they
also passed on their traditions to subsequent generations of sea rovers back
in North America. Libertalia perfected the piratical customs and democratic forms of governance inherited from the Caribbean buccaneers. In turn,
the Madagascar pirates transmitted these habits and institutions to raiders
based at the Bahamas and along North America's Atlantic Coast. Ship's articles, for example, became more detailed and more binding at Saint Mary's,
and it was in Saint Mary's formats that articles were universal among
marauders sailing during the 1720s.

Pirate flags demonstrate how Libertalia recast the symbolism as well as
the actuality of piracy. It is a common belief that every sea raider throughout history flew the Jolly Roger—a flag showing a white skull resting atop
crossed bones on a black background. By extension, the term "Jolly Roger"
has become a generic symbol of all things piratical—and not merely in
English. All around the world, the moniker adorns retail stores, hotels, and
taverns, as well as marinas and vessels.

In fact, few pirates ever used the Jolly Roger. Prior to about 1700,
raiders did not want a special flag identifying them as pirates. Black flags
and death's heads are not mentioned either in Exquemelin's *Buccaneers of
America* or in the French and Spanish records. Despite movies showing Sir

Henry Morgan flying the Jolly Roger, English, French, and Dutch buccaneers flew their national banners. Why would they do otherwise? The
Jolly Roger instantly identifies an approaching vessel as a pirate ship—a
tactic useful only in fiction. In real life, pirates tried until the last minute
to fool merchantmen by flying the flag of a friendly nation. Those with a
privateer's commission attacked under the flag of the nation authorizing
their expedition. (This led to other games. Captain Kidd hoisted the
French flag to trick his prey so he could capture them under an English
privateering commission.)

In addition to national flags, sailors sometimes flew the "bloody flag," a
plain red pennant. A flag was supposed to serve as a rallying point during
battle; in dim light or a haze, a bright red flag is relatively easy to see. In
addition, red directly communicates the symbolism of blood and battle. In
April 1680, when 300 buccaneers marched across the Panama Isthmus, they
divided themselves into several companies, each led by an elected captain.
Each company had its own flag for identification. Four banners were plain
red and two were solid green. "The seventh [division] was led by Edmund
Cook, with red colours striped with yellow, with a hand and sword for his
device."[12] As far as is known, Cook's company was the first to have a special flag of its own design—but the flag was red, not black.

During the seventeenth and eighteenth centuries, flags were important and emotionally charged symbols. During the first years, North
Americans in the Indian Ocean flew their national banner, just as the
buccaneers had done. Indeed, Thomas Tew and others went to considerable effort and expense to acquire a commission as a privateer, just so they
could fly the English flag.[13] They used other flags only later, when they
wanted to tell the world they were citizens of Libertalia and not subjects
of England's king.

As far as is known, Dirk Chivers was the first pirate to claim Saint
Mary's as his nation. Early in December 1696, Chivers held the port at
Calicut to ransom. When English merchants appealed to his sense of patri-
otism, Chivers replied "that they acknowledged no countrymen . . ., and
that they would take no quarter but do all the mischief they could." (The
saying "to take quarter" meant that those surrendering would be spared;
"no quarter" indicated that all captives would be put to death.) To show
that he meant business, Chivers and his men immediately hoisted "bloody
colors"—plain red flags. Chivers had demonstrated a similar mastery of
symbolism a few weeks earlier when he ran up English flags on ships that

had refused to pay ransom. This was done to stress that he knew the vessels were English and would do no favors for his former countrymen.[14]

Despite its practical disadvantages, a black banner instantly conveys the threat of death, since black is the color of funerals in every Christian sect. Thus, pirate warships began to hoist black as well as red flags in battle. This became increasingly common after 1699, as the pirates were embittered by the English government reneging on offers of pardon. It would be fanciful to infer that they thought of Saint Mary's as the kingdom of death, but the black flag did suggest that they no longer considered themselves to be Englishmen. On occasions when they were determined to terrify their foe, ships flew both black and red flags from every mast.[15]

Black and red flags replaced national flags at Saint Mary's. Adding various white images on the black background apparently became common around 1716 at the short-lived pirate haven in the Bahamas. However, the Nassau pirates did not all use the Jolly Roger (the skull and crossbones). Each ship's crew wanted a unique image that would distinguish them from every other company of raiders.

After the Nassau pirate haven was suppressed in 1717, some pirate gangs fled east to Africa and then to Madagascar. They carried with them individualized flags—both black and red. When Captain Snelgrave was captured in April 1719, he reported that Captain Howell Davis came into the river showing the "black Flag at the Main-top-mast-head, which Pirate Ships usually hoist to terrify Merchant-Men."[16] Three weeks later, the same pirates captured a French merchantman. Its captain reported that the mainmast of one vessel carried a black flag with the figure of death stabbing a heart. On the front mast of the same warship appeared a red flag bearing a hand that held a saber; "this flag they called Strong Arm or without quarter."[17]

Ships continued to fly both red and black flags after they passed below the Cape of Good Hope to maraud in the Indian Ocean. When Edward England battled the *Cassandra* at Johanna Island, the *Fancy* hoisted red and black banners as well as the cross of Saint George at the ensign staff.[18] While attacking a Portuguese treasure ship in April 1721, Oliver La Buse and John Taylor again flew both red and black flags; this time, each flag showed several death's heads.[19]

Pirate flags became more elaborate on the ships marauding along the Atlantic coast during the 1720s. Black became more common than red. (Perhaps red cloth was difficult to obtain.) Many companies went to great lengths to exhibit a distinctive design. When Charles Harris and his crew were hanged, "Their Black Flag, with the Portraiture of Death having an Hour-Glass in one Hand and a Dart in the other, at the end of which was a Form of a Heart with three Drops of Blood falling from it, was affix'd at one corner of the Gallows. This Flag they call'd Old Roger, and often us'd to say they would live and die under it."[20]

Bartholomew Rogers generally used a flag depicting a death's head and a cutlass. Angered when the governors of Barbados and Martinique tried to arrest him, he ordered a jack-flag to be made which he hoisted together with other banners. The jack portrayed his own figure, with a flaming sword in his hand, standing on two skulls subscribed with the letters ABH and AMH. These signified respectively: "A Barbadian's Head and A Martinician's head."[21]

It was Robert Louis Stevenson who convinced generations of boys that pirates flew the skull and crossbones. (Earlier fiction vaguely alluded to the pirate's "sable flag" without any mention of the death's head.[22]) Stevenson's *Treasure Island* attracted expert illustrators, including Howard Pyle and N.C. Wyeth, who engraved the Jolly Roger on every reader's memory. Vaudeville, musical comedies, and motion pictures have reinforced the image.[23] Although they never hoisted the Jolly Roger, the men at Saint Mary's contributed to the legend by replacing the cross of Saint George with the red and black banners of Libertalia.

ROMANCING THE REAL: DANIEL DEFOE'S PIRACY
In addition to hundreds of half-European children, the Madagascar pirates thus fathered a rich legacy of legend and lore. In pirate mythology, all marauders are similar and act in similar ways. In fact, many stories originally were told about brigands sailing from Saint Mary's. Only later were they borrowed to describe pirates in other regions and eras.

The Madagascar rovers entered the realm of mythology through Daniel Defoe's *General History*. Defoe created compelling and apparently realistic portraits of major captains. Ever since, other authors have simply copied Defoe's fables, often word for word. With *Treasure Island,* Robert Louis Stevenson relocated Defoe's tall tales from the Indian Ocean to the Caribbean. In this way, Jim Hawkins and Long John Silver can be counted among the half-breed children of the Madagascar pirates.

Defoe did not try for veracity in the *General History*. Seventeenth-century authors and readers did not make a rigid distinction between fiction and nonfiction, between history and fable.[24] Throughout his literary career, Defoe deliberately blended fiction and fact.[25] He never knew, for example, that *Robinson Crusoe* was the first English "novel." This generic label was imposed at a later date; as the title page shows, Defoe published the book as an autobiography, and many readers assumed it was a true tale.

Defoe was fascinated by piracy. In addition to the *General History,* at least four additional major works have pirate heroes, and piracy is involved in numerous other books.[26] *The King of Pirates,* published in 1719, is a fictitious autobiography of Henry Every; it was intended as a tall tale even more outrageous than earlier stories about the fabulously successful raider.[27] *The Life, Adventures and Pyracies of the Famous Captain Singleton* (1720) presents an unscrupulous marauder who meets Every. *A New Voyage Round the World* (1724) describes a plunder raid by a coolly murderous captain, who stops at Madagascar to purchase a ship and recruit crewmen.

But generations of readers have agreed that *A General History of the Robberies and Murders of the most Notorious Pyrates* is more exciting and readable than Defoe's other pirate books. Fictitious biographies of criminals had long been an established form of entertainment—albeit entertainment often with an edifying moral message. But Defoe raised the format to new heights, and the *General History*'s biographies are among the most intrinsically interesting works in Defoe's entire vast output.[28] The full title shows Defoe's understanding of his audience. He included the gore, sex, and grotesque comic relief his readers expected, but he embedded these details in powerful stories.[29] Even when they are entirely fictional, the events described seem very real.[30] In one form or another, the *General History* has remained in print for almost three centuries,[31] and hundreds of authors have paid the book the additional compliment of plagiarism.

The first volume, published in 1724, includes biographies of seventeen captains. Except for Henry Every and Edward England, all had cruised the Atlantic Ocean during the preceding ten years. Fortunately, the book enjoyed considerable success, for Defoe was in desperate financial need. In July 1728, he published a sequel largely devoted to the pirates at Madagascar and Saint Mary's Island.

The second volume starts with a wholly fanciful description of Captain Misson's pirate utopia on Madagascar.[32] Thomas Tew and William Kidd each get a chapter. A series of interlinked biographies follows, presenting captains active from 1699 to 1707, including Bowen, Halsey, White, Burgess, North, and a fictional David Williams.[33]

Whereas the first volume probably contains as many true as imaginary events, invented stories prevail in the sequel. Defoe had little information about events thirty years earlier. He compensated by concocting pirate communities and conversations with fictitious native chiefs. In the process he created two enduring myths and added to the public image of piracy: fiend and hero.

Thanks to the *General History,* therefore, Madagascar captains have a fictional twin or *doppleganger,* who more or less closely resembles the real man. Once they were published, Defoe's stories entered the public domain, and later writers were free to add new details to his account, thereby creating the pirate mythology of our own day. In a sense, Defoe's portraits of pirates are like those of a graphic artist. From time to time, subsequent painters retouched the canvas, but Defoe's original sketch can still be discerned underneath the later layers of pigment. As John Robert Moore remarked, "It is hardly too much to say that the author of the *History* has created the modern conception of Pirates."[34]

During the early nineteenth century, a Boston retailer named Charles Ellms turned to compiling almanacs with catchy titles. The *Pirates Own Book,* his most profitable product, went through at least nine editions. Ellms was a cut-and-paste editor, and he took at least half his stories from the *General History.* To suit his purposes, he plagiarized only those captains Defoe had portrayed as fiends. Heroic figures such as Captain Misson were left out.

Even Defoe's monsters were not sufficiently frightening for Ellms's purposes, and he inserted new details of ravaging and gore. He copied Defoe's biography of Captain Kidd, for example, but made telling additions. Kidd was totally evil, Ellms asserted, an "animal of the ocean" from his birth. Because it condemned the crimes he wanted to commit, Kidd buried his Bible in the sand—a nice touch that fascinated pious readers. Always eager to play up buried treasure, Ellms also added tales about Kidd's booty.

Ellms intended his books for the entire family, and they influenced children especially through their illustrations. The lurid pictures in the *Pirates Own Book* were created by an anonymous artist. During the twentieth century, Ellms' role as pirate fantasist was taken by Howard Pyle, a popular illustrator. The *General History* was also Pyle's preferred source of inspiration for pirate fiction and art.[35] While his stories are restrained, Pyle's drawings of pirate captains emphasize their merciless cruelty.

THE REAL *TREASURE ISLAND*

Robert Louis Stevenson left the most lasting mark on modern conceptions of piracy. Stevenson took Defoe's tall tales about Madagascar and transferred them to the Caribbean. Major characters, including Long John Silver, were lifted straight from the *General History of the Pyrates.* After Edward England captured the *Cassandra,* many men wanted to hang the ship's captain. In Defoe's version, Captain Macrae was saved by a former shipmate. A bluff and hardy fellow with a wooden leg, he "comes swearing and vapouring upon the Quarter-Deck . . .; *shew me the Man,* says he, *that offers to hurt Captain* Mackra, *for I'll stand by him.*" It is this one-legged man, renamed Long John Silver, who dominates the plot of *Treasure Island.*[36]

Stevenson indirectly acknowledges his debt when Jim Hawkins overhears Long John Silver plotting mutiny. Addressing the crew, Silver boasts of his piratical career. Before going with Flint, Silver says, he had sailed under Edward England. "So it was with the *Cassandra,* as brought us all safe home from Malabar, after England took the Viceroy of the Indies."[37] Silver earlier had told Jim that his parrot had learned to say "Pieces of eight" while sailing with England. There are many other references (not always accurate) to the *General History.* As Francis Watson points out, "Even minor bits of phraseology, and the swing of the prose rhythm of Jim Hawkins' narrative go back to the redoubtable captain [Johnson]—who was probably Daniel Defoe."[38]

If he took characters and details from the *General History,* Stevenson transformed his borrowings through his own imagination. *Treasure Island* has been a standard boy's book for generations, and numerous motion pictures and television programs have been taken from it.[39] Thanks to this powerful outpouring of pirate fiction—all ultimately derived from the *General History*—nearly everyone thinks of pirates in the same way. The "Pirate" has become a protean archetype, deeply embedded in popular culture. The word instantly evokes a mental image or icon, appropriated by everyone, both male and female. Only the image of the "Cowboy" is as powerful. Even Robin Hood is less well-known. Among modern icons, only Elvis Presley and Marilyn Monroe come close.

For the English-speaking world, the Caribbean buccaneers dominate pirate mythology, as if no other marauders ever roamed the seven seas. Equipped with an eye patch, hoop earrings, head band, and parrot—and probably with a wooden leg—the buccaneer of song and story stands posed over a smoking cannon beneath the skull n' crossbones. One hand flourishes a bottle of rum mixed with gunpowder; the other waves a cutlass.

Soon he will pounce on his prey, fiendishly torturing his victims and reveling in their agony. For all his crimes, he will die penniless—-his loot either buried in the sand or robbed by some buxom wench.

HUNTING FOR PIRATE TREASURE

Although everyone associates them with the Caribbean, the modern image of the pirate does not resemble the real-life buccaneers. Fictionalists have imposed these legends on West Indian pirates, but their origins in Defoe's *General History* remain apparent. Even in their exaggerated form, they are more suitable to the Indian Ocean of Captain Kidd than the Caribbean of Sir Henry Morgan.

Caribbean villains, to take one example, are surrounded by great heaps of gold coins and gems. But mythical pirates do not spend their treasure; they instead bury it in the sand. They die with the gold still hidden, awaiting discovery by modern-day treasure hunters. This buried treasure myth was created during the eighteenth century, with Captain Kidd being the first man credited with secreting vast wealth. Culminating in *Treasure Island,* pirate fiction elaborated the legends and moved them to the Caribbean. Movies and television routinely show Sir Henry Morgan and other Caribbean buccaneers hiding treasure. But neither Exquemelin nor any other contemporary ever mentions anything of the sort.

Away from Madagascar, buried treasure makes no sense at all. Caribbean and North American pirates rarely captured gems or gold and silver coins. (Any other form of loot would rot away if buried.) And, when they did take plunder, North American rovers had no reason to conceal it. Their voyages were brief and they were never far from home. Local officials did not enforce laws against pirates, who were welcome to spend their take in a dozen ports. Ambitious men used their booty to buy sugar plantations, while less provident ones enjoyed gambling and other pleasures. Why would any man have chosen instead to lose his gold by burying it in the sand?

Although no one has found Captain Kidd's buried treasure, there were sensible reasons to hide loot on Madagascar—and only on Madagascar. The marauders in the Indian Ocean did seize golden treasure on many occasions, taking far more money than they could spend quickly. They were far from home, and many lived on Madagascar for years at a time. There were many motives for putting money aside. Robert Culliford might well have hidden loot from one cruise before embarking on another. Adam Baldridge and Edward Welch had to store coins while waiting for Samuel Burgess to bring supplies from North America. Some men might have wanted to send money to their families. Others might have hidden it because they did not entirely trust their Malagasy wives and dreamed of going home some day. When Samuel Burgess was captured at the Cape of Good Hope in December 1699, his nineteen pirate passengers carried a total of £11,400 (about $5.7 million).[40] There was no way to spend that much money on Saint Mary's, and it made good sense to store it away while waiting to return to North America.

SAINT MARY'S AND THE PIRATE HERITAGE

The young men that made the difficult passage across the oceans were a remarkable lot. Sailing from Saint Mary's, they stole more loot than any other criminals in history. With rare exceptions, they escaped capture and lived to enjoy their booty. They created a uniquely democratic form of government, perfecting customs inherited from the Caribbean buccaneers and passing these along to later generations of raiders. When not attacking their prey, they managed to be on good terms with everyone from colonial governors to Indian merchants and the Malagasy of Madagascar. They seem to have been particularly attractive to the already "liberated" women of Saint Mary's, who willingly took them as husbands. Their memory was cherished by their mixed blood children, who imitated their piratical raids.

The Madagascar raiders represented the final Golden Age of European piracy. It surely is fitting that Daniel Defoe—a man of equal genius in his own field—turned their exploits into enduring myths. Even if this were desirable, it is not possible at this late date to erase the pirate mythology created by great artists. Once firmly established, popular legends are not abandoned, no matter how much evidence is presented to the contrary. For two centuries, nearly everyone has believed that Captain Kidd spent his life murdering and plundering. It would do no good to point out that, prior to his ill-fated voyage, Kidd had fought heroically alongside the English navy. More recently, novels and plays have turned Anne Bonny and Mary Read—two fictional characters in the General History of Pyrates—into overwhelmingly powerful Amazon warriors. Again, it would be useless to prove that, in real life, neither women ever fought a battle or looted a ship.[41] Nothing can be gained by arguing with long-established myths. Nevertheless, it is but simple justice to note that the memory of the Madagascar pirates was preserved in these curious ways—that, for example, anyone that spends time with Silver and Jim Hawkins actually is visiting Saint Mary's, the real "Treasure Island."

NOTES

ABBREVIATIONS USED THROUGHOUT
Benjamin Franks' Narrative
  Deposition made at Bombay on October 20, 1697. Printed in *Privateering and Piracy in the Colonial Period: Illustrative Documents*, ed. John Jameson (New York: Macmillan, 1923), pages 190–195.
Bucquoy
  Jacobus de Bucquoy. *Zestien Jaarige Reis nass de Inidien gedan door Jacob de Bucquoy.* (Haarlem: Bosch, 1744). Reprinted in part in *Grandidier,* vol. 5, pages 103–139.
CSPC
  Calendar of State Papers, Colonial Series, America and West Indies.
Documentary History of New York
  Documentary History of the State of New York, ed. Edmund B. O'Callaghan, 4 vols. (Albany: Weed, Parsons, 1849–1853).
Documents, Colonial History of New York
  Documents Relative to the Colonial History of the State of New York, comp. John Romeyn Brodhead, ed. Edmund B. O'Callaghan and Berthold Fernow, 15 vols. (Albany: Weed Parsons, 1853–1887).
Cape of Good Hope: Journal
  Précis of the Archives of the Cape of Good Hope: Journal, 1699–1732, ed. Hendril Carel Vos Leibbrandt (Cape Town: Richards, 1896).
Grandidier
  Collection des Ouvrages anciens concernant Madagascar, ed. Alfred Grandidier and Guillaume Grandidier, 9 vols. (Paris: Comité de Madagascar, 1903–1920).
General History of the Pyrates
  Daniel Defoe. *A General History of the Pyrates*, 2 vols. (London: Rivington, 1724–1728). New edition in one volume by Manuel Schonhorn (Columbia: University of South Carolina Press, 1972. Schonhorn edition reprinted with a new postscript, Mineola, N.Y.: Dover, 1999).
Lazenby's Narrative
  Deposition by Richard Lazenby made at Bombay in 1721. Printed in part in Charles Grey, *Pirates of the Eastern Seas* (London: Low, Marston, 1933), pages 316–18, 320–25.
Luttrell
  Narcissus Luttrell. *A Brief Historical Relation of State Affairs from September 1678 to April 1714*, six volumes (London: Oxford University Press, 1857).
Kidd's Narrative
  Deposition by William Kidd made at Boston, July 17, 1699. Printed in *Privateering and Piracy*, pages 205–13; *Trial of Captain Kidd*, pages 194–99. Slightly abbreviated version printed in *CSPC, 1699* (London, 1908), pages 375–79.

Papers of Thomas Bowery
> *The Papers of Thomas Bowery 1669–1713*, ed. Richard Carnac Temple (London: Hakluyt Society, 1927).

Privateering and Piracy
> *Privateering and Piracy in the Colonial Period: Illustrative Documents*, ed. John Jameson (New York: Macmillan, 1923).

Robert
> *Description en général et en détail de l'Iâle de Madagascar . . . par le sieur Robert* (1730), published in part in *Grandidier*, vol. 5, pages 61–71.

Robert Drury's Journal
> Daniel Defoe. *Madagascar; Or, Robert Drury's Journal, during Fifteen Years' Captivity on That Island*. New edition by Pasfield Oliver (London: Fisher Unwin, 1890).

State Trials
> *A Complete Collection of State-Trials and Proceedings upon High-Treason, and other Crimes and Misdemeanors; from the Reign of King Richard II to the End of the Reign of King George I*, second edition in six volumes (London: Walthoe, 1730).

Trial of Captain Kidd
> *Trial of Captain Kidd*, ed. Graham Brooks (London: Hodge, 1930).

Villers Diary
> *Isle de Bourbon (Réunion): Documents 1701–1710*. New York Public Library, 1909. [Includes the diary of Jean-Baptiste de Villers, governor of Réunion from 1701–1709.]

INTRODUCTION

1. Sir Francis Drake took almost as much booty when he captured the *Cacafuego* off Peru in 1579. However, Queen Elizabeth I seized almost all the treasure, leaving only a tiny part for Drake and his men. In contrast, because they ruled themselves, raiders from Saint Mary's got to keep almost everything they took.
   The quotation at the beginning of this chapter is taken from *Bucquoy*, pages 107, 116.
2. Some historians say homosexuality was prevalent among Caribbean buccaneers and North Atlantic marauders. See B. R. Burg, *Sodomy and the Pirate Tradition* (New York University Press, 1984); Hans Turley, *Rum, Sodomy, and the Lash: Piracy, Sexuality, and Masculine Identity* (New York University Press, 1999). However, the mariners sailing from Saint Mary's seem to have been largely heterosexual. Whatever they did on the way to Madagascar, most married one or more Malagasy women soon after they hit the beach. One can be confident in asserting that most of the men were straight precisely because they took a rather tolerant attitude toward homosexuality. No attempt was made, for example, to hide the fact that some men were gay, including Captain Robert Culliford, who was extremely popular with his crew. (On a cramped ship without separate sleeping quarters, how could his comrades have avoided noticing Culliford's sexual predilections?)
3. Many of the French pirates retiring at Réunion Island, just east of Madagascar, were Protestants, a religious minority under attack in France since the 1680s.
4. Antoine Boucher, *Mémoire pour servir a la connoissance particulière de chacun des habitans de l'isle de Bourbon*, ed. Jean Barassin (Aix-en-Provence: Association des Chercheurs de l'Ocean Indien, 1978), page 316.
5. *Documents, Colonial History of New York*, vol. 4, page 447.
6. See John Robert Moore, *Defoe in the Pillory and other Studies* (Bloomington: Indiana University Press, 1939), page 133. "Although the majority of 'Johnson's' [Defoe's] statements are substantially good history . . . there are many things which could not possibly be known, even if true. The *History* tells what a man is thinking about before he dies, and it contains long speeches and dialogues (quoted verbatim) which had no reporters. A ten-paragraph statement is remembered word for word by a man who saw it only once. He is later killed by a cannonball, and yet in some mysterious way pre-

serves a record of it for posterity. The marvelous journal of Captain Misson is carried through all dangers and posted up to date, only to escape drowning with its author by being in the possession of a man on another ship. . . ."

7. William Minto, *Daniel Defoe* (New York: Harper, 1887), page 169. "He was a great, a truly great liar, perhaps the greatest liar that ever lived."

8. In his famous and immensely successful *History of England* (1849–1861), Thomas Macaulay accepts the stories that Captain Kidd committed countless acts of shameless cruelty. Since he was an historian of ancient Greece, perhaps Henry Ormerod—*Piracy in the Ancient World* (Liverpool, 1914), page 157—may be forgiven for believing the pirate colony in Madagascar "was founded by the Frenchman Mission and our Captain Tew." Ormerod added that "The fullest account of both men is that given by Chas. Johnson, *History of the Pirates*, Vol. II (1725)."

   Historians of New York, New England, and Madagascar also have perpetuated legends about other Saint Mary's men as well as about the fictitious Captain Misson. Mervyn Brown thus recites Defoe's fictions about Thomas White as if they actually took place; see *Madagascar Rediscovered: A History from Early Times to Independence* (Hamden, Conn.: Archon Books, 1979), page 84.

9. In *Between the Devil and the Deep Blue Sea* (New York: Cambridge University Press, 1987), Marcus Rediker describes the wretched social and economic status of merchant seamen. Failing to find examples of sailors criticizing this oppressive social system, Rediker quotes from speeches Defoe put into the mouths of his imaginary creatures. As Manuel Schonhorn notes in his postscript to the 1999 edition of the *General History*: "Unfortunately, like the gullible popularizers, Professor Rediker is obliged to cite the mock trials of Antis's crew and the radical rodomontade of Captain Bellamy as evidence of their contempt for authority and their quest for social justice."

10. Professor Rediker gives statistics created by comparing real and imaginary pirate captains both in *Between the Devil and the Deep Blue Sea* and also in "Under the Banner of King Death," in *William and Mary Quarterly*, vol. 38 (1981), page 208. In the same way, in "Legitimacy and Authority," *American Neptune*, vol. 37 (1977), pages 44–45, B. R. Burg created a chart showing the birth place, "class origin," and early seafaring experience of Defoe's fictional pirate commanders. He goes on to analyze these totally fictitious characteristics as if they provided evidence about the marauders who actually lived at Saint Mary's Island.

11. Created in Defoe's biographies of Henry Every (Chapter Six below), the stereotype of the noble hero was perfected in Charles Kingsley's *Westward Ho* (1855) and the novels of Rafael Sabatini published during the 1920s.

12. In W. S. Gilbert and Arthur Sullivan's *The Pirates of Penzance* (1879), for example, the audience is told that the pirates always let their captives go. In Robert Louis Stevenson's *Treasure Island* (1883) and James Barrie's *Peter Pan* (1904), the audience knows from the beginning that no one will be harmed.

13. See Roger Bootle, *The Death of Inflation: Surviving and Thriving in the Zero Era* (London: Brealey, 1996), page 169; David Hackett Fischer, *The Great Wave: Price Revolutions and the Rhythm of History* (New York: Oxford University Press, 1996) pages 4–6. Both authors provide citations to studies of the primary sources for data on price changes.

14. Fischer, *Great Wave*, page 120.

15. Henry Wilkinson, *Bermuda in the Old Empire* (London: Oxford University Press, 1950), page 15.

16. Niall Ferguson thus argues that Nathan Rothschild was richer at the time of his death than any person is today. When he died in 1836, Rothschild had £3.5 million—equivalent to 0.62 percent of the total Gross Domestic Product of Great Britain in that year. Rothschild's income and wealth were, moreover, comparatively untaxed. See *The House of Rothschild: Money's Prophets, 1798–1848* (New York: Viking, 1998).

17. See Philip N. Furbank and W. R. Owens, *The Canonisation of Daniel Defoe* (New Haven: Yale University Press, 1988). See below, Chapter Fourteen, note 9, for a discussion of the historical accuracy of *Robert Drury's Journal*.

CHAPTER ONE

1. John Ovington, *A Voyage to Surat in the Year 1689,* ed. H. G. Rawlinson (London: Oxford University Press, 1929), page 64. Ovington's book was first published in London in 1696. The quotation from the beginning of this chapter is taken from CSPC, *1700,* page 211.
2. See A. P. Thornton, *West-India Policy under the Restoration* (Oxford: Clarendon, 1956), Chapter Three.
3. Richard Dunn, *Sugar and Slaves: The Rise of the Planter Class in the English West Indies, 1624–1713* (Chapel Hill: University of North Carolina Press, 1972), pages 151–165. For overviews, see Jan Rogoziński, *Pirates! Brigands, Buccaneers, and Privateers in Fact, Fiction, and Legend* (New York: Facts on File, 1995) under the words *Buccaneers* and *Port Royal* as well as Rogoziński, *Brief History of the Caribbean* (New York: Facts on File, 1999), pages 92–104. Charles H. Haring, *The Buccaneers in the West Indies in the XVII Century* (London: Methuen, 1910) remains a useful narrative of events incorporating archival research.
4. Lionel Wafer, *A New Voyage & Description of the Isthmus of America,* ed. L. E. Elliot Joyce (London: Hakluyt Society, 1934), page 155. Haring, *Buccaneers,* page 267, notes that the town already had been sacked eight times by 1671.
5. Oskar Spate, *Monopolists and Freebooters* (Minneapolis: University of Minnesota Press, 1983), pages 140–159, provides an overview tracing the successive waves of invaders. Peter Kemp and Christopher Lloyd, *Brethren of the Coast: Buccaneers of the South Seas* (New York: Saint Martin's, 1961) examines the printed journals published by some of the buccaneers. Peter Bradley used these journals as well as the Spanish and colonial archives for *The Lure of Peru: Maritime Intrusion into the South Sea, 1598–1701* (New York: Saint Martin's, 1989), pages 103–166. Peter Gerhard also investigated Spanish and Mexican records for *Pirates on the West Coast of New Spain, 1575–1742* (Glendale, Calif.: Clark, 1960), pages 135–194.
6. William Schurz, *The Manilla Galleon* (New York: Dutton, 1939) is the most comprehensive account of these treasure ships.
7. Bradley, *Lure of Peru,* page 159.
8. Kemp and Lloyd, *Brethren of the Coast,* page 27.
9. William Dampier's *A New Voyage Round the World* originally was published by Knapton (London, 1697). N. M. Penzer published a new edition in 1927 (London: Argonaut). The Penzer edition has been reprinted by Black (London, 1927), by Dover (New York, 1966), and possibly by others.
10. Dampier, *New Voyage,* pages 340–341, for the *Cygnet's* final days.
11. Virginia Platt, "The East India Company and the Madagascar Slave Trade," *William and Mary Quarterly,* 3rd series, vol. 26 (1969), page 549.
12. Martin, *Mémoires,* vol. 2, page 549: *"Ces corsaires sont Anglais, filbustiers des iles Antilles et mêlés apparemment d'autres nations."* (These pirates are buccaneers from the Caribbean islands, mostly English but accompanied by men from other nations.) See *Grandidier,* vol. 3, page 456.
13. S. B. Miles, *The Countries and Tribes of the Persian Gulf* (London: Frank Cass, 1966), page 227.
14. Antoine Boucher, *Mémoire,* pages 22, 230, 258, 333.
15. Bradley, *Lure of Peru,* pages 129–130.
16. In a deposition given in April 1700, Edward Davis said that he was, at that time, a "mariner aged about 49 yeares old." See Harold Wilkins, *Captain Kidd and His Skeleton Island* (New York: Liveright, 1935), page 211.
17. Wafer, *New Voyage,* page 124.
18. Wafer, *New Voyage,* page 125 and footnote 1; Bradley, *Lure of Peru,* page 154; Spate, *Monopolists,* page 472, note 44.
19. Wafer, *New Voyage,* page 130.

20. *CSPC, 1689–1692,* page 20.
21. Wafer, *New Voyage,* page xiv. Donald Shomette describes their arrest and imprisonment in *Pirates on the Chesapeake* (Centreville, Md.: Tidewater Publishers, 1985), Chapter Three. See also Bradley, *Lure of Peru,* page 155; Lloyd Williams, *Pirates of Colonial Virginia,* (Richmond: Dietz, 1937), pages 33–34; *CSPC, 1689–1692,* page 20.
22. Davis (said to be an extraordinarily stout man) bought a passage with Captain William Kidd, when he left Saint Mary's Island in November 1699; see Lord Bellomont to the Council of Trade, October 24, 1699: *CSPC, 1699,* page 488. Davis was arrested with Kidd, sent to England, jailed in the Marshalsea and later in the Newgate prison, and apparently released on bail in June 1700: Wilkins, *Captain Kidd,* pages 157, 203, 213. For his April 1700 deposition telling how he came to be on Saint Mary's when Kidd arrived, see Wilkins, *Captain Kidd,* page 212.
23. The English buccaneers took advantage of the pardon James II had granted in May 1687 (*CSPC, 1685–1688,* numbers 1,277–1,278). French pirates fared less well with Jamaican officials; the latter arrested and tried several Frenchmen who had served in the South Sea (on a different vessel than the *Cygnet* or the *Delight*): *CSPC, 1685–1688,* number 1,796.
24. Haring, *Buccaneers,* pages 200–201.
25. Charles Grey, *Pirates of the Eastern Seas (1618–1723): A Lurid Page of History* (London: Low, Marston, 1933), pages 113–114.
26. Captain William Kidd described Baldridge's mistreatment of the Malagasy to Lord Bellomont during Kidd's interrogation after his arrest in July 1699. See *CSPC, 1699,* page 404. See also *Documents, Colonial History of New York,* vol. 4, page 413, and the deposition of Samuel Perkins (August 25, 1698), printed in *Privateering and Piracy,* page 176.
27. *Documents, Colonial History of New York,* vol. 4, page 333.
28. *Documents, Colonial History of New York,* vol. 4, page 413 (October 25, 1698).
29. *CSPC, 1699,* page 229, (item 384.II). Also published in *Privateering and Piracy,* pages 180–187.
30. Deposition of Samuel Perkins (August 25, 1698), printed in *Privateering and Piracy,* page 176.
31. Perhaps Adam Baldridge joined the raids on South America's Pacific coast, but he is not mentioned as a captain or leader in the copious accounts of those raids.
32. Testimony of Henry Watson, a naval surgeon and pirate prisoner in 1696: *CSPC, 1697–1698,* page 108.
33. Martin, *Mémoires,* vol. 1, pages 146–171, describes Malagasy customs on Saint Mary's and the mainland immediately to the east of the island, where Martin lived from 1665–1668. See vol. 1, page 34 for the French fort erected on Madagascar during Martin's stay.

    The *ravenala madagascariensis* popularly is known as the "traveler's-tree" (*arbre de voyageur*). It produces huge leaves in two ranks, giving the appearance of a gigantic symmetrical fan; small white flowers are held in erect series of canoelike bracts. In Madagascar the *ravenala* typically is a secondary-growth plant, growing in poor soil after the original forest has been destroyed. It has been imported to Florida, where it is planted to suggest a "tropical" ambiance.
34. Few Malagasy lived on the island when François Martin visited during the 1660s. At that time, the small population lived by fishing and traded their catch for rice with tribes on the mainland. Martin, *Mémoires,* vol. 1, pages 29–31.
35. Baldridge's deposition, *Privateering and Piracy,* page 181. When she arrived at Saint Mary's, the *Delight* carried only fourteen cannon, fewer but perhaps larger guns than when she had been a slaver.
36. Shirley Hughson, *The Carolina Pirates and Colonial Commerce, 1670–1740* (Baltimore, 1894), page 32.
37. *CSPC, 1696,* page 73.

38. For South Carolina's lack of "hard money," see Converse Clowse, *Economic Beginnings in Colonial South Carolina, 1670–1730* (Columbia: University of South Carolina Press, 1971), pages 144–147.

39. Edward Randolph to the Board of Trade: *CSPC, 1696,* page 73.

40. See Adam Baldridge's deposition in *Privateering and Piracy,* page 181. The *Delight's* total take during a three-year cruise thus exceeded £80,000, with a buying power of about $400 million in today's money.

41. Cyrus Karracker, *Piracy was a Business* (Rindge, N.H.: Richard Smith, 1953), page 150.

42. Adam Baldridge's deposition, *Privateering and Piracy,* page 182. Baldridge calls the visiting vessel the *Nassau.* However, it is clear that this ship is identical to the *Jacob.* Edward Coates is named as captain in both cases, the description of the two ships is similar, and both are said to have returned to New York from Saint Mary's.

43. Governor Christopher Codrington to the Board of Trade, March 1, 1690, *CSPC, 1689–1692,* pages 225–229. See also Robert Ritchie, *Captain Kidd and the War Against the Pirates* (Cambridge, Mass.: Harvard University Press, 1986), pages 30–31.

44. In reporting to the Board of Trade, Governor Codrington attached a description of the battle written by "a gentleman on board Hewetson's ship": *CSPC, 1689–1692,* pages 229–231.

45. Deposition by Robert Culliford, London, October 1701, printed in Wilkins, *Captain Kidd,* page 92. Governor Codrington reported (*CSPC, 1689–1692,* page 227) that "They took their opportunity when Captain Kidd (who has behaved himself well) was ashore and have carried off goods of his to the value of £2,000 ($1 million). Most of the crew were formerly pirates and I presume liked their old trade better than any that they were likely to have here."

46. Chapin, *Privateer Ships,* pages 116–117; James Lydon, *Pirates, Privateers, and Profits* (Upper Saddle River, N.J.: Gregg Press, 1970), pages 61–63, 75. Leisler's commission to "William Masson" is printed in *Documentary History of New York,* vol. 2, pages 250–251.

47. Leisler's commission is mentioned in a Board of Trade report of October 1698, in *Documents, Colonial History of New York,* vol. 4, page 385. It also is mentioned in Samuel Burgess's deposition (May 1698), *CSPC, 1697–1698,* page 227.

48. Robert Culliford's deposition (October 1701), printed in Wilkins, *Captain Kidd,* page 93.

49. In Pondicherry, French officials heard that pirates had seized four Surat vessels in the Red Sea. The Muslim governor of Surat imprisoned the English traders in the city and demanded that the Dutch and French East India Companies help defend the sea traffic lanes from Mocha to Surat: Martin, *Mémoires,* vol. 3, pages 252–253.

50. In his 1698 deposition, Baldridge says each man had £500. Taylor and Burgess, in depositions also taken in 1698, speak of 1,800 pieces of eight, equivalent to about £400: *Documents, Colonial History of New York,* vol. 4, page 386.

51. Deposition of Edward Taylor (May 7, 1698), printed in *CSPC, 1698–1698,* page 118.

CHAPTER TWO

1. Schurz, *Manilla Galleon, passim.* For the quotation at the beginning of this chapter, see *CSPC, 1696–1697,* page 260.

2. The Trade Winds receive their name from their opposing directions of flow, the term *trade* being used in the otherwise obsolete sense of direction or course (compare the word *tread*). Their force is greatest in the springtime. Above the equator, the northeast trades are strongest in April, while the southeast trades below the equator reach their maximum in September.

3. Matthew Maury, *The Physical Geography of the Sea, and its Meteorology,* 8th ed. (1862), ed. John Leighly (Cambridge, Mass.: Belknap, 1963), page 291.

4. The Asian monsoon system has not been fully explained. One theory attributes it to the oceans being hotter or colder than the land, depending on the season. It also may

be significant that the Indian Ocean is open toward the South Pole only, whereas the Atlantic and Pacific are open from one pole to the other. See K. N. Chaudhuri, *Trade and Civilisation in the Indian Ocean* (Cambridge, Eng.: Cambridge University Press, 1985), pages 127–128.

5. Chaudhuri, *Trade and Civilisation,* page 127. See also G. Bastian, *Madagascar: Etude géographique et économique* (Paris: Nathan, 1967), pages 18–19.
6. Auguste Toussaint, *History of the Indian Ocean,* trans. June Guicharnaud (Chicago: University of Chicago Press, 1966), page 10.
7. Teak offers the best resistance to the teredo worm. See Toussaint, *Indian Ocean,* page 10.
8. Eleven vessels brought slaves to Barbados during the 1680s, and at least three more sold their cargo at Jamaica. See Virginia Platt, "The East India Company and the Madagascar Slave Trade," *William and Mary Quarterly,* 3rd series, vol. 26 (1969), page 549.
9. Holden Furber, *Rival Empires of Trade in the Orient, 1600–1800* (Minneapolis: University of Minnesota Press, 1976), page 92; Jonathan Israel, *Dutch Primacy in World Trade, 1585–1740* (Oxford: Clarendon, 1989), pages 329–333.
10. Furber, *Rival Empires,* page 91.
11. Toussaint, *Indian Ocean,* page 121.
12. K. N. Chaudhuri, *The Trading World of Asia and the English East India Company* (New York: Cambridge University Press, 1978), pages 50–51.
13. By 1709, the East India Company also had permanent factors in the Persian Gulf at Gombroon and Basra as well as a base overseeing the spice trade at Bantam in Java. See Philip Lawson, *The East India Company: A History* (London: Longman, 1993), page 48.
14. Israel, *Dutch Primacy,* page 336.
15. Furber, *Rival Empires,* pages 91, 102; John Keay, *The Honourable Company: A History of the English East India Company* (New York: Macmillan, 1991), page 150.
16. Israel, *Dutch Primacy,* 338; Om Prakash, *The Dutch East India Company and the Economy of Bengal, 1630–1720* (Princeton, N.J.: Princeton University Press, 1985), pages 159, 212.
17. Kaeppelin, Paul. *Les Origines de l'Inde française: La Compagnie des Indes Orientales et François Martin* (Paris: Challamel, 1908), pages 223–232; Furber, *Rival Empires,* pages 119–120.
18. Chaudhuri, *Trading World,* pages 202–203.
19. Once it had built up its own trade in a given area, the Dutch East India Company applied pressure to freeze out Asian competitors. For example, Gujarati ships destined for Indonesian ports had to have passes, which were issued very sparingly. See Furber, *Rival Empires of Trade,* page 77; Chaudhuri, *Trading World,* pages 199, 208.
20. Furber, *Rival Empires of Trade,* page 273.
21. Chaudhuri, *Trading World,* 205–207.
22. See below, Chapter Seven, note 23.
23. Surat did not lose its commercial preeminence to Bombay until the end of the eighteenth century. Chaudhuri, *Trading World,* page 195.
24. Chaudhuri, *Trading World,* page 194.
25. Chaudhuri, *Trading World,* page 194; *Asia Before Europe* (Cambridge: Cambridge University Press), page 305.
26. Chaudhuri, *Trade and Civilisation,* page 305. See Thomas Barlow, *Barlow's Journal of His Life at Sea,* Basil Lubbock, editor (London: Hurst & Blackett, 1934), vol. 2, page 484 (1697). "The Great Mogul's ships are generally employed most for carrying passengers to and from Mocha, which only go in devotion's sake to their great prophet Mahomet's tomb, it lying three or four days' journey from 'Judda.' That Mogul's ship in our company had no less than 700 and odd passengers and seamen on board, men, women, and children, and upon the rest of the ships were several passengers as well as merchants."
27. Chaudhuri, *Trade and Civilisation,* page 108.
28. Chaudhuri, *Trading World,* pages 197–198.
29. Chaudhuri, *Trading World,* page 193.

30. Chaudhuri, *Trading World*, pages 201–203; *Trade and Civilisation*, page 126.
31. *Privateering and Piracy*, page 168 (testimony of John Dann).
32. *Privateering and Piracy*, page 159 (Letter from Venice, May 25, 1696).
33. Chaudhuri, *Trading World*, page 201.
34. K. N. Chaudhuri, *The English East India Company: The Study of an Early Joint-Stock Company, 1600–1640* (London: Frank Cass, 1965), page 107.
35. Chaudhuri, *Trade and Civilisation*, page 131.
36. Chaudhuri, *Trade and Civilisation*, page 131; J. M. Filliot, *La Traite des Esclaves vers les Mascareignes au XVIIIe siècle* (Paris: Orstom, 1974), pages 92–94.
37. Furber, *Rival Empires*, page 89.
38. *CSPC, 1697–98*, page 463.

CHAPTER THREE

1. Bastian, *Étude géographique et économique*, page 20. Bastian's work is richly illustrated with many maps. There are overviews in Mervyn Brown, *Madagascar Rediscovered,* Chapter One; and Nigel Heseltine, *Madagascar* (London: Pall Mall, 1971), Chapter One.
2. Bastian, *Étude géographique*, page 20.
3. Doctor Watson reported (*CSPC, 1697–1698*, page 108) that the *John and Rebecca* had a crew of 116 "plus blacks." In this case, the latter phrase could mean either (or both) African or Malagasy servants. Similarly, William Willock, a prisoner on board the *Mocha*, described the crew as about sixty-five men "plus blacks": *CSPC, 1697–1698*, page 366.
4. It is necessary to be tentative in describing the origins and culture of the Malagasy peoples. Archaeological exploration began only after World War II, and scholars argue about many aspects of Madagascar's history. For overviews, see Heseltine, *Madagascar,* Chapters Two and Three; Raymond Kent, *Early Kingdoms in Madagascar* (New York: Holt, Rinehart, and Winston, 1970), Chapters One and Two; Brown, *Madagascar Rediscovered*, Chapters Two and Three; John Mack, *Madagascar, Island of the Ancestors* (London: British Museum Publications, 1986); Pierre Verin, *The History of Civilisation in North Madagascar* (Rotterdam: Balkema, 1986), Chapter Two; Pierre Verin, "L'Imerina et le peuplement de Madagascar: Les hypothèses confrontées aux nouvelles découvertes," *Taloha*, vol. 12 (1994), pages 25–28. Hilary Bradt, *Madagascar* (Oxford, Eng.: Clio, 1993) is a comprehensive bibliography including additional references to the academic literature.
5. Verin, *History of Civilisation*, Chapters Three and Four; Filliot, *Traite des Esclaves*, page 115.
6. "If one Englishmen goes with the Prince with whom he lives to war, he has half the slaves that are taken for his pains." Testimony (1696) of Henry Watson, ship's surgeon: *CSPC, 1697–1698*, page 108.
7. Martin, *Mémoires*, vol. 1, page 154. For a modern overview, see Jørgen Ruud, *Taboo: A Study of Malagasy Customs and Beliefs* (Oslo: Oslo University Press, 1960).
8. Martin, *Mémoires*, vol. 1, page 154.
9. Martin *Mémoires*, vol. 1, page 164; see *Bucquoy*, page 136. The chief was a senior member of the senior family in that clan's village; often he was the previous chief's son.
10. If the woman left, her family had to return the purchase price to her former husband: Martin, *Mémoires*, vol. 1, page 162. During the 1820s, polygamy remained common, and marriage required merely the consent of the bride and her family; see B. F. Leguével de Lacombe, *Voyage a Madagascar et aux iles Comores* (Paris: Desessart, 1840), pages 144–146.
11. Martin, *Mémoires*, vol. 1, page 164; see *Bucquoy*, page 135.
12. 1 Kings 20.
13. Herodotus, *The History*, 4.42.
14. Herodotus, *The History*, 4.44.

15. The overland trade routes survived the Portuguese invasion of India in the early 1500s, and valuable Asian commodities continued to travel west in caravans to the Ottoman Empire. It was the Dutch and English East India Companies that finally killed off Asian land commerce during the seventeenth and eighteenth centuries. See Niels Steensgaard, *The Asian Trade Revolution of the Seventeenth Century* (Chicago: University of Chicago, 1974).
16. Brown, *Madagascar Rediscovered,* page 31.
17. When Governor Flacourt took possession of Mascarin for France in 1649, he renamed the island Bourbon after France's ruling family. With the French Revolution, Bourbon was renamed Réunion in 1793 and later became Ile Bonaparte. The name *Bourbon* was restored in 1815, but the island again became Réunion in 1848. Although anachronistic, the modern name is used throughout to avoid confusion. For the Fort Dauphin settlement, see Brown, *Madagascar Rediscovered,* pages 49–54; Hubert Deschamps, *Histoire de Madagascar,* 4th ed. (Paris: Berger-Levrault, 1972), pages 67–76; Henri Froidevaux, "Madagascar du XVIe siècle . . ." in *Histoire des Colonies Françaises,* Gabriel Hanotaux and Alfred Martineau, editors, vol. 6 (Paris: Plon, 1934), pages 13–81.
18. Martin, *Mémoires,* vol. 1, page 157.
19. After returning to France, Flacourt published in 1658 the *Histoire de la Grand Ile de Madagascar* ("History of the Great Island of Madagascar") describing the country, its vegetation and animals, and the customs and beliefs of the Malagasy. It remained the most useful guide to the island for a century and a half.
20. Deschamps, *Histoire de Madagascar,* page 71.
21. Deschamps, *Histoire de Madagascar,* page 76: "Le petit groupe de Français s'est résigné à vivere péniblement de razzias, en pur parasite, sans apporter au pays aucun progrès, même matériel."

CHAPTER FOUR

1. Chaudhuri, *East India Company,* page 107; Filliot, *Traite des Esclaves,* page 86.
2. Bastian, *Madagascar: Étude géographique,* pages 112–115. In modern times a port and harbour have been created at Tamatave.
3. Saint Mary's Island still was heavily wooded in the 1820s. See Leguével de Lacombe, *Voyage a Madagascar,* page 282: "On rencontre dans les forêts de Sainte-Marie des beaux arbres propres à la construction des vaisseaux."
4. Deschamps, *Histoire de Madagascar,* page 105.
5. Martin, *Mémoires,* pages 162–164.
6. *CSPC, 1696–1697,* page 260; *Privateering and Piracy,* page 175.
7. Jacob Judd, "Frederick Philipse and the Madagascar Trade," *New York Historical Society Quarterly,* vol. 55 (1971), page 357.
8. Adam Baldridge's testimony in *Privateering and Piracy,* page 182. A "horn book" was a beginning primer, consisting of a single page protected by a transparent sheet of horn. A book of this type could also have been used to teach the Malagasy how to read, but some mariners were themselves illiterate; see below Chapter Eleven at note 9.
9. Ritchie, *Captain Kidd,* page 113.
10. See deposition by Henry Watson, prisoner on the *John and Rebecca* in 1696 (*CSPC, 1697–1698,* page 108): "During my residence with the pirates, whose chief rendezvous is at an island called St. Mary's near Madagascar, I understood they were supplied with ammunition and all sorts of necessaries by one Captain Baldridge and Lawrence Johnston, two old pirates that are settled in the above islands, and are factors for one Frederick Phillips, who under pretence of trading to Madagascar for negro slaves, supplies these rogues with all sorts of stores, consigning them to Baldridge and Johnston."
11. Judd, "Frederick Philipse," page 363. See also John Pantree's deposition in June 1698, (*CSPC, 1697–1698,* page 286): "I went sailor on the ship Fortune about seventeen months ago to Madagascar. We took in a cargo of sugar, liquors, pumps, hats and stock-

ings, arms and gunpowder at Turtle Bay, and at Madagascar we traded for negroes and also with a vessel formerly commanded by one Hore (who was then dead) for East India goods. We brought the said goods to Long Island Sound, where they were taken off by two New York sloops."

12. Warren's November 1697 letter: CSPC, 1697–1698, page 71. See below, Chapter Eleven.

13. Theophilus Turner, a crewman on Robert Culliford's Mocha, testified that there were "near an hundred English, French and Dutch" on Saint Mary's when he came into port in December 1699: CSPC, 1699, page 289. Otto Van Toyle, who served on John Hoar's John and Rebecca, guessed at a population of approximately 170 at the same time: CSPC, 1699, pages 289, 407. But neither witness included the men on his vessel in his estimate.

14. CSPC, 1699, page 129.

15. During the 1760s, a Malagasy chief told a French official that he had seen underground cellars with walls of stone walls used to store gun powder: Grandidier, page 62, note 1.

16. John Hoar's men told Dr. Henry Watson that there were seven or eight guns on Saint Mary's: CSPC, 1697–1698, page 102. Perkins, who had personally visited Saint Mary's, said the fort carried twenty-two guns: Privateering and Piracy, page 177.

17. Deposition of Theophilus Turner, CSPC, 1699, page 289.

18. CSPC, 1699, page 289: "Edward Welch has 6 guns at his house, which have no command of the place where the shipping lie." Captain Kidd claimed that his mutinous crew ransacked his sea chest, which was stored at Welch's house about four miles from the harbor; see Kidd's Narrative.

19. Wilkins, Captain Kidd, page 212.

20. Robert, page 62. French settlers on Madagascar and Réunion Island also erected elevated bamboo huts in the Malagasy fashion. See Martin, Mémoires, vol. 1, page 165; Jean Barassin, La vie quotidienne des colons de l'île Bourbon à la fin du regne de Louis XIV, 1700–1715 (Sainte-Clotilde: Dionysienne, 1989), page 174; Albert Lougnon, Sous le signe de la tortue: Voyages anciens à l'Ile Bourbon (Paris: Larose, 1958), page 179; Patrick Lizé, "Le naufrage du Speaker," Vues sur La Piraterie, ed. Gérard Jaeger (Paris: Tallandier, 1992), pages 334–335.

21. Robert Drury's Journal, pages 297–298.

22. In 1693, Adam Baldridge bought forty-three pairs of shoes and pumps to sell at Saint Mary's: Privateering and Piracy, page 182, section 4. It is not obvious why the mariners wanted shoes; there are no poisonous snakes on Madagascar, and they were used to walking barefoot on the rough surfaces of ships.

23. For "speckled" shirts, see Baldridge's deposition, Privateering and Piracy, page 182, section 4; Barassin, Vie quotidienne, page 111. Embroidered coats: William Snelgrave, A New Account of Some Parts of Guinea, and the Slave-Trade (London: Knapton, 1734), pages 255–256.

24. See Rogoziński, Pirates!, at the words clothing, earrings, and tattoos.

25. In 1697, Adam Baldridge incurred the hatred of the Malagasy on Saint Mary's by selling their members of their families into slavery. See above, Chapter One; CSPC, 1699, page 404; Documents, Colonial History of New York, vol. 4, page 413; Privateering and Piracy, page 176.

26. Martin, Mémoires, vol. 1, page 170. François Martin, the founder of the French settlement at Pondicherry, was an astute and careful observer who visited Saint Mary's and lived on the mainland to the west of the island in 1668.

27. Testimony of Henry Watson, CSPC, 1697–1698, page 108: "[Captain Baldridge and Lawrence Johnston] are both of them married to country women, and many of the others are married at Madagascar."

28. Robert Drury's Journal, page 298.

29. See above, Chapter Three. Deschamps, Histoire de Madagascar, page 105, reports that, when the Europeans arrived, there already were numerous fair-skinned Malagasy among the tribes along the coast directly to the west of Saint Mary's.

30. Clement Downing, *A History of the Indian Wars* (New edition by William Foster, London: Oxford University Press, 1924), page 105.
31. See testimony of Henry Watson, *CSPC, 1697–1698*, page 108.
32. In December 1717, Cape of Good Hope officials ordered that a soldier, sailor, and field-guard be smothered for committing "sodomy"; a fourth man was to be flogged and sent back to Holland: *Cape of Good Hope: Journal*, page 274. On four occasions between 1684 and 1732, Cape officials drowned men in the bay (with weights attached to their bodies) to punish the "abominable crime of sodomy." The victims included free men, negro slaves, and native Africans. The records do not specify what is meant by "sodomy," but it is clear that the men were killed because the Dutch officials believed they had had some sort of sexual intercourse with each other. See Donald Bozarth, "Burgher, Boer, and Bondsman" (Ph.D. thesis, University of Maryland, 1987), page 356.
33. Hector Saint John de Crèvecoeur, *Letters from an American Farmer* (New York: Dutton, 1957 [originally London, 1782]), page 209. James Axtell has written several books, drawing on the original sources concerning the interaction between Europeans and Indians in North America. See especially *The European and the Indian* (New York: Oxford University Press, 1981) and *The Invasion Within* (New York: Oxford University Press, 1985). See also Richard Drinnon, *White Savage: The Case of John Dunn Hunter* (New York: Schocken Books, 1972).
34. It is striking that runaway African slaves in the Caribbean did not try either to copy European ways or to recreate African customs. Instead they enthusiastically adopted the culture of the Indians while they were overwhelming them genetically, thus creating the numerous group called the "Black Carib." See Jan Rogoziński, *A Brief History of the Caribbean* (New York: Facts on File, 1999), page 160.
35. See below, Chapter Seven at note 23.
36. This is the version reported by a Captain Coin, commanding the Dutch ship *Tamboer*, who docked at Port Dauphin in July 1699: Grey, *Pirates of the Eastern Seas*, pages 182–183. *Robert Drury's Journal*, pages 102–106, has a garbled version of the same tale. This story—of a native princess who identifies a European visitor as her long-lost son—also has been told about other mariners. Nevertheless, even if some of the details may have been romanticized, Abraham Samuel undoubtedly did become ruler of the Port Dauphin region. See *CSPC, 1699*, page 289.
37. For Commodore Littleton's expedition, see below Chapter Eleven at notes 40–45.
38. *Manual of the Corporation of the City of New York*, ed. David Valentine (New York: Bell, 1853), pages 406–408.
39. See *Cape of Good Hope: Journal*, page 131; Ritchie, *Captain Kidd*, pages 84–85.

CHAPTER FIVE

1. See James Leamon, "Governor Fletcher's Recall," *William and Mary Quarterly*, 3rd series, vol. 20 (1967), pages 527–542.
2. In the introduction to his edition of *Calendar of State Papers Colonial* for 1697–1698, J.W. Fortescue describes Lord Bellomont's frenzied efforts to destroy former governor Benjamin Fletcher.

> So far the evidence produced by Bellomont against Fletcher, Nicoll and Brooke fully justified his action; but very soon he lost sight of his true objects, namely the suppression of illegal trade and piracy, in the delight of persecuting Fletcher and his associate. In the madness of party-spirit which prevailed at the time, he was not content with preparing punishment for genuine evil-doers, but must needs espouse the cause of the deceased ruffian, Jacob Leisler. . . . Moreover he exhausted himself in collecting proofs that everything that Governor Fletcher had ever done in New York was wicked and felonious. . . .

> Adding that Bellomont trusted Adam Baldridge, the chief fence at Saint Mary's, Fortes-

cue concluded that "The natural inference is that Bellomont was more zealous than wise, which indeed seems to have been the fact." See *CSPC, 1697–1698*, page xix.

3. Richard Tew migrated from England to Newport in 1640. He became a prominent citizen and is named in the charter granted to the Rhode Island colony in 1663. Thomas Tew, a mariner and probably Richard's brother, lived at Newport in 1643. See Chapin, *Privateer Ships*, page 58; Dow, *Pirates of the New England Coast*, page 84.

4. In February 1697, John Graves reported that he had known Tew "living in Jamaica twelve years before": CSPC, *1696–1697*, page 379. During the prosecution of Governor Fletcher, an attorney for the crown claimed that "it was a thing notoriously know to everyone that Tew had before then been a pirate": *CSPC, 1699*, page 33.

5. The *Amity* had been impressed as a warship at Barbados in 1691: Chapin, *Privateer Ships*, page 57.

6. *General History of the Pyrates*, page 422.

7. Edmund Randolph to Board of Trade, August 17, 1696, "Thomas Tew, a pyrate, came thither [Rhode Island] from the Read Sea in the year 1694 and brought with him £100,000 in Gold and Silver, he shared £12,000 for himself and his sloop." *The Colonial Records of North Carolina*, ed. William L. Saunders and others (Raleigh: Hale, 1886–1907), vol. 1, page 469 (abridged version in *CSPC, 1696–1697*, page 74).

8. Adam Baldridge (*Privateering and Piracy*, page 183) said the *Amity* carried a crew of sixty when she reached Saint Mary's. Only forty-five men signed the ship's articles in Bermuda, but Tew may well have picked up additional men along the way east.

9. *CSPC, 1697–1698*, pages 260. Under the ship's articles, Tew was entitled to two and one half shares as captain and an additional amount as part owner.

10. *CSPC, 1697–1698*, page 326. Various owners were said to have received sums ranging from £3,000 to £4,000: *CSPC, 1703*, pages 154, 624. However, Colonel William Outerbridge reportedly earned £550 for a one-ninth interest in the *Amity* (Wilkinson, *Bermuda in the Old Empire*, page 65); this would bring the total paid to the owners to £4,950.

11. Wilkinson, *Bermuda in the Old Empire*, page 65. The owners in Bermuda got back fourteen times the original cost of the *Amity*.

12. *General History of the Pyrates*, page 423.

13. Pringle, *Jolly Roger*, page 138. See the governor of New Jersey to the Board of Trade, July 26, 1697 (*CSPC, 1696–1697*, page 563): "and carried with him one Want in a Brigantine and another vessel."

14. Deposition by John Dann, *Privateering and Piracy*, page 167.

15. Karracker, *Piracy was a Business*, page 150.

16. *CSPC, 1696–1697*, page 260; Karracker, *Piracy was a Business*, page 140; Chapin, *Privateer Ships*, page 60.

17. Chapin, *Privateer Ships*, pages 61, 72–73.

18. According to a ship's doctor captured by Dirk Chivers: *CSPC, 1697–1698*, page 70.

19. The *Susana*'s owners were said to reside in Boston: *CSPC, 1696–1697*, pages 259–260.

20. *CSPC, 1697–1698*, page 205: "William May is the only man commissioned by this Government who has been to the south of the Cape of Good Hope." After Henry Every's rape of the *Gunsway* made piracy a public scandal, the London government investigated Tew and his associates. Rhode Island's governor claimed that he had turned down Tew's request for a privateer's commission, despite Tew's offer of £500. By then, Captain Tew was dead and could not contradict the governor's story. See *Records of the Colony of Rhode Island*, vol. 3, page 341. Also printed *CSPC, 1697–1698*, 477, and mentioned *CSPC, 1696–1697*, page 315.

21. Sydney V. James, *Colonial Rhode Island: A History* (New York: Scribner's, 1975), pages 116–117. See *CSPC, 1700*, pages 277–278 for the privateering commissions to Want and Wake. Greene's commission to Banks is dated December 10, 1694: Chapin, *Privateer Ships*, page 71.

22. Governor Fletcher's commission to Tew is dated November 2, 1694. See Fletcher to Board of Trade, *CSPC, 1696–1697*, page 518.

23. Lord Bellomont to Board of Trade, May 18, 1698, *Documents, Colonial History of New York*, page 310.
24. A privateer's commission also was called a *letter of marque*. See in general Rogoziński, *Pirates!* under the words *Privateer* and *Reprisal, Letters of.*
25. The London government hanged Captain Kidd in 1701 for violating the terms of his commission—granted in Kidd's case by the king rather than a mere governor. After this, most pirates decided a privateering commission no longer had much value.
26. Deposition of John Dann, *Privateering and Piracy*, page 167.
27. *CSPC, 1697–1698*, page 205.
28. *CSPC, 1700*, page 278. Captain Want made it back to South Carolina, where he held a privateer's commission in 1696: Chapin, *Privateer Ships*, page 60. Two of the *Dolphin's* crew, Daniel Smith and William Griffith, had joined Tew's 1693 cruise, which had left from Bermuda. When they returned to Bermuda from the Bahamas, Smith had about £800 ($400,000) in coins and jewels. For Smith and Griffith, see Wilkinson, *Bermuda in the Old Empire*, page 69; *CSPC, 1699*, page 182; *CSPC, 1700*, page 503.
29. Grey, *Pirates of the Eastern Seas*, pages 164, 168; deposition by John Dann, August 1696, in *Privateering and Piracy*, page 171.
30. *Privateering and Piracy*, page 184.
31. *Privateering and Piracy*, page 169. See below, page 88.
32. Grey, *Pirates of the Eastern Seas*, page 131.
33. Governor of Rhode Island to Council of Trade, May 8, 1698, *CSPC, 1697–1698*, page 205. "William Mayes had his clearance here for Madagascar and a commission from this Government to fight the French. By the best information that we have Captain Every plundered him, and we very much suspect has destroyed him and his company, for none of them are returned and there is no news of any one of them."
34. Attorney general of New York to Lord Bellomont, May 4, 1698, *CSPC, 1697–1698*, page 456.
35. *General History of the Pyrates*, page 439.
36. Adam Baldridge's deposition, *Privateering and Piracy*, page 184.
37. Robert Livingston to the duke of Shrewsbury, September 20, 1695, quoted in Wilkins, *Captain Kidd*, page 57. See also Chapin, *Privateer Ships*, page 120: "Richard Glover was an inhabitant of New York, who had served as a privateersman in the West Indies under a Jamaica commission. He was commissioned by Governor Fletcher as a privateers man and went to Barbadoes where he obtained from the Governor a commission of letter-of-marque for a trading voyage to go to Madagascar to get a cargo of negroes."
38. It also is possible that the theft of the *Charming Mary* was a ruse to fool English officials by disguising a surreptitious sale. There were reports that the *Amity's* crew sent money to the *Mary's* owners through Adam Baldridge. See *CSPC, 1696–1697*, page 563; *1697–1698*, page 367.
39. *CSPC, 1697–1698*, page 70.
40. Deposition by Robert Culliford, London, June 1700; printed in Wilkins, *Captain Kidd*, pages 94–95. Deposition by William Willock, held prisoner aboard the *Mocha* from January through December 1697: *CSPC, 1697–1698*, pages 366–367. Willock describes the *Mocha's* consort as "130 tons from Madagascar, with about twenty men, all old privateers."
41. Grey, *Pirates of the Eastern Seas*, page 130. The men correctly believed that they could bring the *Charming Mary* back to Barbados without fear of arrest, even though the island's governor was part owner of the *Mary*. This suggests that they had (as suggested in note 38 above) paid the *Mary's* owners for the use of their ship.

CHAPTER SIX

1. *The Life and Adventures of Capt. John Avery* (London: Hills, 1709; reprinted Augustan Reprint Society, 1980), page 6. The version of the 1696 ballad "A Copy of Verses, Composed by Captain Henry Every," which is quoted at the beginning of Chapter Six,

is taken from *Naval Songs and Ballads,* ed. C. H. Firth (London: Naval Records Society, 1908), page 131.

2. Charles Johnson, *The Successful Pyrate* (London: Lintott, 1713; reprinted Augustan Reprint Society, 1980), page 9.

3. *Grandidier,* vol. 5, pages 146–155; Joel Baer, "Piracy Examined: A Study of Daniel Defoe's *General History of the Pirates* and its Milieu" (Ph.D. Thesis, Princeton University, 1970), pages 121–134. See also *La Suede & Madagascar au debut du XVIIIème Siècle,* Jacques Macau, editor (Aix-en-Provence: Insitut d'histoire des pays d'outre-mer, 1973).

4. See the deposition of John Dann, August 1696, *Privateering and Piracy,* page 165: "The Shipps Company mutinied at Corunna for want of their pay, there being 8 months due to them; some of the men proposed to Captain Every, who was master of the *Charles,* to carry away the Shipp, which was agreed on and sworn too. . . ." Another copy of Dann's deposition is in *CSPC, 1696–1697,* pages 262–264.

5. Testimony of David Creagh, *State Trials,* vol. 5, page 7. Dann's deposition, cited in the previous note, provides other testimony concerning the mutiny, as does the deposition by Philip Middleton before the Lords Justices of Ireland (August 1696), *CSPC, 1696–1697,* pages 260–262.

6. Deposition by Peter Claus, *CSPC, 1697–1698,* page 185.

7. Peter Claus, *CSPC, 1697–1698,* page 185.

8. See May's testimony, *State Trials,* vol. 5, page 12. When Edgcumbe reached Bombay, Ralph Stout and other Saint Mary's pirates seized his vessel and killed its cruel captain. See below, Chapter Seven.

9. *Privateering and Piracy,* page 154; William Hedges, *The Diary of William Hedges,* ed. R. Barlow, 3 vols. (London: Hakluyt Society, 1887–1889), vol. 2, page 138.

10. Dann's deposition, *Privateering and Piracy,* page 167.

11. Dann's Testimony, *Privateering and Piracy,* page 167; *State Trials,* page 8.

12. Hamilton, *New Account,* vol. 1, page 89: "*Abdul Gafour,* a *Mahometan* that I was acquainted with, drove a Trade equal to the *English East-india* Company, for I have known him to fit out in a Year, above twenty Sail of Ships, between 300 and 800 Tuns." See Das Gupta, Ashin, "The Merchants of Surat, c. 1700–1750," *Elites in South Asia,* ed. Edmund Leach and S. N. Mukherjee (Cambridge, Eng.: Cambridge University Press, 1970), pages 208–209.

13. Dann's deposition, *Privateering and Piracy,* page 168; Muhammed Hashim Khafi Khan, *Muntakhabu-l Lubáb* in *The History of India as Told by its Own Historians,* ed. Sir H. M. Elliott and John Dowson (London: Trübner, 1867–1877), vol. 7, page 350.

14. Khafi Khan, *The History of India,* page 350.

15. Khafi Khan, pages 350–351.

16. East India Company Bombay to EIC London, *Privateering and Piracy,* page 159. An "umbraw" (*Urdu amar*) was a nobleman and official at the Mogul's court.

17. The earliest contemporary versions of this rumor are less romantic. According to Robert Snead, a Pennsylvania merchant writing in September 1697 (*CSPC, 1696–1697,* page 614): "They ran away from Jamaica with a ship, went to the Persian seas, and took and murdered many. A princess, who was given in marriage to a great man, was on her way to him by sea when they took the ship; they killed most of the men and threw her overboard. They brag of it publicly over their cups."

18. *The King of Pirates* (New York: Jenson, 1907), page 54.

19. Middleton's deposition, *CSPC, 1696–1697,* page 261.

20. Hamilton, *New Account,* vol. 1, page 88. Dann testified (*Privateering and Piracy,* page 169) that 180 men received a share worth about £1,000. Middleton (*CSPC, 1696–1697,* page 261) said 180 men joined in the share out. This would indicate a total take of under £200,000 ($100 million).

21. Middleton's deposition, *CSPC, 1696–1697,* page 261.

22. Dann's Deposition, *Privateering and Piracy,* page 169. The witnesses are silent as to why the *Amity's* crew did not share in the booty, since she was damaged by gunfire. Perhaps

this occurred during the first minutes of the battle, so that her crew were unable to chase after and board the *Gunsway.*
23. *Privateering and Piracy,* page 169.
24. A French naval squadron reached Réunion in July 1696. The admiral reported that twenty-five of the seventy men landing in November 1695 were French; the rest were English and Danish. See Guët, *l'île Bourbon,* pages 202–205. The East India Company reported that Every's crew included fifty-two Frenchmen and fourteen Danes, the remainder being "English, Scotch, and Irish": *Diary of William Hedges,* vol. 2, page 139.
25. At least seven of these men were still living on Réunion in 1709. They had used their booty to purchase land, and some had become respected citizens. Denis Turpin, for example, was appointed to the island's judicial council in 1712 and served on the provincial council from 1713–1717: Boucher, *Mémoire,* page 251.
26. Samuel Annesley to Sir John Gayer, printed in Arnold Wright, *Annesley of Surat and his Times* (London: Melrose, 1918), pages 164–165.
27. Wright, *Annesley of Surat,* pages 179, 189.
28. *Acts of the Privy Council, Colonial Series,* vol. 2, pages 299–302.
29. Middleton says (*Privateering and Piracy,* page 172) that about 100 men aboard the *Fancy* contributed to Trott's bribe, each man giving twenty pieces of eight and two pieces of gold. After the fact, some accused Trott of taking £1,000; other rumors spoke of £7,000 ($3.5 million): *CSPC, 1697–1698,* pages 208, 506.
30. *CSPC, 1697–1698,* page 506.
31. *CSPC, 1696–1697,* page 20.
32. *CSPC, 1697–1698,* page 208.
33. A number of men were arrested and released. In April 1696, Josiah Rayner landed on the east end of Long Island, carrying a chest holding over £1,000 in treasure. In return for £50, Governor Benjamin Fletcher ordered the sheriff to release Rayner and return his chest: *CSPC, 1697–1698,* page 288. John Elston went to New Jersey where he was arrested in 1698; Elston claimed he was a cabin boy of thirteen, forced to accompany Every and his band: *CSPC, 1697–1698,* page 313; cf. *Documents, Colonial History New York,* vol. 4, 332. Two men named Cornish and Downe were arrested in Rhode Island; they escaped from prison, possibly with the aid of the sheriff: *Records of the Colony of Rhode Island* (Providence: Greene, 1856–1865), vol. 3, page 365.

Daniel Smith and William Griffin returned to Bermuda, where they paid £900 for property: *CSPC, 1697–1698,* page 326. Peter Claus, Robert Clinton, and Edmund Lacel purchased land in Pennsylvania. A magistrate wrote to London that each man had brought home £1,000 and had given £100 to Governor Markham to buy his protection: *CSPC, 1696–1697,* page 613.
34. *CSPC, 1702,* page 442.
35. *Privateering and Piracy,* pages 171, 174.
36. *State Trials,* vol. 5, page 2.
37. *General History of the Pyrates,* pages 53–57.

CHAPTER SEVEN
1. *CSPC, 1697–1698,* pages 68–69.
2. Grey, *Pirates of the Eastern Seas,* page 172.
3. An East India Company official described the *Resolution* as a 300-ton vessel carrying twenty guns and one hundred men: *CSPC, 1697–1698,* page 70. Another source credits the ship with 250 tons and twenty-eight guns: John Biddulph, *The Pirates of Malabar* (London: Smith, Elder, 1907), page 49. Samuel Perkins remembered the *Resolution* as having eighteen guns and sixty men when it left New England: *Privateering and Piracy,* page 175. As Tew had done in 1693, Glover sold shares to the merchants outfitting the vessel; Adam Baldridge thus described Glover as "part owner" of the *Resolution* (*Privateering and Piracy,* page 184).

4. Governor Jeremiah Basse of New Jersey, July 26, 1697, *CSPC, 1696–1697*, page 563. See Chapin, *Privateer Ships*, pages 86–93, for Glover's activities in the Caribbean and the coast of Canada.
5. Chapin, *Privateer Ships*, pages 92–93, prints the consortship agreement between the *Dragon* and the *Dolphin*.
6. Captain Harrison sued Glover for the *Dolphin*'s share. Some aboard the *Dragon* tried to deprive other crewmen of their cut, and the latter brought suit for recovery. One man had been killed during the cruise, and his heirs wanted the dead man's portion. Masters of runaway servants that had joined the expedition tried to take away their shares. The surgeon had served on both ships and thus claimed two shares.
7. The *John and Rebecca* was taken "near the river of Canada," according to a deposition by Dr. Henry Watson, who was Hoar's captive throughout 1696: *CSPC, 1697–1698*, page 108. In a December 1698 deposition, Benjamin Fletcher, former governor of New York, also mentions Hoar's commission by the governor of Jamaica: *Documents, Colonial History New York*, page 446. Samuel Perkins served aboard the *Resolution*, consort to the *John and Rebecca*; Perkins's deposition (*Privateering and Piracy*, page 176) describes the latter as a vessel of two hundred tons and fourteen guns. Adam Baldridge (*Privateering and Piracy*, page 185) speaks of twenty cannon. An East India Company official reported that Captains Hoar and Glover commanded "two small pirates, one of fourteen and one of thirteen guns, with each about 150 men, almost all English." See *CSPC, 1697–1698*, page 68.
8. Chapin, *Privateer Ships*, page 71. See Sydney V. James, *Colonial Rhode Island: A History* (New York: Scribner's, 1975), pages 116–117.
9. *CSPC, 1697–1698*, page 108. Governor Fletcher later was criticized for giving Glover a privateer's commission when the latter did not have a ship berthed at New York: *CSPC, 1697–1698*, page 225.
10. In 1698, the attorney general of New York wrote to Lord Bellomont (*CSPC, 1697–1698*, page 456) that "Hore . . . took his prizes to Rhode Island. He came to New York and gave out that he was bound for the Red Sea, which procured him many men, and obtained a commission from Governor Fletcher." Hoar's commission is dated July 16, 1695; Lord Bellomont wrote the Board of Trade that Hoar had given Fletcher a £3,000 bond for good behavior: *Documents, Colonial History New York*, page 310. Samuel Perkins also mentions Fletcher's commission to Hoar: *Privateering and Piracy*, page 116. Robert Glover is said to have paid Fletcher £500 for his commission: *CSPC, 1697–1698*, page 463. See also *CSPC, 1697–1698*, page 108; *Documents, Colonial History of New York*, vol. 4, page 447.
11. Grey, *Pirates of the Eastern Seas*, page 169.
12. Doctor Henry Watson said that both Hoar and Glover were based at Saint Mary's: *CSPC, 1697–1698*, page 108.
13. If the testimony of John Eldridge is to be believed. See *CSPC, 1700*, page 278.
14. In his deposition, Henry Watson said the *John and Rebecca* was alone, and the *Resolution* came to the scene only after the capture: *CSPC, 1697–1698*, page 108. Watson was an eyewitness, unlike the East India Company official who later said the two pirate ships acted together: *CSPC, 1697–1698*, page 68.
15. Doctor Watson says the *John and Rebecca* had a crew of 116 "plus blacks." In this case, the latter phrase could mean either (or both) African or Malagasy servants.
16. *CSPC, 1697–1698*, pages 68, 107.
17. Doctor Watson said Hoar asked for 35,000 pieces of eight, equivalent to £7,875. The East India Company valued the ship's cargo at 60,000 pieces of eight or £13,500. During the 1690s, a piece of eight typically traded at four shillings, six pence. About 4.5 pieces of eight thus were equivalent to one pound sterling, and a piece of eight was worth about $112. See Holden, *Rival Empires of Trade*, page 386; Judd, "Frederick Philipse and the Madagascar Trade," page 362, note 15.
18. Hamilton, *New Account of the East Indies*, vol. 1, page 34.

19. When the *Resolution* attacked shipping at Calcutta in November 1696, its captain said he expected a consort ship commanded by Captain Hoar: *CSPC, 1697–1698,* page 70.
20. Deposition by Adam Baldridge, *Privateering and Piracy,* pages 184–185. In his testimony, given in 1698, Baldridge said Glover and the Indian ship arrived at Saint Mary's on December 19, 1695. But the sequence of events makes it clear that 1696 is the correct date.
21. Baldridge's Deposition, *Privateering and Piracy,* page 185. Since Dr. Watson, Hoar's captive, does not mention the capture of the Indian vessel, it presumably was taken after Watson was freed and put ashore on October 30, 1696.
22. Deposition by Doctor Henry Watson, *CSPC, 1697–1698,* page 107.
23. Lord Bellomont to the Lords of the Treasury, July 1, 1698, *Documents, Colonial History New York,* vol. 4, pages 354–355. Lord Bellomont estimated that the *Fortune* carried East India goods worth some £20,000 ($10 million).
24. Edward Randolph to the Council of Trade, May 30, 1698: *CSPC, 1697–1698,* page 256.
25. Glover's death is mentioned by Samuel Perkins, *Privateering and Piracy,* page 176. Glover's will, dated September 5, 1697, at "Island St Mary, nigh to the Island of Madigascar" bequeathed his "silver and gold, coyned and in dust" to his two sons: Chapin, *Privateer Ships,* page 92. John Eldridge, one of the crew, bought passage to New York on the *Nassau* in 1699; Eldridge was arrested and testified to Hoar's death and the wreck of the *John and Rebecca: CSPC, 1700,* page 278.
26. East India Company, Calcutta, to Board of Trade in London, November 30, 1696: *CSPC, 1697–1698,* pages 69–70. Quoting page 69.
27. It is possible that this was the William Mason who had commanded the pirate ship *Jacob* when it left New York in 1690. During the ship's cruise along India's west coast, Mason and eighteen others left the ship at Mangalore and went to work for the East India Company. It would be sensible to send out a former pirate to negotiate with pirates. However, both because pirates often used pseudonyms and also because Mason is a common name, the identification is not certain.
28. *CSPC, 1697–1698,* page 70.
29. Adam Baldridge's deposition in *Privateering and Piracy,* pages 185–186.
30. Biddulph, *Pirates of Malabar,* page 49; Grey, *Pirates of the Eastern Seas,* pages 172–173.
31. For the history of the post at Saint Thomas, see Henry Weber, *La Compagnie française des Indes (1604–1875),* (Paris: Rousseau, 1904), page 168.
32. Grey, *Pirates of the Eastern Seas,* page 173.
33. Leckie's letter concerning Edgcumbe is printed by Grey, *Pirates of the Eastern Seas,* pages 133–135.
34. Hamilton, *New Account,* page 134.
35. Deposition by Robert Culliford, London, June 1700; printed in Wilkins, *Captain Kidd,* page 91. See Biddulph, *Pirates of Malabar,* page 32.
36. Hamilton, *New Account,* page 134.
37. Lord Bellomont to the Board of Trade, November 29, 1699: *CSPC, 1699,* page 551; *Privateering and Piracy,* page 237.
38. Grey, *Pirates of the Eastern Seas,* page 136.
39. East India Company to the Board of Trade, December 15, 1696: *CSPC, 1697–1698,* page 69. See also *CSPC, 1697–1698,* page 113.
40. Kelley used the name James (or John) Gilliam during these years.
41. Miles, *Persian Gulf,* page 227. See also Grey, *Pirates of the Eastern Seas,* page 133; Biddulph, *Pirates of Malabar,* pages 14–15. Mangrol is on the Kathiawar Peninsula northwest of Surat and Bombay. The Nawab ruled Mangrol as a vassal under the Prince of Jamnagar.
42. After his arrest, Kelley claimed he was an honest seaman and no pirate. Lord Bellomont had him examined by a physician and a Jewish leader. Both testified that he had been circumcised, "but not after the manner of the Jews": *CSPC, 1699,* page 556.

43. Deposition by James Knott, Kelley's shipmate aboard the *Batchelor's Delight,* November 1699: *CSPC, 1699,* page 557.
44. See Chapter One above.
45. *CSPC, 1697–1698,* page 69.
46. *CSPC, 1697–1698,* page 113.
47. Grey, *Pirates of the Eastern Seas,* page 148.
48. Deposition by Robert Culliford, London, June 1700; printed Wilkins, *Captain Kidd,* pages 94–95. See also the deposition by William Willock, captain of the *Satisfaction,* who was held prisoner aboard the *Mocha* from January through December 1697: *CSPC, 1697–1698,* pages 366–367. Willock's deposition is the most reliable source for the *Mocha's* cruise in the Bay of Bengal.
49. See Captain Willock's deposition, *CSPC, 1697–1698,* page 366.
50. The quotation is taken from Willock's deposition. For the battle with the *Dorrill,* see also the depositions by William Reynolds, the *Dorrill's* supercargo, and by William Soames, East India Company representative at Achin in Sumatra. These are printed in Grey, *Pirates of the Eastern Seas,* pages 138–146. Reynolds's deposition also is printed by Arnold Wright, *Annesley of Surat* (London: Melrose, 1918), pages 203–206.
51. Reynold's deposition, Grey, *Pirates of the Eastern Seas,* page 141.
52. Willock's deposition, Grey, page 145.
53. Culliford's June 1700 deposition, Wilkins, *Captain Kidd,* page 94.
54. Testimony by Robert Bradinham and Joseph Palmer in *Trial of Captain Kidd,* pages 99, 106.

CHAPTER EIGHT

1. For Jacob Leisler's government, see Michael Kammen, *Colonial New York: A History* (New York: Scribner, 1975), pages 120–126; Lawrence Leder, *Robert Livingston, 1654–1728, and the Politics of Colonial New York* (Chapel Hill: University of North Carolina Press, 1961), pages 57–76. The printed primary sources are cited by Jerome Reich, *Leisler's Rebellion: A Study of Democracy in New York, 1664–1720* (University of Chicago Press, 1953).
2. See Lawrence Leder, "Records of the Trials of Jacob Leisler and His Associates," *New York Historical Society Quarterly,* vol. 36 (1952), pages 431–457.
3. Kammen, *Colonial New York,* 148–153.
4. Kammen, *Colonial New York,* 140.
5. Peter Delanoy's letter, dated June 13, 1695, is printed *CSPC, 1695,* page 503; *Documents, Colonial History of New York,* vol. 4, pages 221–224. Under the Leisler regime, Delanoy had been collector of customs and a member of the governor's council: Reich, *Leisler's Rebellion,* page 132.
6. *CSPC, 1693–1696,* page 506, for the announcement of Bellomont's appointment as governor of Massachusetts.
7. Memorial of the Lords Justices of England, July 16, 1695, *CSPC, 1693–1696,* page 541. See James Leamon, "Governor Fletcher's Recall," *William and Mary Quarterly,* 3rd Series, vol. 20, pages 527–542.
8. Leder, *Livingston,* pages 91–101.
9. Leder, *Livingston,* page 105; Leamon, *Fletcher's Recall,* page 534.
10. *Documents, Colonial History of New York,* vol. 4, pages 127–130, 143–145.
11. Paul Lorain, the pastor of Newgate Prison, attended Kidd while he was in jail. Lorain wrote that "Captain Kidd, born in Scotland, [was] about fifty-six years of age" when he was hanged in 1701. For the evidence about Kidd's early years, see Wilkins, *Captain Kidd,* pages 17–26.
12. *CSPC, 1689–1692,* page 227; *Trial of Captain Kidd,* page 149.
13. Captain Kidd later said that Governor Codrington gave him the *Antegoa* as a reward for his services against the French in the Caribbean: Ritchie, *Captain Kidd,* page 32, note 10.
14. Lawrence Leder, "Captain Kidd and the Leisler Rebellion," *New York Historical Society Quarterly,* vol. 38 (1954), pages 48–53.

15. Isaac Phelps-Stokes, *The Iconography of Manhattan Island, 1698–1909* (New York: Dodd, 1916–1928), vol. 4, page 363.

16. *Journal of the Votes and Proceedings of the General Assembly of the Colony of New York* (New York: Gaine, 1764–1766), vol. 1, page 13. See Lawrence Leder, "Captain Kidd and the Leisler Rebellion" and "Records of the Trials of Jacob Leisler and His Associates."

17. *Documentary History of New York,* vol. 2, pages 250–251, 291–295, 304–307.

18. Phelps-Stokes, *Iconography,* vol. 2, page 329; vol. 6, page 133.

19. Phelps-Stokes, *Iconography,* vol. 4, page 341, 345, 349; vol. 6, pages 21, 133. It is possible that Kidd met his future wife as early as 1688, when some records suggest he was associated with her in selling a house at 56 Wall Street. See *New York's Land-Holding Sea Rover* (New York: Lotus Press, 1901).

20. In August 1691, he brought in a prize and paid the fees due to the king and governor: Phelps-Stokes, *Iconography,* vol. 4, page 370. He was still operating as a privateer in 1694. See Wilkins, *Captain Kidd,* page 34; Ritchie, *Captain Kidd,* page 39, note 27.

21. Phelps-Stokes, *Iconography,* vol. 2, page 329; vol. 3, pages 950.

22. Leder, *Livingston,* pages 93–95. Since most of the evidence has been lost, it is not possible to know whether Livingston was guilty as charged.

23. The articles between Bellomont, Livingston, and Kidd (October 10, 1695), as well as the performance bonds given by Kidd and Livingston are in *Documents, Colonial History of New York,* vol. 4, pages 762–765.

24. Printed in *Trial of Captain Kidd,* pages 14–15. Kidd was charged to "set forth in warlike manner in the said ship called the *Adventure Galley,* under his own command, and therewith, by force of arms, to apprehend, seize, and take the ships, vessels and goods belonging to the French King and his subjects, or inhabitants within the dominions of the said French King. . . ."

25. *Trial of Captain Kidd,* page 15.

26. *Trial of Captain Kidd,* page 193.

27. R. C. Anderson, *Oared Fighting Ships, From Classical times to the Coming of Steam* (London: P. Marshall, 1962), pages 86–87. For the speed under oars of this type of vessel, see Bruce Ingram, *Three Sea Journals of Stuart Times* (London: Constable, 1936), pages 116–117.

28. At Kidd's trial, Captain Hewetson testified that Kidd had told him this story about Bellomont's threats about the time the agreement was signed in October 1695: *Trial of Captain Kidd,* pages 149–150.

29. Bellomont to Vernon, October 18 and December 6, 1700, *Documents, Colonial History of New York,* vol. 4, pages 760, 815–817.

30. Livingston first mentioned the Red Sea expedition in his diary on August 10, but he may well have come up with the concept somewhat earlier. In his biography of Livingston, Lawrence Leder concludes that Livingston invented the scheme, partly because Leder believed "Kidd was too rough and unpolished to court the favor of some of the highest nobles in the land" (Leder, *Livingston,* page 109). However, there is no reason to think that Livingston enjoyed any greater social "polish" than Kidd. Both men were members of the commercial elite of New York province; as such, both were socially inferior to the peers of the realm they met in London.

31. Even legal depositions are remarkably imprecise in their references to timing. Mariners accustomed to voyages that took many months did not place much importance on precise chronology. John Dann, a member of Every's crew, says the attack on the *Gunsway* occurred sometime in August 1695 (*Privateering and Piracy,* page 168). The East India Company office in Bombay reported Every's depredations in a letter dated October 12 (*Privateering and Piracy,* pages 156–159), which took several months to reach the Company's London headquarters. Moreover, Every's crimes did not become widely known until the arrest of several crewmen in June and July 1696.

32. Because they ignore this crucial matter of timing, Kidd's biographers tie his expedition to outrage over Every's attack. See, for example, Graham Brooke's introduction to *Trial of Captain Kidd,* page 6; Dunbar Hinrichs, *The Fateful Voyage of Captain Kidd* (New York: Bookman, 1953), page 25.

33. There is no extant information about "John Ireland," who also is listed in the king's January 1696 commission to Kidd. It is likely that the staff preparing the document misspelled the name.

34. For the pirate-catching activities of Sir Robert Holmes, see Wafer, *A New Voyage,* page xviii. For Holmes's royal commission and other relevant documents, see *CSPC, 1685–1688.*

35. Bellomont's letter is printed in Brooke, *Trial of Captain Kidd,* pages 16–17. It is likely that ship's articles were signed by Kidd and crewmen joining the *Adventure Galley* in England, but these have not survived. Ritchie erroneously assigns to this London period the ship's articles Kidd signed in New York on September 10, 1696. Ritchie has the New York articles being assented to in London a year earlier on September 10, 1695 (*Captain Kidd,* pages 58–60). But Kidd had not yet agreed to make the voyage in September 1695.

36. Edmund Drummer, surveyor to the royal navy, letter written in 1699 and printed in Wilkins, *Captain Kidd,* pages 50–51.

37. Bellomont to the Board of Trade, March 6, 1699: "When ordered by the Admiralty to restore them, captain Steward did not mind to restore the same men to Kidd, but the same number." Wilkins, *Captain Kidd,* page 51.

38. Bellomont, *Documents, Colonial History of New York,* vol. 4, pages 199, 815–816.

39. Governor Fletcher to the Lords of Trade, June 22, 1697, *Documents, Colonial History of New York,* vol. 4, page 275.

40. When it was registered in England, the *Adventure Galley* was said to carry thirty-four guns. At least four or five men were needed to service each gun, and two or three dozen more were required to man the sails during battle. See John Ehrman, *The Navy in the War of William III* (Cambridge, Eng.: Cambridge University Press, 1953), page 109.

41. The ships articles are printed in *CSPC, 1700* page 199; Wilkinson, *Captain Kidd,* pages 53–54, prints a similar version from a different source. Assuming that all 152 crewmen survived till the final cut, the booty would be split into 193 shares. Kidd's patrons would receive 35 of those or 18 percent of the total after expenses. As it turned out, able seamen received a full share, while novices and apprentices received a half share. Kidd and his patrons received 40 out of a total of 160 shares, or 25 percent. See testimony of Robert Bradinham and Joseph Palmer, *Trial of Captain Kidd,* pages 101 and 108.

42. *Documents, Colonial History of New York,* vol. 4, page 275; *CSPC, 1696–1697,* page 518.

43. Both men tended to act imperiously, and Kidd probably treated Governor Fletcher with only formal and limited respect. Kidd was immensely proud of his commission, signed by the king himself. He knew, moreover, that Bellomont would replace Fletcher as governor before the *Adventure Galley* returned from the Indian Ocean.

44. Ritchie, *Captain Kidd,* pages 63–67, provides information about some of the crewmen. Kidd recorded the names of those sailing with him from New York, but there is no extant evidence about some men.

45. *Benjamin Franks' Narrative* is among the most impartial sources for the voyage. Franks deserted the ship at Carwar in India and he gave a deposition at Bombay on October 20, 1697. Unlike most of those testifying about Kidd's expedition, Franks had no reason to lie. His connection to Kidd and journey on the *Adventure Galley* was over and done with forever. He owed nothing to the East India Company or Kidd's other foes, and he had no particular love for Kidd, either. Franks was physically unwell when he left the *Adventure Galley* at Carwar, and he had not enjoyed the voyage. He felt that Kidd was a stern, hard captain to sail under, and he did not like his shipmates, who were much younger and generally less educated.

CHAPTER NINE

1. Firth, *Naval Songs,* pages 135–137. This is the English version of the ballad "Captain Kidd's Farewell to the Seas; or, the Famous Pirate's Lament," probably published on the

day of Kidd's execution. A modified version appeared in North America somewhat later and remained popular for two centuries; see Willard Bonner, *Pirate Laureate: The Life and Legends of Captain Kidd* (New Brunswick, N.J.: Rutgers University Press, 1947), pages 85–112.

2. *Benjamin Franks' Narrative;* Deposition by John Clerke, *CSPC, 1697–1698*, page 364.

3. Hendril Carel Vos Leibbrandt, *Précis of the Archives of the Cape of Good Hope.* (Cape-town: Richards, 1896–1919), vol. 3, pages 34–36. On this episode, see also Biddulph, *Pirates of Malabar,* pages 42–43.

4. Quoting Wilkins, *Captain Kidd,* page 78; another copy in *CSPC, 1697–1698,* pages 363–364. In their *Narratives,* neither Kidd nor Franks mentions any antagonism during the encounter with the company vessels at Johanna.

5. Kidd's *Narrative* reports the incident with extraordinary terseness. "And from thence [Johanna] about the Twenty-second of March, sailed for Mehila, an Island Ten Leagues distant from Johanna, where he arrived next morning, and there careened the said Galley; and about Fifty men died there in a Week's time." Although he survived the disease, Benjamin Franks became "mortall sick" and remained in bed for months, struck down by "Feaver, Ague, and Flux."

6. Testimony of Joseph Palmer, *Trial of Captain Kidd,* page 102. See also *Benjamin Franks' Narrative.* Hugh Parrot, who was tried with Kidd for piracy, was one of the men recruited in Johanna at this time: *Trial of Captain Kidd,* pages 113, 202.

7. The narrative of the voyage Kidd wrote for Governor Bellomont omits, probably deliberately, all events from April to September 1697.

8. If they had followed the script of an Errol Flynn movie, Kidd and his men would have snuck up on the pirates and captured them as they lay comatose after a drunken orgy.

9. Testimony of Robert Bradinham and Joseph Palmer, *Trial of Captain Kidd,* pages 96 and 102.

10. Testimony of Joseph Palmer, *Trial of Captain Kidd,* pages 102–103.

11. Nicholas Alderson, who deserted the *Adventure Galley* at Carwar, stated that she was chased by a man-of-war: Deposition taken at Bombay, October 19, 1697, *CSPC, 1697–1698*, page 370.

12. *Barlow's Journal of His Life at Sea,* vol. 2, pages 484–485. Barlow's account is similar to the testimony given by Robert Bradinham and Joseph Palmer at Kidd's trial. *Benjamin Franks' Narrative* also says much the same, although with less detail because Franks was sick and below in bed throughout the day.

13. Testimony of Bradinham and Palmer, *Trial of Captain Kidd,* pages 96, 103; *Benjamin Franks' Narrative.*

14. Letter from the East India Company representative at Carwar, September 22, 1697, Grey, *Pirates of the Eastern Seas,* page 198; *Notes on Piracy in Eastern Waters,* ed. S. Charles Hill (Bombay: British India Press, 1923–1928), page 115. See also *Benjamin Franks' Narrative;* testimony of Bradinham and Palmer, *Trial of Captain Kidd,* pages 96 and 103; *Barlow's Journal,* vol. 2, page 490.

15. Letter from Fort Saint George to EIC London, January 26, 1697–1698, Wilkins, *Captain Kidd,* page 77.

16. The date is as given in *Kidd's Narrative.* Three of the crewmen deserting at Carwar reported Kidd's plans to the viceroy at Goa, who sent out the ships specifically to seize the *Adventure Galley.* See letter of September 1697, cited above, note 14.

17. *Barlow's Journal,* vol. 2, page 490, reports that the small frigate was badly damaged. *Kidd's Narrative* resumes the voyage's chronology with this incident, about which Kidd boasted "that no Portuguese will ever attack the King's Colours again, in that Part of the World especially."

18. *Barlow's Journal,* vol. 2, page 492. Testimony by Bradinham and Palmer, *Trial of Captain Kidd,* pages 97, 104.

19. There is some confusion about the timing of these events. Kidd's *Narrative* says the *Galley* encountered the *Loyal Captain* at "the beginning of the month of November, 1697."

At his trial in 1701, Kidd was convicted of killing William Moore on October 30. Since Moore's murder took place about two weeks after the meeting with the *Loyal Captain,* the court's indictment would place the latter about October 15. This is impossible, since it leaves too little time for careening the ship at the Maldives. Although it may be off by a day or two, Kidd's chronology seems more plausible than that of the indictment.

These sources give the date according to the Old Style or Julian calendar, which was used in England until 1752. By the 1690s, the Gregorian calendar (still used today) was ten days ahead of the Julian; November 1, 1697, was November 11 by the modern calendar.

20. *Trial of Captain Kidd,* page 76. Under cross-examination, Joseph Palmer, a witness hostile to Kidd, corroborated Parrot's account (*Trial of Captain Kidd,* page 71): "Captain Kidd was aboard that ship, and there were eight or nine men that had muskets and other arms, and they were for taking the ship, but Captain Kidd was against it, and so it was not done."

21. Testimony of Hugh Parrot, *Trial,* pages 76–77.

22. Testimony of Joseph Palmer, *Trial,* page 70.

23. However, this trick might not work if the captured vessel was brought before an honest prize court. The pass or passes carried aboard did not establish a vessel's nationality, which was determined by the nationality or domicile of the owners and not that of the captain. See below at the conclusion of this chapter.

24. This clearly was a different *Rouparelle* from the one burned by John Hoar in August 1696.

25. Testimony of Robert Bradinham, *Trial of Captain Kidd,* page 97. Note, however, that the *Rouparelle* flew the Armenian flag: Deposition of William Jenkins, *Trial of Captain Kidd,* page 205.

26. Depositions of Hugh Parrot and William Jenkins, *Trial,* pages 202, 204.

27. Bradinham, *Trial,* page 97. The indictment for piracy against the *Rouparelle* valued her cargo at £105: *Trial,* page 131. Quilon (known at that time as Caliquilon) was considered a safe place to fence pirate booty. See Hamilton, *New Account,* vol. 1, page 184.

28. Testimony of Joseph Palmer, *Trial of Captain Kidd,* page 146.

29. Palmer, *Trial,* page 178.

30. Deposition of Hugh Parrot, *Trial,* page 202.

31. See below, Chapter Ten, note 27.

32. Bradinham guessed that Kidd received £7,000 or £8,000 for the goods sold at Quilon; Palmer estimated the receipts at £10,000 to £12,000: *Trial of Captain Kidd,* pages 98 and 105. These estimates do not seem to be accurate. Palmer also says each man with a full share received £200 at this time. But this contradicts his estimate of the total value; since there were 160 shares, the total take thus would have amounted to £32,000 ($16 million).

33. It was perhaps during this encounter with Kidd that the *Dorrill*'s surgeon was killed and several other men wounded. Citing this attack "by pirates," the captain of the *Dorrill* asked the governor to a lend him a surgeon when the ship reached Mauritius in July 1698. See André de Chapuiset Le Merle, *Précis d'histoire de l'îsle Maurice* (Port Louis, Île Maurice: Nouvelle Imprimerie Coopérative, 1950), page 174.

34. Kidd's *Narrative.*

35. Deposition of Hugh Parrot, *Trial of Captain Kidd,* page 202.

36. *Privateering and Piracy,* pages 224–232.

37. *Privateering and Piracy,* page 251; Cornelius Dalton, *The Real Captain Kidd* (New York: Duffield, 1911), page 315.

38. *The Book of Buried Treasure* (London: Heinemann, 1911), page 104.

39. *Trial of Captain Kidd,* pages 204–208.

40. Lord Birkenhead, *Famous Trials of History* (London: Hutchinson, 1926), page 107. Graham Brooks's introduction to *Trial of Captain Kidd* summarizes the legal issues involved.

CHAPTER TEN

1. For the purposes of his defense, Kidd's *Narrative* says all those leaving the *Adventure Galley* moved over to Robert Culliford's *Mocha*. But some are known to have instead transferred to the *Margaret*; see note 11 below. Moreover, this would have given the *Mocha* a much larger crew than it actually had. The *Mocha* carried about 125 Europeans when it captured Captain Willock's *Satisfaction* in January 1697; see *CSPC, 1697–1698*, page 114. If, therefore, all of the approximately 100 men leaving Kidd had joined up with the *Mocha*, her crew would have increased to more than 200. However, only about 130 men sailed from Saint Mary's with Culliford in June 1697, according both to Kidd's *Narrative* and to the deposition by Edward Buckmaster (June 6, 1699), printed in *Privateering and Piracy*, page 198.
2. Deposition of William Jenkins, *Trial of Captain Kidd*, page 204.
3. *Trial of Captain Kidd*, page 26.
4. Kidd's *Narrative* is an accumulation of evasions and outright lies. For example, Kidd says the *Adventure Galley* went directly from the Comoros to the Indian Coast, omitting to mention the meeting with the *Sceptre* at the mouth of the Red Sea. Kidd actually looted six vessels. His *Narrative* admits to attacking only the two with French passes, the *Rouparelle* and the *Quedah Merchant*. (He also mentions the peaceful meeting with the *Loyal Captain*.)
5. *Trial of Captain Kidd*, page 108.
6. However, Palmer declared that Kidd sold the guns to Culliford for £400 or £500: *Trial of Captain Kidd*, pages 99, 106.
7. *Trial of Captain Kidd*, pages 100, 105.
8. On this point, Kidd's *Narrative* is confirmed by the deposition of Gabriel Loff taken in Boston by Lord Bellomont, *Trial of Captain Kidd*, page 209.
9. Kidd's *Narrative* appears to understate the crew's size. In his June 1700 deposition, Robert Culliford says ninety-six men deserted Kidd at Saint Mary's: Wilkins, *Captain Kidd*, page 94. William Jenkins remembered that "about 115 men" made it to Saint Mary's (*Trial*, page 205), and a crew of 115 to 120 would be consistent with the division into 160 shares.

    Kidd had left New York with a crew of over 150. As many as fifty died of fever in the Comoro islands, but this loss partly was made up by new recruits taken aboard at Johanna and from some of the prizes. When Kidd arrived at Carwar in September 1698, the East India Company's representative guessed that the *Adventure Galley* carried "140 well men and 30 guns": Grey, *Pirates of the Eastern Seas*, page 198.
10. It is impossible to be precise since Kidd's *Narrative* presents a confusing chronology of these events.
11. *Trial of Captain Kidd*, page 108.
12. *Trial of Captain Kidd*, page 197.
13. For the inventory of the goods Bellomont recovered, see *Trial of Captain Kidd*, pages 200–201.
14. Grey, *Pirates of the Eastern Seas,* page 199.
15. Deposition by Nicholas Alderson, taken at Bombay in October 1697, *CSPC, 1697–1698*, page 370.
16. Above, page 100.
17. The owners of the ship and cargo estimated their value at £45,000. The East India Company—from which the owners demanded compensation—set their value at £22,500: Grey, *Pirates of the Eastern Seas*, page 209. Kidd carried £14,000 ($7 million) in highly portable loot even after he abandoned the *Quedah Merchant* and its cargo of fine cloth and other spoils.
18. Ritchie, *Captain Kidd*, page 120.
19. About 120 men split some £12,000 taken from two prizes. Captain Willock's *Satisfaction* mainly carried rice. In June 1700, Culliford testified that he took £12,000 in gold and silk from the Portuguese ship *Loretta*: Deposition by Culliford printed Wilkins, *Captain Kidd*, page 94. In comparing this booty to that taken by Kidd, it must be

remembered that Kidd had been at sea for many more months than Culliford. For the number of men on the *Mocha*, see above, note 1.

20. Culliford could sign his name. He was employed by the East India Company as a gunner from 1691 until 1696, when he took part in a mutiny aboard the Company vessel *Josiah*.

21. Culliford's June 1700 deposition, printed in Wilkins, *Captain Kidd*, page 94.

22. Deposition by Theophilus Turner, printed in *Privateering and Piracy*, page 201.

23. Depositions by Culliford and Turner, cited notes 21 and 22 above; East India Company at Madras to London, January 1699, quoted Grey, *Pirates of the Eastern Seas*, page 148. Annesley, the Company representative at Surat, gave the value of the cargo at 185,000 rupees (about £41,000): Harihar Das, *The Norris Embassy to Aurangzib (1699–1702)* (Calcutta: Mukhopadhyay, 1959), page 33.

24. Wilkins, *Captain Kidd*, page 95.

25. Culliford's June 1700 deposition, printed in Wilkins, *Captain Kidd*, page 95.

26. At least 100 men were aboard the *Resolution/Soldado*, and the *Mocha* carried another 130 men. Fewer than forty took passage on the *Margaret* and the *Vine*.

27. Wright, *Annesley of Surat*, pages 210–212.

28. Culliford's June 1700 deposition, printed in Wilkins, *Captain Kidd*, pages 94–95. In June 1699, Theophilus Turner, a seaman aboard the *Mocha*, gave a deposition before Governor Blakiston of Maryland; see *Privateering and Piracy*, pages 200–201. Since they had been promised immunity before they testified, Culliford and Turner would have gained little by lying about the incident. Moreover, it is unlikely that the *Great Mahomet* carried hundreds of passengers.

29. Das, *Norris Embassy*, page 33.

30. East India Company report to London, quoted Das, *Norris Embassy*, page 33.

31. Das, *Norris Embassy*, pages 33–35; Wright, *Annesley of Surat*, pages 232–238.

CHAPTER ELEVEN

1. Judd, "Frederick Philipse," pages 368–370. See also Robert Ritchie, "Samuel Burgess, Pirate," *Authority and Resistance in Early New York,* ed. William Pencak and Conrad Wright (New York: New York Historical Society, 1988), pages 114–135. See Grey, *Pirates of the Eastern Seas,* page 207 for the quotation at the beginning of this chapter.

2. *Cape of Good Hope: Journal*, pages 17–20.

3. Judd, "Frederick Philipse and the Madagascar Trade," page 369.

4. Judd, "Frederick Philipse and the Madagascar Trade," page 369.

5. Grey, *Pirates of the Eastern Seas,* page 174.

6. Deposition by Theophilus Turner, a seaman on the *Mocha, CSPC, 1699*, page 289. Daniel Defoe later invented an improbable history of the *Pelican*, which he inserted into Nathaniel North's biography in the *General History of the Pyrates*, page 515. Defoe says the vessel had been captured from French mariners off Newfoundland. According to Theophilus Turner's deposition, however, the *Pelican* was acquired and outfitted at Rhode Island.

7. The term *pink* (derived from the Ditch word *pincke*) was used for any relatively small vessel with a narrow stern. The East India Company used ships such as the *Vine* to tend to and accompany larger East Indiamen.

8. For the text of the pardon, see *Trial of Captain Kidd*, pages 88–89.

9. Another man signed and came board when the *Vine* stopped at Port Dauphin on October 16. Culliford's petition was recorded by the secretary of the Admiralty Court on March 26/April 5, 1700: Wilkins, *Captain Kidd*, pages 96–97.

10. *Cape of Good Hope: Journal*, pages 17–21. The Dutch governor of the Cape colony prevented Lowth from repeating his seizure of the *Margaret*. The governor had protested to Lowth about his arrest of Burgess and his passengers. But Lowth refused to turn them over, and the governor was unwilling to take on a vessel of the East India Company, especially one as strongly armed as the *Loyal Merchant*.

11. *CSPC, 1701*, pages 44, 730, 737.
12. Wilkins, *Captain Kidd*, pages 98–101.
13. *Trial of Captain Kidd*, page 90.
14. See Chapter Nine, page 125. The meeting adversely affected Kidd's plans. At the Cape of Good Hope, Warren caught up with three Company vessels and told their captains of his misgivings. When they ran into the *Galley* near the Comoro Islands, they thus avoided Kidd as much as possible and refused to give him any assistance or supplies.
15. *CSPC, 1697–1698*, pages 67–71.
16. Warren's November 1697 letter: *CSPC, 1697–1698*, page 71. Warren had recently returned to England: Biddulph, *Pirates of Malabar*, page 55.
17. *CSPC, 1697–1698*, page 67. James Vernon was an assistant to Lord Shrewsbury and acting Secretary of State.
18. I. K. Steele, *Politics of Colonial Policy: The Board of Trade in Colonial Administration, 1696–1720* (Oxford: Clarendon, 1968), page 45.
19. *CSPC, 1697–1698*, pages 83–84.
20. *CSPC, 1697–1698*, page 122.
21. *CSPC, 1697–1698*, page 88.
22. *CSPC, 1697–1698*, pages 121–122, 340; Steele, *Politics*, page 52.
23. *CSPC, 1697–1698*, page 355. Captain Warren had suggested the addition of a fourth vessel so that the squadron could be divided into two when needed: see page 352.
24. Steele, *Politics*, page 52. The Lords Justices delayed preparation of the instructions by irrelevantly proposing that the squadron establish settlements at Madagascar, Saint Mary's, or any other place at useful for trade and not occupied by Christians.
25. The Board of Trade proposed that pirates should not be pardoned for crimes after they learned of the proclamation. The king replied that there was no way of knowing when a person first heard of the proclamation; he instead inserted specific dates into the document. See *CSPC, 1697–1698*, pages 445–446.
26. At one point during the process of approval, the Board of Trade itself suggested that the Company bear half the expenses of the expedition: Steele, *Politics*, page 52.
27. The Lords Justices told the king they were not in favor of the project, but he approved it anyway. Professor Steele notes that three of the Lords Justices were among those sponsoring Kidd: Lord Somers, the Lord Chancellor; Lord Orford, First Lord of the Admiralty; and Lord Shrewsbury, the secretary of state. Steele suggests that these men feared that the proposed pardon would hinder Kidd from pillaging the pirates; "delay in executing this plan can best be understood in terms of the personal interest of [these] three prominent politicians." Steele, *Politics*, page 51.
28. *Trial of Captain Kidd*, page 26.
29. Das, *Norris Embassy*, pages 75–88; *Luttrell*, vol. 4, pages 452, 456, 467.
30. *Luttrell*, vol. 4, pages 428–429.
31. Opposition to the company had both economic and political motives. Influential private merchants (the so-called interlopers) wanted to share in the wealth. The Company also had become identified with the Tory party and its policy of strong relatively strong monarchy. During the first years of their reign, William and Mary placed their greatest trust in politicians belonging to the Whig party. These Whig leaders resented the Company's privileges, and some also sought to assert the constitutional claim that Parliament and not the crown should control trading privileges. See Lawson, *East India Company*, pages 51–53.
32. *Journal of the House of Commons*, vol. 11, page 64.
33. Lawson, *East India Company*, pages 54–57; Das, *Norris Embassy*, pages 39–42.
34. The largest ship in the squadron was the 989-ton *Harwich*, built in 1674 and listed at sixty-six guns and four hundred men. See Das, *Norris Embassy*, page 91, note 2; "List of the Royal Navy as delivered by Pepys to the House of Commons, 1675," *Diary of Henry Teonge*, ed. G. N. Manwaring (New York: Harpers, 1927), page 296.
35. Das, *Norris Embassy*, pages 94–109.
36. *Cape of Good Hope: Journal*, pages 8, 10.

37. Das, *Norris Embassy*, pages 109–113.
38. *Luttrell*, vol. 4, page 662.
39. Above at note 9.
40. Biddulph, *Pirates of Malabar*, page 55; Steele, *Politics*, pages 52–53.
41. This is the story Littleton told when the *Hastings*, *Anglesey*, and *Lizard* reached the Cape of Good Hope on February 21 on their way back to London. *Cape of Good Hope: Journal*, page 35.
42. Hamilton, *New Account*, page 21. See Biddulph, *Pirates of Malabar*, pages 56–57.
43. The most notorious crimes—such as the theft of the *Gunsway*, *Quedah Merchant*, and *Great Mahomet*—all involved ships and cargo owned by Indians.
44. See the examples cited Ritchie, *Captain Kidd*, page 278, note 93.
45. They were at Mauritius from early January to March 25, 1701. See Chapuiset Le Merle, *Précis d'histoire de l'isle Maurice*, page 175.
46. Carey's remarks are quoted at the beginning of this chapter.

CHAPTER TWELVE

1. Unless they fell into the hands of the law, ordinary men were not included in official records. At the end of the seventeenth century, a man's birth and death might be recorded in parish registers, but little track was kept of what went on between the beginning and the end of life. Even when pirates used their original names it would be the work of decades to track down the family of each individual in these thousands of parish registers.
2. *Documents, Colonial History of New York*, vol. 4, page 447.
3. Governor Fletcher told the Board of Trade (*Documents, Colonial History New York*, vol. 4, page 446): "As to the four commissions which I granted to Captain Tew, Richard Glover, John Hoar, and Thomas Moston, they were men in reputation for their bravery and courage, and what I did therein was with advice and full approbation of the Councill. . . . And if Tew and Hoar did abuse the commissions they had and turned pirates afterwards, 'tis an event of which like instances doe some times happen, but it not being in my power to foresee, I was not able to prevent."
4. Officials in France began to keep dossiers on individuals earlier than in other countries. With their laudable penchant for hanging on to even the smallest and most tattered pieces of paper that get into their hands, French bureaucrats have preserved these obscure records. Antoine Boucher was secretary and treasurer for the royal governor of Réunion Island from 1702 to 1709; returning to France, he prepared reports for the East India Company regarding the island and its people. Among these was his *Mémoire pour servir a la connoissance particulière de chacun des habitans* written in 1710. More than two centuries later, Jean Barassin published Boucher's work for the first time, after checking his assertions against archival records preserved in France as well as on Réunion.
5. Boucher, *Mémoire*, page 25; Reydellet, *Bourbon et ses gouverneurs*, page 17. Former pirates were designated by such terms as *fourban, flibustier,* or *venu sur vaisseau fourban.* Some of these men, it is true, may have claimed to be "forced men," captured by pirates and required to work with them.
6. Boucher, *Mémoire*, pages 23–24, 230.
7. Albert Lougnon, *L'Ile Bourbon pendant La Régence* (Nerac: Couderc, 1956), page 162.
8. Below, Chapter Fourteen, note 29.
9. Ages ranged from 17 to 45. The mean age was 29.3; the median was 27. Because men in the seventeenth century were less likely than then they are today to know their precise birth date, all ages are approximate within a year or two.
10. Rediker, *Between the Devil and the Deep Blue Sea*, page 299, provides the ages of 198 sailors as given in depositions between 1700 and 1750 before the Admiralty court and vice-admiralty courts in the American colonies. Although Rediker does not say so, these ages reported in these depositions are approximations or guesses.

11. Richards, *Black Bart,* pages 113–114. All these victims were again much the same age. The youngest man was 19, the oldest 45. Twenty-nine men were in their 20s, fifteen in the 30s. Only five were 40 or older.

12. Boucher, *Mémoire,* page 229.

13. For Jacques de Lattre, see Boucher, *Mémoire,* page 97. An analysis made in 1706 found similar antecedents among pirates at France's Caribbean colony of Martinique. There were a sprinkling of young men from the best families and a number of impoverished settlers; perhaps the largest number were deserters from merchantmen. See J. S. Bromley, "Outlaws at Sea, 1660–1720: Liberty, Equality, and Fraternity among the Caribbean Freebooters," in *Corsairs and Navies 1660–1760* (London: Hambledon Press, 1987), page 7.

14. Easy access to the sea may be sufficient to explain why only a small number of nations —including England, France, Holland, Italy, and Greece—have supplied the bulk of pirates throughout history. Men raised in Switzerland and Poland might join brigands on land, but it would not occur to them to become pirates.

15. For the drunkards, see Boucher, *Mémoire,* pages 69, 80, 127–128, 234.

16. Lougnon, *L'Ile Bourbon,* page 169. The text of Beauvollier de Courchant's regulation is printed by M. I. Guët, *Les origines de l'île Bourbon et de la colonisation Française à Madagascar* (Paris: Bayle, 1888), page 221.

17. Lougnon, *L'Ile Bourbon,* page 172.

18. *CSPC, 1696–1697,* pages 73–74.

19. *CSPC, 1697–1698,* page 181. For additional complaints about Governor Markham's alleged failure to arrest pirates, see *CSPC, 1696–1697,* page 614; *1697–1698,* page 228.

20. Ritchie, *Captain Kidd,* page 100.

21. See, for example, *Bucquoy,* page 116.

CHAPTER THIRTEEN

1. The Swiss cantons were the only place in Europe with anything remotely resembling a democratic form of governance. By the seventeenth century, city governments— relatively egalitarian centuries before—were now ruled by oligarchies.

2. *Precis of the archives of the Cape of Good Hope: Letters received, 1695–1708,* ed. H. C. V. Leibbrandt (Cape Town: Richards, 1896), page 135.

3. For Lazenby and Bucquoy, see below, Chapter Fifteen.

4. Introduction by Percy Adams to Woodes Rogers, *A Cruising Voyage Round the World,* ed. George Manwaring (New York: Dover, 1970), pages ix–x.

5. Ralph Davis, *The Rise of the English Shipping Industry in the Seventeenth and Eighteenth Centuries* (London: Macmillan, 1962), pages 131–132. See also George Steckley, "Litigious Mariners: Wage Cases in the Seventeenth-Century Admiralty Court," *The Historical Journal,* 42 (1999): 315–345.

6. *Cape of Good Hope: Journal,* pages 59, 78.

7. Marcus Rediker, *Between the Devil and the Deep Blue Sea,* pages 212–227. Sir Evan Cotton, *East Indiamen: The East India Company's Maritime Service* (London: Fawcett, 1949), page 60.

8. Under the prize laws of 1702, the crown received one-fifth; by 1705, the charge had risen to one-third. Before 1702, the crown took only one-tenth, but colonial governors skimmed off an additional one-fifteenth. In New York in 1708, officials of the admiralty court demanded another 25 percent. See Lydon, *Pirates, Privateers, and Profits,* pages 56–57.

9. Bromley, *Corsairs and Navies,* page 4; Bryan Little, *Crusoe's Captain* (London: Odhams, 1960), page 48.

10. Woodes Rogers, *Cruising Voyage,* pages 21–23.

11. A. O. Exquemelin, *The Buccaneers of America,* trans. Alexis Brown (Harmondsworth, England: Penguin, 1969), page 71.

12. Exquemelin, *Buccaneers of America,* pages 171–172. However, all the men, as well as the

officers, were asked to agree to giving Morgan 1 percent of the total take before divisions into shares.

13. Bradley, *Lure of Peru,* page 154.
14. *General History of the Pyrates,* page 131; see below, Chapter Fifteen.
15. Patrick Pringle, *Jolly Roger: The Story of the Great Age of Piracy* (New York: Norton, 1953), pages 110–111.
16. Wilkinson, *Bermuda in the Old Empire,* pages 63–64, note 2.
17. Kidd's articles are printed in *CSPC, 1700,* page 199; Wilkins, *Captain Kidd,* pages 53–54, prints a version that is similar although taken from a different source.
18. For various reasons, New York's economy was depressed in 1696.
19. Wilkins, *Captain Kidd,* pages 53–54, sentences numbered 4, 6, 8, and 14.
20. The long history of voluntary association through sworn oaths is outside the scope of this study. In the sacrament of hommage during the Middle Ages, a man knelt before his lord and pledged faithfulness on the Bible or a holy relic. When urban life revived during the eleventh century, towns began as "communes," revolutionary associations created through sworn oaths. Similarly, in Latin canon law, a marriage came into existence solely through the oaths sworn by bride and groom. The author is not implying that seventeenth century mariners were familiar with the history of law. What is clear is that all these various associations reflected and grew out of a profound belief that it is a shameful abomination for a man to break his pledge or oath.
21. See below, Chapter Fifteen, page 207.
22. *Bucquoy,* pages 114–116.
23. Edward Low's articles were printed in the *Boston News-Letter,* August 8, 1723. They have been reprinted by George Dow and John Edmonds, *The Pirates of the New England Coast* (Salem, Mass.: Marine Research, 1923), pages 146–147; Edward Spence, *Shipwrecks, Pirates, and Privateers* (Charleston, S.C.: Narwhal, 1995), page 44. Daniel Defoe published the articles adopted on vessels commanded by George Lowther (1721) and John Phillips (1723): *General History of the Pyrates,* pages 307–308, 342–343.
24. Richards, *Black Bart,* pages 33–34.
25. Maurice Besson, *Les "Frères de la coste": Flibustiers & Corsaires* (Paris: Duchartre & Van Buggenhoudt, 1928), pages 17–20.
26. Grey, *Pirates of the Eastern Seas,* page 129. See above, page 76.
27. The pirates sailing from Nassau in the Bahamas continued to demote captains for serious shortcomings. Thus Samuel Bellamy was elected to replace Benjamin Hornigold because the latter refused to take and plunder English vessels: Deposition of John Brown, May 1717, *Privateering and Piracy,* page 294.
28. Snelgrave, *New Account,* page 216.
29. Downing, *Indian Wars,* page 99.
30. Kemp and Lloyd, *Brethren of the Coast,* page 37.
31. Kemp and Lloyd, *Brethren of the Coast,* pages 47–48; Spate, *Monopolists and Freebooters,* page 142.
32. *CSPC, 1697–1698,* page 367; see above, page 108.
33. See below, Chapter Seven, page 98.
34. See below, Chapter Fifteen, page 214.
35. See below, Chapter Fourteen, page 195.
36. *Bucquoy,* page 103.
37. Deposition by Robert Culliford (October 1701), printed in Wilkins, *Captain Kidd,* page 93.
38. Burgess later served as a ship's captain and slave trader on behalf of Frederick Philipse, the wealthiest merchant in New York. See pages 198–199.
39. Snelgrave, *New Account,* page 199.
40. Pringle, *Jolly Roger,* page 108.
41. Snelgrave, *New Account,* page 250.
42. *Bucquoy,* pages 111, 115.

43. Snelgrave, *New Account*, page 257.
44. Rediker, *Between the Devil and the Deep Blue Sea*, page 85; Davis, *Rise of the English Shipping Industry*, page 113.
45. Kemp and Lloyd, *Brethren of the Coast*, page 82; Bradley, *Lure of Peru*, page 129–130.
46. Hamilton, *New Account*, page 134; Deposition by Robert Culliford, printed in Wilkins, *Captain Kidd*, page 91.
47. The quartermaster's role among the pirates resembles that of a land army's quartermaster, who also saw to the billeting, feeding, clothing, and booty of a body of troops. One may speculate that former soldiers played a role in increasing the power and responsibilities of the quartermaster among the Caribbean buccaneers. If so, it is curious that no one drew this connection at the time. Some of the pirate's captives, such as Captain Snelgrave, surely would have been acquainted with the customs of the English and French armies.
48. B. R. Burg, "Legitimacy and Authority," pages 50–51.
49. Christopher Hill, "Radical Pirates," *The Origins of Anglo-American Radicalism*, ed. Margaret Jacob and James Jacob (London: Allen & Unwin, 1984), pages 20–26.
50. Bromley, *Corsairs and Navies*, page 11.
51. Above, Chapter Twelve, page 160.
52. There is another obvious problem with the theory that the pirate democracy was inspired by the traditions of Protestant dissenters. North American pirates grew up in several different colonies with very different types of Protestantism, some of which had highly undemocratic customs. See, for example, David Hackett Fischer, *Albion's Seed: Four British Folkways in America* (New York: Oxford University Press, 1989).
53. Manuel Schonhorn, *Defoe's Politics: Parliament, Power, Kingship, and Robinson Crusoe* (Cambridge, Eng.: Cambridge University Press, 1991), pages 4–5.
54. For a variety of reasons, I do not agree with the revisionists who deny that Daniel Defoe wrote the *General History of the Pyrates*. (See the Introduction, note 7.) Among the facts suggesting Defoe's authorship is the close similarity—both in substance and in literary style—between the *General History* and works that Defoe certainly wrote. Defoe's uncommon theory of charismatic kingship thus is found both in the *General History* and in other works that he signed with his own name.
55. Schonhorn, *Defoe's Politics*, page 151.
56. *General History of the Pyrates*, pages 388–391.
57. *General History of the Pyrates*, pages 526–528. Unlike the totally fictitious Misson, there really was a Captain North. As so often in the *General History*, however, Defoe freely mixes fantasy and fact, and there is no first-hand evidence corroborating Defoe's description of North's utopia.
58. *CSPC, 1697–1698*, page 70.
59. When the early inhabitants of Saint Domingue got together to cultivate a plot jointly, they were said to be acting like matelots: *il's'amatelotient*.
60. Bromley, *Corsairs and Navies*, page 15. For matelots and the logwood cutters see Rogoziński, *Pirates!*, under those words. Both Honduras and Campeche, Mexico, were Spanish colonies, so the English and French log cutters—like the pirates at Saint Mary's —had either to govern themselves or live in anarchy.
61. In the same way, the Carib, Cuna, and other Indian peoples may have inspired the practices of the Caribbean buccaneers. However, I am unaware of any systematic investigation of Indian influences on Caribbean marauders. See pages 191 and 197 for Nathaniel North as onshore captain.

CHAPTER FOURTEEN

1. Boucher, *Mémoire*, page 235.
2. See Captain George Whaley's November 1703 deposition as printed in Richard Carnac Temple, *New Light on the Mysterious Tragedy of the "Worcester"* (London: Benn, 1930), page 136. In March 1703, Bowen's gang captured the *Pembroke* and kept Captain Wha-

ley (or Wooley) for some months to serve as pilot (see below at note 14). While Whaley was with them, Bowen and his confederates talked freely of their earlier exploits. On November 7, 1703, Whaley wrote about his experiences to a Mister Penning, head of the New East India Company factory at Calicut. Whaley's letter was first printed in 1705 along with the record of the trial of Captain Thomas Green for piracy on the ship *Worcester*. It served as the underlying basis for Daniel Defoe's anecdotes about Bowen and other captains.

3. *General History of the Pyrates,* pages 476–479. There is no documentary evidence supporting Defoe's story. One wonders why Booth would have gone to Zanzibar when the Comoro Islands were closer and traditionally hospitable. A fort guarding the harbor at Zanzibar was built after 1698 (when Arab solders seized the place) and before 1710 (when it was described by a Portuguese spy). See John Gray, *History of Zanzibar* (London: Oxford University Press, 1962), pages 82–83.

4. The pirates told Captain George Whaley that "They took Captain Conway [and the *Borneo* in October 1702], selling ship and goods in shares; viz. one third part to merchant of Callequilon [Quilon], another third to a merchant of Porca [Purakadda], the other third to Malpa, the Dutch broker of this place [Rajapura]." Quoting Temple, *New Light,* page 126; see also the Professor Schonhorn's annotations to *General History of the Pyrates,* page 686.

5. Captain George Whaley's November 7 deposition, printed in *New Light,* page 134.

6. Chapuiset Le Merle, *Précis d'histoire de l'îsle Maurice,* page 177. To excuse his cooperation with known pirates, the Dutch governor later told his superiors that he had intended to massacre the castaways after he had gained their trust. But this self-serving story is not borne out by the Mauritius records cited by Chapuiset Le Merle.

7. Boucher, *Mémoire,* pages 183, 236, 242, 265, 290, 320.

8. The ship's articles, signed just before the two vessels sailed, are printed in George Insh, *Papers Relating to the Ships and voyages of the Company of Scotland Trading to Africa and the Indies* (Edinburgh: Constable, 1924), pages 245–248. Both vessels were about one hundred tons burden, according to the deposition by Edward Fenwick, supercargo of the *Pembroke,* printed in Grey, *Pirates of the Eastern Seas,* pages 236–237.

9. Somewhat later in 1702, Drummond and Steward were encountered by Robert Drury, a youth who also had been shipwrecked on Madagascar. Drury later was separated from the both men but ran into Captain Drummond again two years later. Drury escaped to England in 1717, but the two captains died while still living on Madagascar.

   A book purporting to be an autobiographical account of Drury's captivity appeared in 1729 entitled *Madagascar, or Robert Drury's Journal During Fifteen Years Captivity in that Island.* In 1890, Pasfield Oliver published a new edition of *Robert Drury's Journal.* Oliver pointed out that some of the descriptions of tribal customs are almost word-for-word translations of passages in an earlier French account by Etienne Flacourt. In addition, Drury's publisher also published many books by Daniel Defoe, and the work is interspersed with philosophical speculations similar to those in Defoe's works. Pasfield Oliver thus concluded that *Robert Drury's Journal* was a work of fiction, most likely by Daniel Defoe, the undoubted author of *Robinson Crusoe,* another tale of shipwreck.

   In more recent years, documentary evidence has been found proving that Robert Drury existed and was shipwrecked on Madagascar. At least some of the events described in the *Journal* probably did occur. However, while he may have prepared a first draft or dictated his story, Drury did not write the book himself. The organization and much of the writing are the work of a professional author, either Daniel Defoe himself or one of his collaborators or imitators.

   See Arthur Secord, *"Robert Drury's Journal" and Other Studies* (Urbana: University of Illinois Press, 1961). Mervyn Brown summarizes *Robert Drury's Journal* in Chapter Six of *Madagascar Rediscovered.*

10. The trial records are printed in *State Trials,* vol. 5, pages 576–614. See Temple, *New Light,* for a detailed account of this incident.

11. Temple, *New Light,* page 134. See also the ship's log of the *Galley Mary,* kept by Captain Thomas Tolson, in *Papers of Thomas Bowery,* pages 244–245, 251. The 230-ton *Prosperous* was owned by Thomas Bowery and five others. In 1701, she was licensed by the New East India Company to trade "for Negroes" at Madagascar, where she arrived in May 1702. Twenty-eight of those left on shore got away in the ship's boat, the *Linnet,* which touched at Johanna in the Comoro Islands, where five men stayed. The rest, after a voyage of five weeks, reached Surat in September 1702. On arrival, the Muslim governor of Surat suspected them of piracy and imprisoned them for nearly six months, despite the efforts of the New East India Company's consul to free them. They were released to help defend the town against a threatened attack by Maratha forces hostile to the town's government.

12. Howard probably was one of the attackers and not a member of the crew of the *Prosperous.* Daniel Defoe in *The General History of the Pyrates,* pages 487–492, presents a biographical sketch of Howard, beginning with his youth in London. There is no corroboration for Defoe's tale, which is entirely fictitious.

13. Deposition by Edward Fenwick, supercargo of the *Pembroke,* Grey, *Pirates of the Eastern Seas,* page 235. See also Captain Whaley's deposition, Temple, *New Light,* page 134.

14. Captain Whaley's November 7 deposition, printed in Temple, *New Light,* page 134.

15. Temple, *New Light,* pages 134–135.

16. Whaley's November 7 deposition.

17. Grey, *Pirates of the Eastern Seas,* page 239.

18. *General History of the Pyrates,* page 494.

19. Chapuiset Le Merle, *Précis d'histoire de l'isle Maurice,* page 184. The Dutch settlers again remarked on how punctiliously Bowen and his men paid for their purchases.

20. Boucher, *Mémoire,* pages 138, 186, 229, 241. One of those disembarking at Réunion at this time was Joseph de Guigné, who had been supercargo aboard the French vessel commanded by Julien Forget and captured by George Booth in 1697 (above at note 1). De Guigné thus had shared the adventures of Booth and John Bowen aboard the *Speaker, Speedy Return,* and *Defiance* from 1697 to 1704. De Guigné married in November 1704 and later purchased tracts of land in three separate locations on Réunion: Boucher, *Mémoire,* page 235.

21. Boucher, *Mémoire,* page 229; quoting *General History of the Pyrates,* page 524.

22. Deposition by Edward Fenwick, supercargo of the *Pembroke,* Grey, *Pirates of the Eastern Seas,* page 236–237.

23. *General History of the Pyrates,* page 525. Defoe throughout refers to "Nathaniel" North, but witnesses at the time write only of John North.

24. *General History of the Pyrates,* page 527. See above, Chapter Thirteen at note 56. At one point in his tale, Defoe tells us that North commanded this utopia for five years; elsewhere he says the community lasted only two years before the arrival of John Halsey disturbed its torpor.

25. *Villers Diary,* pages 33–35. Pierre Tiré, the pirates' new recruit, was wealthy enough to possess a horse, which Governor Villers confiscated after his departure. According to Villers, the vessel captured from the French captain was stocked with *"eau de vie,"* which may have been either brandy or rum.

26. *General History of the Pyrates,* pages 483–485. The capture of the *Dorothy* in August 1706 is mentioned in a letter from the New East India Company's agents at Masulipatam, *Diary of William Hedges,* vol. 3, page 10.

27. *General History of the Pyrates,* page 485. See also Hill, *Notes on Piracy in Eastern Waters,* page 138.

28. *Villers Diary,* pages 44–45. The dates are those given by Governor Villers. As so often is the case in the *General History of the Pyrates,* Defoe does not indicate where and when the actions he describes took place. Defoe says that White had given up his original vessel and transferred to the *Dorothy.* However, Governor Villers reports that the vessel

arriving in December 1706 carried thirty guns, whereas, by Defoe's own reckoning, the *Dorothy* had only six cannon.

29. In his 1709 list of inhabitants, Antoine Boucher names fourteen men who settled on the island when Thomas White visited in 1706. These are Jacques Boyer, Patrick Droman, Jean de Lattre, Jean Janson (Johnson), Jacques Pitou, Pierre Bouché, Edward Robert, Thomas Elgar, Giles Fontane, André Rauld, Pierre Heros, Jean Le Roy, Jean "Miclatchy," and a man named simply Robert. See Boucher, *Mémoire,* pages 69, 79, 97, 179, 193, 236, 256, 292, 303, 304, 320, 384.
30. A man named Thomas Yousen, according to *Villers Diary,* page 45.
31. Male settlers at Réunion were expected to marry, and they did not enjoy full citizenship until they had done so. Because marriage was a condition of acceptance by the colony's government, buccaneers married very soon after retiring at Réunion.
32. See above, Chapter Twelve, note 15.
33. Boucher, *Mémoire,* pages 69, 233–234.
34. Foulpointe is a French name, and does not mean what it appears to mean in English. It is not known whether the English name is derived from the French name or vice-versa. In modern French, *fou* has the sense of excess, foolishness, silliness; but the meaning may have included "hopeful" during the seventeenth century. Mervyn Brown thinks, in contrast, that Foulpointe is a French mispronunciation of Hopeful Point; see *Madagascar Rediscovered*, page 291, note 17.
35. *General History of the Pyrates*, pages 526, 535.
36. Halsey was born in Boston on March 1, 1670, the son of James and Dinah Halsey. In the early years of King William's War, he served as a sailor on HMS *Nonesuch* and subsequently became a merchant seaman and captain. See Chapin, *Privateer Ships*, pages 178–179.
37. *CSPC, 1704–1705*, pages 212, 445, 592–593, 663.
38. *Boston News-Letter* report of the execution, printed in *Privateering and Piracy*, pages 278–284.
39. Contemporary documents about this incident are found in *CSPC, 1704–1705*, pages 212, 445, 592–593, 663; *Records of the Colony of Rhode Island*, vol. 3, pages 508–510, 535–540; Deposition of Paul Dudley August 15, 1705, printed in *Privateering and Piracy*, pages 285–286. See also Chapin, *Privateer Ships*, pages 178–181.
40. Chapin, *Privateer Ships*, page 181.
41. *General History of the Pyrates*, pages 465–467. Defoe provides no dates for these events. Halsey was off the Azores early in 1706, and he probably reached Saint Augustine's Bay about the middle of the year. Nevertheless, Defoe claims he picked up castaway sailors from the *Degrave*, which had foundered in 1703. It is unlikely that these survivors would have lingered in the area around Saint Augustine's, as it has a harsh climate and was sparsely populated.
42. Deposition of Captain Collins of the *Calicut*, February, 1707, printed Grey, *Pirates of the Eastern Seas*, pages 271–273. Collins says the *Charles* carried sixteen guns and a crew of fifty Europeans at this time. *General History of the Pyrates*, pages 465–467. Defoe provides no dates for these events. Halsey was off the Azores early in 1706.
43. The *Calicut* was stripped of its planking and sunk: Grey, *Pirates of the Eastern Seas*, page 271.
44. *Villers Diary*, pages 47–48. The corsair warship is said to have carried thirty cannon and one hundred men commanded by Captain "Ion Loüis." Ion is clearly *Jan*, the normal English pronunciation of the name *John*. "Loüis" is not, however, a close translation of Halsey (even given that the letter *h* was not pronounced before *a*). But there was no other corsair warship near Réunion in May 1707. Halsey used the pseudonym John Jones when he captured the *Buffalo* and *Calicut*; see the deposition by Captain Collins of the *Calicut* cited note 42 above. Presumably the early eighteenth-century English pronunciation of Jones sounded like Loüis to an early eighteenth-century Frenchman.
45. Governor Villers reports that "Captain Loüis" (John Halsey) was on his way to Saint

Mary's when the *Charles* stopped at Réunion Island. Defoe's *General History* says that Halsey met up with the *Buffalo* and *Dorothy* at Hopeful Point. Although only Villers is a firsthand witness, there are several scenarios under which both Villers and Defoe could be accurate.

46. Nathaniel North served as quartermaster, according to Defoe.

47. Deposition of Thomas Adams, September 17, 1707, printed in Grey, *Pirates of the Eastern Seas*, page 275. Captain Jago was forced to leave the merchant marine because of his cowardly flight from Halsey's attack; see Hill, *Episodes of Piracy in the Eastern Seas*, page 55.

48. Adams' deposition, printed in Grey, *Pirates of the Eastern Seas*, page 275.

49. Diary of Henry Smith, September 1707, printed in Temple, *New Light*, page 322.

50. Captain Jones of the Greyhound, June 1708, printed in Grey, *Pirates of the Eastern Seas*, pages 278–279, 283.

51. *General History of the Pyrates*, pages 470–471.

52. Captain Jones's June 1708 deposition, Grey, *Pirates of the Eastern Seas*, page 283.

53. *General History of the Pyrates*, page 471.

54. Jones's June 1708 deposition, Grey, *Pirates of the Eastern Seas*, page 283; compare *General History of the Pyrates*, page 536.

55. *General History of the Pyrates*, pages 536–539.

56. The Malagasy had driven out both the English colonists at Saint Augustine's Bay and the French settlement at Fort Dauphin; see above, Chapter Three, pages 51–53. The documentary evidence often refutes Defoe's narrative. To take one example, Defoe says Nathaniel North transported the *Neptune's* Scottish purser to the French colony at Réunion (*General History of the Pyrates*, pages 536–537). Had this visit taken place, it would have left some trace in Réunion's records. Maritime visitors were rare, and the officials living at that sparsely inhabited colony paid close attention to every ship that arrived at the island.

57. See above, pages 16, 177.

58. Judd, "Frederick Philipse," page 360. Burgess could speak Dutch as well as English, which increased his value as an employee of the Philipse family. Although there is no firm evidence about his origins, his knowledge of both languages suggests that he may have previously lived in the linguistically mixed community of New York. At the time of his trial in London, he was said to have come from a seafaring family of good repute. See Ritchie, "Samuel Burgess," page 133, note four.

59. Judd, "Frederick Philipse," pages 360–361; Ritchie, "Samuel Burgess," page 120.

60. For Burgess's deposition before Governor Bellomont on May 3, 1698, see *CSPC, 1697–1698*, pages 227–228.

61. See above, Chapter Eleven, page 147.

62. Until 1700, English law required that pirates be sent to England for trial before the High Court of Admiralty. In that year, Parliament passed a new piracy statute, which created a vice admiralty court system covering the entire empire. Even if English officials in India were aware of the new law, they had not yet set up the requisite procedures. Thus Burgess and the others were returned to England. See Steele, "Politics," pages 55–59; P. Bradley Nutting, "The Madagascar Connection: Parliament and Piracy, 1690–1701," *American Journal of Legal History*, 22 (1978), pages 202–215; Helen Crump, *Colonial Admiralty Jurisdiction in the Seventeenth Century* (London: Longman's Green, 1931).

63. Captain Lowth was less than scrupulous in accounting for funds due the crown. As late as 1705, he had not turned over any of the various types of coins confiscated from the *Margaret*. There is no evidence that either Burgess or the Philipses ever got their money back. However, it is possible that some private agreement between Lowth and the Philipses was reached out of court. See Judd, "Frederick Philipse," page 373.

64. On July 26, 1698, the Board of Trade had asked the King to approve Bellomont's pardon for Burgess and Edward Taylor. Although it requested royal approval, the Board was of the opinion that Bellomont's commission as governor had given him the power

to pardon pirates "according as he shall find them to deserve." See *Documents, Colonial History of New York*, vol. 4, page 360.

65. For William Dampier's career, see Rogoziński, *Pirates!*, pages 93–94.
66. *CSPC, 1702–1703*, pages 633–635.
67. See above, Chapter Five, note 21.
68. *CSPC, 1702–1703*, Number 1150.
69. *An Account of Her Majesty's Revenue in the Province of New York, 1701–1709: The Customs Records of Early Colonial New York*, ed. Julius M. Bloch and others (Ridgewood, New Jersey, 1966), page 113.
70. For Samuel Burgess's command of the Mary, see *An Account of Her Majesties Revenue*, page 127.
71. Thomas Duckett testified before Parliament in 1707 about Burgess: *Journals of the House of Commons*, vol. 15, pages 382–384. Thomas Bowery wrote a description of the slave trade for the king of Prussia, citing Burgess as an expert. For Bowery, see the introduction to *Papers of Thomas Bowery*.
72. Drury's many adventures in Madagascar are described in *Madagascar; or, Robert Drury's Journal*, a ghost-written autobiography published in 1729. See above, note 9.
73. *Madagascar; or, Robert Drury's Journal*, pages 297–298.
74. The *General History*, page 510, asserts that Burgess decided to return to the West Indies and enlisted as third mate on the *Henry*, another English slave ship. As agent for the *Henry*'s captain, Burgess irritated King Dick, who fed him "Honey Toke, in which it is supposed he was poison'd, for he fell ill and died soon after, leaving what he had to the Care of the chief Mate, for the use of his [Burgess's] Wife and Children." This anecdote is highly improbable, particularly because there is no evidence that Burgess had a wife and children, either in New York or in London. It undoubtedly was inserted into the *General History* as a comic interlude and perhaps also to make the point that "crime does not pay."

CHAPTER FIFTEEN

1. For descriptions of the *Fancy*, see Captain Kirby's log for the *Greenwich*, printed in Downing, *Indian Wars*, page 43, note 2; Macrae's deposition, *General History of the Pyrates*, page 118.

   The chapter on Edward England in Daniel Defoe's *General History* is wholly fictional until the encounter with the Captain Macrae's *Cassandra* in August 1720. The supposedly factual testimony in Clement Downing's *History of the Indian Wars* also turns out to be untrustworthy about England's career.

   Downing's book describes the 1722 expedition to Saint Mary's and the nearby coast of Madagascar led by Commodore Theodore Matthews. Downing was a seaman aboard one of Matthews's warships, and he personally interviewed John Plantain, a European living at Antongil Bay. Before coming to Madagascar, Plantain told Downing, he had served on the *Fancy* under Edward England throughout its adventures in the Indian Ocean (*Indian Wars*, pages 97–104).

   Plantain said he enlisted on a sloop which left Rhode Island, with John Williams as captain and Bartholomew Roberts as quartermaster. On the way to West Africa and along the African coast, the sloop captured a number of prizes. Command of the *Fancy*, a Dutch slave ship, was given to Edward England. The crew trusted England because he had been with them since leaving Rhode Island and he was "a Man who had been Mate of several good Ships."

   England proposed that the squadron go on to the Indian Ocean. Since Bartholomew Roberts strongly opposed this suggestion, the crews of the various ships went ashore to discuss the matter. They could not come to a consensus, so some stayed in Africa with Roberts, while others enlisted under England on the *Fancy* and *Victory*.

   Plantain's story about this stage of his cruise with Edwards is not believable. Plantain is the only source to suggested that Bartholomew Roberts came to Africa on a Rhode

Island sloop. But several firsthand witnesses testify that Roberts instead sailed from London in the 1719 as third mate of the slave ship *Princess*. In June, the *Princess* was captured by Howell Davis, and Roberts enlisted on Davis's vessel. (See note 22 below.)

There are various explanations for Plantain's errors in this segment of his story. Plantain may have been lying to Downing. For example, he may not have joined the crew of the *Fancy* until it reached Madagascar. It also is possible that Downing did not report Plantain's tale correctly. Downing published his book in 1737, fifteen years after the events described. And the entire work is marked, in the words of its modern editor, by many "inaccuracies, both willful and involuntary" *(Indian Wars,* page xxxi).

2. Documents in French refer to this captain as La Buse, "the Buzzard," certainly an appropriate nickname for a brigand. In English sources, he is called La Bouche and, in one ship's log, Lepouse. These appear to be efforts to record the sounds the Englishmen heard when La Buse said his name—although La Bouche ("the Mouth") would also be a fitting pirate's nickname.

3. Said to be from Calais, France (Biddulph, *Pirates of Malabar,* page 134), La Buse was among the pirates sailing from Nassau on Providence Island in the Bahamas. In 1716, his warship cruised in consort with a vessel initially commanded by Benjamin Hornigold and later by Samuel Bellamy. La Buse and Bellamy captured British and French vessels near the Virgin Islands but were separated early in 1717: Examination of John Brown, May 1717, *Privateering and Piracy,* page 294. After Woodes Rogers became governor of the Bahamas in July 1718, La Buse fled to the West African coast, where he joined forces with ships commanded by Thomas Cocklyn and Howell Davis; see below, note 21; Snelgrave, *New Account,* pages 198–199.

4. *General History of the Pyrates,* page 114.

5. *General History of the Pyrates,* pages 581, 583. Some books on pirates give Condent's name as John, others call him Edmund. But the primary source always refer to him simply as "Captain Condent" and do not mention a first name.

6. Rogoziński, *Pirates!,* pages 117–123, for an overview of pirate fiction. Exquemelin's *Buccaneers of America* was published in England in 1684; see Jack Beeching's introduction to the Penguin translation by Alexis Brown, page 17. As portrayed by Exquemelin, both François l'Olonnais and Sir Henry Morgan gloat over savage and even insane acts. While torturing a prisoner to obtain information, l'Olonnais became enraged. "Then l'Olonnais, being possessed of a devil's fury, ripped open one of the prisoners with his cutlass, tore the living heart out of his body, gnawed at it, and then hurled it in the face of one of the others, saying, 'Show me another way, or I will do the same to you.'" (Brown translation of *Buccaneers of America,* page 107.)

7. *General History of the Pyrates,* page 121.

8. Snelgrave, *New Account,* page 272.

9. *Lazenby's Narrative,* printed in Grey, *Pirates of the Eastern Seas,* page 321.

10. Taylor is first mentioned in April 1719 as sailing master under Howell Davis. The story Taylor told Bucquoy is contradicted by the fact that Davis took up piracy only a few weeks before the gang captured Captain Snelgrave's *Bird Galley.* Queen Anne had died in 1714; and there is no evidence about Taylor's activities—piratical or otherwise—during the intervening five years before he shipped with Davis. However, it is not impossible that Taylor had been aboard another pirate ship and transferred to Davis's vessel, just as he later left Davis and went over to Edward England.

11. *Bucquoy,* page 107: "Certes, ils ne pouvaient trouver pour remplir cette function un homme plus capable que lui, car, abstraction faite du caractère de son infâme et odieuse profession et de ses vices privés, il réunissait tout ce qu'on peut desirer dans un marin, un soldat, et un capitaine."

12. Lougnon, *L'Ile Bourbon,* page 165, notes 19 and 20. The *Dauphine* was captured at the end of 1718.

13. Lougnon, *L'Ile Bourbon,* page 166, note 21. In 1722, Plantain welcomed a naval squadron to Antongil Bay. At that time, according to Clement Downing (*Indian Wars,* pages

103–104), Plantain claimed he had come to Madagascar with Edward England and John Taylor. But Downing's story is full of chronological and factual errors; see note 1 above. Plantain may well have set up his fortress at Antongil Bay years earlier. Indeed, it is difficult to see how he could have become intimate with the local chief and built an extensive habitation during the few months elapsing between Taylor's visit to Saint Mary's and the arrival of the naval squadron.

14. Downing, *Indian Wars,* page 45 and note 5; Biddulph, *Pirates of Malabar,* pages 186–187. For the cargo's value, see also Lougnon, *L'Ile Bourbon,* page 166, note 22; Grey, *Pirates of the Eastern Seas,* page 302. Stories reaching British India blamed England and Taylor instead of Condent for the loss of the Indian merchantman; Downing reports these rumors but is corrected by his editor. Relying on some version of the same misinformation, Defoe also confuses England, Taylor, and Condent: *General History of the Pyrates,* page 584. But Condent stayed at Saint Mary's island before the other two captains, and he had already had left when they arrived.

15. Lougnon, *L'Ile Bourbon,* page 166. Baker had to leave five of his crew as hostages for his return, but he was allowed to take away to Réunion three physicians that Condent had kidnaped from various prizes.

16. See above, Chapter Twelve, notes 5–8.

17. Lougnon, *L'Ile Bourbon,* page 168. See also Froidevaux, "Madagascar du XVI siècle à 1811," *Histoire des Colonies Française,* ed. Hanotaux and Martineau, vol. 6, page 324.

18. Downing, *Indian Wars,* page 45 (see also page 87).

19. *Lazenby's Narrative,* page 302; Lougnon, *L'Ile Bourbon,* page 180.

20. Lougnon, *L'Ile Bourbon,* page 180, note 58. The commander's testimony was given in connection with Condent's quarrel with officials of the government tobacco monopoly. It is not possible to determine who was at fault in the incident.

21. Lougnon, *L'Ile Bourbon,* page 164.

22. Davis was off on his own by about June 5, 1719, when he seized three English slave ships at Annamabo, on the Gold Coast. The third mate of one captured vessel was Bartholomew Roberts, who took over at the end of July after Davis was murdered by the Portuguese on Principe Island. Cruising from Africa to Brazil to Canada, Roberts is said to have looted some four hundred vessels of various size. See Rogoziński, *Pirates!,* pages 96, 292; Richards, *Black Bart.*

23. Several sources—including Richard Lazenby, who was held captive for ten months (*Lazenby's Narrative,* page 316)—say that "Jasper Seager" had the chief command while Taylor was in charge of the *Victory.* Edward England and Jasper Seager clearly were the same person; if Seager was an alias, then England may have been his original name.

24. The *General History of the Pyrates* (pages 115–117) claims they captured more than twenty vessels, looting them all and burning some.

25. Lougnon, *L'Ile Bourbon,* page 165, note 18.

26. Captain Kirby's log book for the *Greenwich,* printed in Downing, *Indian Wars,* page 43, note 2.

27. For La Buse wrecking his ship on Mayotte Island, see the deposition by James Macrae, printed in *General History of the Pirates,* page 118. Cf. Lougnon, *L'Ile Bourbon,* page 173. Cocklyn is not mentioned again by the sources, and his fate is unknown.

28. *General History of the Pyrates,* page 117.

29. *General History of the Pyrates,* page 125.

30. East India Company records, printed Grey, *Pirates of the Eastern Seas,* pages 307–308.

31. The *General History of the Pyrates,* page 117, states that England and Taylor went from Africa to Madagascar, headed east to India's Malabar Coast (where they captured the *Fancy*), and then went back west to the Comoro Islands. Since this itinerary would have taken them against the monsoon winds both going to India and coming back, Defoe's account is highly unlikely.

According to John Plantain (as reported in Downing's *Indian Wars,* page 102), the *Fancy* and the *Victory* went to Saint Augustine's Bay, Johanna, and the mouth of the

Red Sea. At the last place they captured a very rich Indian treasure ship and took it to Saint Mary's, where they massacred the men and "abused their women in a very vile manner." They then went back to Johanna and attacked the *Cassandra*. Plantain's story is a naive retelling of Henry Every's capture of the *Gunsway*. Like Defoe's version, moreover, it includes too many activities to fit into seven months.

32. Captain Macrae's account of the battle, dated at Bombay, November 16, 1720, is printed in the *General History of the Pyrates*, pages 118–121. For Captain Kirby's report and the log of the *Cassandra*, see Grey, *Pirates of the Eastern Seas*, page 313; Downing, *Indian Wars*, page 43, note 1.

33. Downing, *Indian Wars*, page 45, note 6. The *Cassandra*'s cargo included gold and silver coins for trading purposes as well as a large quantity of fine cloths and European liquors.

34. *General History of the Pyrates*, page 123.

35. Biddulph, *Pirates of Malabar*, pages 140–141.

36. This encounter took place on October 22, 1720. See Downing, *Indian Wars*, pages 47–49; Biddulph, *Pirates of Malabar*, pages 150–152. The editor of Downing's *Indian Wars* confirms (page 48, note 1) that the British naval squadron "acted in a cowardly manner."

37. While Brown remained the nominal head of the squadron, Captain Macrae was second in command and "in reality the moving spirit" of the expedition": Biddulph, *Pirates of Malabar*, page 154.

38. *Lazenby's Narrative*, page 321.

39. Lazenby clearly is exaggerating when he states that the men aboard the *Victory* and *Cassandra* paid £6,000 to £7,000 (about $3 million) for these goods: *Lazenby's Narrative*, page 322. Arrack is a relatively strong alcoholic drink of the Middle East and nearby regions of the Orient, usually distilled from rice or molasses.

40. Lougnon, *L'Ile Bourbon*, page 173, note 41.

41. Lazenby does not specify when these events took place, and there is no certainty about where England was put off from the *Cassandra*. The *General History of the Pyrates* says he was left at Mauritius, without specifying when this event took place. In the context of a dishonest story, Taylor later told Jacob de Bucquoy that England was put off at Madagascar near Ampasindava (*Bucquoy*, page 109).

England's punishment was more severe if he was marooned on Mauritius rather than on Madagascar. A significant number of former pirates lived on Madagascar and Saint Mary's Island, and many Malagasy chieftains were hospitable. Mauritius, in contrast, had been abandoned by the Dutch East India Company in 1710; French officials took possession in 1715 but did not begin to send settlers until after 1721. The island thus had no government and perhaps no permanent residents in 1720; see Guët, *Les origines de l'île Bourbon*, pages 264–265.

42. There are several contemporary accounts of the capture of *Nostra Senhora de Cabo* and its rich cargo. Clement Downing (*Indian Wars*, page 103) reports the rumors about the *Cabo* that reached the English in India. *Lazenby's Narrative* (Grey, *Pirates of the Eastern Seas*, pages 324–325) provides the source closest in time to the events, but Lazenby tailored his report to please East India Company officials. As Defoe's editor indicates (page 672, note 10), the version in the *General History of the Pyrates* depends on Lazenby, whose *Narrative* reached England in March 1722.

In *Lettres curieuses sur divers sujets* (Paris, 1725), François Duval published an account of the taking of the *Cabo* written in 1722 and allegedly containing information given by the count of Ericeira himself. Albert Lougnon reprinted Duval's version in *Sous le signe de la tortue*, pages 167–171.

In April 1722, the men of the *Victory* and the *Cassandra* occupied a small fort in Mozambique built by the Dutch East India Company. When they left two months later, they took with them several company employees. Among them was Jacob de Bucquoy, a specialist in maritime mapmaking who was held captive on the *Victory* for several months, sleeping in Taylor's cabin. Bucquoy's memoirs were published in the Netherlands in 1744; the sections dealing with Madagascar and Réunion are printed in *Grandidier*, vol. 5, pages 103–139.

43. The *Cabo* carried mountings for seventy-two cannon, but only thirty had been installed when it left Goa: Lougnon, *L'Ile Bourbon*, page 174.

44. Lougnon, *L'Ile Bourbon*, page 175.

45. Taylor told Bucquoy (*Bucquoy*, page 110) that the *Victory* and *Cassandra* ranged up along side the *Cabo*, one on either side, so she was sandwiched between them. This may be true, although a maneuver of this type ran a significant risk that the two attackers would shoot over the *Cabo* and hit each other.

46. François Duval in Lougnon, *Sous le signe de la tortue*, page 169. This self-serving story did not assuage the wrath of the king of Portugal, who banished Ericeira from the royal court for ten years.

47. *Bucquoy*, page 111; François Duval in Lougnon, *Sous le signe de la tortue*, page 170; Lougnon, *L'Ile Bourbon*, page 175, note 46.

48. *Lazenby's Narrative*, page 325.

49. François Duval in Lougnon, *Sous le signe de la tortue*, page 171.

50. Duval in Lougnon, *Sous le signe de la tortue*, 171; see also Lougnon, *L'Ile Bourbon*, page 176.

51. *Lazenby's Narrative*, page 324; Lougnon, *Sous le signe de la tortue,* page 171.

52. Deposition by John Freeman, second mate of the *Ville de Ostende,* printed in Grey, *Pirates of the Eastern Seas,* page 325. The ship was retaken by its crew on July 22, 1721, and brought to Mozambique: Norbert Laude, *La Compagnie d'Ostende et son activité commerciale au Bengale, 1725–1730* (Brussels: G. van Campenhout, 1944), page 230.

53. *Bucquoy*, page 111.

54. It was the king's personal financial losses that led to Ericeira's disgrace and exile from court. In fairness to the unlucky count, it is difficult to see what he could have done differently. Perhaps he might have taken some of the cannon off the *Cabo* and made them ready to defend the vessel from the shore. (Réunion has no really secure harbors.) But the diamonds would also have been lost if the *Cabo*—already weakened by the storm—had sunk because Ericeira defended it, thereby tempting the attackers to use their guns.

55. Taylor told Bucquoy (page 110) the plunder was worth more than 30 million Dutch gulden, equivalent at that time to 60 million French francs. Lazenby says Count Ericeira claimed the diamonds were worth 3 or 4 million rupees: *Lazenby*, page 325. See also Lougnon, *L'Ile Bourbon,* page 178, note 51.

56. Macrae reported that, in August 1721, the *Victory* and the *Fancy* together held about 300 men with a share in the booty: *General History of the Pyrates,* page 120. When they attacked Réunion in April 1722, the *Victory* was said to carry thirty-six cannon and 200 men, and the *Cassandra* had thirty-eight guns and 280 crewmen: François Duval in Lougnon, *Sous le signe de la tortue*, page 168. The pirates may well have enlisted more men in India and Madagascar and on Saint Mary's after taking the *Cassandra*.

57. *General History of the Pyrates*, page 131.

58. Lougnon (*L'Ile Bourbon*, page 178) says eighty men died of "frenzied debauchery." This is a misreading of *Robert*, page 64, who says the eighty men died in quarrels and while fighting in tribal wars. But Robert was not captured until after the men left Saint Mary's; his statement is hearsay, and the pirates may have exaggerated the number of deaths to amuse themselves at Robert's expense.

59. *Robert*, page 64; *Bucquoy*, page 111. Compare *General History of the Pyrates*, page 131.

60. For the specific date of December 30, 1721, see Lougnon, *L'Ile Bourbon*, page 179, note 53.

61. *Robert*, pages 64–65.

62. Governor Dumas of Réunion, December 10, 1730, cited *Grandidier*, page 65, note 1.

63. For the sea rovers led by the Angria family, see Rogoziński, *Pirates!*, pages 11–12.

64. Downing, *Indian Wars*, page 51.

65. Downing, *Indian Wars*, page 76.
66. A hooker was a short, tubby little vessel with main- and mizzenmasts; in the Netherlands during the early eighteenth century, the mainmast usually was square-rigged while the mizzenmast carried a small topsail above a fore-and-aft sail hosted on a gaff. The vessel owes its name (Dutch *hoeker* from *hoek*, "fishhook") to its frequent use as a fishing craft.
67. See note 41 above.
68. *Bucquoy*, page 103.
69. *Bucquoy*, page 104. "Si l'on pouvait monter à l'assaut du ciel, je tirerai mon premier coup de fusil sur Dieu. . . . Pourquoi vous êtes vous faits pirates? N'est ce pas parce que vous ne craignez pas le danger et que vous voulez faire du butin. Or, à Mozambique, il y en a et beaucoup, mais je vois qu'j'ai affair à des gens lâches, trop lâches pour se lancer dans des enterprises viriles!"
70. *Bucquoy*, page 107.
71. *Bucquoy*, page 113; Lougnon, *L'Ile Bourbon pendant La Régence*, page 179, note 55.
72. *Bucquoy*, page 115; Grey, *Pirates of the Eastern Seas*, pages 328–329. Compare *General History of the Pyrates*, page 134.
73. After Taylor put Bucquoy ashore at Bombétouke, eyewitness testimony ceases. Various rumors circulated about the *Cabo*'s demise. The English in India heard that the vessel had been burned after the men got back to Saint Mary's: Grey, *Pirates of the Eastern Seas*, page 328. *Robert* (page 67) says the men destroyed it because they could not maneuver it around Madagascar's *northern* coast. But French officials report that the men ran the ship aground because they could not get around the *southern* coast: Lougnon, *L'Ile Bourbon*, page 179.
74. Lougnon, *L'Ile Bourbon*, page 179.
75. Guët, *Les origines de L'île Bourbon*, page 219; *Grandidier*, vol. V, page 48, note 1. See also Charles de La Roncière, *Le Flibustier Mystérieux: Histoire d'un trésor caché* (Paris: Editions Le Masque, 1934), page 103. The governor of Réunion had been authorized to pardon pirates by a royal decree of 1716, sent to the colonies in 1719: Lougnon, *L'Ile Bourbon*, page 168. In a letter dated October 10, 1725, the newly reconstituted French East India Company ordered the island's government to stop receiving pirates as settlers. A letter of October 1727 modified this prohibition: Réunion could accept pirates that surrendered but was to send these men on to France as soon as possible: *Correspondance du Conseil Supérieur de Bourbon et de la Compagnie des Indes*, ed. Albert Lougnon (Saint-Denis, Réunion: Imprimerie Drouhet, 1934), pages 21, 33.
76. Henri Froidevaux in *Histoire des Colonies Française*, ed. Hanotaux and Martineau, vol. 6, page 86.
77. *Correspondance du Conseil Supérieur*, page 131. See also Guët, *Les origines de L'île Bourbon*, pages 219–220; Dureau Reydellet, *Bourbon et ses gouverneurs* (Saint-Denis, Réunion: Cazal, 1978), page 21. La Buse's grave is located in the cemetery at Saint-Paul, behind the mausoleum of the Panon-Desbassyns family.

CHAPTER SIXTEEN

1. For Commodore Matthews' expedition, see above Chapter Fifteen, note 64. The quotation at the beginning of this chapter is from *Robert,* page 61. "Personne ne doute qu'il y a en plusieurs endroits de Madagascar un quantité de forbans qui s'y sont retirés et établis, particulièrement à la côte de l'Est, dans la province de Mangabé, les uns depuis un temps considérable, les autres depuis dix à douze ans. . . . Il est vrai que la plupart y sont considérés comme de petits sourverains, avant chacun sous sa domination deux ou trois villages; cette autorité ne leur est venue que parce qu'ils ont pris pour femmes les principals negresses, celles qui étaient les plus in dignité du pays et qui étaient déjà presque toutes riches par la fréquentation du tout temps des forbans."

2. Downing, *Indian Wars,* page 60.
3. Downing, *Indian Wars,* page 105; see above, Chapter Fifteen, note 1, for the credibility of Plantain's stories.
4. In 1723, local authorities told the French government that there were forty to fifty pirates near Antongil Bay. Twenty-three men moved to Réunion the following year. See *Grandidier,* page 61, note 2; above, Chapter 15, note 75.
5. Deschamps, *Histoire de Madagascar,* page 105; Heseltine, *Madagascar,* page 14.
6. Brown, *Madagascar,* page 97.
7. This was the legend accepted by the Malagasy in the 1770s, according to Nicholas Mayeur, a French trader and explorer. Whether or not it is literally true, the story nicely symbolizes the attitude of hundreds of European pirates who turned their backs on European civilization and elected to remain at Madagascar.
   There have been various attempts to identify this "Pirate Tom," Ratsimilao's father. Some say he was none other than Thomas Tew. Another theory says he was "Mulatto Tom," described by Clement Downing as the son of Henry Every and the Indian princess captured on the *Gunsway.* Based on a story in the *General History of the Pirates* (pages 485–486), yet others think Thomas White was the generous father who tried to give Ratsimilao an English education.
8. Brown, *Madagascar,* pages 97–106; Deschamps, *Histoire de Madagascar,* pages 105–107; Mack, *Madagascar: Island of the Ancestors,* pages 43–44. For the documents concerning the French occupation of Saint Mary's Island, beginning in 1750, see Raymond Decary, *L'établissement de Saint-Marie de Madagascar sous la Restauration* (Paris, Société d'éditions, géographiques maritimes et coloniales, 1937).
9 Vêrin, *History of Civilisation in North Madagascar,* page 125. Vêrin lists and describes the sources for the history of these slave raids.
10. Decary, *L'Établissement de Saint-Marie de Madagascar sous la Restauration,* pages 60–61: "[Les naturels qui habitant cette partie] sont en outre de braves soldats, et les plus hardis navigateurs de tout l'île. Chaque expédition maritime qui se fait contre Anjouan, Comores ou autres lieux, au Sud de Madagascar, sont toujours dirigées par ces peuples qui fournissent à eux seuls les deux tiers de entreprise, soit en hommes, soit en fortes pirogues de guerre." See also Leguével de Lacombe, *Voyage a Madagascar,* 274.
11 Brown, *Madagascar,* page 109.
12. Journal of Basil Ringrose published with the first English translation (1684–1685) of A. O. Exquemelin, *The Buccaneers of America,* ed. W. S. Stallybrass (New York: Dutton, 1924), page 300.
13. Some books and Internet web sites show a flag—said to be that of Thomas Tew—with a black background and the white image of a hand holding a sword. However, the authors of these stories do not (and cannot) cite a source for this fictional banner, which was invented long after Tew died.
14. *CSPC, 1697–1698,* pages 69–70, for Dirk Chivers. According to some authors (who do not, however, cite any eyewitness sources), Henry Every in 1695 fought under the English flag as well as his own personal flag—four silver chevrons against a red field. When this flag flew at the masthead, it meant that he was willing to give quarter; if resistance was offered, he hoisted a plain red flag, signifying that he had withdrawn the offer of quarter.
15. Deposition of Thomas Adams, September 17, 1707, printed Grey, *Pirates of the Eastern Seas,* page 275. See above, Chapter Fourteen, page 196.
16. Snelgrave, *New Account,* page 199.
17. Lougnon, *L'Île Bourbon pendant la Régence,* pages 164–165.
18. Pringle, *Jolly Roger,* page 228.
19. Eyewitness testimony of Monsieur Duval, cited by Lougnon, *Sous le signe de la tortue,* page 168.
20. *New England Courant,* July 22, 1723.
21. *Privateering and Piracy,* page 317; Richards, *Black Bart,* page 53.

22. It is obvious that pirate mythology had not yet adopted the "skull and cross bones" as late as the 1820s. For example, Sir Walter Scott—obviously confused about the entire matter of pirate flags—referred to the "Jolly Hodge, the old black flag, with the death's head and the hour glass." See *The Pirate* (Edinburgh: Constable, 1822), vol. III, page 309.

23. In the *Pirates of Penzance,* the stage directions tell the pirate king to unfold a black flag with the skull and cross bones as he sings "Oh better far to live and die / Under the brave black flag I fly."

24. Robert Mayer, *History and the Early English Novel; Matters of Fact from Bacon to Defoe* (Cambridge, Eng.: Cambridge University Press, 1997). See also Everett Zimmerman, *The Boundaries of Fiction: History and the Eighteenth-Century British Novel* (Ithaca, N.Y.: Cornell University Press, 1996), page 1: "In a letter to William Warburton, Samuel Richardson protests Warburton's open reference to *Clarissa's* fictionality. . . . Other writers of eighteenth-century fiction indicate a similar reluctance to have their fictions definitely separated from history."

25. John Robert Moore (*Defoe in the Pillory,* page 41) argued that Defoe did not see any difference between writing history and fiction; everything he wrote was a sort of historical Romance. "Defoe was a romancer, as well as moralist, satirist, controversialist, journalist, and historian, *all at the same time.*"

    Defoe's strongly held religious beliefs influenced his practices. He believed that God's Providence guides the course of human history. If real events were not available to prove his conclusions, then it was legitimate to make fictional events do the job. See Maximillian Novak, *Realism, Myth, and History in Defoe's Fiction* (Lincoln: University of Nebraska Press, 1983), page 55: "And most important, . . . [Defoe] had faith in fiction as exemplifying history. To introduce fictional events into his History of the Pirates in the form of a contrast between the Communist, Captain Misson, and the practical colonialist, Captain Tew, was to force history to do its job by way of providing examples."

26. In *Robinson Crusoe* (1719), the hero is captured by Muslim corsairs, and a mutiny aids his escape from the desert island. Pirates also capture the leading character in *Colonel Jacques* (1722). In *The Four Years Voyages of Capt. George Roberts,* the hero is plundered by Edward Low and Francis Spriggs and a Portuguese pirate nicknamed John Russell. *Madagascar; or Robert Drury's Journal* (1729) describes the hero's 16 years of slavery on that island. Like the *General History,* it cunningly mixes fact and fiction; see above, Chapter Fourteen, note 9.

27. Moore, *Defoe in the Pillory,* page 155. See above, Chapter Six, page 91.

28. In addition to many newspaper articles, Defoe is credited with writing more than 500 books and pamphlets. As I indicate in the preface, I accept the traditional view that Defoe wrote both volumes of the *General History of Pyrates* under the pseudonym Captain Charles Johnson. For the history of criminal biographies, see Lincoln Faller, *Turned to Account: The Forms and Functions of Criminal Biography in Late Seventeenth- and Early Eighteenth-Century England* (Cambridge, Eng.: Cambridge University Press, 1987).

29. Compare Manuel Schonhorn's postscript to the 1999 edition of *General History of the Pyrates,* page 711: "We can recognize in his *Pyrates* the unique Defovean voice, once again able to overcome the moral scruples of his day, questioning the ethical, even religious, considerations of his readers, and yet catering to their hidden pleasures in the illicit, the immoral, and the profitable. . . ."

30. Literary critics differ as to why the reader finds Defoe's criminal fiction so "realistic." It is true that Defoe had considerable experience as a convicted criminal and was more than once a fugitive from justice. He barely escaped capture following Monmouth's Rebellion in 1685. He was imprisoned in Newgate and the Queen's Bench Prison, exhibited to the public in the pillory, and threatened with hanging. For an accurate yet accessible biography, see Richard West, *Daniel Defoe: The Life and Strange, Surprising Adventures* (New York: Carroll & Graf, 1998).

    However, Defoe's personal experiences with crime and punishment are not sufficient to explain why the reader thinks the events really happened, even when (or especially when) they are imaginary. See Lincoln Faller, *Crime and Defoe: A New Kind of Writing* (Cambridge, Eng.: Cambridge University Press, 1993), page 37: Defoe "wrote narratives so full of 'real truth' that to this day there are those who believe there must have been a 'real' Moll Flanders, that is, an actual person who served as her model. . . . But Defoe's other criminals have a richness as well. . . ." [It is difficult to account for] "the powerful sense of authenticity projected by Defoe's novels, particularly the criminal novels."

See also Novak, *Realism, Myth, and History*, page 9: "The charm of Defoe's fiction has certain magical qualities as well. Realism was one element in a tendency to build convincing fictional worlds."

31. Philip Gosse lists versions published up to 1926 in *A Bibliography of the Works of Capt. Charles Johnson* (London: Dulau, 1927). Subsequent editions are recorded in the catalogs of the Library of Congress and the British Library.

32. See above, Chapter Thirteen, pages 181–182.

33. After the Madagascar biographies, Defoe inserts the adventures of a mulatto seaman held captive at the African kingdom of Magadoxa, northwest of Madagascar. He concludes with four biographies of Caribbean captains, two of whom (Cornelius and Lewis) are totally imaginary.

34. Moore, *Defoe in the Pillory*, page 127.

35. *Jack Ballister's Fortunes* (1895) depicts Blackbeard, and *The Rose of Paradise* (1888) describe Edward England's plundering of the East Indiaman *Cassandra*. In addition, Pyle drew on Defoe for short stories and numerous illustrated articles in *Harper's Magazine*.

36. Defoe also was the source for Long John Silver's enigmatic psychological traits. The Silver of *Treasure Island* is an ambiguous character, both bad and good, cruel and generous, despicable and admirable. In creating his most memorable character, Stevenson combined several of Defoe's Madagascar pirates into one many-faceted hero-villain.

37. This is poetic license on Stevenson's part. In fact, England was ousted as captain, and John Taylor captured the viceroy's treasure. Taylor afterwards took the *Cassandra* to the West Indies and not to England.

38. Harold Watson, *Coasts of Treasure Island* (San Antonio, Texas: Naylor, 1969), pages 150–151.

39. In the English language alone, five full-length movies directly based on *Treasure Island* appeared between 1917 and 1991. In addition, other films present sequels containing the "further adventures" of Jim Hawkins and Long John Silver.

40. Above, Chapter Eleven.

41. It is bizarre that writers styling themselves Feminists should insist that "women were pirates too." They seem determined to prove that women as well as men were included among the cruel, demented, and bloodthirsty fiends of pirate mythology. One would think that Feminists instead would take pride in the fact that—except perhaps among the Chinese—no woman is known to have committed piracy at sea. Among authors that erroneously assert that Bonnie and Read committed piracy (and that also invent other female pirates), see John Carlova, *Mistress of the Seas* (1964); Jessica Salmonsen, *The Encyclopedia of Amazons: Woman Warriors from Antiquity to the Modern Era* (New York, 1991); Jo Stanley (editor), *Bold in Her Breeches: Women Pirates Across the Ages* (London, 1995).

BIBLIOGRAPHY

This bibliography lists historical and fictional works about the pirates plying their trade from Madagascar during the seventeenth and eighteenth centuries; it also cites studies of British North America, Madagascar, and the Indian Ocean. The number of books about "pirates" approaches infinity, but most repeat the same hoary tall tales found in earlier compilations. For information on specific topics as well as a selective bibliography of piratical literature, see Jan Rogoziński, *Pirates! Brigands, Buccaneers, and Privateers in Fact, Fiction, and Legend*. New York: Facts on File, 1995.

PRIMARY SOURCES

An Account of Her Majesty's Revenue in the Province of New York, 1701–1709: The Customs Records of Early Colonial New York. Julius Bloch, ed. Ridgeway, New Jersey: Gregg, 1967.

Acts of the Privy Council, Colonial Series. William Grant and James Munro, eds. 6 vols. London, 1908–1912.

Barlow, Edward. *Barlow's Journal of His Life at Sea*. Edited by Basil Lubbock. 2 vols. London: Hurst & Blackett, 1934.

Boucher, Antoine. *Mémoire pour servir a la connoissance particulière de chacun des habitans de l'isle de Bourbon*. Edited by Jean Barassin. Aix-en-Provence: Association des Chercheurs de l'Océan Indien, 1978.

Bowery, Thomas. *A Geographical Account of Countries Round the Bay of Bengal, 1669–1679*. London: Hakluyt Society, 1905.

———. *The Papers of Thomas Bowery 1669–1713*. Edited by Richard Carnac Temple. London: Hakluyt Society, 1927.

Calendar of State Papers, Colonial Series. America and West Indies, 1574–1738. Noel Sainsbury and others, eds. 42 vols. London: Her Majesty's Stationery Office, 1860–1969.

Collection des Ouvrages anciens concernant Madagascar. Alfred Grandidier and Guillaume Gradider, eds. 9 vols. Paris: Comité de Madagascar, 1903–1920.

Collections of the South Carolina Historical Society. Charleston: South Carolina Historical Society, 1857–1897.

A Complete Collection of State-Trials and Proceedings upon High-Treason, and other Crimes and Misdemeanors; from the Reign of King Richard II to the End of the Reign of King George I. 2nd ed. 6 vols. London: Walthoe, 1730.

Correspondance du Conseil Supérieur de Bourbon et de la Compagnie des Indes. Albert Lougnon, ed. Saint Denis (Réunion): Imprimerie Drouhet, 1934.

Dampier, William. *A New Voyage Round the World.* London: Knapton, 1697. Edited by N. M. Penzer. 1927. Reprint. London: Black, 1937.

Defoe, Daniel. *Defoe's Review.* Edited by Arthur Secord. 22 vols. New York: Columbia University Press, 1938.

Documentary History of the State of New York. Edmund B. O'Callaghan, ed. 4 vols. Albany: Weed Parsons, 1849–1853.

Documents Relating to the Colonial History of the State of New Jersey. W. A. Whitehead and others, eds. 21 vols. Newark: 1880–1899.

Documents Relative to the Colonial History of the State of New York. Edmund B. O'Callaghan and Berthold Fernow, eds. Compiled by John Romeyn Brodhead. 15 vols. Albany: Weed Parsons, 1853–1887.

Downing, Clement. *A History of the Indian Wars.* London: Cooper, 1737. Edited by William Foster. London: Oxford University Press, 1924.

Ellis, William. *Three visits to Madagascar during the years 1853–1854–1856. Including a journey to the capital, with notices of the natural history of the country and of the present civilization of the people.* New York: Harper, 1859.

Exquemelin, A. O. *The Buccaneers of America.* Edited by W. S. Stallybrass. New York: Dutton, 1924.

———. *The Buccaneers of America.* Translated from the Dutch by Alexis Brown. Harmondsworth, England: Penguin, 1969.

Firth, C.H., ed. *Naval Songs and Ballads.* London: Naval Records Society, 1908.

Foster, William, ed. *The Red Sea and Adjacent Countries at the Close of the Seventeenth Century as Described by Joseph Pitts, William Daniel, and Charles Jacques Poncet.* London: Hakluyt Society, 1949.

Hamilton, Alexander. *A New Account of the East Indies.* 2 vols. Edinburgh, 1727. Reprint. London: Argonaut Press, 1930.

Hedges, William. *The Diary of William Hedges, Esq. (afterwards Sir William Hedges), during his agency in Bengal: as well as on his voyage out and return overland (1681–1687)*. 3 vols. Edited by R. Barlow and Henry Yu. London: Hakluyt Society, 1887–1889.

Herodotus. *The History.* Translated by David Grene. Chicago: University of Chicago Press, 1987.

Hill, S. Charles, ed. *Notes on Piracy in Eastern Waters.* Bombay: British India Press, 1923–1928.

Ingram, Bruce, ed. *Three Sea Journals of Stuart Times.* London: Constable, 1936.

Isle de Bourbon (Réunion): Documents 1701–1710. New York: New York Public Library, 1909.

Journal of the Votes and Proceedings of the General Assembly of the Colony of New York. 2 vols. New York: Gaine, 1764–1766.

Journals of the House of Commons. 56 vols. London: Reprinted by order of the House of Commons, 1803–1813.

Khafi Khan, Muhammed Hashim, *Muntakhabu-l Lubáb* in volume seven, *The History of India as Told by its Own Historians,* 8 vols. Edited by Sir H. M. Elliott and John Dowson. 1867–1877. Reprint. Allahabad, 1972.

La Suede & Madagascar au debut du XVIIIème Siècle. Jacques Macau, ed. Aix-en-Provence: Insitut d'histoire des pays d'outre-mer, 1973.

Lougnon, Albert. *Sous le signe de la tortue: Voyages anciens à l'Ile Bourbon (1611–1725).* Paris: Larose, 1958.

Luttrell, Narcissus. *A Brief Historical Relation of State Affairs from September 1678 to April 1714.* 6 vols. Oxford, Eng.: University Press, 1857.

Manual of the Corporation of the City of New York. Compiled by S. J. Willis, D. T. Valentine, and others. 28 vols. New York: Bell, 1841/1842–1870.

Martin, François. *Mémoires de François Martin, Fondateur de Pondichéry (1665–1696).* Edited by A. Martineau. 3 vols. Paris: Société d'éditions géographiques, maritimes et coloniales, 1931–1934.

Ovington, J. *A Voyage to Surat in the Year 1689.* 1696. Edited by H. G. Rawlinson. London: Oxford University Press, 1929; New Delhi: Associated Publishing House, 1976.

Papers Relating to the Ships and Voyages of the Company of Scotland Trading to Africa and the Indies 1696–1707. Edinburgh: Scottish History Society, 1924.

The Periplus Maris Erythraei. Translated by Lionel Casson. Princeton, N.J.: Princeton University Press, 1989.

Précis of the Archives of the Cape of Good Hope: Journal, 1699–1732. Hendril Carel Vos Leibbrandt, ed. Capetown: Richards, 1896.

Précis of the archives of the Cape of Good Hope: Letters received, 1695–1708. Hendril Carel Vos Leibbrandt, ed. Capetown: Richards, 1896.

Privateering and Piracy in the Colonial Period: Illustrative Documents. John Jameson, ed. New York: Macmillan, 1923.

Records of the Colony of Rhode Island. 10 vols. Providence: Greene, 1856–1865.

Rogers, Woodes. *A Cruising Voyage Round the World.* 1712. Edited by George Manwaring. London: Cassell, 1928; New York: Dover, 1970.

Saunders, William L. and others, eds. *The Colonial Records of North Carolina.* 26 vols. Raleigh: Hale, 1886–1907.

Snelgrave, William. *A New Account of Some Parts of Guinea, and the Slave-Trade.* 1734. Reprint. London: Frank Cass, 1971.

Teonge, Henry. *The Diary of Henry Teonge, Chaplain on board H.M.'s Ships Assistance, Bristol, and Royal Oak, 1675–1679.* Edited by George Manwaring. New York: Harper & Brothers, 1927.

The Tryal of Capt. William Kidd for Murther & Piracy Upon Six Several Indictments. Don Seitz, ed. New York: Wilson, 1936.

Trial of Captain Kidd. Graham Brooks, ed. Toronto: Canada Law Book Company, 1930.

Valentine's Manuals: A General Index to the Manuals of the Corporation of hte City of New York, 1841–1870. Compiled by Otto Hufeland. New York: Harper, 1900.

Vos Leibbrandt, Hendril Carel. *Rambles through the Archives of the Colony of the Cape of Good Hope, 1688–1700.* Cape Town: Jut, 1904.

Wafer, Lionel. *A New Voyage and Description of the Isthmus of America.* Edited by L. E. Elliot Joyce. London: Hakluyt Society, 1934.

BIOGRAPHIES OF MADAGASCAR PIRATES WRITTEN DURING OR SOON AFTER THEIR LIFETIMES.

Anonymous [attributed to a fictitious Captain Adrian Van Broeck]. *The Life and Adventures of Captain John Avery.* London, 1709(?). Reprint. Los Angeles: University of California at Los Angeles, Augustan Reprint Society, 1980.

Defoe, Daniel. *A General History of the Pyrates.* 2 vols. London: Rivington, 1724–1728. Reprint (2 vols. in 1). Edited by Manuel Schonhorn.

Columbia: University of South Carolina Press, 1972; New York: Dover, 1999.

———. *The King of Pirates, being an account of the famous enterprises of Captain Avery, with lives of other pirates and robbers.* London, 1719. Edited George Aitken. London: Dent, 1895. Edited as vol. 16 of *The Works of Daniel Defoe.* New York: Jenson, 1907.

———. *Madagascar; Or, Robert Drury's Journal, during Fifteen Years' Captivity on That Island.* London: W. Meadows, 1729. Edited by Pasfield Oliver. London: Fisher Unwin, 1890; New York: Negro Universities Press, 1969.

Hayward, Arthur. *Lives of the Most Remarkable Criminals Who have been Condemned and Executed for Murder, the Highway, Housebreaking, Street Robberies, Coining or other Offences.* 3 vols. London: Osborn, 1735. Reprint (3 vols. in 1). New York: Dodd, Mead, 1927.

Johnson, Charles. *The Successful Pyrate: A Play as it is acted at the Theatre-Royal in Drury-Lane.* London: Lintott, 1713. Reprint. Los Angeles: University of California at Los Angeles, Augustan Reprint Society, 1980.

HISTORICAL AND GEOGRAPHICAL STUDIES.

Andrews, Charles M. *The Colonial Period of American History.* 4 vols. New Haven: Yale University Press, 1934–1938.

Archdeacon, Thomas. "The Age of Leisler—New York City, 1689–1710: A Social and Demographic Interpretation." In *Aspects of Early New York Society and Politics,* edited by Jacob Judd and Irwin Polishook. Tarrytown, N.Y.: Sleepy Hollow Restorations, 1974.

Arnold-Forster, F. D. *The Madagascar Pirates.* New York: Lothrop, Lee, and Shepard, 1957.

Arasaratnam, Sinnappah. *Maritime India in the Seventeenth Century.* Delhi: Oxford University Press, 1994.

Auber, J. *Histoire de l'océan Indien.* Tananarive, Madagascar: Société Lilloise d'imprimerie de Tananarive, 1955.

Axtell, James. *The European and the Indian: Essays in the Ethnohistory of Colonial North America.* New York: Oxford University Press, 1981.

———. *The Invasion Within: The Contest of Cultures in Colonial North America.* New York: Oxford University Press, 1985.

Barassin, Jean. *Bourbon, des origines jusqu'en 1714. Naissance d'une chrétienté.* Paris, 1953.

————. *La vie quotidienne des colons de l'île Bourbon à la fin du regne de Louis XIV, 1700–1715.* Sainte-Clotilde: Dionysienne, 1989.

Bastian, G. *Madagascar: Étude géographique et économique.* Paris: Nathan, 1967.

Béchet, Roger. *La Piraterie dans l'Ocean Indien; quelques dates, les pirates aux Mascareignes.* Paris, 1953.

Besson, Maurice. *Les "Frères de la coste": Flibustiers & corsaires.* Paris: Duchartre & Van Buggenhoudt, 1928.

Biddulph, John. *The Pirates of Malabar.* London: Smith, Elder, 1907.

Birkenhead, Frederick Edwin Smith, First Earl. *Famous Trials of History.* London: Hutchinson, 1926.

Bonner, Willard. *Pirate Laureate: The Life and Legends of Captain Kidd.* New Brunswick: Rutgers University Press, 1947.

Bootle, Roger, *The Death of Inflation: Surviving and thriving in the Zero Era.* London: Brealy, 1996.

Bozarth, Donald. "Burgher, Boer, and Bondsman: A Survey of Slavery at the Cape of Good Hope under the Dutch East India Company, 1652–1795." Ph.D. diss., University of Maryland, 1987.

Bradley, Peter. *The Lure of Peru: Maritime Intrusion into the South Sea, 1598–1701.* New York: Saint Martin's, 1989.

Bromley, J. S. *Corsairs and Navies, 1660–1760.* London: Hambledon, 1987.

Brown, Mervyn. *Madagascar Rediscovered: A History from Early Times to Independence.* Hamden, Connecticut: Archon Books, 1979.

Burg, B. R. "Legitimacy and Authority: A Case Study of Pirate Commanders in the Seventeenth and Eighteenth Centuries," *American Neptune* 37 (1977): 40–51.

————. *Sodomy and the Pirate Tradition: English Sea Rovers in the Seventeenth-Century Caribbean.* New York: New York University Press, 1984.

Chapin, Howard. *Privateer Ships and Sailors: The First Century of American Colonial Privateering, 1625–1725.* Toulon: Mouton, 1926.

Chapuiset Le Merle, André de. *Précis d'histoire de l' ísle Maurice (XVe au XVIIe siècle).* Port Louis (Île Maurice): Nouvelle Imprimerie Coopérative, 1950.

Chaudhuri, K. N. *Asia before Europe: Economy and Civilisation of the Indian Ocean from the Rise of Islam to 1750.* Cambridge, Eng.: Cambridge University Press, 1990.

————. *The English East India Company: The Study of an Early Joint-Stock Company, 1600–1640.* London: Frank Cass, 1965.

————. *Trade and Civilisation in the India Ocean: An Economic History from the*

Rise of Islam to 1750. Cambridge, Eng.: Cambridge University Press, 1985.

———. *The Trading World of Asia and the English East India Company.* Cambridge, Eng.: Cambridge University Press, 1978.

Cochran, Hamilton. *Freebooters of the Red Sea: Pirates, Politicians and Pieces of Eight.* Indianapolis: Bobbs-Merrill, 1965.

Cotton, Sir Evan. *East Indiamen: The East India Company's Maritime Service.* Edited by Sir Charles Fawcett. London: Batchworth, 1949.

Craton, Michael. *A History of the Bahamas.* London: Collins, 1962.

Crump, Helen. *Colonial Admiralty Jurisdiction in the Seventeenth Century.* London: Longman's Green, 1931.

Dalton, Cornelius. *The Real Captain Kidd: A Vindication.* New York: Duffield, 1911.

Das, Harihar. *The Norris Embassy to Aurangzib (1699–1702).* Calcutta: Mukhopadhyay, 1959.

Das Gupta, Ashin. "The Merchants of Surat, c. 1700–1750." In *Elites in South Asia,* edited by Edmund Leach and S. N. Mukherjee. Cambridge, Eng.: Cambridge University Press, 1970.

Davis, Ralph. *The Rise of the English Shipping Industry in the Seventeenth and Eighteenth Centuries.* London: Macmillan, 1962.

Decary, Raymond. *Coutume guerrieres et organisation militaire chez les anciens Malagaches.* Paris: Éditions maritimes et d'outremer, 1966.

———. *L'Établissement de Saint-Marie de Madagascar sous la Restauration et le rôle de Sylvain Roux.* Paris: Société d'éditions, géographiques maritimes et coloniales, 1937.

De Peyster, Frederic. *The Life and Administration of Richard, Earl of Bellomont, Governor of the Provinces of New York, Massachusetts, and New Hampshire, from 1697 to 1701.* New York: New York Historical Society, 1879.

Deschamps, Hubert. *Histoire de Madagascar.* Paris: Berger-Levrault, 1972.

———. *Les Pirates à Madagascar aux XVIIe et XVIIIe siècles.* Paris: Berger-Levrault, 1972.

Distances Between Ports. 10th ed. Bethesda, Md.: National Imagery and Mapping Agency, 1999.

Dow, George and John Edmonds. *The Pirates of the New England Coast, 1630–1730.* Salem, Mass.: Marine Research, 1923.

Duncan, T. Bentley. *Atlantic Islands: Madeira, the Azores, and the Cape Verdes in Seventeenth-Century Commerce and Navigation.* Chicago: University of Chicago Press, 1972.

Ehrman, John. *The Navy in the War of William III, 1689–1697: Its State and Direction.* Cambridge, Eng.: Cambridge University Press, 1953.

Filliot, J. M. *Pirates et corsaires dans l'Ocean Indien.* Tananarive, Madagascar: Office de la Recherce Scientifique et Technique Outre Mer, 1971.

————. *La Traite des Esclaves vers les Mascareignes au XVIIIe siècle.* Paris: Orstom, 1974.

Fischer, David Hackett. *The Great Wave: Price Revolutions and the Rhythm of History.* New York: Oxford University Press, 1996.

Fitzpatrick, Gary and Marilyn Modlin. *Direct-line distances—international edition.* Metuchen, N.J.: Scarecrow Press, 1986.

Furber, Holden. *Rival Empires of Trade in the Orient, 1600–1800.* Minneapolis: University of Minnesota Press, 1976.

Gardiner, Robert and Brian Laver, eds. *The Line of Battle: The Sailing Warship, 1650–1840.* Annapolis, Md.: Naval Institute Press, 1992.

Gilbert, Arthur. "Buggery and the British Navy, 1700–1861," *Journal of Social History,* 7 (1976): 72–98.

Gray, John. *History of Zanzibar from the Middle Ages to 1856.* London: Oxford University Press, 1962.

Great Britain, Hydrographic Office. *Admiralty Weather Manual 1938.* London: Admiralty, 1941.

Grey, Charles. *Pirates of the Eastern Seas (1618–1723): A Lurid Page of History.* 1933. Reprint. Port Washington, N.Y.: Kennikat, 1971.

Guët, M. I. *Les origines de l'île Bourbon et de la colonisation Française à Madagascar.* Paris: Bayle, 1888.

Hanotaux, Gabriel and Alfred Martineau. *Histoire des colonies françaises et de l'expansion de la France dans le mode.* 6 vols. Paris: Plon, 1929–1934.

Heseltine, Nigel. *Madagascar.* London: Pall Mall Press, 1971.

Hill, Christopher. *The World Turned Upside Down: Radical Ideas during the English Revolution.* London: Smith, 1972.

Hinrichs, Dunbar. *The Fateful Voyage of Captain Kidd.* New York: Bookman Associates, 1953.

Hughson, Shirley. *The Carolina Pirates and Colonial Commerce, 1670–1740.* Baltimore: Johns Hopkins University Press, 1894.

Insh, George. *Papers relating to the Ships and voyages of the Company of Scotland Trading to Africa and the Indies, 1696–1707.* Edinburgh: Constable, 1924.

Israel, Jonathan. *Dutch Primacy in World Trade, 1585–1740.* Oxford: Clarendon, 1989.

Jacob, Margaret and James Jacob, eds. *The Origins of Anglo-American Radicalism.* London: Allen & Unwin, 1984.

Jaeger, Gérard, ed. *Vues sur la Piraterie.* Paris: Tallandier, 1992.

Jolly, Alison, Philippe Oberle, and Roland Albignac, eds. *Madagascar (Key Environments).* Oxford, Eng.: Pergamon, 1984.

Judd, Jacob. "Frederick Philipse and the Madagascar Trade," *New York Historical Society Quarterly* 55 (1971) 355–374.

———. "Lord Bellomont and Captain Kidd: A Footnote to an Entangled Alliance," *New York Historical Society Quarterly* 47 (1963): 67–74.

Kaeppelin, Paul. *Les Escales françaises sur la Route de l'Inde, 1638–1731.* Paris: Challamel, 1908.

———. *Les Origines de l'Inde française: La Compagnie des Indes Orientales et François Martin.* Paris: Challamel, 1908.

Kammen, Michael. *Colonial New York: A History.* 1975. Reprint. New York: Oxford University Press, 1996.

Karracker, Cyrus. *Piracy was a Business.* Rindge, New Hampshire: Richard Smith, 1953.

Keay, John. *The Honourable Company: A History of the English East India Company.* New York: Macmillan, 1991.

Kemp, Peter and Christopher Lloyd. *Brethren of the Coast: Buccaneers of the South Seas.* New York: St Martin's. 1961.

Kent, Raymond. *Early Kingdoms in Madagascar 1500–1700.* New York: Holt, Rinehart and Winston, 1970.

La Roncière, Charles de. *Le Flibustier Mystérieux: Histoire d'un trésor caché.* Paris: Editions Le Masque, 1934.

Laude, Norbert. *La Compagnie d'Ostende et son activité commerciale au Bengale, 1725–1730.* Brussels: G. van Campenhout, 1944.

Lavery, Brian. *The Ship of the Line.* Two vols. Annapolis, Md.: The Naval Institute Press. 1983–1985.

Lawson, Philip. *The East India Company: A History.* London: Longman, 1993.

Leamon, James S. "Governor Fletcher's Recall," *William and Mary Quarterly* 20 (1967): 527–542.

Leder, Lawrence. "Captain Kidd and the Leisler Rebellion," *New York Historical Society Quarterly* 38 (1954): 48–53.

———. "Records of the Trials of Jacob Leisler and His Associates" *New York Historical Society Quarterly* 36 (1952): 431–457.

———. *Robert Livingston, 1654–1728, and the Politics of Colonial New York.* Chapel Hill: University of North Carolina Press, 1961.

Leguével de Lacombe, B. F. *Voyage a Madagascar et aux îles Comores (1823–1830)*. Paris: Desessart, 1840.

Little, Bryan. *Crusoe's Captain: Being the Life of Woodes Rogers, Seaman, Trader, Colonial Governor*. London: Odhams, 1960.

Lougnon, Albert. *L'Ile Bourbon pendant La Régence*. Nerac: Couderc, 1956.

Lydon, James. *Pirates, Privateers, and Profits*. Upper Saddle River, N.J.: Gregg, 1970.

Mack, John. *Madagascar: Island of the Ancestors*. London: British Museum Publications, 1986.

Maury, Matthew. *The Physical Geography of the Sea, and its Meteorology*. 8th ed. 1862. Edited by John Leighly. Cambridge, Mass.: Belknap, 1963.

McPherson, Kenneth. *The Indian Ocean: A History of People and the Sea*. Delhi: Oxford University Press, 1993.

Miles, S. B. *The Countries and Tribes of the Persian Gulf*. London: Frank Cass, 1966.

Milligan, Clarence. *Captain William Kidd, Gentleman or Buccaneer?* Philadelphia: Dorrance, 1932.

Morehouse, Clifford. *Trinity: Mother of Churches, An Informal History of Trinity Parish in the City of New York*. New York: Seabury, 1973.

Morris, Richard. *Fair Trial*. New York: Knopf, 1952.

———. *Government and Labor in Early America*. New York: Columbia University Press, 1946.

Nutting, P. Bradley. "The Madagascar Connection: Parliament and Piracy, 1690–1701," *American Journal of Legal History* 22 (1978): 202–215.

The Oriental Annual. London: E. Churton, 1834–1840.

Paine, Ralph. *The Book of Buried Treasure*. London: Heinemann, 1911.

Pencak, William and Conrad Wright, eds. *Authority and Resistance in Early New York*. New York: New York Historical Society, 1988.

Phelps-Stokes, Isaac. *The Iconography of Manhattan Island*. 6 vols. 1916–1918. Reprint. New York: Arno Press, 1967.

Platt, Virginia. "The East India Company and the Madagascar Slave Trade," *William and Mary Quarterly* 26 (1969): 548–577.

Prakash, Om. *The Dutch East India Company and the Economy of Bengal, 1630–1720*. Princeton, N.J.: Princeton University Press, 1985.

———. *The New Cambridge History of India. Part Two, Number Five: European Commercial Enterprise in Pre-Colonial India*. Cambridge, Eng.: Cambridge University Press, 1998.

———. *Precious Metals and Commerce: The Dutch East India Company in the Indian Ocean Trade*. Aldershot, Eng.: Variorum, 1994.

Pringle, Patrick. *Jolly Roger: The Story of the Great Age of Piracy.* New York: W. W. Norton, 1953.

Rediker, Marcus. *Between the Devil and the Deep Blue Sea: Merchant Seamen, Pirates, and the Anglo-American Maritime World, 1700–1750.* New York: Cambridge University Press, 1987.

Reich, Jerome. *Leisler's Rebellion: A Study of Democracy in New York, 1664–1720.* Chicago: University of Chicago Press, 1953.

Reydellet, Dureau. *Bourbon et ses gouverneurs.* Saint-Denis, Réunion: Cazal, 1978.

Richards, Stanley. *Black Bart.* Llandybie, Wales: Davies, 1966.

Ritchie, Robert. *Captain Kidd and the War against the Pirates.* Cambridge, Mass.: Harvard University Press, 1986.

Rubin, Alfred. *The Law of Piracy.* 2nd ed., Irvington-on-Hudson, N.Y.: Transnational, 1998.

Runcie, John. "The Problem of Anglo-American Politics in Bellomont's New York," *William and Mary Quarterly* 25 (1969): 191–217.

Ruud, Jørgen. *Taboo: A Study of Malagasy Customs and Beliefs.* Oslo, Norway: Oslo University Press, 1960.

Saintoyant, J. *La Colonisation Française sous l'Ancien Régime.* 2 vols. Paris: Renaissance du Livre, 1929.

Shomette, Donald. *Pirates on the Chesapeake.* Centreville, Md.: Tidewater, 1985.

Spence, Edward. *Shipwrecks, Pirates, and Privateers: Sunken Treasures of the Upper South Carolina Coast, 1521–1865.* Charleston: Narwhal, 1995.

Steckley, George. "Litigious Mariners: Wage Cases in the Seventeenth-Century Admiralty Court," *The Historical Journal* 42 (1999): 315–345.

Steele, I. K. *Politics of Colonial Policy: The Board of Trade in Colonial Administration, 1696–1720.* Oxford, Eng.: Clarendon, 1968.

Steensgaard, Niels. *The Asian Trade Revolution of the Seventeenth Century: The East India Companies and the Decline of the Caravan Trade.* Chicago: University of Chicago Press, 1974.

Temple, Richard Carnac. *New Light on the Mysterious Tragedy of the "Worcester" 1704–1705.* London: Benn, 1930.

Thomson, Janice. *Mercenaries, Pirates, and Sovereigns: State-Building and Extraterritorial Violence in Early Modern Europe.* Princeton, N.J.: Princeton University Press, 1994.

Toussaint, Auguste. *History of the Indian Ocean.* Translated by June Guicharnaud. Chicago: University of Chicago Press, 1966.

————. *La Route des îles: Contribution à histoire maritime des Mascareignes.* Paris: S.E.V.P.A.N., 1967.

Turley, Hans. *Rum, Sodomy, and the Lash: Piracy, Sexuality, and Masculine Identity.* New York: New York University Press, 1999.

Van den Dool, Pretorius. *The Dutch East India Company, A Business History.* Master's thesis, University of Oregon, 1962.

Vérin, Pierre. *Histoire ancienne du nord-ouest de Madagascar.* Tananarive: Université de Madagascar, 1972.

————. *The History of Civilisation in North Madagascar.* Rotterdam: Balkema, 1986.

————. "L'Imerina et le peuplement de Madagascar: Les hypothèses confrontées aux nouvelles découvertes," *Taloha* 12 (1994): pages 25–28.

————. "Problèmes de la Naissance de l'Etat Ancien aux Comores et dans le Nord de Madagascar." Paper presented at symposium, Pre-Colonial Madagascar, Centre for African Studies, University of London, 28 November 1986.

Villiers, Alan. *Monsoon Seas: The Story of the Indian Ocean.* New York: McGraw-Hill, 1952.

Weber, Henry. *La Compagnie française des Indes (1604–1875).* Paris: Rousseau, 1904.

Wilkins, Harold. *Captain Kidd and his Skeleton Island.* New York: Liveright, 1935.

Wilkinson, Henry. *Bermuda in the Old Empire: A History of the Island from the Dissolution of the Somers Island Company until the end of the American Revolutionary War, 1684–1784.* London: Oxford University Press, 1950.

Wright, Arnold. *Annesley of Surat and his Times.* London: Melrose, 1918.

STUDIES OF DANIEL DEFOE AND OTHER 17TH- AND 18TH-CENTURY AUTHORS

Baer, Joel. "Piracy Examined: A Study of Daniel Defoe's *General History of the Pirates* and its Milieu." Ph.D. diss., Princeton University, 1970.

Bernbaum, Ernest. *The Mary Carleton Narratives, 1663–1673: A Missing Chapter in the History of the English Novel.* Cambridge, Mass.: Harvard University Press, 1914.

Davis, Lennard. *Factual Fictions: The Origins of the English Novel.* New York: Columbia University Press, 1983.

Faller, Lincoln. *Crime and Defoe: A New Kind of Writing.* Cambridge, Eng.: Cambridge University Press, 1993.

————. *Turned to Account: The Forms and Functions of Criminal Biography in Late Seventeenth- and Early Eighteenth-Century England*. Cambridge, Eng.: Cambridge University Press, 1987.

Furbank, Philip and W. R. Owens. *The Canonisation of Daniel Defoe*. New Haven: Yale University Press, 1988.

————. *Defoe De-attributions: A Critique of J. R. Moore's Checklist*. London: Hambledon Press, 1994.

Gosse, Philip. *A Bibliography of the Works of Capt. Charles Johnson*. London: Dulau, 1927.

Main, C. T. "The German Princess; or, Mary Carleton in Fact and Fiction," *Harvard Library Bulletin,* 10 (1956): 166–185.

Mayer, Robert. *History and Early English Novel; Matters of Fact from Bacon to Defoe*. Cambridge, Eng.: Cambridge University Press, 1997.

Moore, John Robert. *A Checklist of the Writings of Daniel Defoe*. 2nd ed. Hamden, Conn.: Archon Books, 1971.

————. *Daniel Defoe, Citizen of the Modern World*. Chicago: University of Chicago Press, 1958.

————. *Defoe in the Pillory and other Studies*. Bloomington: Indiana University Press, 1939.

————. *Defoe's Sources for Robert Drury's Journal*. Bloomington: Indiana University Press, 1943.

Novak, Maximillian. *Economics and the Fiction of Daniel Defoe*. Los Angeles: University of California Press, 1962.

————. *Realism, Myth, and History in Defoe's Fiction*. Lincoln: University of Nebraska Press, 1983.

Peterson, Spiro. *The Counterfeit Lady Unveiled and other Criminal Fiction of Seventeenth Century England*. Garden City, N.Y.: Doubleday, 1961.

Richetti, John. *Defoe's Narratives: Situations and Structures*. Oxford, Eng.: Clarendon, 1975.

————. *Popular Fiction before Richardson*. Oxford, Eng.: Clarendon, 1969.

Roosen, William. *Daniel Defoe and Diplomacy*. Selinsgrove, Pa.: Susquehanna University Press, 1986.

Secord, Arthur. *"Robert Drury's Journal" and Other Studies*. Urbana: University of Illinois Press, 1961.

Schonhorn, Manuel. "Defoe's Pirates: A New Source." *Research in English Studies,* 14 (1963): 386–389.

————. *Defoe's Politics: Parliament, Power, Kingship, and Robinson Crusoe*. Cambridge, Eng.: Cambridge University Press, 1991.

Singleton, Robert. "English Criminal Biography, 1652–1722," *Harvard Library Bulletin* 18 (1970): 63–83.

Warner, John. *Joyce's Grandfathers: Myth and History in Defoe, Smollett, Sterne, and Joyce*. Athens: University of Georgia Press, 1993.

Watson, Harold. *Coasts of Treasure Island: A Study of the Background and Sources for Robert Louis Stevenson's Romance of the Sea*. San Antonio, Texas: Naylor, 1969.

West, Richard. *Daniel Defoe: The Life and Strange, Surprising Adventures*. New York: Carroll & Graf, 1998.

Zimmerman, Everett. *The Boundaries of Fiction: History and the Eighteenth-Century British Novel*. Ithaca, N.Y.: Cornell University Press, 1996.

INDEX

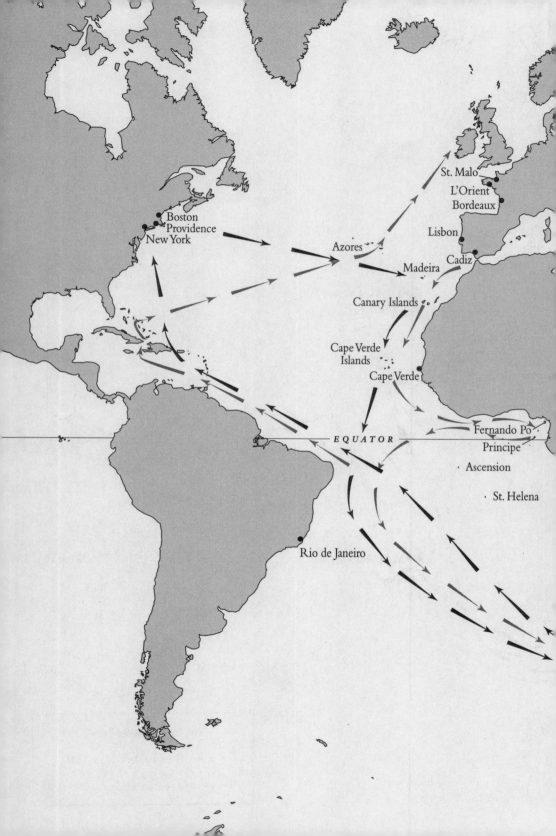

St. Malo
L'Orient
Bordeaux

Lisbon

Cadiz

Boston
Providence
New York

Azores

Madeira

Canary Islands

Cape Verde
Islands

Cape Verde

Fernando Po

Principe

Ascension

St. Helena

EQUATOR

Rio de Janeiro